A Social History of the Welsh Clergy

circa 1662-1939

Roger Lee Brown

PART TWO

SECTIONS SEVEN TO FOURTEEN

in THREE VOLUMES

The cover picture depicts
LLANGELYNIN CHURCH, MERIONETH
Depicting an early nineteenth century arrangement of the interior.

A Social History of the Welsh Clergy
circa 1662-1939

Roger Lee Brown

PART TWO

VOLUME TWO

SECTIONS NINE AND TEN

Published by Roger Lee Brown, 2018
Cartref, 14 Berriew Road, Welshpool, SY21 7SS

ISBN: 978-1-9996156-5-9

Part 2 Volume One ISBN: 978-1-9996156-4-2
Part 2 Volume Three ISBN: 978-1-9996156-6-6

Book Design by Russell Holden
www.pixeltweakspublications.com

Printed by Ingram

CONTENTS
VOLUME TWO

A SOCIAL HISTORY OF THE WELSH CLERGY
LIST OF THE OTHER SECTIONS OF PART TWO

A SOCIAL HISTORY OF THE WELSH CLERGY

SECTION 9: PASTORALIA

Chapters

CHAPTER ONE: INTRODUCTION

The visiting of parishioners and the care of the sick and dying were some of the responsibilities of the clergy,[1] and these tasks were duly emphasised in many visitation sermons and charges. As the Word of God was preached in the services, so it needed to be applied in the homes. Both were aspects of feeding the flock.[2] Bishop Bull, for example, in his 1708 Charge, reminded his clergy of their duty of not only visiting at times of acute illness, but of acquainting themselves with their flock when they were in health, "in order to promote the great end of their own function, the salvation of souls."[3] His contemporary at St Asaph, William Fleetwood, told his clergy they were not to be busy-bodies nor meddlers with other people's domestic and temporal concerns, as this was distasteful to people. Nevertheless, "unless they be most diligent and heedful Observers of the Lives and Manners of their People, they will neither preach pertinently to them in their Churches, nor discourse properly in their Houses, nor rightly apply to them, on their Sick Beds. To do these Patients the best Service, one must thoroughly know, and be well acquainted, with their condition."[4]

Peter Williams, who reprinted Archbishop Hort of Tuam's instructions to his clergy for the benefit of the Welsh clergy, reminded the clergy of their obligation to visit the sick and all parishioners regularly, to learn about the true state of their souls and their spiritual wants. In church they heard, but in their homes they could speak about their fears, doubts and temptations, and if the clergy failed to so visit then the greater part of their duty was undone.[5] This advice was carried out by John Wesley's father, whose view of pastoral duty included visiting each house in his parish.[6] An unknown writer of the 1770s desired the clergy to teach repentance and faith from house to house in order to enforce the preaching of the Church and to impart the first principles of Christianity in plain and familiar conversation.[7] After a lengthy discussion about pulpit oratory, Richard Evans, vicar of Llanbadarn Fawr, in an essay of 1807 about promoting a more regular attendance at worship, went on to make clear that part of the clerical duty was to visit their sick parishioners, without waiting to be asked, and praying with them and for them and exhorting them to pray for themselves.[8]

The nineteenth century took another angle. This was to make clear that pastoral work was as important as preaching. This emphasis was because Nonconformity seemed to be built upon pulpit oratory, many clergy felt they should imitate them to regain the multitudes to their side and thus ignored their pastoral work. Hence the Welsh bishops continually emphasised this aspect of the clerical duty. Ollivant in his 1854 Charge was concerned that the clergy should invite the sick to ask for the prayers of the Church and to give thanksgiving for their recovery in the midst of the congregation.[9] By 1875 he suggested that one way of winning the masses back to the Church was by a pastoral house to house visitation and manifesting loving sympathy with them in their troubles rather than reproving and exhorting them. Able preaching could not do this for those who were dead in their trespasses and sins, but care for them, especially in affliction, might eventually draw people to Christ.[10] Possibly speaking from his own experience at Merthyr Tydfil, Bishop Campbell of Bangor in 1863 reminded the clergy how much they might learn at the bedside from the humblest of parishioners who had a living faith in the Redeemer.[11] Archdeacon John Evans of Carmarthen suggested to his clergy in 1864 that if the Church prayed its prayers rather than read them, laboured out as well as in the pulpit, and strove to bring people to Christian maturity, then the churches would be crowded.[12]

Bishop Basil Jones was even more emphatic in his 1877 Charge. Accepting that many of his clergy, faced with the onslaught of Nonconformity, felt that preaching was their main task, he made it clear that fine oratory from the pulpit was as nothing compared to heart searching talks with men at their own fireplace. While preaching might gather a good congregation it was pastoral care that would keep it together. Equally, the clergy belonged to a National Church, and they had a commission to visit all their parishioners who would receive their visits, not just the church-going, for otherwise they would be ministers of a sect. The bishop added that in those parishes in which sound evangelical teaching and diligent pastoral care had been given by some good man a large proportion of the population remained loyal to the Church.[13] The spiritual nature of these visits was also emphasised by both Bishop Short and Bishop Hughes of St Asaph. Short made it clear that if the visitation of parishioners for "spiritual supervision" was neglected, then the benefit of public worship would soon cease.[14] Hughes suggested that an organised plan of visitation was required and the clergy should guard against the temptation of making the visits a matter of courtesy and idle gossip. In addition, they should seek out the afflicted and sick and bring them the comforts of Christ.[15] Yet for many clergy this spiritual aspect of their pastoral visiting was outside their personal remit. In a report to Archbishop Benson, Joseph Cullin, his Tate missioner who was working with the Welsh clergy in the 1880s, noted that for many of the clergy pastoral visitation meant gossip and tea drinking.[16] This tallies with Charles Wilkins' description of John Griffith as rector of Merthyr. "His *forte*," he wrote, did not lie in visitation in the way generally understood, that is, in making calls on Church-going ladies and interchanging the gossip of the day." Rather, if any parishioner was sick, whatever their denomination, he would go to cheer and comfort, but his real sympathies were with the miserable and the poor children rather than the well-to-do.[17]

A number evaded this duty. Amongst them was the incumbent of Llandderfel in 1730, whose rural dean, John Wynne, wrote that he feared the sick were not visited frequently, in contrast to his colleague at Gwyddelwern, where the sick were visited constantly.[18] By contrast the 1720 returns for Carmarthenshire affirmed that the clergy did visit the sick, although for Llanfihangel Cilfargen it was suggested this was better known to the curate than to the warden.[19] Erasmus Saunders in his work on the state of the diocese of St Davids noted several clergymen to be as eminent for their pastoral care and diligence as others were for their neglect and scandal.[20]

CHAPTER TWO: THE VICTORIAN OUTWORKING OF PASTORAL VISITATION

The Victorians believed, in the later words of Bishop Edwards, that a house-going parson produced a church-going people, and this was probably true as the parson was a man of authority if not of persuasion. Edwards believed that it knit people and the clergyman together in fellowship.[1] As Walsham How put it, if the people would not come to the parson he should go to them and show them how important he believed were the things he spoke about from the pulpit.[2] Although there were exceptions, such as John Kenrick, vicar of Llangernyw, 1730-55, who visited every home in his parish but found it a thankless task,[3] and John Hughes of Aberystwyth, 1827-60, who apparently took a great delight in pastoral visiting,[4] an earlier generation of clergy did not see this as part of their duty. In some instances the need was not there, as they were involved in the life of their small villages and their parishioners all attended the Church and they knew them well. Henry Alford, though serving an English parish, Wymeswold, 1838-53, was not a regular visitor as it was alleged on his behalf that it was not then general practice and parishioners did not expect it.[5] This was equally so in Wales. David Owen, vicar of Eglwysbach, 1826-69, though kind and polite to his parishioners, hardly ever visited them in their homes, and seldom pressed them to attend his services;[6] George Cunliffe, the aristocratic vicar of Wrexham, 1826-71, was said in 1865 that he had no wish to be pestered by the "vulgar" people of his parish,[7] while an obituary of Griffith Edwards, rector of Llangadfan who died in 1893 and had been previously at Minerva, records that in his day it was not the custom to visit houses. He concentrated instead on his pulpit ministry.[8] Robert Roberts' first curacy was at Cwm, and he related how his vicar, Thomas Griffith, 1858-73, was bored by society and only cared for his reading of the newspaper and his garden walks.[9] Howel Kirkhouse, vicar of Cyfarthfa, 1868-1914, was said never to have done much visiting unless he was specifically wanted, though he built up a large congregation.[10]

The position had changed by the 1840s for those newly ordained due to the exhortations of bishops, evangelical practice, and the increasing expectations of parishioners.[11] In addition, the ending of pluralities and the grant-aid available to incumbents to appoint assistant curates assisted this process. In fact, as early as 1827 house-to-house visiting was encouraged by Bishop Sumner of Llandaff in his visitation charge of that year. He made clear that a clergyman was responsible before God for all his parishioners, and should make no distinction between Nonconformist and Church homes.[12] Thus pastoral visiting became the chief instrument of pastoral care with the provision of church schools as the second.[13] Walsham How was one of many writers who gave practical advice to the clergy as to how they should visit. He regarded afternoon as the best time to do so, and felt that an average of 36 to 40 visits a week was reasonable for a town parish, but 22 in a rural parish where people were scattered. One great danger of visiting was that the men would be at work, and there was a need to reach out to them, but on the other hand women and children also had souls. An evening visit was to be avoided for then the men would be tired. In upper class houses there should be a concern for the servants though permission from the head of the family must be sought for this. The cleric should speak of spiritual things, ask about family prayer and Bible reading, and leave a pastoral letter.[14]

Further advice came from R.W. Evans, a Welsh clergyman who became archdeacon of Westmorland, about visiting Nonconformist families. He clearly took the position that the cleric had a responsibility for all his parishioners, and advised that rather than argue with dissenters it was better to show pastoral concern, though to make clear that the cleric's ministry was done in the name of the Church.[15] Others asked how could the priest know his people and so minister effectively in the pulpit or at the sick-bed unless he knew where they lived and worked, or deal with moral wickedness and error, if he confined his ministry to the church building or to the faithful.[16] Yet as many recognised, visiting parishioners often required some social interaction as well as spiritual input, such as signing club certificates, writing a letter, providing a ticket for the dispensary, a good word to the Board of Guardians, or an order for a parish coffin.[17]

The *Ecclesiastic* published an amusing but serious article on parish visiting in 1863.

It described some of the methods used by clergy, and district visitors, in visiting homes. "A gentle tap on the door, a gliding entrance, a smirking nod of recognition, a bland persuasiveness of tone"; an offer or even the demand to read a portion of the Bible sometimes accompanied by an intrusive examination into spiritual experience, was one example. Another was the "blunt, bluff, free-and-easy, neighbourly, gossiping, jocose method, in which there is much small-talk of family affairs and all kinds of personal minutiae" with little spiritual substance; and another "the patronising, pompous, dictatorial, peremptory *genus clericorum* ... ordering and scolding, or with cold polished courtesy tendering an alms, and laying down the law... as to spending it. In short, almsgiving, gossiping, lecturing, supply the staple of ordinary Visiting."

The writer regarded this kind of visiting as absolutely useless. It failed to reach those who most needed pastoral instruction, for many were working during the day or resented such rude visits, so leaving a small select circle of those willing to receive them, generally the aged and the infirm, for whom such visits would be a harmless comfort. Often, he continued, an inquisitorial and intrusive style of visiting resulted in alienation from the Church, or the *bonhomie* of the parson means that he sacrificed his dignity in order to win popularity. Rather, the clergyman was more than an educated gentleman or a justice of the peace, because his "one great work and all absorbing purpose ... is *the salvation of their souls, their edification in spiritual-mindedness and sanctity.*" All his efforts should be directed to this end, and while he should concentrate on his priestly function with the sacraments, prayers and intercessions, and use the time spent for general visiting in holding classes for catechumens, district visitors (who would undertake most of the visiting) and Sunday School teachers, he should give two hours a day when he might be available for private consultation, and visit the sick in a sacramental sense. Indeed, he should be prepared to leave the ninety-nine in the wilderness, presumably to the care of his more active parishioners, and concentrate on the one who needed his priestly ministry. "The *sick* souls, and not the whole among his people, will engage his tenderest treatment and most assiduous care."[18] Though this was a voice of a High Churchman, his concern for a limited but effective pastoral rather than social visiting was echoed by many, including Bishop Edwards of St Asaph.[19]

A number of examples may be offered of this pastoral care and visitation. Jane

Williams records of Thomas Price, Carnhuanawc, that while he was at Llangatwg, 1816-22, he regarded house to house visiting as one of his most important duties, even if the families he visited choose not to attend his public ministry.[20] Henry Vaughan of Crickhowell, 1830-7, is described by his biographer as visiting both rich and poor throughout his parish, and ceased not to warn and entreat them about their spiritual lives.[21] Appointed to the Crown livings of St Dogmael's in 1826, Henry James Vincent later wrote "there is scarcely a day in which I am not called to the bed of sickness, though the duty of visiting the parish is arduous, yet I can truly say that I have received more benefit from it to my soul than from any part of the ministerial functions."[22] Dean Cotton, as senior vicar and later dean of Bangor (1810-62) was said to be untiring in his visiting of the sick and poor.[23] When the Church Pastoral-Aid Society gave a grant for a curate in an unknown south Wales colliery area in 1841, it resulted in an increase in the number of services, the number of families visited increased threefold and the number of communicants doubled. The report added that if their grantees expected to be useful they must visit and make themselves known to their people, as clearly this unknown cleric had done.[24]

David Howell was ordained to the curacy of Neath in 1858 for the specific task of conducting the "pastoral visitation" of the Welsh families of that parish.[25] At Pwllheli he was known as an able preacher and, more importantly, a laborious pastor, as a report on church attendance in north Wales of 1865 declared. The report described Howell as working from day to night, consoling the sick, admonishing the reckless, and contributing towards the necessities of the poor, while he not only preached the "everlasting Gospel" from the pulpit, but from door to door.[26] According to Robert Roberts, William Hicks Owen of Tremeirchion in the 1850s worked his parish well, obtaining the best curates to assist him, and never allowing the Church fire to die out.[27] Canon Evans of Rhymney (1856-1908) was said to have visited all his parishioners, including Nonconformists, but this must have been an immense undertaking in his large industrial parish. Nevertheless, he built up and maintained one of the largest congregations in Wales. It is said he visited his parishioners from 12.30 until 2.00pm, and then before his evening meetings. If he placed his silk hat on the dresser people knew it was a sign he would welcome a cup of tea.[28] A new incumbent of Newborough, Anglesey, Thomas Meredith, arrived in 1866, and re-charged the parochial batteries. Visiting house to house, persuading people to attend the church, he soon had two rather than one Sunday service and a Sunday school and a chapel of ease. Nonconformists were envious of his success, especially as some of their adherents had become church members.[29] It was generally accepted that Non-conformists gave the clergy a cordial welcome when they visited them in their homes.[30]

The diary of John James Turner for 1857-8, when he served as curate of Berriew, notes how he visited all his parishioners, including Nonconformists, walking considerable distances to do so. He writes of numerous occasions when he was called to visit the sick, one at 6.00am in the morning, and records many instances of tragic illness and mental sickness.[31] We note from Kilvert's diary during his years as curate of Clyro, 1864-76, how active he was in visiting his parishioners, especially the elderly and the sick. He prayed with them, read the Scriptures, offered tracts, distributed blankets and left gifts, and was frequently called out to care for the sick and dying. He read to Sarah Probert the story of the raising of Lazarus, and asked John Morgan if he trusted he was forgiven by God. He repeated some of the Church prayers to old Whitcombe, deaf and near blind, and his joining in them was "very touching". He read the last chapter of Revelation to Thomas Meredith, going up on a ladder to the loft where he lay. It has been estimated that of the 130 families of that parish 90 are noted in the edited version of his diary though this does not mean he visited each one. Toman suggests that of the 68 homes of labourers he only visited twenty.[32]

Speaking in 1879 the vicar of Swansea, Samuel Christopher Morgan, said how impressed he had been with the great knowledge many people had of the Bible and the great eagerness in which they received the visits of a pastor, as well as the hearty way in which they would respond when he spoke to them about spiritual things. In an English parish he sometimes had the door shut in his face, but he had never experienced anything of this kind in Wales.[33] W.J. Bronham of St Matthew's, Swansea (1927-43), had such a concern for this pastoral ministry that it meant he was out all hours visiting homes.[34] The vicar of the docks area in Llanelli during the 1930s would visit every house in a street regardless of denomination after the Sunday service. If anyone in the house was using a sewing machine it had to be put away for that kind of work on a Sunday was seen as sinful.[35] Charles Phelps, vicar of St Martin's, Haverfordwest, 1888-1907, aimed to visit every home in his parish twice a year (and more frequently in case of sickness).[36] On leaving the parish of Hawarden in 1904, Stephen Gladstone personally called at every one of its 1,800 houses to say farewell,[37] and Cecil Lillingston, as he entered his new parish of Sketty in 1903, visited every family in the parish in his first few months.[38] The four curates of St John's, Canton, each had their own district and visited house to house, although their visits to church people were more frequent, as their incumbent told the 1906 royal commission.[39] Canon Thomas Jones, vicar of Abergele 1904-13, though famed as a preacher throughout Wales, is said to have been a constant visitor of his parishioners, both church and chapel.[40] When he left his previous parish of Llanfyllin, he spoke to a farewell meeting in these words, which may sum up the devotion of many clergy to their pastoral work:

> The sympathy which my pastoral visits met with in your homes made me feel that God was with me. To Him is due the praise for whatever has been done during my ministry. … If my ministrations in this dear old Church have been comforting and edifying, He it is who has blest the words I have uttered. If I have brought calmness and consolation and spiritual strength to the sick and dying, He inspired me. If I have cheered many a heart broken by grief, and trouble and sorrow, He supplied the healing influence. I have been in close touch with almost all the families who are in the habit of worshipping within these walls. … I have been closeted with many at a time of some great anxiety, when their hearts have gone out to me in the fullest confidence, eagerly expecting from me some word of hope, some word of relief, some word of strength. I have been present in many a chamber of sickness and sorrow, where we have knelt together at the bedside of a loved one and broken the stillness of the room with accents of prayer. I have stood at the open grave and helped many to lower their dear ones to their last resting-place. Sad, indeed, my friends, is the breaking of the bond which binds a pastor to his people.[41]

It is not surprising that the report of the Royal Commission of 1906 quoted the testimony of Bishop Edwards about the value of the Church's pastoral ministry: "whether amid 'the loneliness of the crowded town or the isolation and remoteness of the small rural parishes. In most of our parishes pastoral visitation is thorough and systematic and is not limited to Church people only. The universal experience of the parochial clergy is that their visits are valued and welcomed in every home, as a rule, in the parish.'" In nearly one third of the parishes of his diocese of St Asaph the clergyman was the only resident minister.[42] Even with this in mind many clergy found it difficult to find the time for pastoral visiting, due to their duties in the church school and their preparation for the pulpit. This was stated at a meeting of the Newtown Clerical Association in 1877, though it was also urged that a register of parishioners be kept, and the whole parish, including Nonconformists, be visited every three months.[43]

PARISH VISITING ASSOCIATIONS

With this belief that the Church had the pastoral care of all people within a parish, not just the churchgoers, it meant a general visitation throughout the parish. This was obviously impracticable for a single man to accomplish, even with curates, in a large parish, and hence a system developed by which district visitors were appointed from within the congregation. Most were women who had the leisure to do so, and their task was to visit in an assigned district a number of streets, give out tracts, promote family prayer and Bible reading, persuade parents to attend the worship of the Church, to have their children baptised and sent to the Sunday School, to offer help and charity when required and to let the clergy know of cases of sickness and deprivation or where spiritual help was required. In one sense it was the outworking of the sympathy of the rich for the poorer parishioners and a point of contact between the Church and non-attenders. These societies (and one at Brighton) were noted in his 1828 Charge by Bishop Sumner of Chester, who encouraged them in his vast and industrialised diocese, by which time a General Society for the Promotion of District Visiting had been established, though it seems to have had little impact in Wales.[44] Arthur Burns suggests that the first visiting society was formed by Daniel Wilson in 1812 at Islington, but their antecedents went back further than that, though in some cases, as W.M. Jacob maintains, they were more concerned to relieve the poor than to be an evangelising agency.[45] The system was clearly developed and used by Thomas Vowler Short when he was vicar of St George's, Bloomsbury, and it was one he recommended to his clergy in his Charge of 1850. From his experience as bishop of Sodor and Man, Short claimed that in this way ten times more houses could be visited by the use of these district visitors, the inhabitants relieved and sufferers directed to Christ. In his *Parochialia* of 1843, describing his work at St George's, he claimed that his district visitors were often led to a deeper sense of holiness by their exertions.[46]

Edward Squire of Swansea divided his parish into units of forty homes for his district visitors, the visitors being ladies of the parish, and held monthly meetings with them for prayer and the distribution of relief. The object of his Parochial Visiting Association was to bring to the notice of the vicar every family in his parish, to induce them to attend the ministrations of the Gospel, comfort them in sorrow, and relieve them in poverty and sickness. In the accounts for 1858 it was noted that in twelve years 23,743 cases had been relieved by the distribution of money, blankets, sheets, baby clothes and flour tickets, and in that year 4,000 tracts had been distributed, while two lay visitors (probably stipendiary) had made 5,559 visits plus 903 visits to the sick, and had held 180 cottage Bible readings. Yet there were problems as the then vicar, Samuel Christopher Morgan, divulged in 1879. Though districts were mapped out too often the poorest districts were left unsupplied, as some visitors said they feared scarlet fever or cholera, and others "that poor people smell so". He now took young men to be district visitors, and gradually taught them to take cottage meetings and conduct services in mission halls. By 1892 there were 62 district visitors, and another 19 in the St Mark's area of the parish, all of whom were women.[47]

Many other parishes possessed district or parochial visiting societies, as did Hawarden;[48] Caernarfon (where lay people went out in pairs, with a younger probably gaining experience from an older);[49] Cowbridge,[50] St Mary's, Cardiff, under the ministry of William Leigh Morgan;[51] Gresford (where its vicar, Robert Wickham, wrote in 1854 that its existence would lighten his anxieties and secure the requisite assistance to the poor in all parts of the parish);[52] Welshpool by the 1890s if not before (where each of the curates had a district allocated to them which they "worked" with lay visitors);[53] Rhymney (which had 187 lay workers, including district visitors, by 1897);[54] St Gabriel's,. Swansea;[55] and Wrexham (where in 1906 there were 47 district visitors, and the parish had been divided into districts each headed by a curate). In these places the clergy made a systematic visitation of church people, while the sick visiting was arranged from the written reports of the district visitors. A less formal situation existed at Penmaenmawr, with its vicar, David Jones, declaring that the lay people often visited and prayed with the sick.[56] What seems clear is that some associations were more concerned to extend the social care of the Church, while others had a more spiritual object. A comment made by Marshall Dugdale, a layman, at the 1885 St Asaph Diocesan Conference suggests the former. Ladies would obtain more sympathy for the Church in talking to cottagers about the baby and other domestic things than the parson would get if he talked religion for twelve months.[57]

Yet Anthony Russell remarks that many clergy felt that the results of such systematic visiting, by themselves or with the aid of district visitors, was disappointing.[58] The writer of the *Ecclesiastic* article mentioned above argued this was because of "random, helter-skelter sort of Visiting" that many practised, and because the clergy trusted too much to their own personal activity and zeal, rather than discharging "their *sacerdotal* functions duly and as efficiently as possible".[59] Though it was widely believed that the clergy should visit all their parishioners, and any substitute was seen as an evasion of this duty, by the 1900s it was clear that many were wearing themselves out with this pastoral visitation and ignoring more important duties, such as a proper preparation for worship and preaching and even caring for their own families.[60]

THE VISITATION OF THE SICK

Visiting the sick had its dangers and often the need for a strong stomach, but also had its opportunities at a time when much sickness led to death. It was the priestly task to enable a sick person to face the possibility of death, bringing some to repentance and others to a deeper assurance of faith. The Prayer-Book service for the Visitation of the Sick directed the pastor to inquire whether a person had repented of their sins and, if thought necessary, to make a special confession of them, and admonish them to make a will if they had not done so. There might be dark tidings, but "the brightest daylight lies beyond" might be the message given by the the clergy as they took advantage of these times of illness to awaken faith and probe the conscience.[61]

John Warren, in his 1784 Bangor Charge, pointed out that as people were "most susceptible of religious impressions, and have the truest sense of their spiritual concerns, when they are visited with sickness", the diligent pastor would take advantage of such occasions.[62] In a charge to the Rochester clergy of 1800, Samuel Horsley, formerly of St Davids and later of St Asaph, added to this testimony and reminded his clergy not only to repeat the prayers of the Church at the bedside of the sick, but to make inquiry into the actual state of their soul in order to minister such advice and consolation as required and offering them all the assistance they needed to make their peace with God. He added that nothing would attach their parishioners to their minister as much as performing this duty.[63] In his lectures on pastoral work, Walsham How advised the clergyman to prepare the sick for holy communion if that was practicable, and also about confession, not as a father confessor but as a spiritual friend able to assist them in their doubts and assure them that their sins had been forgiven. This presumably was his practice at Whittington.[64] A former vicar of Conway, Henry Rees, produced *The Welsh Clergyman's Vade Mecum* in 1898, describing it as a collection of Scripture and other readings and prayers for use with the sick, in both Welsh and English. His introduction noted there was no part of a clergyman's life which required so much tact and discernment, as well as a ready sympathy, as visiting the sick, and if he did so conscientiously it would make great demands on his resources. He hoped that his book might make the visitation of the sick spiritual rather than secular, and in it he provided short services to meet a number of cases. His prayers included those for resignation and restoration, confession and bereavement, the communion of the sick, while his non-Scriptural readings came from such sources as Wilberforce, Blunt, Newman, Trench, Kempis and even Wordsworth.[65]

Bishops and pastoral writers gave advice to their clergy about the practicalities of visiting the sick. In his 1710 Charge, William Fleetwood of St Asaph suggested that a minister should be told not only about sickness, but regarding the best time to visit: "when are the intervals of greater ease, from Pain or Sickness; when they are most awake and sensible; and when the Operations of Medicines best permit".[66] More practical advice came from John Gott in a pastoral handbook for clergy. In visiting infectious cases one should visit soon after eating, but not visit another house until one had changed one's dress and had an hour's "blow" in fresh air. Nor should one touch anything touched by the infected person, nor bend over them and so catch a whiff of their breath. Above all, one should leave all fear behind.[67] Many followed the precept that visits to the sick should be on a weekly basis, and daily in those cases where death was imminent.[68]

Sadly, little is recorded of this visitation of the sick, save that most clergy were conscientious in their duty, as was Kilvert, already noted. One of the few recorded instances is noted in Squire Bulkeley of Llanfechell's diary of 1752. He wrote on one occasion that after 5.00 pm word was brought to the rector that William Davies was near expiry. He went there, and having read to him and scarce finished the "Recommendary Prayer" he died soon after.[69] John Williams, Ab Ithel, rector of Llanymawddwy from 1849-62, a scattered parish, visited his parishioners even in cases of malignant fever, often lighting fires, preparing meals, giving medicines, praying with the dying, and bringing them communion. Perhaps it is no wonder he suffered from acute stress.[70] Another was David Howell, who was noted for his ministry to. and prayers with. the sick, amongst all classes of people and without reference to denomination.[71] Walsham How, along with many other stories of his pastoral ministry, related one about a dissenting minister refusing to enter a room where a person lay sick of smallpox, but the incumbent of the parish came and prayed at the bedside with the patient.[72]

What is clear is that many clergymen were extraordinarily faithful in their pastoral work during the various cholera outbreaks of the early Victorian period.[73] Cholera was the great horror of the nineteenth century. It struck with little warning, and it killed many. Its causes were not known at that time, and so people were frightened of any contact with its victims. These people were still parishioners, and many clergy became revered for their devotion to duty at times like these. Philip Constable Ellis, as curate of Holyhead in 1846, faced such an epidemic, and not only cared for its victims spiritually but actually put those who had died into their coffins as the undertakers declined to do so.[74] John Griffith at Aberdare in 1849 and David Lewis at Briton Ferry in 1854 were also conspicuous for their devotion to duty during these times,[75] as were J.C. Campbell of Merthyr and Evan Jenkins of Dowlais during the 1849 epidemic,[76] and Lodwick Edwards at Rhymney during the two epidemics of 1849 and 1854.[77] Evan Jones records that during the 1854 cholera outbreak at Llandaff the curate, David Morgan, was asked if he felt nervous about visiting those afflicted. He replied he did not as he would eat a good dinner and trust in God.[78] During the 1865-6 outbreak at Caernarfon it vicar, J.C.

Vincent, visited all the haunts of the disease and attended the bedsides of the dying. He was assisted by a Baptist minister, Robert Ellis, who resisted calls for prayer meetings by stating that sanitary reforms were needed instead. It is thought that Vincent's exertions during this time led to his early death.[79]

National fasts were called for, and Russell Davies notes those that took place in Swansea, Cardiff, Merthyr, Pembroke, Carmarthen, Milford and Pontypool.[80] A sermon of 1849 on such an occasion was preached, and later published, by Charles Williams, vicar of Holyhead. If they had been spared, they should rejoice in the Lord, though he reminded his congregation of the rubric that in times of infectious sickness the clergy should press upon their parishioners their duty of often partaking of the holy communion.[81] Others took practical measures. During the 1854 epidemic Campbell of Merthyr published a sermon he had preached, informing people if they wished to be delivered from the scourge, they needed to be practical, and this included cleanliness in addition to repentance. While it was a warning to those careless of their future state, Christians should have no fear about exposing themselves for their neighbour's good and should show a quiet trust in God.[82]

When cholera broke out in Lampeter Velfry in 1865 Richard Lewis had a letter printed and distributed enclosing a prayer to use but also reminding people about sanitary precautions and their spiritual obligations.[83] As a result of these outbreaks many clergy, such as Evan Jenkins at Dowlais and William Clive of Welshpool, were instrumental in obtaining local Public Heath Acts for their areas,[84] while Thomas Stacey and William Leigh Morgan, of the two Cardiff parishes, endeavoured with others to improve the sanitary condition of that town through their membership of the health committee of the Board of Guardians.[85]

Another aspect of the ministry to the sick was taking them Holy Communion or celebrating it in their homes. Again, the evidence, though it does not amount to much, points to considerable faithfulness on the part of the clergy. The 1705 return for the Carmarthenshire parish of Llangain notes that its minister "administered" communion in private homes at the request of the sick and the dying.[86] The parish of Llanfor in Merioneth in 1748 possessed a small silver chalice and paten used for house communions, though in 1729 the wardens of Llansanffraid Glan Conwy had refused the minister the use of the surplice to administer the sacrament to the sick, but promised not to do so thereafter.[87] In the parish of Llanfechell its squire, Bulkeley, noted sick house communions on Easter Monday and Tuesdays in the 1730s and 1740s.[88] In the early 1850s Robert Roberts described a dying man receiving Holy Communion at his bedside on a Christmas day.[89] In his diary of 1857-8 John James Turner, curate of Berriew, frequently administered communion to the sick, apparently celebrating at the bedside, though he records one instance when, called to give communion to a dying woman, he had to officiate at a service first and by the time he arrived at the home she had died.[90] The Cardiff clergy chapter of 1896 heard a paper whose writer suggested that the sick should be reminded about their obligation to receive holy communion in their homes.[91]

Although some workhouse unions allowed a local incumbent to provide services and pastoral assistance for their inmates, especially in rural areas, it was not always the case, especially in large towns. Pwllheli was an exception, for in the 1850s and probably thereafter there was a weekly service held at the workhouse.[92] In the Llandaff diocese with eleven workhouses, four had no chaplain, though in two others local clergy held services and in others the inmates were allowed to go to a local church. The Llandaff Diocesan Conference during the 1890s had a number of debates about this poor provision, when it was pointed out that there was a need for a dedicated chaplain rather than the work being left to the local incumbent, whose Sunday duties might preclude taking a service at the workhouse, even if a room was available. At Pontypridd workhouse the two local curates visited weekly, but the guardians only allowed them to take thirteen services a year, and this had been a recent concession. If more were provided, and these were of a bright and cheery nature, it was believed many more would attend.[93]

Another aspect of the clerical life was the giving of foodstuffs, clothing and material assistance to parishioners in need. Many believed this assistance was part of the clergyman's duties, and many a clerical household was immersed in making soups for the poor during harsh times, making clothing for children, and distributing the product of orchard and glasshouse. It was said of the rector of Cilrhedyn in north Pembrokeshire in 1897 that his family assisted all the parishioners in affliction with baskets of delicacies without distinction of sect or party.[94] Some clergy learnt sufficient medicine to help doctor their parishes, as did George Birkett of St Florence. As a curate in Oswestry a local doctor told him instead of coming to him for assistance with every ailment he ought to learn something of medicine himself. This he did, to the benefit of to his parishioners.[95] Similarly, Thomas Price, Carnhuanawc, acquired a sufficient knowledge of medicine to treat ordinary ailments and casualties.[96]

TOWN VERSUS RURAL MINISTRY

In a letter to the *Western Mail* of 1890, one *Cymro Eglwysig* wrote that in rural areas few could attend guilds and other meetings, so the rural pastor had more time to visit his flock than his contemporary in a town parish. He accepted that a town incumbent could visit his flock in a reasonably short time, but this would take months in the country.[97] D. Parry-Jones calculated that a town parson might manage fifty or sixty visits a week, but in rural areas twenty-five was probably the maximum and that required far greater physical exertion, especially in days before most clergy had their own cars.[98] In a previous generation many clergy rode on horseback around their parish visiting their parishioners, as did Walsham How at Whittington.[99]

Many bishops expressed the concern that the incumbent of a rural parish had little to do, and it was easy for him to fritter away his time and do nothing at all. For example, Basil Jones was concerned that incumbents would become dispirited at the lack of response to their ministries and as a result idle away their time, so he suggested that the rural clergy should adopt a scheme of work for each day to keep themselves occupied.[100] The reality for many was indicated by A.H. Grey-Edwards, himself a rural incumbent. He put it this way: the rural incumbent had to be choirmaster, advisor, organiser, trustee, chairman, as well as the regular factotum.[101] A rector of Hope, Thomas Evan Jones, speaking in 1891, dismissed the idea that a rural clergyman never did a hard day's work. Rather, he was expected to "peddle" with the secular affairs of the parish, as it had no man of business; tramp the parish with a collecting box, and still take services like Socrates or Sankey on Sundays.[102] The truth was probably in between as D. Parry-Jones suggested. The rural parson needed to know something or be ready to learn about farming, and also needed hobbies to occupy his time apart from reading.[103] There were others who suggested he would be immersed in the life of the village rather than running numerous organisations as did his town colleague.[104]

Bishop John Owen, in presenting evidence to the Royal Commission of 1906, accepted that the work of a rural clergyman was far different from that of a town incumbent, with the visiting he had to undertake and the numerous societies he had to look after. He added, however, that while the work in the countryside was different from the town, it should not be undervalued for, quoting a remark of a country priest of great academic distinction, rural parishes had a "small congregation but a large class". Rural clergy worked as hard as their town counterparts, and often because of depopulation had to see their younger people move away, and so had to start all over again building up a choir or a new set of confirmees. Their pastoral care had implications far wider than their own area, for many of their people found their way to the industrial areas and kept up their Welsh character and churchmanship there to the benefit of those places. Indeed, Owen asserted, the spiritual life of Wales depended on this rural ministry.[105]

A speaker at the Brighton Church Congress of 1901, P.P. Pennant of St Asaph, suggested that to be successful a rural incumbent had to be a quiet person, know everyone in his parish and the names of the children, be a family lawyer to his parishioners, and advise them if they got into trouble.[106] In this estimate it seems he was to be more a social worker than a priest. In reality he was both, and often faced isolation and depression. Marshall Dugdale applauded the rural clergy in 1903 who continued preaching to a small congregation week by week.[107] By this time, as Haig makes clear, rural ministry had become a little unfashionable for the up-and-coming new clergymen, who wished to be involved in the large town churches. They realised the loneliness and isolation of a rural parish, the lack of congenial company, the apparent lack of work (which was untrue in many cases), though many were reminded that at some time in the future their preferment would lie in such parishes in which they could cultivate holiness, a matter difficult for the town parson whose life was filled with activity.[108]

The large industrialised areas were difficult to manage pastorally, and besides, were generally centres of Nonconformity on the one hand and radical protest on the other. John Gott, in his *The Parish Priest of the Town*, described how the town parson differed from his rural contemporary. Haig notes he answered under four headings: organisation, high pressure, "the intricacies of conscience" (created by trade, theatres, factory life, dissent), and a hostile indifference of many to his ministry.[109] Heeney notes a comment that the town parson was required to be a combination of an athlete, showman, popular lecturer, relieving officer, savings bank manager, district visitor and general advisor, with the fear that he would become secularised as a result.[110] A more poignant note was made by Frederick Edmondes, speaking at the 1890 Llandaff Diocesan Conference. He said:

> There are parishes with six, ten, fifteen and sometimes twenty thousand people, and very often there is only one man to perform all the varied ministrations which a parish requires. He must preach, conduct all services held in Church, administer Holy Communion, baptize, catechise the young, marry, bury – the latter frequently at a distance from his parish – visit the sick and the whole, search out the sick and impotent folk of the parish, superintend the charities and charitable organizations, keep the parish registers, search for, and give certificates, send copies to the registrar, beside a whole host of other occupations, partly secular, which the double aspect of the Church, as a spiritual society and a legal institution, thrust upon him. And no one, except perhaps a brother Priest, where what we call a "Curate" can be "kept," as we say, can give him the slightest assistance. No voice must be heard in Church but his, however many services may be held there, save that the reading of the Scriptures has frequently of late, through not at first without some protest, been committed to Lay hands. The wonder is, not that these multifarious duties are ill done, as perforce they must be, but that they are ever done as well. In my own case, as my physical strength is not, and never has been, great, I find it a great strain, and one which seriously interferes with my performance of the office of preaching, to go through the whole service unassisted; and especially I feel the being alone at the administration of Holy Communion. But if this is the case in a small parish, how a Clergyman in a large parish can ever find the leisure or the strength necessary to instruct his flock properly, I have never been able to understand.[111]

After the consecration of Dowlais Church in 1827 Bishop Sumner is supposed to have remarked to its new vicar, Evan Jenkins, "I leave you as a missionary in the heart of Africa."[112] Many such parishes were missionary areas. The life of a Victorian town parish is noted further in this chapter, and the difficulties of establishing a new church plant in an industrialised region is discussed in a further section.

CHAPTER THREE: NURTURING THE SPIRITUAL LIFE

Another aspect of pastoral care was the nurturing of the spiritual life of the parishioners entrusted to the care of the parish incumbent. This included such matters as prayer, reading the Bible, weekday services for instruction and teaching, establishing guilds and similar societies, and supporting missionary societies together with a concern for the wider Church at home and overseas.

FAMILY PRAYER

Many of the pamphlets produced by the SPCK commended family prayer and frequent attendance at, together with proper preparation for, the communion service. It was a theme emphasised by many of the bishops in their Charges, and no doubt by clergy in their sermons and pastoral ministrations. In his letter to the clergy of the diocese of St Davids, the archbishop of Canterbury in 1703 urged them to exhort parents to undertake "family duty", to teach their children to pray, as well as to obtain spiritual books for them.[1] Many writers throughout the centuries commended family prayer to their readers. Amongst them was Bishop Bull of St Davids who did so in a circular letter to his clergy of 1708,[2] Richard Bassett of Colwinston,[3] and Daniel Nihill, curate of Forden, whose *The Farmer's Guide to Happiness* published in 1843 exhorted the farming community to commence family prayer. The circulating schools of Griffith Jones encouraged family prayer and taught adults and children about its practice.[4]

Family prayer was commended by both Bishop Burgess in his 1807 Charge (informing the clergy they should give an example)[5] and Bishop Short of St Asaph. In an appendix to his 1853 Charge he advised his clergy how to ascertain if family prayer was carried out in the homes of their parishioners and how to encourage it, along with hints about providing Bibles and forms of prayer. In addition, he suggested that children in the schools should be assisted to pray, and be taught prayers to say at their bedside morning and night, thus establishing a lifetime habit.[6] In that same year Short wrote a letter to Archdeacon Clough, which was printed for distribution, commending family prayer in both gentry and humble homes, and teaching the children to pray at home.[7] A speaker at the St Asaph Diocesan Conference of 1892 suggested that in the previous thirty years the custom of family worship and the saying of grace over meat had been lost in Wales. As a result there were many attempts to revive the practice.[8] In his parish circular of 1884, J.G. Gauntlett of Holy Trinity, Swansea, asked people to adopt family prayer, and if not communicants, to remedy this deficiency,[132] while David Howell wrote a tract, published by Home Words in 1891, entitled *Prayer as an Aid for Godliness*, promoting prayers at home. Howell encouraged what he described as "family duty" throughout his ministerial life. Family worship was one of the essentials of a peaceful home but a family without an altar was like a house without a roof. Public worship might become a habit, but family worship was a sign of spiritual life. He was equally concerned to promote individual private prayer. In an address given to the St Davids Diocesan Conference of 1902 he encouraged family worship, suggesting that Bishop Ken's morning and evening hymns could be sung, Scripture read and extempore prayer given. Not only would this instruct the whole family, it would allow a spiritual influence to pervade the whole household and have an effect on a person's speech and behaviour.[10] The whole matter of religion in the home was discussed at the Llandaff Diocesan Conference of 1892, and by the Bangor Conference in 1910.[11]

It is impossible to say to what extent family prayers took place in private homes, although John Elias, the Methodist leaders' grandfather of the same name, a faithful churchman, had family worship in his home morning and evening. This would be in the 1750s and thereafter.[12] The Victorians, especially the upper and professional classes, are known to have practised it, and one assumes this might have been a continuation from previous generations. Numerous devotional books were produced at this time, such as Henry Thornton's *Family Prayer* of 1834, or Edward Bickersteth's *Family Prayers* of 1842.[13] Similar Welsh publications are noted below, while the devotional books written by Griffith Jones were still in print in the early nineteenth century. A description of such family prayer, albeit in a gentry house, is recorded by Joseph Romilly in the 1840s. Four were present plus five servants. Romilly read prayers and selected a sermon by Fenton he had found in the house which he altered and shortened. At night he read Matthew 18 and expounded it, and abridged the service of evening prayer.[14]

THE DISTRIBUTION OF BOOKS

Bibles and religious books in Welsh were in short supply, and Thomas Gouge, who died in 1681, having founded the Welch Trust for establishing charity schools in Wales, also procured at great expense a new impression of the Bible and Prayer Book in Welsh, of which 8,000 were printed and 1,000 freely given to the poor. The others were sold at 4s. each and were said to be well bound and clasped and cheaper than the equivalent English version.[15] But this was insufficient for the expected need. The position was greatly assisted by the foundation of the SPCK which produced Bibles for distribution, and it had local correspondents in many areas to whom they were sent for distribution. A new edition of the Welsh Bible was produced by the society in 1718 under the editorship of Moses Williams, and a further edition in 1727. There were numerous pirated versions published at Shrewsbury, cheap, convenient but defective. All these, including the pirated copies, had a wide circulation. In 1750, for example, 14,704 Welsh Bibles published by SPCK were distributed and a reprint of 15,000 copies of that year of the Bible with the Prayer Book cost 4s.6d. per copy, and in addition 5,000 New Testaments with the Prayer Book were produced, and the same number of the Prayer Book on its own. Morris Pritchard Morris of Dulas, in Anglesey, as a correspondent, received 50 Bibles and 56 New Testaments which he distributed to fourteen parishes, including 40 New Testaments to the rector of Llaneugrad, Lewis Owen.[16] Griffith Jones benefited immensely from the support of SPCK in providing his circulating schools with Welsh Bibles and literature, especially catechisms and Welsh psalter. Five thousand copies of an impression of the church catechism were printed in 1740. The text was broken into short sections with Scriptural proofs placed on the opposite side of the column.[17]

Thomas Parry, in his seminal work, *A History of Welsh Literature*, notes the numerous devotional books which appeared between 1630-91. These were either original works in Welsh or translated from the English,. Their subjects ranged from prayer, morality, the need for preparation for Holy Communion, and the prospect of death. Most were written by Churchmen.[18] Between 1699-1738 SPCK published 31 books of devotion in Welsh, some of them translations from English.[19] These included Tillotson's *Persuasives to Frequent Communion* and Gibson's *Family Devotions*, Nelson's *Festivals and Fasts* (translated by Thomas Williams, rector of Denbigh), Lewis Bayly's *Practice of Piety* and Rowland Vaughan's translation of it. Bayly's work was a popular guide to the spiritual life and devotion, and even included instructions for making a will.[20]

Throughout this period the SPCK produced a large number of tracts, a number in Welsh, while the Religious Tract Society, founded in London in 1799, followed suit. The SPCK's tracts included ones on Christian duties, against various vices, and many were directed to particular occupations. Bishop Gibson of London encouraged clergy to have them in hand for widespread distribution.[21] Between 1804-12 the Bangor Diocesan Tract Society produced numerous tracts for distribution on Sabbath observance, family prayers, the Welsh Catechism, a selection of psalms and sermons, and it was also concerned with the distribution of Bibles. These tracts were sent to parishes where they were lent out to parishioners, and when returned another one was given in its place. It seems to have been based on the lines of the St David's Church Union Society, which also produced tracts and pamphlets, and was followed by a similar, though short-lived, society in the diocese of St Asaph before 1830. This was probably promoted by Rowland Williams, who was one of the main organisers of the Bangor society.[22] Richard Davies, archdeacon and vicar of Brecon, who died in 1859, encouraged the distribution of these tracts throughout his parish, even producing some of his sermons in this format.[23]

As we noted earlier, district visitors were encouraged to give out tracts to the homes they visited, but in addition a number of town parishes possessed colportage associations, though these were generally interdenominational affairs. The report for the Swansea branch survives for 1878-9. The colporteur visited a large number of families, selling Christian books to them and encouraging them to subscribe to Christian periodicals rather than reading sensational literature about crime and disgusting heroism. He had a stall in the market on Saturdays.[24]

By the late nineteenth century the parish magazine had become a means of educating the laity as well as informing them about local events. Many of these parochial magazines were accompanied by insets provided by various societies which had a missionary or evangelistic aim.[25] In commencing a magazine for his Cardiff parish in

1870, David Howell saw it as an extension of his own parochial ministry. His aim was to provide cheap literature "on the side of morality", bearing in mind that so much literature was on the other side. He included articles on Sabbath observance, almsgiving, aspects of Church teaching, and on disestablishment and ritualism.[26] Some magazines were produced for a rural deanery or archdeaconry: the archdeaconry of Brecon had such a magazine in 1885, and one for the rural deanery of Llanfyllin was started in 1888.[27] A number of church periodicals were commenced as well. Brutus (David Owen) was long connected with *Yr Haul*, which savaged Nonconformity with a biting tongue, and William Evans of Rhymney, edited *Y Cyfaill Eglwysig*, which had been commenced by David Howell. Dean Cotton was on the committee which established *Y Cymro*, but the management of the paper neglected its finances and Cotton was sued by the printers and judgment was obtained against him. Had it not been for Lord Penrhyn, associated with him on the committee, who paid these debts, Cotton would have been in serious trouble.[25]

The British and Foreign Bible Society was an interdenominational society, and as such caused some difficulties to High Churchmen. They felt that the Church's own society, SPCK, was sufficient for the purpose of distributing Bibles, and disliked the idea of Bibles being sold without the Book of Common Prayer. The story of its foundation, and the prominent part taken in it by Thomas Charles of Bala, is too well known to be repeated here. In spite of the distaste of many bishops, including Bishop Marsh of Llandaff, who argued that the Bible needed to be accompanied by the Prayer Book as its interpreter, and feared the illiterate teachers who would find their own interpretations,[29] a large number of Welsh clergymen were supporters of the Society. Bishop Burgess, for example, refused to accept the arguments made against Anglican involvement in the Society. To co-operate with so-called "unbelievers", that is, dissenters, was not an act of heresy or schism, and he would not decline to do good in distributing Scripture as he accepted the resources of SPCK were inadequate to supply the demand.[30] Reginald Heber, later bishop of Calcutta, whilst at Hodnet, 1807-23, also supported and defended the Bible Society against its critics.[31] Thomas Price, Carnhuanawc, preached on its behalf at Liverpool, and was deeply concerned with a translation of the Breton Bible.[32] Many localities had their own branches, such as Berriew. A notebook belonging to this branch survives for the period of 1819-25. Within it is a letter to David Richards of Llansilin, stating that as the writer was in the midst of dissenters he was anxious that the Church should come forward and maintain its proper ground, presumably through that branch society.[33]

WEEKDAY SERVICES AND LECTURES

By the 1840s there were more clergy and a greater conscientiousness amongst clergy and laity about spiritual life. This led to the growth of weekday evening services and meetings, as a means of enriching and growing the spiritual life. Consequently, many churches held weekday services, generally Evening Prayer with a sermon, as did Aberystwyth in the 1840s,[34] Caernarfon in 1851 (with an evening lecture once a week, communicants' meetings, and numerous Bible classes for men, boys and females),[35] and Pwllheli in the 1860s. Here the services were in Welsh on Thursday and English on Friday, while a communicants' class met on Mondays (possibly a Bible class), and there was another weekly class during which the collects were discussed.[36]

Though Griffith Jones endeavoured to persuade the clergy to establish weekly lectures in their parishes in 1737, it never seems to have happened, and this had to wait for another seventy years, though there seems to have been a precedent for them in the dioceses of St Asaph and St Davids at the beginning of the century, according to G.H. Jenkins.[37] The origin of the circulating schools came from Jones' experience of holding a lecture on the Saturday evening previous to the sacrament Sunday, when he would catechise in the church and apply its teaching to their lives.[38]

A variant of these services were the so-called weekly lectures, which consisted of a service together with an address. These were designed for those who found it difficult to attend the Sunday worship, either because of other commitments, or there was no room in the church building for them, or because they lacked decent clothes to do so. As they often used a simpler service than that provided by the Book of Common Prayer they were termed lectures, for if they were held in a consecrated building such a truncated service would be regarded as an ecclesiastical offence. Until 1855, under the Conventicle Act, it was also an offence to publicly use the services of the Prayer Book outside a consecrated building when more than twenty people were present.

In his *Sunday Evening Lectures recommended to the Clergy of the Diocese of St*

David's, of 1806, Bishop Burgess advocated the use of these as a means of bringing in people who were unable to attend the main Sunday services, and to offer an alternative to those who attended the Nonconformist evening services. He suggested as a form of service psalmody, of the plainest sort, interspersed with parts of evening prayer, together with a lecture or address.[39] It is not known if churches adopted this at the time, though presumably some did. But by the 1820s a number of churches held these Sunday evening lectures. Wrexham commenced one in 1820, when subscriptions were raised and an evening lecturer paid £50 per annum.[40] St Julian's, Shrewsbury, also did so in 1828, and its regular congregation consented to give up their pews for those who attended, mainly from the poorer classes.[41]

In many parishes the congregation was scattered geographically and as a result many of the parishioners were unable to be regular churchgoers. To remedy this deficiency cottage meetings were established. Thus there arose the cottage service or lecture which was seen as another means of teaching the faithful and extending the influence of the Church. Walsham How provided the format for such a cottage lecture service in his *Pastor in Parochia* published in the 1870s if not earlier, as did John Ellerton in his *Manual of Parochial Work* for a service lasting one hour.[42] These lectures were certainly in existence by 1815, albeit at Wellington, Shropshire,[43] and were commended by John Bird Sumner, bishop of Chester from 1828, as a way by which the exposition of the Bible could be thoroughly undertaken, suggesting he was writing about a long existing practice.[44]

Henry Vaughan introduced these cottage meetings into the parish of Crickhowel during his ministry, 1830-7. He often held impromptu meetings in homes where there had been a bereavement and invited the neighbours to attend.[45] In a large south Wales parish (possibly Eglwysilan), noted in a CPAS report of 1846, there were three cottage meetings, or, as they were termed, "lectures". Two were held at considerable distances from the church, and these attracted many who previously had never attended a church service. The curate took one of them, in an area filled with persons prejudiced against the Church, found that people crowded to hear him, "and while he speaks their attention seems riveted, and they appear at the time completely subdued".[46] John Williams, ab Ithel, also introduced them to his parish of Llanymawddwy between 1849-62, and though he was a High Churchman he even allowed laymen to take prayer meetings at different cottages.[47] Robert Roberts, whilst at Tremadoc on an extended holiday, seems to have commenced a weekly lecture with some friends there in the 1850s, using first the English church, until its righteous members objected that "the plebeians contaminated the cushions and hassocks", and then the Town Hall, but the congregation was small and there was no external support.[48]

Cottage lectures took place at Gwersyllt, then in the parish of Gresford, in 1849, on each Friday at 2.00pm when around fifteen people attended,[49] and at Berriew in the late 1850s. Here, however, the curate, J.J. Turner, had to insist that the Scripture reader, who he had reluctantly agreed could take the service in the schoolroom, should check with him what prayers, Bible readings and hymns would be used.[50] The 1851 census noted several: at Llandysul, Cardiganshire, where a cottage lecture was delivered every other Sunday evening in a distant part of the parish, as was another at Llanthetty, Breconshire, which was held in a schoolroom and attended by about one hundred people.[51] Though Kilvert wrote of a cottage meeting at Langley Burrell, Wiltshire, of which he was then curate, there is little mention of them otherwise in his diary.[52] Cottage meetings were recorded in the parishes of Lampeter in the early 1870s,[53] Welshpool in 1875 at some of its more outlying areas,[54] Ruabon in the 1880s,[55] and Hawarden in the early 1900s,[56] and another, linked to St Mark's Church, Swansea, was mentioned as late as 1905.[57] Today, they would be described as house meetings. A number of these cottage meetings became the nucleus of a mission room and sometimes of a church. This happened in the 1880s for the Ebbw Mission in the parish of St Paul's, Newport.[58]

SPIRITUAL SOCIETIES

There were many clergy in the eighteenth century who realised more was needed than just church services, among them Dr Woodward, who was instrumental in forming a number of religious societies and in 1712 wrote a manual for them, *An Account of Religious Societies*. These societies were more personal than the lectures, and promoted discussion of the religious life. His example was followed by numerous evangelical clergy in England though many were cautious until they had episcopal approval. One such society was known at Wrexham in the 1700s, and others at Carmarthen,

Llanddeiniolen in Caernarfonshire, and at St Asaph, though some of these appear to have been linked with the Society for the Reformation of Manners.[59] A reflection of these societies is possibly noted by Erasmus Saunders in his book of 1721, *A View of the State of Religion in the Diocese of St David's* makes mention of a similar though informal society. He notes how groups of people would assemble outdoors or in private homes to instruct themselves privately, and for young people in particular to sing spiritual carols for want of any more formal instruction. This was, he notes, a religious exercise they were used to, and they did the same on public occasions such as wakes, festivals and funerals.[60] Perhaps a continuation of these societies was the Saturday evening catechetical lectures given at Llantrisant, Glamorgan, by Richard Harris in 1763. Guy suspects these may have been started by Harris's father, though they were not continued by his successor.[61]

It could be argued that some of the adult night classes held by Griffith Jones' schoolmasters formed a quasi-religious society, and it is reasonably clear that a number of these became the nucleus of Methodist societies, which, though they believed themselves associated with the Church, were seen by many churchmen as a breakaway movement. William Williams, Pantycelyn, wrote a handbook for these societies.[62] Sadly, the Church, in response, often discontinued what meetings it had organised, or allowed them to move into the Methodist orbit. This occurred with the private societies established by David Jones, Llangan, a Methodist cleric, who died in 1810, where young converts were nurtured and the older ones edified, and brought into spiritual union with one another.[63]

Even so, it was soon realised that similar meetings were needed for Church members as they provided something more intimate and personal than the formality of a service. They took the form of communicants' meetings, even though sometimes they resembled the society meetings of the evangelical revival, where hearts were bared and secrets revealed for spiritual counsel to be given.

David Howell, writing to his bishop in 1886, urged that parishes should have a fortnightly meeting of communicants, to teach them to pray and speak, and also meetings for extempore prayer,[64] though many might have regarded such matters as more akin to Nonconformity than the Church. There was an element of distaste, for example, from

Bishop Carey in a letter to his friend, Thomas Griffith Roberts of Llanrwst, when he told him that Griffith Howel, junior, informed him that he was holding "a sort of evening prayer meeting" in a schoolroom in 1832. The bishop desired him to discontinue it.[65] In a pamphlet of 1842 entitled, *What says the Church?* a Welsh rector declaimed against those whose hearts were really in conventicles and who held prayer or preaching meetings in school room and private houses, and thus sanctioned dissent. A return to Church principles was required. A pamphlet written in support of this publication, which had aroused a pamphlet war, allegedly by Evan Lloyd, rector of "Llangelynys", added private societies to the list of concerns, claiming that only those who attended these society meetings would be admitted into the Church. Those who engaged in such matters were "worse than traitors in the camp".[66]

John Griffith, recently appointed to Aberdare, writing as *Cambro Sacerdos* in 1846, condemned these meetings outright, arguing they had been introduced into the Church by the Cardiganshire born clergy of Methodist stock who had become curates in the south Wales valleys. After a comment on the psalms, the cleric would encourage the men to relate their experiences, which would be "loathsome and offensive to every discreet ear" He alleged that if they refused to go through such an ordeal, communion would be denied them. Those clergy who held such meetings and allowed prayer "by the Spirit" were thoroughly condemned by Griffith, with Griffith commenting that to serenade "the Holy Ghost to such rhapsodies as you hear uttered, and which you countenance, is nothing but to defend *boldness* with *blasphemy*."[67]

Archdeacon James of Carmarthen was equally unimpressed, arguing that the prayer meeting in a schoolroom was not a sufficient alternative to holding weekday services. These, he believed, even if attended by eight or twelve people, would repay the minister as they would quicken the spiritual life of the parish.[68] However, a defence of communicants' meetings came from Bishop Campbell in his 1860 Charge. While he accepted that some regarded those who attended as forming a church within a church and as becoming elitist, and conceded the liturgy made no provision for these meetings, no-one was required to attend, they were not opposed to the spirit of the liturgy, could extend the catechetical office of the Church and promote the fellowship of pastor and communicants.[69]

Bishop Campbell was not alone among the bishops in commending these activities. Following the Methodist break-away in 1811, Bishop Cleaver of St Asaph permitted the clergy, especially those evangelicals he ordained as literates as part of his policy of strengthening the Church against Methodism, to hold meetings for the deepening of devotional life without the danger of their being branded with opprobrious names.[70] If Thirlwall of St Davids did not commend these meetings, at least he permitted his clergy to hold them and to adopt the style of teaching most suited to their members, but he warned them not to allow these meetings to become an occasion for schism.[71] Short of St Asaph in his 1850 Charge considered that the best way for preparing Sunday School teachers for their work was through a Bible class, and also spoke in favour of communicants' meetings and holding family prayers in large farmhouses attended by people in the locality.[72]

In spite of this opposition to them these communicants' meetings gained strength. It is said that John Williams, ab Ithel, was one of the first to start such meetings in his parish of Llanymawddwy in the 1850s,[73] though a communicants' meeting, on Wednesday mornings, was noted in a Welsh valley parish (possibly Eglwysilan), in 1846, as having beneficial results.[74] At Rhymney, Lodwick Edwards, 1843-56, held a weekly communicants meeting during which he trained his congregation in prayer and Bible reading. This was continued by William Evans, his successor, who regarded this meeting as the backbone of his spiritual work.[75] In the early 1850s Robert Roberts noted such meetings at Bethesda and in neighbouring parishes.[76] In the 1870s such meetings were held on a monthly basis at Welshpool,[77] and around the same time at Lampeter during the curacy of J.A. Jackson.[78] The 1906 royal commission noted further examples at Llanfihangel-ar-Arth and Pencader, where they were held monthly, but in addition the latter parish had prayer meetings and Bible classes.[79] The pastoral letter of Christ Church, Swansea, for 1887-8, made clear that the communicants' guild required its members to read a portion of Scripture each day, to examine themselves, offer up morning and evening prayer, attend Holy Communion frequently, preferably weekly, to be reverent in church, honest and upright, strive against impure thoughts, be obedient to parents and employers and to undertake some Christian work.[80]

Akin to a communicants' meeting was the prayer meeting. This had a long pedigree in evangelical and Methodist circles. They were not only used to edify those who attended them but also to teach them to conduct their own household worship.[81] David Herbert of Llanrhystud and Llansanffraid, who died in 1835, is said to have kept his parishes loyal to the Church in spite of the Methodist secession and the persuasive influence of nearby Llangeitho, the Methodist centre, by adopting Methodist ways, including congregational singing, an all-age Sunday school, and a prayer meeting that resembled the Methodist *seiat* or experience meeting.[82] Many of these meetings were held on Sundays as this was the only day most people could assemble, though the meetings might also have prayed for God's blessing on the services of the day. At Cardiff St John's in 1871 an early morning Sunday prayer meeting was held at 7.30am, attended by over 200 people.[83]

Daniel Richards records such a communicants' meeting at Llanbadarn Trefeglwys in the early 1900s. Although it appears to have taken the place of the Sunday evening service, it was conducted by laymen. Its leader, Benjamin Evans, would invite a number of members to offer prayer, knowing who would be long winded and who would be short to ensure the meeting would be finished within an hour. Sometimes up to eighteen laymen might be involved in these meetings. The service began with a hymn, recalled from memory, and generally only one verse was sung though the last lines might be repeated. In between the prayers there would Scripture readings and further hymns.[84] In other places free prayer might be permitted. The 1906 Royal Commission was told by Archdeacon Albert Owen Evans that while the Church's liturgy forbade such meetings, many parishes in the diocese of Bangor held them. One was held at Penmaenmawr whose vicar, Canon David Jones had described his prayer meeting to the commission which, apart from a section of Biblical exposition, was indistinguishable from a Nonconformist one. It commenced with the Lord's Prayer and a hymn, followed by short responses; a chapter of scripture was read and expounded for fifteen minutes, and then various laymen were asked to give out a hymn or to pray, sometimes extempore, sometimes not. Between twelve and fifty attended. The bishop of St Davids also gave evidence that similar meetings were held in many parishes of his diocese as well.[85]

Bishop Edwards of St Asaph, giving evidence before the same Royal Commission, stated that in nearly all the parishes of his diocese Bible classes or guilds for young people were held.[86] There were probably few parishes without such a class by the 1900s. David Howell formed a Bible class soon after his entry to the parish of Wrexham in 1878, and by 1886 there were a number of these, with separate ones for men, women and children (as was general at the time), as well as another one for Welsh speakers. He regarded these classes as an essential part of his ministry, urged those attending to let them take precedence of all other engagements, and to regard them as a means of grace from which a blessing might be prayerfully expected. Furthermore, they were a means of expounding the Scriptures, clearing up apparent difficulties, removing prejudices, and showing the harmony between the Bible and the teaching of the Church.[87] Welshpool had a number of Bible classes in the 1890s. The men's class, which met on Sundays at Christ Church, a daughter church, had 130 members, and occasional talks on such subjects as Sabbath observance and on the value of the Book of Common Prayer. It was said their presence gave life to this church and ensured there was a large congregation at the evening service.[88]

A leaflet advertising the Christ Church, Swansea, men's Bible class survives from 1901. It advised that the method used in its Sunday afternoon meetings did not show whether a man could read or not, so those who could not read should not hesitate about joining. Admission was for those over seventeen, there were prizes for good attendance, and it was linked to a social club. The 180 members studied the Acts of the Apostles, but on the first Sunday of each month there was a talk about a noted Christian, such as Lord Shaftesbury, George Herbert, St Francis of Assisi, Edward Denison or Charles Kingsley.[89] We perhaps should also note the Girls' Instruction Class, noted in Christ Church, Swansea's, pastoral letter of 1891-2. Girls from twelve to seventeen years old were taught thrift, singing, reciting, spelling and sewing at its meetings, but above all the Bible was read and explained and the Catechism taught with a view to confirmation.[90]

The Tractarian parishes had guilds which served a similar purpose. By 1882 the parish of Roath had guilds for men, young men and boys, young women and girls, as well as branches of the Confraternity of the Blessed Sacrament.[91] David Williams, vicar of Llanelli, established guilds in his parish soon after his arrival in 1867.[92] By 1872 St Mary's Church, Cardiff, had mothers' meetings, Bible classes, various guilds, and the East Grimstead sisters, who worked within the parish among the female population and the children.[93] At Whittington Walsham How established a guild of church workers, and gave his cook membership, claiming she made delicacies for the poor in her own time, with the result that her work was as valuable as that of any district visitor who took them in person to the recipient.[94]

QUASI-SPIRITUAL PAROCHIAL ORGANISATIONS

By the end of the nineteenth century a number of quasi-Church organisations had come into being. Most had been started in a parish, but had grown into national movements, with the local parochial group being affiliated to a diocesan association. Amongst their number were the Mothers' Union (MU), Girls' Friendly Society (GFS), Church of England Men's Society (CEMS), and such Anglo-Catholic fraternities as the Society of St David and of the Blessed Sacrament. The MU and CEMS receive some notice below, while the others are briefly noted in the text. In addition there were the missionary societies many of which were organised in the same way with diocesan organisations and local branches. As noted in another chapter, most parishes had temperance associations and other societies with the more secular aim of keeping church members, especially the young, sufficiently occupied and away from temptation.

The Mothers' Union, which became almost a quasi-Church, developed from the various mothers' meetings that had started in the 1860s. Brecon had one by 1868 to encourage the habits of thrift and industry, and Swansea by 1885. At these meetings various ladies sought to assist the poorer classes who attended them by relieving their home cares, teaching household skills, and promoting their spiritual welfare. Many of these mothers' meetings organised clothing clubs or provided cloth for garments at a reduced price, and while members sewed during the meeting a book was generally read. At Christ Church, Swansea, there was Bible reading, a hymn and a prayer, plus an address by the clergy, and various domestic activities took place as a book was read bearing upon the homes and hearts of the members. The aim was to assist mothers to save money for clothes but also to provide for them a means of grace.[95] The Mothers' Union swept many of these mothers' meetings under its umbrella and also took over some of their aims. They thus promoted prayer and spiritual life, especially by assisting mothers in bringing up their children in the Christian faith, praying for them, and seeking by their own example to lead their families in purity and holiness of life. One of its first branches in Wales was at Llandrindod Wells in 1884, and by 1894 Llandaff diocese had eleven branches, but its growth was rapid thereafter. By 1899 Bangor had seven branches, Llandaff 45, St Asaph 39 and St Davids 56 (where a speaker at its diocesan conference that year said that a branch in a parish would transform it), but by the 1920s there was rivalry from the newly introduced Women's Institutes.[96]

The Church of England Men's Society, founded in 1899, and which required a rule of life from its members specifying prayer and forwarding the work of the Church, was organised on a diocesan basis in Llandaff during 1912 as a means of further promoting the Society's work in that diocese.[97] Pritchard Hughes, bishop of Llandaff, in the following year commended the organisation, stating that it was deepening the spiritual life of its members, and was banding Churchmen together for the glory of God.[98] The Girls' Friendly Society, founded in 1875, which though it had a social and educational motive also had a spiritual purpose in addition to its aim of encouraging morality. Many of its members came from the servant classes, and it acted as an honest agency for girls wishing to enter service. The organisation possessed sick clubs, a rest home at Criccieth, and an employment office.[99] The Church Lads' Brigade, founded in 1891, had a military set-up, but gave Christian teaching and required its members to attend the services of the Church, generally in uniform. Many branches had drum and fife bands, which often led church processions.

By the end of the nineteenth century most parishes had many of these societies, and other organisations, including temperance and missionary societies. Bishop Watkin Williams of Bangor, in his 1900 visitation, asked his clergy about their parish organisations. Frances Knight has analysed a sample of the answers of 35 mainland parishes, and notes the most common were associations to raise money for mission work, young men's organisations (which will be discussed in another chapter) and GFS. Surprisingly, the MU was not mentioned in many of these returns, possibly as its impact was still to come.[100] It is not surprising, therefore, that a well-worked town parish, such as Hawarden, even by the 1880s, had a number of directly spiritual organisations and others with a quasi-spiritual character. These consisted of a ward of the Confraternity of the Blessed Sacrament, the MU and GFS, and in addition there was a Communicants'

Association and a Missionary Association with a children's missionary guild.[101] In the 1870s Llanfairfechan had both a communicants' guild for Welsh speakers, and a children's guild attached to it as a preparatory society,[102] while in the 1890s the parish of Llanfyllin had numerous social societies, a Band of Hope and temperance society, branches of GFS, MU, SPG, and the Waifs and Strays (now the Children's' Society).[103] Penarth had numerous Bible classes, and branches of the MU, CLB, and GFS,[104] and St Martin's, Haverfordwest, had at various times in the 1890s and beyond a Bible class, confirmation guild, a Guild of St Martin and in the late 1910s a branch of the Society of St David, an Anglo-Catholic fraternity founded at St David's College, Lampeter.[105]

By the 1900s a parish such as Holy Trinity, Aberystwyth, had in addition to the MU and GFS, branches of CEMS and CLB, as well as the King's Messengers – a children's missionary society, and in the 1930s a Young Communicants' Guild.[106] During the same period the parish of St Paul's Newport had prayer meetings, a Bible Reading on Tuesdays, a branch of CEMS, a Band of Hope, and a men's Bible class which had a membership of over one hundred.[107] The parish of Holy Trinity, Ystrad Mynach, had in 1914, branches of the CEMS and GFS, a young men's Bible class, a Welsh service on Thursday evenings, and by 1924 a CLB.[108] Similarly, the large Tractarian parish of St Theodore, Port Talbot, had such organisations as the MU, CEMS, GFS, a men's Bible class, and later a Church Defence League (to protest about disestablishment), a Fraternity of the Resurrection, and a Guild of the Servants of the Sanctuary.[109] The Greenhill Mission in Swansea, which later moved to St Matthew's Church, and was a centre of evangelical churchmanship, had by contrast no secular or even quasi-spiritual organisations, but instead held throughout the week a Band of Hope, Bible and prayer classes, a Gospel meeting, and an open air witness on Saturdays.[110]

Weekly Bible classes were held at St Mary's, Swansea, as a result of the 1905 Welsh revival's impact on that parish, but this appears to have been an addition for converts, as in 1878 there were prayer meetings in the National Schoolroom on the first and fourth Sundays after the evening service and on Tuesday evenings, with an address, in addition to several others in the daughter churches. By 1894 there were six Bible classes on Sundays (divided between men, boys, girls and women), and another two on weekdays for young women, two mother's meetings and a Sunday School teachers meeting. Two of the district churches, at least, had Bible classes and prayer meetings, while St Thomas had a boys' brigade together with its drum and fife band, as well as temperance organisations.[111] A rural parish such as Prendergast had a strong branch of CEMS, having a weekly meeting and a monthly service.[112]

It was probably the task of the individual clergyman to establish such societies, and this may be why a valley parish such as Senghenydd was late in starting a MU branch in 1916, and a GFS branch nine years later.[113] It was certainly true of Penley, where a new incumbent, R.W. Foulger, instituted in 1874, commenced branches of the GFS (founded the following year), a temperance society, and various other societies.[114] It was also true of Oystermouth, where a new vicar, Harold Williams, appointed in 1898, started numerous social and other organisations including a Bible Class as well as a parish magazine, which had a circulation of 800 copies.[115] The evangelical Cecil Lillingston, appointed to Sketty in 1903, immediately organised Bible classes, started a MU branch, and commenced a parish magazine.[116]

Rural parishes, by contrast, had few organisations, either pastoral or social, as a speaker declared at the 1885 St David's Diocesan Conference, though most had Sunday Schools, and a few had Bible classes and clothing clubs.[117] It might have been in this connection that H.A. James, then dean of St Asaph, could assert in 1888 that while the Church in Wales could compare favourably with England in its Bible classes and number of communicants, it was much inferior in guilds, Sunday Schools and social institutions.[118] In these areas meetings were confined to the winter months when agriculture was at a low ebb. This occurred in the parish of Pentraeth, Anglesey, when David Griffith was curate, 1884-94. Though there was a regular Sunday School, the communicants' class only met in winter and then on alternative Saturday evenings.[119] It was also suggested that in these parishes the Sunday Schools were combined with an adult Bible class, as was the custom in Nonconformity.[120]

OVERSEAS MISSION

The missionary movement was a major concern of the Victorian Church for as the Empire expanded and Africa was opened, numerous missionary societies were founded to spread the Gospel into "heathen lands". Indeed, the Victorian age was the great age of missionary expansion overseas, although both the SPG and the SPCK had been in this field since their foundation in 1698 and 1701 respectively. The SPG, by its charter, was confined to English plantations. A large number of Welshmen, including Bishop Humphreys of Bangor, Sir Humphrey Mackworth, and Sir John Philipps were associated with these two societies. By the nineteenth century many parishes had become linked to a missionary society in what was termed a missionary auxiliary, whose purpose was to raise awareness of, and funds for, them. An early one was at Welshpool for the SPCK in 1812.[121] Ollivant's Charge of 1857 suggested that groups of clergy could form themselves into missionary associations, seeking contributions from their parishioners, and dividing the proceeds between the two main missionary societies, CMS and SPG.[122] The clergy of the Arllechwedd deanery expressed a desire that every parish should have a branch of at least one missionary society as part of its activities, and the deanery was also concerned to raise funds for the mission in Patagonia to the Welsh settlers.[123]

Many clergymen acted as local correspondents or area secretaries for these societies, as did John Hughes of Aberystwyth for CMS,[124] while Edward Smart, while rector of Henllan 1840-76, acted in a voluntary capacity as CMS associate secretary for Wales, employing a curate for his parish from his own resources to cover his many absences. As a fluent Welsh speaker he was especially welcomed in many parishes.[125] Thomas Price, Carnhuanawc, supported and preached for CMS,[126] and Henry Vaughan of Crickhowel, who advocated the claims of CMS and the Moravian missions, made frequent tours into England to preach for these societies, where he emphasised "the sweet savour of the name of Jesus".[127] Richard Richards, who died in 1860, while at Caerwys and Meifod, acted as a speaker for both CMS and the Bible Society in the diocese of St Asaph and beyond,[128] and the evangelical David James of Panteg was an associate secretary for CMS.[129] Hugh Jones, vicar of Holywell 1844-68 was another associate secretary of CMS, and travelled all over Wales on horseback in order to preach for the society.[130] A memorial to Charles Arthur Albany Lloyd, rector of Whittington 1799-1851 describes him as one who "most zealously preached Christ crucified … and energetically advocated the cause of the Church Missionary Society, remembering and obeying the Scriptural precept, 'Tell it out among the heathen that the Lord is king'." His son, Albany Rossendale Lloyd, vicar of Hengoed until 1895, held an annual three day mission festival for CMS and always amazed his chosen speakers by his generous hospitality and the substantial attendance at these meetings.[131]

David Williams, who held livings at Nannerch and Castle Caereinion and who died in 1882, not only translated works into Welsh for SPCK, and compiled for SPG a Welsh work on Christian mission, *Cenhadeuthau Eglwysig,* he also acted as organising secretary for SPG in the diocese of St Asaph from 1850. He persuaded many of the mission leaders of the day to come to speak in the diocese, including Bishop Selwyn of New Zealand, and through his activity St Asaph was said to have contributed more in subscriptions to that society than many wealthier English dioceses, often to the extent of £1,000 per annum.[132] Canon Eleazar Williams, vicar of Llangefni 1877-1901, collected thousands of pounds for CMS and held public meetings in its Town Hall on behalf of the society addressed by "giants of the Church", and with his wife organised missionary sales and house to house collections. When in residence at Bangor he held drawing room meetings for the society, though his colleagues in the chapter were not favourably inclined to CMS. It is said that many young clergy were drawn to missionary work through his influence.[133] The life of James Davies, the schoolmaster of Devauden, whose generosity to the CMS almost exceeded his means and who laboured to collect funds for the it, was recorded in two books as an example to lay people of their own obligation to support foreign mission.[134] The work of an association secretary is described by A.H. Grey-Edwards in his Reminiscences.[135]

Parishes were expected to contribute to missionary work, whether they had a local auxiliary or not. Special collections in the diocese of St Asaph in 1856 for non-parochial objects indicated that out of a total of £1,067, just under half went to two societies, CMS and SPG.[136] A survey of the diocese of St Davids in 1897 revealed that while 128 parishes supported SPG, 141 CMS, and another 41 supported both, a further 187 supported neither society. David Howell, then dean of St Davids, thought this was deplorable.[137] In a pamphlet he argued that the Church was neglecting the King's command to support foreign mission and there was a need to place missionary duty and vocation before the people. The United Kingdom gave less than £1.5m. for foreign mission, compared to spending £9m. on tobacco and £140m. on alcoholic drinks.[138] The duty of supporting foreign mission was emphasised at the St Asaph Diocesan Conference of 1901, as well as on other occasions.[139] Each year the Llandaff Diocesan Conference had a report from its Board of Missions, formed in 1904, which calculated how much was sent to these societies in any given year. A resolution of regret was passed in 1911 that foreign mission was not better supported. In 1913-14, for example, 53 parishes made no contribution, 115 contributed to CMS and 145 to SPG, and 90 to other societies. The total sum collected was £4,832.[140] Missionary festivals and exhibitions were also arranged by local committees, assisted by the diocese. Welshpool was the centre for one such festival in 1874 when Bishop Selwyn of Lichfield was the guest preacher. The next year Canon Gregory of St Paul's visited the area as the deputation speaker for SPG, and spoke in Welshpool and at some of the outlying village churches. There was also an annual day of intercession for mission.[141] Another festival was held in Cardiff in 1907.[142]

A number of examples of this parochial concern for foreign mission may be given. The parish of Swansea, whose evangelical witness was nurtured by its vicar, Edward Squire, a former missionary in India, had a host of such associations in 1866: CMS, SPCK, Jews' Society, the Irish Church Mission to Roman Catholics, Missions to Seamen (when it was an evangelistic society), and CPAS as a home mission society, amongst others. By 1892 the list included the Colonial and Continental Church Society, the Moravian Mission, the Bible Society, and the Church of England Zenana Society.[143] Its neighbour, Holy Trinity, had auxiliaries of CPAS and CMS, and also announced the commencement of a juvenile branch of CMS in 1884.[144] St Theodore's, Port Talbot, had a branch of the UMCA (United Mission to Central Africa).[145] Welshpool had a SPG auxiliary, and some of its meetings in the 1840s and 1860s were presided over by the earl of Powis.[146] By the 1900s this parish mainly though not exclusively supported SPG, and had both a Ladies Group and a Children's Guild connected with this society. The children were urged to collect one shilling a year for the cause and to pray daily for foreign mission. One collection a year was given to SPG and another to CMS. In one particular year the amount collected for foreign mission amounted to £82, though the parish also supported the Jews' Society and the Universities Mission to Central Africa.[147]

In addition, many auxiliary societies were formed for a locality, such as Cardiff, for example, and the reports of their annual meetings, including CMS, SPCK, SPG, the Moravian Missions, duly appeared in the local press.[148] Both Monmouth and Glamorgan had district auxiliaries for SPG and SPCK, whose meetings were often held together, and in the 1830s held an annual service with an address.[149] In the archdeaconry of Brecon, according to its 1885 magazine, there was much local support for CMS and SPG as well as the Zanzibar Mission. One missionary representative, the Revd. J. Cook, gave a missionary lecture with "dissolving views" at Rhaeadr, while Llandrindod had a working party to make clothes for the mission field.[150]

There were a large number of clergy and laypeople who became missionaries overseas and who had been nurtured within the Welsh dioceses. Mary Clement notes a number who served in India, Virginia and Newfoundland during the last quarter of the seventeenth century.[151] Henry Nichols became the first resident missionary at Pennsylvania in 1703, serving with SPG. By 1708 others were serving in the Leeward Islands and Jamaica.[152] In the 1700s Evan Evans, followed by Griffith Hughes, 1732, served as missionaries to the Welsh-speakers of Radnor, Pennsylvania. Thomas Barton, an itinerant missioner to the Welsh from 1758 had to flee in 1776 because of his refusal to omit the state prayers in the Prayer Book.[153] The originator of the circulating schools, Griffith Jones, almost became a missionary in Malaber but felt that Wales was equally a missionary country.[154] George Lewis, who was rector of Dolgellau 1715-23, had previously served as a chaplain with the East India Company in India from 1692-1714, where he was held in high esteem.[155] In the 1770s Edward Vaughan of Llandaff was serving in New Jersey, dying there after 30 years' service,[156] and between 1823-38 David Thomas Jones served as a missionary in Canada's Red River settlement, but ill-health brought him home and he died in 1843 as professor of Welsh at St David's College, Lampeter.[157]

Henry and William Williams, two brothers, departed for New Zealand in 1822, and Griffith Griffiths to Jamaica in 1825; Thomas Thomas to Tinevelly, India, 1836, and the first missionaries to Madagascar were natives of Cardiganshire, Thomas Bevan and David Jones.[158] Elected to a specific fellowship of Jesus College, Oxford, endowed for overseas work, John David Jenkins was one of its few holders who fulfilled its obligation by becoming a missionary in Natal 1852-8. He was later vicar of Aberdare.[159] Born in Fishguard in 1815, John Bowen became bishop of Sierra Leone 1857-9, but failed to survive its climate, though he was one of the first to set forward the concept of an indigenous clergy,[160] and Mesac Thomas, a native of Llanbadarn Fawr, Cardiganshire, was the first bishop of Goulburn, Australia, 1863-92. He became prominent in the activities of that colonial church, and established one of the first diocesan synods within the Anglican Church.[285] Another missionary bishop, who died in 1893, was Walter Chambers of Labuan and Sarawak, who was born in the neighbourhood of Aberystwyth.[162] Charles Alun Smythies, a former rector of Roath, became bishop in Zanzibar in 1884, and died in post ten years later.[163] Alex Goldwyer-Lewis, born at Gwynfa, Carmarthenshire, and educated at St David's College, Lampeter, was archdeacon of Bombay until he returned to England in 1896,[164] and John Roberts, who graduated from St David's College, Lampeter, became a missionary to the Indian population in 1883 at Wyoming, Colorado, and translated parts of the Bible and communion service into Shoshone, enabling it to become a written language.[165] By the twentieth century a number of Welshmen served as overseas bishops: Llewelyn Henry Gwynne, of Swansea, became bishop of Khartoum and later of Egypt, 1908-46:[166] John Charles Jones served in Uganda from 1934-44 as a theological teacher, and from 1948 until his early death in 1956 as bishop of Bangor,[167] the same year in which J.R. Richards, who had served in Iran 1927-45 with CMS, became bishop of St Davids.

DISCIPLINE

The Church believed itself to be the guardian of moral behaviour, and its ecclesiastical courts controlled these matters and enforced penance on those who offended against its rules. Often, these would be matters reported in visitation queries, taken to a court, and the offenders, if found guilty, would be sentenced to undergo penance. This meant they would be required to attend their parish church, sometimes dressed in a white sheet, and during the service, be required to confess their sins and request the pardon of the Church and congregation. Although bishops endeavoured to enforce these matters, they died out by the late eighteenth century, though the Church still retained its probate rights, that of proving wills, its matrimonial jurisdiction, and the right to adjudicate in cases of defamation, until early Victorian times. It lost its right to deal with cases of defamation by the Ecclesiastical Causes Act of 1855, which was due partly to the publicity given to a case in the ecclesiastical court of Llandaff, presided over by the chancellor, Hugh

Williams, vicar of Bassaleg and Radyr.[168] Ten years later these courts lost their other jurisdictions to the secular courts.

Many such cases are noted in the diocesan consistory court records held at the National Library of Wales, for defamation or incontinence, for example, though on occasions it appears that the parish authorities took the law into their own hands. In the 1830s the parish authorities of Llanegryn, presumably the incumbent and churchwardens, punished those guilty of falsehood and slander by walking them around the church robed in a white sheet, and requiring them to publicly express contrition and to distribute so many white loaves to the poor.[169] At Ystradgynlais a woman who had an illegitimate child was compelled to walk with her paramour, if known, to the church during the hour of divine service, covered by a white sheet. This was last recorded in 1790.[170]

An even stranger custom was practised at St Ishmael, Carmarthenshire. Until around 1860 a chair was kept in the church designed for two persons to sit on, and this was used as a chair of penance for married couples. Carved on it were the words: "husbands love your wives", and "let the wife reverence her husband". If there was marital disharmony the couple were placed in it, with a white sheet over their heads, the chair being placed in the midst of the congregation. If one was judged to be at fault, he or she sat alone.[171]

By the nineteenth century such public penance had gone, but in one sense it had been replaced in some Anglo-Catholic churches by the confessional. This was a matter of great controversy, and will be noted in another section, but the whole matter was discussed rather favourably by the Cardiff clergy chapter in 1906.[172]

CHAPTER FOUR: WORKING WITHIN SOCIETY

It has been stated repeatedly that the Church was seen as the agent of the State for social control in an age when the police force was rudimentary and there was no standing army. It is hardly surprising, therefore, that the Church, nationally and locally, sought to control public opinion and prevent public disorder.[1] Although this conception was dated by early Victorian times, with the existence of a police force and an effective judicial system, the growth of elementary education and the spread of Nonconformity (which had taken into its fold a proportion of the otherwise unruly masses and subdued them), the concerns of an earlier age still lingered in the minds of many. Indeed, in some cases they were reinforced by the industrial and agricultural unrest of the 1840s and the fear that the events of 1830 and 1848 on the Continent could spread into this country.

The response of the Church to these concerns was an endeavour to promote its mission not only in an ecclesiastical field, by evangelistic mission and the expansion of the Church's work in the newly developing industrial areas, but also to bring into its community and retain the allegiance of those who might not necessarily be church-goers. This meant tackling the growing social "evils" of the day, such as drunkenness, Sabbath-breaking, juvenile delinquency, and providing healthy recreations for church members and others, especially youth, not only to keep them within the Church fold but also to provide an alternative to the public house and other undesirable places. It is significant that these organisations were often started around the time when muscular Christianity was at its height, ensuring Christian men and boys were fit in body as well as mind and spirit. We look at these in turn.

A CONCERN FOR THE POOR

Many parishes possessed their own charities given by benefactors in the past, and these were often recorded on tablets placed in the church or more generally in its porch.[2] Some of these charities, as at Welshpool, stipulated the provision of blankets or clothing, and sometimes bread, but by the 1890s this giving had become more organised, and instead money was distributed on New Year's Day in the form of vouchers to outfitters and drapers.[3] In addition, the offertory given at the communion service was dedicated to the relief of the poor and needy. Furthermore, clergy often gave from their own pocket relief in kind or in money to those in need.[4]

At times of depression many clergy obtained subscriptions for the relief of the poor, as did Richard Davies of Brecon in 1820. He obtained £196 to distribute in coal, bread and blankets, and at a time of considerable unemployment paid from his own pocket for poorer people to clean the streets of snow, make drains and whitewash houses.[5] A rector of Llanaber, John Jones, obtained subscriptions in 1844 to distribute to the poor of his parish five sacks of good oatmeal.[6] Walsham How at Whittington started an Old Men's Dinner in 1856, as well as an annual tea for the older women, during which, after the entertainment, he was able to speak some solemn words to his guests.[7] One of David Howell's first acts as vicar of Cardiff was to start a Christmas dinner for the poor of the parish, irrespective of creed or race. In 1870 over 400 people attended, while during the winter months a cheap dinner for the poor was provided three times a week. While these cost two pence each, one penny was charged, though members of the congregation were sold books of tickets at five shillings each which they could distribute to the needy. Three thousand meals were served in the winter of 1870-1.[8]

Though John Griffith of Merthyr had little sympathy for trade unions, he had great sympathy for those who were the victims of industrial action. During the recession in the iron industry of the 1870s, which closed a number of works, industrial relations became tense, and the employers, endeavouring to break the various unions, closed down their enterprises and locked out over 60,000 employers until they capitulated to their terms and accepted a substantial reduction in their wages. Not only did Griffith organise relief work for those affected by this lockout, assisted by local ministers, he did so on a national scale, but he was almost alone in criticising a society that allowed such destitution to take place. Though he was accused by the employers of prolonging the strike by giving aid to its innocent victims, he maintained that the children should not suffer. Soup kitchens were established for over 5,000 children and appeals were made for used clothing to meet their bodily needs during a harsh and cold winter. A further appeal was made in 1877-8 during a period of great depression in the iron trade, and once more Griffith resumed his activities and his comments. During it, as a result of another national campaign assisted by the London press, Griffith claimed he had received £2, 300 in clothing and foodstuffs, and over £4,000 in donations which enabled over 5,000 children to be assisted with good quality food. As a result, Griffith claimed, many had been nursed back from the illnesses indigenous to poverty.[9]

During the trade depression of 1885-6 Christ Church, Swansea, gave 2,000 different "relief" of food, clothes, blankets and coal, during the three months of winter. The value of these gifts came to £75, and was presumably met by subscriptions.[10] A winter soup kitchen was organised in Welshpool from 1891 onwards; the Church House, built in 1895, having had a kitchen specifically designed with this requirement in mind. Children received a bowl of soup for a halfpenny and during one winter 3,141 bowls had been purchased, though the full cost had to be met from subscriptions and the proceeds of a concert.[11] Other parishes held rummage sales to assist the poor, and many private individuals often gave their own discreet assistance to the poor. The Welshpool parish magazine, for example, often had obituaries stating that a deceased lady would be much missed by the poor.[12] The 1834 Poor Law act which forced the poor into workhouses may have relieved the parish from some of its responsibilities, but the system was regarded as so harsh than many clergy declined to act as poor law guardians while those who did often caused the poor to feel alienated from the Church.[13]

The parochial visiting associations, with their subsidiary concern for relieving the poor in sickness and hardship, have already been noted.[14] Other parishes had Dorcas Societies, when well-bred ladies made clothes for poverty stricken women and children. Holy Trinity Church, Swansea, had one in 1884, while Christ Church, in the same town, had such a society that made 160 garments for the deserving poor some years earlier.[15] A Good Samaritans' Society to meet the needs of the sick and poor was commenced in Oystermouth in the 1900s.[16]

SELF HELP FOR THE POOR

The Victorians believed in being charitable to those they felt deserving, but also wished to encourage self help. In their terminology "deserving" meant those who acquiesced in the role God had assigned them as poor people, were obedient to authority and grateful for small mercies. In his 1850 visitation Bishop Short of St Asaph encouraged the formation of such parochial organisations as clothing clubs, a children's' penny club, and even a pig club.[17] Penny banks were developed to encourage working people to save, rather than to spend their money on drink and other frivolous items. Thrift was replacing indiscriminate charity. A number of penny or savings banks were supported by wealthy subscribers whose subscriptions enabled a small dividend to be paid out, generally at Christmas. Such banks were established during the incumbency of Edward Bolney at Sketty 1865-1903,[18] at Wrexham,[19] and St Gabriel's Swansea in 1888.[20] Dean Cotton of Bangor, for example, established a Savings Bank and a Penny Clothing Club at Bangor, the latter in 1825, while he was also instrumental in the foundation of the Carnarvonshire and Anglesey Infirmary at Bangor in 1844. Sadly, his savings bank failed through the mismanagement of its manager, and he wrote thousands of begging letters and made numerous begging trips to Birmingham and in Cheshire and Lancashire in an effort to assist those who had lost their savings. He had to pay £1,200 himself and his two fellow trustees £1,000 each.[21] At Hawarden Stephen Gladstone had a clothing club, a savings bank, and a school of cookery.[22] A children's penny bank was opened at St Theodore's Church, Port Talbot, possibly in connection with the Sunday School.[23]

Clothing and coal clubs came about from the same concern, allowing people to save small amounts of money so that when new clothing or shoes were required, or a stock of coal needed for the winter months, they would have sufficient money to do so. Caernarfon had such a clothing club by 1853,[24] St John's and St Mary's, Cardiff,[25] and Ystrad Mynach in the 1890s. Presumably using donations from well-wishers this club offered a bonus of one shilling for all those who saved five shillings, and two shillings for fifteen shillings.[26] St Theodore's Port Talbot had another clothing club;[27] St Mark's, Swansea, had a blanket club in 1905,[28] while the clothing club at Welshpool during the 1890s had 163 members on its books, who contributed in small payments over £201 in one year. The interest on this was added, as was subscription income, so that in 1897 the money available for distribution at Christmas amounted to £183, though it was given in the form of tickets to local tradesmen who redeemed the tickets from the club's treasurer, as noted earlier.[29]

The diary of John James Turner as curate of Welshpool during the early 1870s indicates some of the pressures placed upon individual clergymen. Turner records his own generosity to his parishioners. He paid school fees for some children and for flannels for the poor, gave a suit of old clothes to a man, gave innumerable small sums to particular individuals (to enable a person to get to the Salop Infirmary, or five shillings to help a man purchase a horse), and assisted with the distribution of the clothing club monies, the parochial charities, and giving out coal tickets, which he appears to have supervised in the yard of the Royal Oak. Turner and another curate were also made responsible for auditing the accounts of the Savings Bank.[30]

HEALTHY RECREATION

It is noteworthy that during the eighteenth century many of the local clergy joined in the various social events of their people, such as the Mabsant or saint's day celebrations, or the harvest rejoicings, and in so doing managed to ensure that these events did not get out of hand. Games of football might be ended before violence broke out, for example.[31] In the following century many clergy were associated with friendly societies and performed the same sort of function. At the annual dinner of the First Welshpool Friendly Society in 1855, the vicar, Archdeacon Clive, stated he had been a member for thirty-five years, but wanted the business of the society to be transferred from a public house to a neutral place, as using a licensed premises was an inducement for the young to drink. He was not successful.[32] The Aberdovey Benefit Society in 1858 held its annual New Year's procession to the Church where the vicar, W.B. Morgan, preached, followed by a dinner and speeches and reports.[33] The vicar of Newbridge on Wye, in the 1880s, was the chief ranger of the local Forester's Club, and preached its annual sermon.[34] Archdeacon Crawley of Monmouth disliked these friendly societies. Their annual event, even the church service which preceded it, was often disorderly so that many clergymen refused to officiate on these occasions lest they appear to sanction such "open profanation". Crawley also condemned their monthly meetings at public houses and added the societies needed regulating as many had become bankrupt.[35]

Activities of many kinds were organised by clergymen to provide healthy recreation for their parishioners, sometimes as an alternative to other less savoury pursuits. Opposing the annual pleasure fair in his parish, Henry Vaughan of Crickhowel, 1830-7, encouraged the children not to attend, and instead took them for a day of entertainment, with abundant provisions, to the local mountain. One girl even gave him nine shillings for a missionary box which otherwise she would have spent on the fair.[36] Vincent Saulez of St John's, Canton, is noted in 1867 as organising a horticultural show which gave small prizes to its winners.[37]

By the late 1890s the large parish of Penarth had a Young Men's Guild, with over 850 members, and associated with this there were cricket, hockey, bowling and draughts clubs, as well as the CLB drum and fife band.[38] A rugby club was formed at St Francis's Church, Roath, in 1893,[338] while St Theodore's, Port Talbot, had air rifle, rugby, soccer and cricket clubs at various times, and also for some time Penny Readings. These were occasions when the audience actually came and recitated, played musical instruments, sang, or did conjuring or other acts, and became very popular.[40] Kilvert notes these penny readings in his diary,[41] while the parish of Llanfairfechan around the same time had a literary meeting, which might have been somewhat similar.[42] At Oystermouth, football, tennis and cricket clubs were started by a new vicar, Harold Williams,[43] and the vicar of Glanogwen with Bethesda informed the 1906 Royal Commission about the cricket, athletic and football clubs connected with his church.[44] Many parishes by the 1910s and afterwards had scout troops and girl guides, amongst them Swansea.[45]

With a note of disdain the *Record* observed that in the midst of the 1905 Revival the church at Caerphilly persisted with holding popular lectures, cricket and football clubs, and a church club with a refreshment bar. Part of the background was that such activities were declared by many to be sinful in the over-enthusiasm of those revivalist times.[46]

Many parishes also had, apart from Sunday School social events, a specific event for all their members. At Rhymney in the 1860s and thereafter it took the form of a Bank Holiday event, with a procession, games, tea and dancing. Designed for the whole family, one expectation was that it would prevent the men from resorting to other forms of entertainment.[47] St Matthias Church, Treharris, held an annual bachelor's tea in the 1900s, when all the unmarried men put on a tea party for the congregation.[48] The majority of parishes also held social events, such as musical entertainments, lectures, dances, concerts, whist drives, and theatrical events, some in association with existing societies, others to fund raise for the church school, the church itself, or for some specific requirement. They are recorded in parish magazines, but otherwise remain unrecorded and forgotten. We know that at Whittington Walsham How often gave public lectures on such subjects as geology, his visit to Rome, modern poets, or astronomy.[49]

A handbook for the clergy, published in 1887, offered numerous examples, together with advice and rules, for parochial activities. These included allotments; annual parish excursions; athletic sports, benefit, boot and shoe, clothing and coal clubs; debating societies; dorcas societies; dramatic clubs; drum and fife band; emigration; flower and vegetable shows; friendly societies; libraries and reading rooms; penny banks; needlework and sewing societies; soup kitchens; temperance work and working men's clubs, amongst many others.[50] Even organising a few of these must have been exhausting work for the clergy and must have detracted some from their real vocation.

THE NEED FOR ACCOMMODATION

If a church had its own National School, it was able to use its premises for these activities, although many school log books indicate that head teachers were none too happy with these arrangements. By the 1900s, however, many of these schools were either not available as having been closed, had become Board Schools, or were inadequate for these purposes. A movement was thus started to build separate buildings called Church Halls or Church Houses, and by 1906 many parishes in the Brecon area had such a facility.[51] One of the first was the parish room built within the new rectory at Llandrindod Wells in 1884, seating 200 people.[52] St Oswald's Church House, Oswestry, was opened in the 1900s, while the Church House at Welshpool was built as a memorial to the third earl of Powis in 1892, but a projected basement with its own club and billiard rooms had to be curtailed because of cost.[53] In the 1900s the new vicar of Oystermouth, Harold Williams, built a church hall to seat 250 people, but many of the smaller meetings took place in the National School. When the school needed the room for itself he had to extend the parish hall to seat 600 people in 1928, at a cost of £1,750.[54] St Matthias, Treharris, opened its hall in 1908, where the Sunday School and the Band of Hope met, along with other organisations, including at a later date the Scout movement.[55] Ton

Pentre built its church hall in 1905, which placed the parish in debt for many years,[56] Bishopston Church did so in 1909, instead of using the National School,[57] and Senghenydd built its own hall in 1921 by voluntary effort.[58] At Manselton the former church, used as a hall, needed replacement by the 1920s, and the congregation raised the money required by sales of work, collections, and also provided the necessary furniture.[59]

When the church hall was opened in 1923 at Cyfartha the cost was much higher than anticipated, and within a few years a debt of £3,300 had accumulated on it with an annual interest charge of £170. It needed sales of work, bazaars, concerts and other events to simply find this interest money. Eventually interest-free loans were requested from members of the church, and while these loans were found, after having paid over £2,000 in interest charges, it was realised the hall was far too large for the parish's needs.[60] The parish of St Thomas, Swansea, had two men's clubs, one in the Church Hall which included a billiard room, and the other in the hall of a daughter church. There was a combined membership of one hundred.[61] The church hall at Penrhiwceibr, near Pontypridd, opened in 1911, could accommodate 600 people, and had in its basement classrooms and the ever-popular billiard room, while services were performed in the hall for children on Sundays and on Saturdays for those whose parents felt they were too poor or poorly dressed to attend Sunday School or church on Sunday.[62] The Wrenford Memorial Hall was built on the site of the old vicarage of St Paul's, Newport, in 1912. It also contained a Men's Institute (with the hope it might prevent the leakage of youth from the Church),[62] while a church house was built at Colwyn Bay as late as 1936.[64]

TACKLING SOCIAL EVILS

CHURCYARD DESECRATION

A major concern of the eighteenth century church was to ensure the churchyard remained a place of sanctity. In many parishes it was the only open space available. This was long before the cult of erecting tombstones to commemorate the dead had become fashionable. The churchyard was thus the playground of the village, generally of men and youth, and in some places formed part of the local market and fairground. A number of clergymen took advantage of this open space in order to pasture their horses and cattle there, as Parson Bulkeley of Llanfechell wished to do in 1739 to the annoyance of his squire.[65]

The churchyard at Berriew was partly unenclosed and cattle were allowed to graze in that area.[66] In a *Collection of Welch Travels* published in the 1730s it was remarked that the churchyard served the dead as a burying place and the living for a dancing place. Some years later, a writer of *A Journey to Llandrindod Wells* noted a parish wake, with tennis and fives being played against the church walls, and dancing and music in the churchyard with the musicians sitting on the tombstones.[67] Another writer commented on the same position at Diserth: "here we saw common games of ball played against the sacred pile and there was also music playing over the bodies of the deceased".[68]

The Church's concern to end these practices took time, and perhaps only ended when gravestones became fashionable. A number of presentments were made in the ecclesiastical courts, as in 1730 when some men were prosecuted for playing ball and bowls in the churchyard of Gwenddwr, Breconshire.[69] In a number of instances the parish vestry established a system of fines for those who played these games, as at Newtown in 1722 and Llandyrnog in 1753, while a rhyming notice was erected at Llanfair Discoed informing players that if they played on Sundays the devil might take them before Monday.[70] William Thomas in his diary for 1763 records that five men were fined two shillings each for playing ball in Dinas Powis's churchyard on Sunday.[71] The rural dean of Pool in 1729 ordered churchwardens to end the custom of using the churchyard for games, but to what extent this was obeyed is not recorded. As Melvin Humphreys suggests, some may have considered that innocent pleasures were being lost because of moral snobbery.[72] The father of Edmund Jones, who with others would play ball in the churchyard before the Sunday service, was reproved by Howel Williams, the curate of Bedwellte who later preached to them in the church about breaking the Lord's Day.[73] The rector of Merthyr, George Martin Maber, had around the 1800s suppressed the public use of the graveyard for games and public assembly, as well as its use on market day to display china and crockery.[74] Similarly, at Forden, the games and excessive drinking that took place in the churchyard before the Sunday service was ended in the 1830s by Daniel Nihill when he preached a sermon against these "vices" which was not forgotten nearly fifty years later.[75] To prevent these games at Llangranog Church on Sunday mornings, the rector, D.J. Evans, changed the time of the Sunday School from before the morning service to the afternoon,[76] While at Derwen the vicar used to end the games by stating that it was time to commence the service.[77] As late as 1841 a vicar of Skenfrith, George Miller, managed to stop these churchyard games and wakes occurring, though he faced much hostility.[78] Even bishops were unable to wrest control of these churchyards from the mob. Bishop Marsh asked for the intervention of Lord Bute in 1817 to end the practice of people playing ball against the walls of Llandaff Cathedral even during the time of divine service. He had preached against it in vain and the magistrates apparently were not interested in prosecuting the offenders.[79] Surprisingly, in 1677 the churchwardens of Chirk were taken to the quarter sessions for refusing to allow parishioners to play tennis in the churchyard. Tennis was still being played there in 1685, though damage was sometimes caused to the fabric of the church and complaints were made about this in 1725.[80]

One of the most common practices was to use the wall of the church building, often on the unfashionable north side where few burials took place, for playing the game of fives. This is probably meant by playing ball in the churchyard, although it could refer to a game of football. These games of fives took place in the churchyards of Llandysilio, Denbighshire, Whittington and Llanymynech, where it appears the churchyard was also used for other amusements.[81] It was said of William Powell, vicar of Llanfihangel Genau'r Glyn in the 1750s that when he was distracted from the service in church by the noise of men playing ball outside in the churchyard, he would ask his warden to request them to wait and he would come out and join them later.[82] A vicar of Lledrod in 1828 was himself a player, and perhaps a little later a vicar of Llanfeugan would play fives against the tower till the church bell went, and then resume afterwards.[83] This practice continued at Montgomery until the 1870s when a new rector forbade it.[384] At Bedwas it was noted ball games were played against its tower,[85] and at Myddfai quoits were played in the churchyard in the 1740s while the congregation waited for the clergyman to turn up for the service.[86] A common activity at Cwm Eithin, Denbighshire, was leaping from tombstone to tombstone after the morning service.[87] Matthew Owen of Llanrhwydrys in Anglesey, born in 1769, remembered playing football, wrestling, and other games before they went into the Sunday service, and in the afternoon playing tennis against the church roof.[88] James Davies around the same time was pained to see these games played against Llantilio Pertholey Church, and although it was the custom to do so in that area, he felt it produced irreverence.[89] Elias Owen even maintained that two Montgomeryshire churches possessed their own cockpits, namely Pennant Melangell and Llanfechain.[90]

The churchwardens, unable or unwilling to censure or end these practices, placed iron bars and shutters to protect the glass of the windows in many of these churches. John Byng in his tour of Wales of 1787 noted that Pyle Church's windows were protected by shutters to prevent damage from the fives balls, and added that the church was the general place for that sport.[91] At Llandovery wooden shutters were placed against the windows to protect them against the playing of football in the churchyard, and in 1815 posts were set up in an attempt to end the practice.[92] In his tour of Wales in the 1830s John Parker noted that Ffestiniog and many other churches had shutters against their windows.[93] As late as 1865 it was observed that Penarth Church had its windows studded with iron bars giving it the appearance of a prison.[94]

Tenison's visitation of 1710 revealed that there were four fairs held each year in the churchyard at Llandeilo Fawr,[95] and later evidence indicates that five fairs were held each year in the churchyard of the parish of Llangernyw. John Kenrick, its vicar, 1730-55, endeavoured to end the custom, especially as stalls were set up in the church porch and in the churchyard and some even smoked and drank in the church itself as well as using it as a place for paying and receiving money. His efforts had failed even though he had nailed up a church gate and placed stout fellows to prevent the crowds entering, He hoped that his bishop would take action himself as a result of his visitation, while he also suggested that the bishop might suppress another custom. This was a custom of Sunday afternoon fiddling and dancing. The wardens had declined to present this custom at the bishop's visitation, and the magistrates were not concerned about such matters. Eventually, an area outside the churchyard was used for the fairs.[96] The parishioners of St Mary's, Haverfordwest, sought counsel's opinion in 1773 as to the possibility of ending the weekly market with its butchers' stalls held in their churchyard, though it had been sanctioned by immemorial custom. Eventually, the churchwardens persuaded the bishop to end the practice.[97] At Crickhowel the annual fair held in the churchyard with the aid of the magistrates was denounced by Henry Vaughan in the 1830s. He followed the fugitives into the beer houses where once more they heard, in the words of his biographer, his voice of mercy but firm reproof, even though he stood in the midst of an angry disappointed rabble.[98] In a powerful sermon at Ruthin, John Elias, the Methodist preacher, ended the Sunday fair at that place.[99]

Sir John Dillwyn Llewelyn of Penllergaer wrote an account of the annual two-day fair held at Llangyfelach in March, during the time of its patronal festival. Held in the churchyard, tombstones were used for the sale of stockings, flannel and other commodities, while various ball and other games took place there as well. The parson, however, was in absolute control. The cloth dealers had to use the yard measures he supplied at a cost of three pence each, and until the parson opened the fair no selling was permitted. However, horses and pigs were kept outside the churchyard. These customs were ended in 1815 by Daniel Rowland, who became curate of the parish in that year, and turned the fair out of the churchyard, though it continued on the fields opposite it.[100]

The parish wake, or celebration of the patronal saint, normally a rowdy affair with violent football games and excessive entertainment, aroused the concern of many clergy. William Wynne of Lasynys managed to change the wake day at his parish of Llanfair from a Sunday to a weekday by bribery, though he had no objection to attending it and might well have toned down some of its rougher elements.[101] D.W. Howell writes of a football match played on a Sunday, presumably on a wakes day, between two Anglesey parishes, Llanbedr and Llanllechid. The latter team was losing, whereupon notice was sent to those attending the service at its church for its men to leave and join their team, turning the game into a victory.[102]

OBSERVING THE SABBATH DAY

The proper observance of the Sabbath was a theme found in many of the devotional books of the seventeenth and eighteenth centuries published in Wales and also in the Charges of the various bishops. The concern was that not only should that day be a day of rest, but also one of spiritual refreshment and dedication. The readers of these books were informed as to how to prepare for the Sabbath and how to behave during the church service. These, and other works, emphasised the penalties of the non-observance of the Sabbath, such as ending one's days in poverty and squalor, and even worse, as the object of God's wrath and condemnation.[103]

It was noted that until the early nineteenth century the parish constables of

Monmouth endeavoured to enforce the observance of the Sabbath,[104] while Heneage Horsley, as he entered into his ministry at Gresford in 1804 expressed his disgust at the desecration of the Sabbath in his parish, with many riotous young men spending the day shooting in the neighbouring woods, especially those immediately "under" the Church, and others turning up late for the service, even though he had changed the times for their benefit.[105] At Hodnet, then in the diocese of St Asaph, Reginald Heber was more successful in the late 1800s, when with his churchwardens he restrained shopkeepers from selling on Sunday and got the innkeepers to agree not to allow drinking on that day.[106] James Davies of Devauden made his schoolroom into a place of worship to try and counteract the desecration of the Sabbath in his village.[107] Daniel Nihill, noted above, of Forden, in his *The Farmer's Guide to Happiness*, a tract of 1843, contrasted the pious farmer worshipping with his family in church with the non-pious farmer, doing odd jobs on that day and missing God's blessing.[108] In two sermons preached on a day of humiliation for the cholera epidemic of 1849, Edward Squire of Swansea suggested that God was causing them to pause because of their guilt of desecrating the Sabbath, even arguing that one attendance per Sunday was not sufficient, and for refusing to hear God's Word and permitting secret unbelief to enter into their lives.[109] Morgan Morgan, vicar of Conway from 1838, is said to have brought the Sabbath in that town into proper respect, by stopping the rough plays, the games of pitch and toss, the cock fighting on Sundays, and the playing of football and the burning of effigies in the streets.[110] In a sermon preached at Dowlais upon the death of Sir John Guest, the proprietor of the works, in 1853, Evan Jenkins praised him as his was the first works in the district to recognise the divine institution of the Lord's Day, and in the silence of the works came the call to keep holy the Sabbath day.[111]

A debate took place in 1892 at the St Davids Diocesan Conference on how to promote the better observance of Sunday. It was a day for training the mind and body towards duty to God and self. The usual rants were heard against high and low society's desecration of the Sabbath, and such comments were made that while children loved to play on that day a childhood of unrestricted playing was irresponsible. T.E. Walters of Carmarthen suggested clergy should set an example and only eat cold collations on the Sunday, though James Havard Protheroe of Aberystwyth suggested that few would wish to return to the very strict view of Sabbath observance that prevailed until recent times, and others felt that museums might be opened on Sunday for the poor as the rich possessed their own art collections.[112]

This stance was similar to the attitude of Canon J. P. Thompson of Cardiff in 1887, who in a paper attacked Sunday as a day of gloom and penance and wanted wider resources on Sunday for the less fortunate, such as Sunday music in the parks, and the opening of museums and reading rooms.[113] However, the Cardiff clergy chapter had condemned the Sunday opening of museums, claiming this was opposed by divine sanction, while some aspects of art were an incentive to passion.[114] It goes without saying, therefore, that the Sunday opening of museums aroused enormous passion amongst the Christian community, and it is not surprising that the firebrand, John Griffith of Merthyr, should enter the fray on the side of Sunday opening. He had opposed the Cardiff clergy when they petitioned against the Sunday opening of the Crystal Palace in 1851, and the consequent railway excursions to the capital. Sunday was a day of rest, and it was wrong for it to be hedged about with restrictions, besides which it was far better for people to go to such exhibitions than resort to the public house. He was now equally in support of this more local initiative, and had even stated, as witness a complaint made against him, that after attending a service on Sunday it was quite in order to play football in the afternoon.[115]

Sunday observance was the subject of a debate at the 1896 Llandaff Diocesan Conference. Many speakers claimed it was a day of rest and spiritual obligation and expressed concern that the solemnity of the day was being lost in fashionable circles by the use of dinner parties and golf and tennis fixtures. However, Canon Thompson of St John's, Cardiff, argued that Holy Communion was the principal service of the day and he would allow reasonable recreation thereafter, through it ought to be subordinated to the primary concerns of rest and worship. Some years later a further discussion took place. Though Canon Buckley asserted that Sunday golf by the leisured classes set a bad example, it was suggested there should be two conditions for it, namely that those involved should have attended worship beforehand and also carry their own equipment, rather than employ caddies. But it was hard to lay down any "conditions" for Sunday cycling.[116] A similar relaxation was stated at the St Asaph Diocesan Conference of 1901.

Let Sunday be used for relaxation, provided that a person's leisure did not deprive others of their leisure. It was claimed too that there could be no public worship without Sunday rest.[117]

In spite of such liberal remarks individual clergymen made their own gestures. The rector of Begeli, Thomas S. J. Thomas, in the 1830s allowed no work after 6.00pm on the Saturday until Monday morning.[118] Talbot Rice, vicar of Swansea, 1902-19, once walked to Pontardawe to take a service rather than break the Sabbath by taking a cab.[119] In two of his Charges Bishop Pritchard Hughes of Llandaff decried those who required Sunday employment for their own ends and so prevented people from following out their principles, and argued that people wanted Sunday to remain a day of rest.[120] By 1910 Canon Buckley of Llandaff criticised the existence of Sunday dinner parties, bridge parties and visits to the golf links, and even the practice of attending the early service and then doing what one wanted for the rest of the day. The day needed to be preserved for worship and rest.[121]

TEMPERANCE

Drunkenness had become recognised as a social problem by the 1820s, especially in the industrialised parishes where foremen often distributed the wages in a public house. In a small village it might be contained, but in a larger community it meant poverty for a family and social distress. It had been a concern of the Church over many years before, as G.H. Jenkins maintains.[122] Those who drank to excess on the Saturday hardly had the ability to attend a service on the following day, so that temperance also involved Sabbath observance, as Thomas Edwards of Llanllyfni maintained.[123] One of the first sermons known to me on temperance was preached in 1792 by Benjamin Hall to the Melin-Griffith Society of Tradesmen and Manufacturers. He stressed such concerns as body and soul, family and health, and added the necessity of attending a place of worship.[124] As might be expected, clergy were at the forefront of this movement. One of the first temperance societies in Wales was founded by Henry Vaughan at Crickhowel in 1835, who made an appeal for the working men of his parish to join it;[125] William Williams, vicar of Pwllheli, was elected first president of the town's Temperance Society in 1836,[126] and James Francis, the first incumbent of St Paul's, Newport, 1839-43, became the first president of the Newport Total Abstinence Society.[127] Richard Pritchard of Llandaff preached a temperance sermon at Llandaff Cathedral in 1839 and became the first president of the Gwent and Morgannwg Temperance Association.[128] Colonel William Gwynne Hughes of Glancothi, Llanegwad, born in 1841, was an advocate of temperance, and bequeathed £1,000 to the vicar and churchwardens of Carmarthen. Its interest was to be paid to the vicar for an annual sermon on temperance.[129]

The various revivals of the nineteenth century, especially that of 1859 and later of 1904-5, greatly assisted the cause of temperance.[130] In many cases there was active co-operation between Church and Dissent about these matters, with clergy and ministers speaking from the same platform and belonging to the same committees, though this was partly lost when the Liberation Society became a strong influence within Nonconformity after 1862.[131] Possibly as a result of this separation, Meredith Williams, writing in 1903, argued that the general body of Christian believers took little interest in the temperance cause.[132]

Many parishes had branches of the Church of England Temperance Society, whose members had signed a pledge against strong drink. Its aims were to promote the habit of temperance, the reformation of the intemperate, and the removal of the causes which led to intemperance. The society was founded in 1862, and within twenty years had branches in most of the dioceses of the Church of England. Joshua Hughes, bishop of St Asaph, recommended parishes to commence such a branch in 1874. It would awaken enthusiasm for the cause and by force of example break the spell "that bound many a miserable captive in chains".[133] It was not until 1885 that a diocesan branch was inaugurated after which several talks and debates were given at the diocesan conferences.[134]

A debate on the work of the Society took place at the 1881 St David's Diocesan Conference. It urged that local branches be established and coffee taverns and reading rooms be set up. Its effect was limited for in 1899 it was noted that only one in ten parishes of the diocese had a branch of the CETS.[135] A diocesan branch was commenced in the late 1890s for Bangor, which in its 1903 report indicated it had inaugurated four new parochial branches. Canon Hughes of Barmouth had addressed numerous public meetings on its behalf, and a lady lecturer had visited some GFS branches. Its total membership was 2,030.[136] By 1889 the Rev. J.L. Meredith was acting as a district organiser for temperance work in the diocese of Llandaff.[137] The effect was felt on the students at St David's College, Lampeter, whose Principal John Owen claimed that 95 of the 130 men in residence during 1894 were total abstainers.[138]

A branch of this movement at Pwllheli in 1881 had 185 members,[139] another branch at Llantrisant had all the clergy and 720 of the laity as total abstainers in 1891,[140] Daniel Fisher commenced a branch at Rhymney in the 1900s,[141] while Bishop Pritchard Hughes hoped that every parish in his diocese would have its own branch.[142] Another branch was started at Brecon after a Temperance Mission of 1885 produced over 1,200 pledges. It also had women's and juvenile branches and organised tea parties "for the cup that cheers but does not inebriate, and football matches between youth sides.[143] Grimaldi Davis, vicar of Welshpool, established a branch in his parish in 1891, whose speakers included Captain Mytton, who claimed he had contested a parliamentary election without having to take a drink; a rector of Montgomery, R.W. Brown, who maintained that many trades, such as railways and agriculture, were better conducted without alcoholic stimulants; and also a dialogue which included a section about the old pump at the centre of the town, which had never sent any one blaspheming home to harass wife and children or sold the comforts of the home in order to buy more wretchedness and misery.[144]

Though many clergymen supported the temperance movement, others looked on with indifference and even contempt. The teetotallers of Merthyr took their vicar to task for attending and speaking at the Bedwellty Licensed Victuallers Association in 1878,[145] and William Edwards of St James's, Bangor, refused to have a branch of the CETS in his parish, claiming that the Church itself was the society instituted by Christ to cope with evil and bring souls to God.[146]

However, the majority of clergymen seemed to have supported the temperance movement, even if not all of them were total abstainers. At Cardiff David Howell in the 1870s supported a local organisation designed to prevent the Sunday liquor trade, arguing that the better class of publican was glad to close on the Sunday. For some time it appears his parish ran a coffee stall as an aid to temperance.[147] When Thomas Richard Lloyd, known as Estyn, rector of Llanfynydd, died in 1891, he was commemorated as the founder of the Blue Badge movement. A badge was given to reformed drunkards, and the movement spread to the United States and back to England.[148]

Other supporters of the movement included Dean Cotton of Bangor;[149] his successor Dean Edwards, who became a well-known temperance speaker and whose intervention was credited with having aided the passage of the Welsh Sunday Closing Act;[150] and Evan Jenkins of Dowlais, who lectured on the Maine law of total abstinence at the Crown Court in Merthyr Tydfil in 1859 and who became a national speaker, speaking at such places as Bradford, Huddersfield, Leeds, Wakefield and York.[151] In addition we may cite John Griffiths of Neath who took the pledge in 1865 and believed the movement was a means of winning souls to Christ;[152] and Griffith Arthur Jones, of St Mary's, Cardiff, who took a different stance, for while he promoted temperance he hated excessive teetotalism, and preferred to combat drunkenness by use of the pledge reinforced by the sacraments of the Church and holy living.[153] William Leigh Morgan of St Mary's, Cardiff, chaired a public meeting requesting the Cardiff magistrates to grant no further licences for public houses in the town,[154] David Williams, vicar of Llanelli;[155] and Talbot Rice of Swansea, were also involved in the movement.[156] A vicar of Pentre Foelas, Griffith Williams, 1893-1905, composed a short cantata proclaiming the virtues of temperance.[157]

John Griffith of Merthyr became a well-known temperance speaker and it has been suggested that his advocacy of it, both in local and national circles, helped make it a respectable cause within the Church. He often pointed out the results of drunkenness, leading to criminality and other social disorder. For him temperance meant moderation rather than abstinence, and his belief was that people needed alternatives to spending their time drinking. He was also aware that temperance flourished in hard times, and claimed that the 10,000 teetotallers in the Merthyr area, now that good times had come, had all broken their pledge. Why should the devil of drink, he asked, take so much of the enhanced pay given to workmen?[158]

The Band of Hope, a young people's temperance organisation, founded in Leeds in 1847, had become a national institution in 1855. It required its members to sign a pledge never to take "strong drink". Its programme consisted of lectures and songs on the evils of drink, together with social activities, and provided a good night out for many youngsters. Branches were found in most town parishes, such as Penarth,[159] St Thomas' and St Gabriel's Swansea;[160] St John's, Canton, which in 1906 had over 300 persons belonging to it and was unique as it included adults;[161] St Theodore's, Port Talbot (along with a branch of CETS),[162] and St Paul's, Newport.[163] Another branch at Welshpool, established in 1891, had 160 members, and one of its songs had the refrain: "O Father / Mother, stop and think, what do you love best on earth, us children or the drink?" In one of its many entertainments, designed to promote membership, the story of Rip Van Winkle was presented with a temperance theme.[164]

Nonconformity was even more concerned about the alcohol trade, even though at an earlier period chapels often supplied their visiting preachers with a glass of ale, and it was alleged in the 1850s that many male chapel goers in Merthyr would move from the chapel service into the local hostelry.[165] David Jenkins asserts that the chapels became so strict about temperance as a condition of membership that as a result many individuals left the chapel for the church.[166] It was Nonconformist influence that succeeded in obtaining the Sunday Closing Act for Wales in 1881, the first piece of legislation enacted for Wales. Several clergy, however, had campaigned for it, amongst them David Archard Williams of Carmarthen, who edited the *Carmarthen Journal.*[167] The eventual act required all licensed premises to be closed on the Sunday, although bona fide travellers could be served. Many clergy disliked this act as it was effectively obtained by Welsh Nonconformity, and they felt that it might be the prelude to disestablishment, but it was generally admitted the act was a failure, even by Lord Aberdare, who had steered it through the House of Lords.[168]

A number of Welsh clergymen gave evidence to a royal commission of 1890 which enquired into the operations of this Act. John Griffiths of Neath wanted a minimum of ten miles for a bona fide traveller as many used the three-mile limit in order to evade its requirements; Canon Gauntlett of Swansea providing an example of this practice by claiming many went from that town to the Mumbles for their Sunday drink. J. Allan Smith of Swansea also wanted a more stringent approach to this clause, though he insisted the Act should not be repealed. Grimaldi Davis of Welshpool noted the beneficial influence of the Act though it needed amending. At Corwen (his previous parish) many drank on Sundays before it had been enacted, especially young men, but after the act had been passed they had became faithful attenders at the church to the gratitude of their wives and mothers. He had started a temperance society in his present parish. David

Howell of Wrexham noted the Act had caused an increase in the deposits of friendly societies and there had been a decided improvement in the general appearance of the town on Sundays.[169] The result of the Act, suggests W.R. Lambert, was that the Sunday drink trade moved into clubs, which did not need a licence.[170]

Many felt however that alternatives to the public houses needed to be provided, where good non-alcoholic drinks could be obtained and board games provided. A Reformers Tavern was opened at Monmouth in the 1870s as a temperance place serving tea and coffee but had a rather short life.[171] There was a temperance club at Wrexham by the 1880s;[172] Stephen Gladstone had a coffee house and a night school for young men at Hawarden by the 1890s,[173] and Harry Drew at Buckley helped provide a free library, a parish room and a recreation ground, as well as an ambulance van and a parish nurse.[174] John Owen in his presidential address to his St Davids Diocesan Conference of 1901 felt that while temperance was a social concern requiring legislation, some of the remedies for it were in better housing and the elevation of social life.[175]

PURITY AND OTHER ISSUES

From time to time during the eighteenth and early nineteenth centuries there were royal proclamations issued for the encouragement of piety and virtue and for preventing and punishing of vice, profaneness and immorality. In 1813, as a result of one of these proclamations, a Proclamation Society was established for the diocese of St Davids to further these aims. Bishop Burgess required his clergy to distribute the royal proclamation to all alehouse keepers and shopkeepers, reminding the first group of the illegality of encouraging tippling at unlawful hours on Sunday, and the second about opening on Sundays. Hence, his concern was more about Sunday observance than public purity, though the good bishop might have thought there was a connection between the two.[176]

There were also organisations for encouraging and promoting purity, amongst them the White Cross League of Purity, founded in the 1880s. This was claimed to be the Church's purity society, requiring purity amongst men, the preservation of the young from contamination, chivalrous respect for women, upholding the sanctity of marriage but also undertaking rescue work.[177] A men's branch was started at St Theodore's

Church, Port Talbot, in 1905,[178] as one of the few parochial branches in Wales. Nevertheless, John Griffith had commenced such work much earlier in lectures to young men, especially those employed in the drapery trade, who were no longer lodged by their employers above their shops. Too often he discovered a young man had returned home ill, with his mother suggesting his illness had been caused by a damp bed, whereas in reality he had caught some sexual disease.[179]

A more practical approach was the opening of a House of Mercy at Llandaff in 1862, in the hope that prostitutes might be reformed by hard work and spiritual influences. It catered for 25 "penitents" and was housed in an old tucking mill. A lady superintendent and two assistants formed the staff, and the penitents were employed in washing and plain needlework, presumably to keep expenses down and provide them with some employment for the future. John Griffith, rector of Merthyr was the secretary and one of the founders of the institution.[180]

Archdeacon Ffoulkes and his wife showed further practical concern when they established a convalescent hospital for children at Rhyl. By 1880 it had 200 beds, and later became known as the Princess Alexandra Hospital.[181]

The need for better housing was noted by Archdeacon Wickham in his Charge of 1858. He claimed that a single sleeping room for all the members of a family was an affront to decency and modesty, and he expressed equal concern about the morals and habits of young people engaged as farm servants.[182] The same subject was also debated at the Llandaff Diocesan Conference of 1901.[183] John Griffith also had his say, proclaiming one could not make a people civilised and sober unless one attended to their social wants, their houses and their means of recreation. Education could not do so, for how can you teach hygiene to children who cannot practise it in the hovels in which they lived.[184]

THE THEATRE AND POPULAR AMUSEMENTS

Interludes, generally dramatic poetry with a satirical and coarse content, aimed at popular grievances and movements, such as the Methodist movement, were part of the Welsh cultural scene. Many clergy disliked them, but felt unable to condemn them, as appears to have been the position of William Wynne of Lasynys, though Thomas Ellis of Holyhead managed to suppress some of these interludes in the 1740s.[185]

In 1842 the vicar of Llandeilo Fawr, John William Pugh, wrote *An Address to his Parishioners on the Pernicious Effect of Theatrical Amusements*. The strolling players provided no innocent entertainment, he alleged, but rather something that pandered to a corrupt and perverted taste. He disputed the claim that the theatre taught morality, and claimed that many who frequented it resorted afterwards to public houses. He urged his parishioners to boycott these events, but clearly he was jealous as the theatre attracted large crowds for three nights whereas few attended his weekday services.[186] In 1887 a theatre at Exeter burnt down, causing 150 to 200 persons to be burnt to death. Among those who took advantage of the horror caused by this tragedy was J. Allan Smith, vicar of Swansea. In a sermon, later published, he argued that if a person lived for this world they would be theatre-goers, whereas it would be very different for those who lived for God. A Christian should never go to a place in which he would not wish death to find him. Could you take Christ into the theatre? or hope for real good from such a visit? he asked, or ask for God's blessing on it. An actor's occupation was injurious to his spiritual life.[187] His successor, Talbot Rice also condemned the theatre amidst much controversy.[183]

Dancing was also condemned by a number of clergymen, amongst them a Mr Jones, the curate of Merthyr. In her diary for 1835 Lady Charlotte Guest records her discomfort that he had decided it was his duty to refuse the Sacrament to anyone who should go to a ball at Dowlais, even if he was dragged before a court of justice. He made this threat in the presence of Evan Jenkins, rector of Dowlais, who had lent the church's chandeliers for use in the ballroom! She regarded Jones as a bigot.[189]

The Cardiff races were due to take place during Holy Week, 1863, a number on Good Friday, at a time when the Churches had begun to observe Lent in all its fullness. The dean of Llandaff, Thomas Williams, protested, and asked if the passions that races aroused, and its associated gambling, sat well with the thoughts of Calvary. It went ahead, but its organisers, mainly the local gentry, took note.[190] Though the action of Henry Vaughan against a local fair in his parish has been noted, we may note also how the vicar of Montgomery, writing in the parish magazine of 1893, warned the young people of his parish about the temptations of a pleasure fair and asked them to refuse to go with companions who might lead them into sin, especially into excessive drinking, which would prepare the way for future misery.[191]

A motion to check the growing evil of betting and gambling was passed at the 1899 Llandaff Diocesan Conference,[192] while the Cardiff clergy chapter debated the same matter when a question was raised about the legitimacy of raffles.[193] A number of sermons dealt with duelling, amongst them one preached in 1800 at Wrexham by its curate, Edward Edwards, after the death in a duel of Thomas Jones. He argued that the commandment "Thou shalt not kill" also referred to deliberate duelling, while to fight a duel not only testified to a false courage, but was also an act of defiance against God.[194] Edward Celtic Davies of Bishopston hardly endeared himself to his Ilston parishioners by preaching against their smuggling habits in 1817.[195]

Nonconformity was severe on many popular pleasures, including sport, concerts, the theatre and cinema, excursions and even musical evenings, and while the Church was more relaxed on occasions it had to give in to pressure. R. Tudur Jones writes of a Llanelli vicar who offered cyclists a special service in 1894 and invited them to come on their cycles. Nonconformist pressure forced him to give up this plan.[196] Yet some Anglican clergy could be as severe. Cyril Dobson, vicar of St Stephen's, Cardiff, 1910-15, had no place for whist drives, theatricals, or dances, for his was a spiritual work and he would only allow spiritual weapons to be used. But his people supported him as he built up a small congregation into a significant one, both numerically and spiritually.[197] At Greenhill and later St Matthew's, Swansea, W.J. Bronham, from the 1920s to the early 1940s, insisted that his church workers should not compromise themselves with the world by frequenting the theatre, the cinema, whist drives, and should avoid drinking alcohol, betting and gambling.[198]

By contrast, John Griffith of Merthyr took the motto, "all work and no play makes Jack a dull boy". Theatres, he argued, would enable the working man to forget the public house, and in the case of amateur theatricals, were useful for raising money for worthy causes. Circuses and menageries were harmless and innocent amusements, and he could not see what possible harm could come from looking at lions and tigers, or from listening to the broad jokes of a clown. One might learn much from the gentleness of animals and the skill of men. His organised rustic sports for his congregation were popular with them, but had he not been a muscular Christian he would have been crushed to death by the opposition of the Nonconformists.[199]

CHARTISM, LOCKOUTS, WAR AND DEPRESSION

The Church, due to its alliance with the State, lent all its support to the suppression of Chartism, a movement that wanted parliamentary representation for the vast majority of men who were disenfranchised, secret ballots and annual elections. When disorder broke out and riots started, the Church placed itself firmly on the side of reaction, refusing to consider the complaints as legitimate. During the Chartist riots at Newport in 1839 (with other disturbances at Newtown and Llanidloes) , a half-dozen clergymen attended an anti-Chartist meeting in the parish of Christ Church, Newport; James Coles, rector of Michaelston-y-Vedr, a magistrate, presided over the trials of some Chartist prisoners, while a vicious sermon against Chartism was preached by James Francis of St Paul's Church, Newport, in 1839. His sermon was designed to show the evil course into which men were being forced by agitators, even men from his own congregation. Happiness could not come from political agitation, but only through religion, and it was folly to look to the world for satisfaction. He was later to argue that it was only God's intervention that had saved Newport.[200] Evan Jenkins of Dowlais also preached a fiery sermon against the Chartists. He argued in it that men were only equal in so far as they were equally sinful in nature, and Scripture showed that the graduations in society had been appointed by God. Furthermore, poverty was not the result of unjust laws as the Chartists claimed, but part of the everlasting purpose of God. In her diary of 1839 Lady Charlotte Guest wrote that the Chartists had come to the church at Merthyr in a body, and behaved with great order, none attempting to enter anybody's pew without being invited. But she added that her husband, proprietor of the works, had strongly disagreed with Jenkins' Chartist sermon, published as a pamphlet, and refused to allow him to distribute it amongst his workmen.[201]

The Indian Mutiny brought its own reflections, as we have noted from the sermons of Edward Squire. He, and Benjamin Evans, who preached a sermon *Sin, its own Punishment*, at Llanstephan Church in 1857, both argued that humiliation was needed before God as the British in India had allowed idolatry and spell-bound superstitions to continue unchecked. The principal cause of the mutiny, Evans declared, was our timidity in not maintaining our credentials as professing Christians amongst a set of barbarians and deluded men.[202]

What was the Church's attitude to war? John Griffiths of Neath, in a sermon before the Glamorganshire Rifle Volunteers at Neath in 1860 noted that holding this church service had entailed some criticism. He defended himself by saying that while Christianity did not encourage war and bloodshed, the military were required for defence. He urged the assembled soldiers to do their duty to their country and themselves, and so defend both their own country and their own souls.[203] The war in South Africa did not pass unnoticed, with the bishop of Llandaff in 1900 noting this disastrous war, particular affecting areas worked by the SPG.[204]

The First World War brought its own conflict within the Church. Though the leaders of the Church defended the war as a just one, the length and horror of the conflict, the scale of casualties and the assertion that God was on the side of the British prompted a sense of unease. In one sense the integrity of the Church was compromised, though perhaps not so much as Nonconformity where some of its leading ministers, such as John Williams, had become recruiting agents for the army due to their alliance with Lloyd George. Williams was later to be regarded as the one who had sent "our boys" to be killed.[205] A typical example of the reaction of many clergy to the war is seen in the Penrhos entry for November 1914 in the Pool deanery magazine. Nineteen had joined the colours from that parish, and the comment was made that it was a duty and privilege to respond to the call of king and country to defend the motherland against a cruel and relentless foe who threatened our very homes.[206] In Swansea, as in many other places, there were intercessions for the nation throughout those years three times a week.[207]

David Lewis Prosser was vicar of Pembroke Dock when the First World War broke out, and responsible for the spiritual care of the troops stationed there. At one time there were over 7,000 men stationed in the training camps. Prosser brought in members of the Community of the Resurrection to assist him in this work. He was persuaded to suggest to the men who passed through his hands that they should make their confessions as many would face death, which he did himself. It was said that as a result of hearing these confessions he lost his innocence, while he prepared over 1,000 men for confirmation. His addresses to these men were published, and included such short pieces as "What confirmation means", "The Deserter's Returning", and on such topics as cleanliness, abstinence, intemperance, on being a Christian knight, the fear of death, and life beyond death.[208]

The Church's task was to restore harmony, to tell the rich their duties, but also to denounce dissoluteness, drunkenness and sensuality that involved so much misery to the working class, declared Dean H.T. Edwards in an address of 1872 about labour relations. He also noted the position of tenants and landlords.[209] His brother, by then bishop of St Asaph, declared in 1890 that the area of the Church's influence "should be as wide as humanity itself", and demurred at those whose religion was so centred on the afterlife that it was insensible to the claims of the moral and social questions which, in the words of Archbishop Benson, furnished "present, true, worthy problems to the English Church".[210] With this background it is hardly surprising that many clergy were involved in social movements. A number were involved in the anti-slave campaign of the 1820s,[211] and in 1831 there was a complaint from a "Constant Churchman" in the *Cambrian* that an anti-truck shop meeting had been held in Merthyr Tydfil Church. Twenty years later John Griffith joined the Nonconformist Thomas Price in establishing an anti-truck shop society at Aberdare.[212]

Further examples of this concern may be given. Canon J.D. Jenkins, vicar of Aberdare, 1870-6, not only helped promote friendly societies, but also helped conciliate employers and workmen during the 1871 coal strike in Aberdare and district. His concern for railwaymen led him to becoming vice president, and later president, of the Amalgamated Society of Railway Servants, where he sought a peaceful co-operation with employers, especially regarding the workers' requests for a shorter working day and sickness benefit.[213] David Howell in 1873 was asked to arbitrate between the Cardiff building masons and their employers about an increase in their hourly rate, and did so successfully.[214] The farm workers, desperate for better conditions and pay, held a series of strikes between 1917-29, though their revolt failed. They were assisted by a number of clergy, such as J.H. Jenkins, vicar of Cilrhedyn, Gwilym Rees, rector of Llanbrynmair, as well as by a number of Nonconformist ministers, though William Foster Jones, a former naval chaplain and vicar of St Donats, was bitterly reproached by a Nonconformist minister for assisting the farmers to harvest their crops. On the whole, however, it seems that organised religion did little to assist these men to alleviate their conditions, perhaps as there was no wish to offend the farmers.[215]

A further illustration is found in the terrible depression of the 1930s that hit the church extremely hard in the south Wales valleys. At Cyfarthfa nearly all the men of the congregation were out of work.[216] Many of the churches, such as St Barnabas, Penygraig, were still paying off debts contracted for their building, and even to find the necessary money to pay the interest on the capital was almost impossible. Those who were able moved to places where work could be found, such as Slough or the Midlands, leaving many churches bereft of their best members, and many, lacking adequate clothing and believing that you had to be decently dressed to attend a church service, stayed away from these services.[217] Timothy Rees, bishop of Llandaff, with his diocese facing the brunt of this depression, with an average of 43 per cent unemployed throughout the diocese and 63 per cent in Merthyr, encouraged the clergy in these parishes; established "messengers" from his junior clergy to assist in relief work; visited the areas; organised an Industrial Christian Fellowship Crusade in the Rhondda during 1938, and invited groups of unemployed people to his home in Llandaff. At his enthronement in 1931 he said in his address that his heart went out in sympathy to "the broken lives and the broken hearts that are the result of this depression", and he prayed he could make "some contribution to the solution of this crushing problem". For him the Church's social mission was not an optional extra but an essential part of the Gospel. He campaigned for new industry in high places, put pressure on politicians and industrial leaders to provide work for people, and he was instrumental in the creation of the Treforest Industrial Estate which helped alleviate some of the problems.[218] During the famous 1936 Hunger March to London, the vicar of Treherbert gave the seventeen marchers from his parish a religious send-off, with all reciting the Lord's Prayer before they went. He asked them to be well-behaved but assured them the Church in Wales supported their cause.[219]

The Church and socialism was debated at the 1912 Llandaff Diocesan Conference, some years after Keir Hardie won one of the Merthyr seats in 1900 as a socialist. While it was recognised that socialism was concerned about social justice and was not in general hostile to religion, a resolution was introduced that the clergy and laity of Wales should study the application of Christian principles to social questions in order to secure a more just distribution of wealth, leisure and opportunities for living a refined and cultured life.

This resolution was amended, however, as being far too radical, to ensuring a living wage, decent housing, Sunday rest, and opportunities for developing character in accordance with Christ's teaching.[220] There were two debates on socialism at the St Asaph Diocesan Conference, in 1895 and 1907. At the latter a Liverpool cleric, J. Wakefield, alleged he could not find the Liberal and Tory policies in the Bible, but the socialism was all the way through it. The Church was losing out because of its identification with the Tory party and with landlords.[221] Two outstanding socialist clergymen were T.D. James, rector of Llanerfyl 1901-27, a former Tory who now represented Labour on Montgomeryshire County Council, and J.H. Jenkins, rector of Cilrhedyn, 1911-33, who was a prominent platform speaker for the party.[222]

Many clergy were also involved in more social undertakings, sometimes taking a lead or otherwise assisting in such concerns as public health, the provision of clean water and a gas supply, reading rooms, local hospitals and dispensaries, as did Archdeacon Clive of Welshpool, who also blessed the occasion of the cutting the first sod of the Cambrian Railway at Welshpool in 1857.[223] John Griffith was also concerned in such matters as well as providing a children's hospital and an accident ward in Merthyr, and berated the industrial magnates for neglecting this requirement.[224] In his lectures to the working classes and YMCA William Leigh Morgan of St Mary's, Cardiff, stressed the need for good ventilation in houses, good wholesome food, public wash-houses, model lodging houses and savings banks.[225] Thomas Thomas, of Caernarfon, 1835-59, was also chaplain to the local prison, and treated the prisoners as though they were his own parishioners. His "experience of them," wrote his daughter, "led him to condemn most emphatically the system of solitary confinement and the unjust severity of the Game Laws", and to sympathise with their victims.[226]

MISSIONS TO SEAMEN

Seamen, because of the nature of their work, involving frequent turn-arounds at the ports, together with the dangers associated with pimps and agents, became the concern of many clergy associated with seaports. Amongst them was Leigh Morgan of St Mary's Cardiff, who started a mission in 1863, with services (in its own chapel) and social amenities, on board an old wooden vessel. In 1864 within four months over 2,455 seamen had attended its services. Later Morgan started a seamen's hospital on another ship, the *Hamadryad*, having discovered a seaman with smallpox driven from door to door. Later he opened a seamen's hostel and provided a banking service for their money. He would meet ships to preach "the glad tidings of redemption", and his influence was such that it was common to find daily prayers held on board many Cardiff bound ships.[227] The Bristol Channel Seamen's Mission, established by John Ashley in 1856, was later absorbed into the national organisation of the Missions to Seamen.[228] At Swansea, St Nicholas's Church, alongside the docks, held Sunday and weekday services by the 1890s, including a German service on a fortnightly basis, and held temperance meetings, entertainment, prayer meetings, a weekly mothers' meeting for the wives and mothers of seamen, a Sunday School for their children, and opened a daily reading room for the seamen.[229] Other work was carried out at Newport, Porthcawl and Barry, where in 1903 an Institute was being built for the 22,000 seamen who visited that port each year.[230]

CONCLUSION

By way of conclusion it might be suggested that this profusion of activity, especially in town parishes, although it might have retained people within the Church and provided facilities for their increased leisure time, was often accomplished at the expense of the real spiritual work to which the clergy had been called, and made them more into social agents and facilitators and their parish, in Roger Lloyd's words, like a "buzzing hive of furious activity".[231] Rural parishes may have been quieter affairs by comparison, but a parson who discriminated against his parishioners because of some slight to his authority, by declining them admission to his clothing or blanket club, or having the advantage of his personal charity, such as a soup kitchen, stirred up much resentment against the Church.[232] To find the right balance between spiritual matters and social concern was not an easy task, and may have caused the Victorian clergyman considerable anxiety.

ENDNOTES TO SECTION NINE: PASTORALIA

NOTE the abbreviations used in this section:

BFBS: British and Foreign Bible Society
CEMS Church of England Men's Society
CLB Church Lads' Brigade
CMS Church Missionary Society
GFS Girls' Friendly Society
MU Mothers' Union
SPCK Society for the Promotion of Christian Knowledge
SPG Society for the Propagation of the Gospel
UMCA Universities' Mission to Central Africa

CHAPTER ONE: INTRODUCTION

01 The Book of Common Prayer provides an order for the Visitation of the Sick and for the Communion of the Sick (with a rubric suggesting that frequent participation of the Sacrament when a person was well would enable them to be better prepared for a time of sickness). The Ordinal for deacons required them to promise to search for the sick, poor and impotent of the parish and to inform the Curate about them.

02 For some examples see: Jenkinson, *Charge (St Davids)*, 1836, pp. 15-16 (and other charges cited in the text); Edward Davies, *Church Union: A Series of Discourses* (London, 1811), pp. 298-9; H.R. Lloyd, *A Sermon ... at the Primary Visitation of ... Connop, Lord Bishop of St David's* (Llandovery, 1842), pp. 12-14; William Crawley, *The Support and Refreshment of the Faithful Minister of Christ: A Visitation Sermon* (Abergavenny, 1846), p. 13. Jacob cites a number of English examples, including Bishop Wilson of Sodor and Man who in 1715 requested clergy to keep a register of the families of their parishes, and enter into it their visits: *Clerical Profession*, pp. 203-9.

03 Nelson, *The Life of Bishop Bull*, p. 359; L.W. Barnard, "Bishop George Bull of St David's", *JWEH*, 9 (1992), 40.

04 Fleetwood, *Charge (St Asaph)*, 1710, pp. 21-2.

05 Peter Williams, *A Present for a Welsh Clergyman*, 1779. This contains the charge of the Archbishop of Tuam and other similar works. His name is handwritten on the title page of the copy consulted.

06 Hart, *The Eighteenth Century Country Parson*, p. 47.

07 *A Letter to the ... Lord Bishop of St David's concerning the Admission of Unqualified Persons into Holy Orders* (London, 1770s?), pp. 40-1.

08 Richard Evans, *Thoughts on the Most Effectual Ways of Promoting a more General and Regular Attendance at Church* (Church Union Society, Carmarthen, 1807), p. 20.

09 Ollivant, *Charge (Llandaff)*, 1854, p. 21.

10 Ollivant, *Charge (Llandaff)*, 1875, pp. 31-2.

11 Campbell, *Charge (Bangor)*, 1863, p. 26.

12 John Evans, *Charge to the Archdeaconry of Carmarthen*, 1864, p. 32. This is a point emphasised by Bishop Edwards of St Asaph in his 1890 Charge, when he claimed that a clergyman who visited his parishioners would bring new people into the Church: pp. 14, 19-20.

13 Basil Jones, *Charge (St Davids)*, 1877, pp. 14, 17-20.

14 Short, *Charge (St Asaph)*, 1847, p. 15.

15 Hughes, *Charge (St Asaph)*, 1874, pp. 26-8.

16 Lambeth Palace Library, Benson MS. 170, fol. 23. The letter is dated 28 October 1886.

17 Brown, *John Griffith*, pp. 125-6. He left the general visiting to his curates.

18 Griffiths, *Deanery of Penllyn and Edeirnion*, pp. 25, 44.

19 Evans, "Churchwardens' Presentations in Carmarthenshire", *T.Carms.A.S.*, 14 (1919), 12, 14-15. The minister of Conwyl Cayo in 1705 was said to visit the sick when called for: *ibid.*, 11 (1916), 51. Woodforde, the English clerical diarist, was a constant visitor to the sick, but did not visit his parishioners otherwise unless he did so socially: Sykes, *Church and State*, pp. 270-1.

20 Saunders, *A View of the State of Religion*, p. 27.

CHAPTER TWO: THE GRADUAL OUTWORKING OF PASTORAL VISITATION

1 *Proceedings of the St Asaph Diocesan Conference*, 1895, p. 22.

2 W.H. How, *Lectures on Pastoral Work* (Cambridge, 1883), p. 53.

3 Teague and Brown, "Griffith Jones' 'Pious Minister'", p. 32.

4 Jane Ross, *A Light upon the Road* (1989), p. 27. Hughes believed a parish of 2,000 was ideal for such a personal visitation: *Sermons of the late Ven. John Hughes ... [with a] Memoir* (Aberystwyth, 1864), p. vi.

5 Quoted by Hinton, *The Anglican Parochial Clergy*, p. 283. Mrs Gaskell once asked a Yorkshire villager about her parson. She replied he was "a rare good one, he minds his own business and n'er troubles himself with ours": quoted by Hart and Carpenter, *The Nineteenth Century Country Parson*, p. 37. John Longe, vicar of the Suffolk parish of Coddenham, who died in 1834, records little parochial visiting in his diary, though he and his curate would visit the sick, pray and read with them and give them tracts: Michael Stone (ed.), *The Diary of John Longe* (Suffolk Record Society, 51, 2008), p. xxviii.

6 S. Tudor Roberts, *Ysgol Eglwysbach* (1985), p. 13.

7 NLW, MS. 4,318B, for Wrexham (census of attendances at churches, 1865).

8 Elias Owen (ed.), *The Works of the Rev. Griffith Edwards* (London, 1898), p. xiii, and his obituary in *MC.*, 27 (1893), p. 224.

9 Davies, *Life and Opinions of Robert Roberts*, pp. 382-3.

10 F.L.G. Bevan, *History of Christ Church, Cyfarthfa* (1957), p. 15.

11 McClatchey, *Oxfordshire Clergy*, pp. 90-2.

12 Sumner, *Charge (Llandaff)*, 1827, p. 41. For early English precedents see Russell, *Clerical Profession*, pp. 114-5.

13 Obelkevich, *Religion and Rural Society*, p. 166.

14 W.H. How, *Lectures on Pastoral Work* (Cambridge, 1883), p. 53-64; John Ellerton, *A Manual of Parochial Work* (London, 1888), pp. 127-36. R.W. Evans suggested in a rural parish of twelve square miles and a population of 1,500 a clergyman could make 50 visits in six days: quoted by Hinton, *Anglican Parochial Clergy*, p. 282. Many writers suggested regularity and system in visiting, using a parish visiting register and pastoral diary: Heeney, *A Different Kind of Gentleman*, p. 54-5. At the Stoke on Trent Church Congress of 1875 Walsham How advised clergy to seize every pretext for making a visit, especially when there had been a misunderstanding: Brown, *Parochial Lives*, p. 63.

15 R.W. Evans, *The Bishopric of Souls* (London, 1856), pp. 55-61.

16 Heeney, *A Different Kind of Gentleman*, p. 54.

17 Heeney, *A Different Kind of Gentleman*, p. 52.

18 *Ecclesiastic*, 25 (1863), 313-20. By contrast the clerical writer Ashton Oxenden wrote that the pastor must never be intrusive, never enter a house without removing his hat, and show every courtesy

expected of a visitor, while Dean Burgeon reminded the clergy that the feelings of the poor were as acute as their own: Heeney, *A Different Kind of Gentleman*, p. 53.

19 Edwards, *Charge (St Asaph)*, 1890, pp. 14-16.

20 Jane Williams, *Thomas Price, Carnhuanawc*, II, 63.

21 *Memoir and Remains of the Rev. Henry Vaughan* (London, 1841), pp. 26-7. He was described as a bright example of a parish priest: *ibid.*, p. 67.

22 Quoted by Morgan, "Diocese of St David's", B, p. 41.

23 Hughes, *The Very Rev. J.H. Cotton*, p. 161.

24 *Church Pastoral-Aid Society, 8th Report*, 1843, pp. 24-5.

25 Brown, *David Howell*, p. 24. Much later Daniel Parry-Jones had oversight of the Welsh congregation at Pontypridd, plus a district to visit as curate: *A Welsh Country Parson*, p. 23.

26 NLW, MS. 4,316, title, Pwllheli; Brown, *David Howell*, p. 35. In 1875 Howell stated that though the minister's work might be to promote education, help the poor, advise the perplexed, and reconcile differences, his supreme concern was the salvation of his people: *ibid.*, p. 79.

27 Davies, *Life and Opinions of Robert Roberts*, pp. 395-6.

28 *Church and People*, 8 (1897), 221; Brown, *Parochial Lives*, p. 50.

29 E.A. Williams, *The Day before Yesterday* (Llangefni, 1998), p. 177.

30 *Proceedings of the St Asaph Diocesan Conference,* 1893, p. 13.

31 Brown, "The Curate of Berriew", pp. 137-8. Turner refused to write the wills of his parishioners.

32 William Plomer (ed.), *Kilvert's Diary* (London, 1856), I, 251-3, 264; II, 120; Ifans, *The Diary of Francis Kilvert*, pp. 74, 84; Frederick Grice, *Francis Kilvert and his World* (Horsham, 1982), p. 82; David Lockwood, *Francis Kilvert* (Bridgend, 1990), p. 51; John Toman, *Kilvert: The Homeless Heart* (Logaston, 2001), pp. 252-7. Plomer comments that by abbreviating the diary an unjust impression is given about Kilvert's pastoral duties, which were much more extensive than the selections he had made would suggest [quoted Toman, *ibid.*, p. 141].

33 *Report of the Church Congress, Swansea*, 1879, p. 215.

34 I.J. Bronham, *A Record of the Life and Work of the Rev. W.J. Bronham* (1943), p. 20.

35 J. Grenfell-Hill (ed.), *Growing up in Wales* (Llandysul, 1996), p. 144.

36 Smith, *They did it their way*, p. 87.

37 *CT*, 5 August 1904, p. 155. Stephen Gladstone of Hawarden undertook a three-month visitation of his parish in 1890-1, visiting around 1,200 homes. He repeated this in 1898-9 and may have done so annually. It is said people valued this display of interest and concern for their welfare: Ros Aitken, *The Prime Minister's Son* (Chester, 2012), pp. 151, 200.

38 Cowley, *St Paul's, Sketty*, p. 24.

39 *Report of the Royal Commission, 1911*, II, 372 (12299).

40 A.P. Leigh (ed.), *Sermons and Biographical Sketch of the late Rev. Canon T. Jones* (Rhyl, 1913), p. 22.

41 A.P. Leigh (ed.), *Sermons and Biographical Sketch of the late Rev. Canon T. Jones* (Rhyl, 1913), pp. 17-18.

42 *Report of the Royal Commission, 1911*, I-I, 17; IV, 492 (47476).

43 Roger L. Brown, "The Newtown Clerical Association", *MC,* 104 (2016), 79-80. However, clergy should beware of gossip or taking refreshment, and not allow parishioners to send for them as if they were servants.

44 J.B. Sumner, *Four Charges delivered to the Clergy at the Diocese of Chester* (London, 1838): 1828 Charge, pp. 38-44 and 1832 Charge, appendix pp. ii-ix. See also K. Hylson-Smith, *Evangelicals in the Church of England* (Edinburgh, 1988), p. 157, and Russell, *Clerical Profession*, p. 119.

45 S. Taylor (ed.), *From Cranmer to Davidson: A Miscellany* (CERS, 7, 1999), p. 268n. There was a Strangers' Friend Society in London during the 1780s which organised house to house visiting, and John Venn in 1799 divided his parish into districts and assigned lay visitors to them. It is suggested

these societies were based on the work of Thomas Chalmers in Glasgow which he described in his 1821 publication, *Christian and Civil Economy of Large Towns*: D.M. Lewis, *Lighten their Darkness* (Carlisle, 2001), pp. 35-6. See also D.W. Bebbington, *Evangelicalism in Modern Britain* (London, 1989), pp. 118-9; Jacob, *Clerical Profession*, p. 209; R.A. Salway, *Prelates and People* (London, 1969), pp. 320-3. By 1850 it is said that nearly all the 250 London parishes had visiting associations, and by 1889 the *Church of England Yearbook* said there were 47,000 district visitors in Church of England parishes: Doreen Rosman, *The Evolution of the English Church* (Cambridge, 2003), p. 210.

46 T.V. Short, *Parochialia* (London, 1843), see esp. pp. xii, xiv-xv, 54-6. His visitors were regarded by the working class people as agents of the State Church sent to spy on them: R.A. Solway, *Prelates and People* (London, 1969), p. 323.

47 *Parish of Swansea: Abstract of Accounts*, 1858, p. 14; 1866, pp. 26-7; 1892, pp. 33-9; (the 1872 *Abstract of Accounts* notes the provision of three nurses: p. 36); K. Padley, *Our Ladye Church of Swanesey* (2007), pp. 45-6; *Report of the Church Congress, Swansea*, 1879, p. 216; Brown, *Parochial Lives*, pp. 184-5.

48 Pritchard, "The Revd. S.E. Gladstone", pp. 208-9.

49 Thomas Thomas, Caernarfon, *A New Year's Address, 1853,* p. 20; Brown, *Evangelicals in the Church in Wales*, p. 210.

50 *Cowbridge Parish Magazine*, 1885 at South Glamorgan Record Office, F/8/CW/23.

51 Brown, *Ten Clerical Lives*, p. 89.

52 Robert Wickham, *An Address to his Parishioners* (Wrexham, 1854), pp. 5, 1-11.

53 NLW, MS. 4,316, fol. 12; Brown, *Clergy and People in Welshpool*, p. 75. Here the lay visitors always acted in subordination to the clergy.

54 *Church and People*, 8 (1897), 221.

55 Reynolds, *St Gabriel's, Swansea*, p. 28.

56 *Report of the Royal Commission, 1911*, III, 23, 30, 98 (18681, 18900-4, 21369-70). The Wrexham Visitors Association was started by Vicar Cunliffe in 1875 but under David Howell they met monthly, though he combined it with temperance work: Brown, *David Howell*, p. 144.

57 *Proceedings of the St Asaph Diocesan Conference*, 1885, p. 15.

58 Russell, *The Clerical Profession*, pp. 117-8.

59 *Ecclesiastic*, 25 (1863), p. 317. The suggestion about inviting parishioners to call on clergy by appointment was not unknown, especially for those who would not be available when the clergy normally visited homes, such as agricultural workmen and domestic servants: Heeney, *A Different Kind of Gentleman*, p. 50.

60 Roger Lloyd, *The Church of England: 1900-1965* (London, 1966), pp. 161-2.

61 Heeney, *A Different Kind of Gentleman*, pp. 53-4. For a general background see Jacob, *Clerical Profession*, pp. 210-2. He notes that clergy were conscientious about this ministry, which included the baptism of children not expected to live.

62 Warren, *The Duties of the Parochial Clergy*, p. 11.

63 *The Charges of Samuel Horsley* (Dundee, 1813), pp. 153-4; Mather, *High Church Prophet*, p. 149 notes how he realised this kind of ministry could not be achieved in pluralities and with non-resident clergymen. Fleetwood said much the same as Horsley about the response of parishioners to good pastoral care: *Charge (St Asaph)*, 1710, p. 24-5.

64 W.H. How, *Lectures on Pastoral Work* (Cambridge, 1883), pp. 70-1, 76-8.

65 Henry Rees, *The Welsh Clergyman's Vade Mecum* (Bangor, 1898), esp. pp. iii, viii.

66 Fleetwood, *Charge (St Asaph)*, 1710, p. 23.

67 John Gott, *The Parish Priest of the Town* (London, 1890), pp. 132-3,

68 Heeney, *A Different Kind of Gentleman*, p. 54.

69 Evans, *Social Life in mid-Eighteenth Century Anglesey*, p. 175.

70 James Kenward, *Ab Ithel* (Tenby, 1876), p. 62.

71 Brown, *David Howell*, p. 81. Thomas Richardson of Rhyl, 1878-90, had a similar ministry: Brown, *Evangelicals in the Church in Wales*, p. 230.

72 F.D. How, *Lighter Moments from the Notebooks of Bishop Walsham How* (London, 1900), pp. 23-4. He related many anecdotes about his pastoral experiences, including one when he asked for a copy of a Bible to read to an elderly couple, who replied they hadn't needed one for many years ever since the old cow was ill: *ibid.* pp. 16-17, 24-5.

73 Not only cholera: when a throat inflection raged in Hodnet in 1820 Reginald Heber insisted on continuing his pastoral visits, saying he was as much in God's keeping in a sick man's chamber as in his own. He eventually caught the infection and for a time his life was despaired of: *The Life of Reginald Heber, by his Widow* (New York, 1830), II, 1.

74 Neil Fairlamb, *The Clergy of the Beaumaris Parishes* (2007), p. 17.

75 W.O. Wills, "The Clergy and Society in Mid-Victorian South Wales", *JHSCW*, 24 (1974), 38.

76 C. Wilkins, *The History of Merthyr Tydfil* (Merthyr Tydfil, 1908), p. 309. For an account of the cholera at Neath which caused churches and chapels to fill see George Eaton, "King Cholera at Neath", *Transactions of the Neath Antiquarian Society*, 1962-3, p. 16.

77 Islwyn Jenkins, "The Church in Industrial Rhymney", *JHSCW*, 16 (1966), 85.

78 Evan Jones, *Adgofion*, pp. 21-2.

79 G.P. Jones, "Cholera in Wales", *NLW.Jnl.*, 10 (1957-8), 298-9; J.E. Vincent (ed.), *The Memories of Sir Llewelyn Turner* (London, 1903), pp. 187-9. Harriet Thomas notes the first outbreak in Caernarfon when her father, Thomas Thomas, laboured night and day amongst the victims taxing even his moral and physical courage: *Llewelyn Thomas: A Memoir* (London, 1897), p. 21.

80 Russell Davies, *Hope and heartbreak* (Cardiff, 2005), p. 195.

81 Charles Williams, *Sermons* (Oxford, 1866), pp. 71-82, esp. p. 81. He added that few followed this advice.

82 J.C. Campbell, *A Sermon: God's Protection the Support of his People* (Merthyr Tydfil, 1854).

83 M.G.R. Morris, "Bishop Richard Lewis: His Life before Llandaff", *JWEH*, 4 (1987), 85-6.

84 G.P. Jones, "Cholera in Wales", *NLW.Jnl.*, 10 (1957-8), 289; Roger L. Brown, "The Public Health Survey of Welshpool, 1849", *Sayce Papers*, 3 (1997), 10-11.

85 Brown, *Ten Clerical Lives*, p. 94.

86 Evans, "Churchwardens' Presentations in Carmarthenshire", *T.Carms.A.S.*, 11 (1916), 83.

87 SA/RD/26, fol. 141; M.H. Ridgeway, *The Church Plate of the Diocese of St Asaph* (Denbigh, 1997), pp. 146, 187. He adds that Llanbedr Dyffryn Clwyd had obtained similar plate by 1823: *ibid.*, p. 115.

88 Evans, *Religion and Politics in mid-Eighteenth Century Anglesey*, p. 30; Richards, "The Diocese of Bangor during the Rise of Welsh Methodism", p. 206.

89 Davies, *Life and Opinions of Robert Roberts*, p. 69.

90 Brown, "The Curate of Berriew", p. 139.

91 *Cardiff Ruridecanal Chapter Minutes*, October 1896.

92 Hughes, *Pwllheli Church*, p. 24.

93 *Reports of the Llandaff Diocesan Conference*, 1893, pp. 99-116; 1894, p. 56; 1895, pp. 29-30; 1896, pp. 21-6, 135. D. Parry-Jones was later, as curate of Pontypridd, responsible for visiting the workhouse: *A Welsh Country Parson*, p. 23.

94 *Record*, 8 January 1897, p. 37.

95 Huntington, *Random Recollections*, pp. 111-2; cf. Hinton, *Anglican Parochial Clergy*, pp. 288-90.

96 Williams, *Thomas Price, Carnhuanawc*, II, 283-4.

97 *WM*, 8 March 1890, p. 3. Bishop Pritchard Hughes argued it took longer to visit three rural farms than twenty houses in a town parish: *Report of the Royal Commission, 1911*, IV, 523 (48187).

98 Parry-Jones, *A Welsh Country Parson*, p. 149.

99 F.D. How, *Bishop Walsham How* (London, 1899), p. 49.

100 Basil Jones, *Charge (St Davids)*, 1886, pp. 69-70. For eighteenth-century comments about the lack of suitable employment see Jacob, *Clerical Profession*, p. 206.

101 A.H. Grey Edwards, *Reminiscences of an Unknown Man* (1940), p. 117. Bishop Pritchard Hughes of Llandaff partly agreed with him: *Report of the Royal Commission, 1911*, IV, 523 (48491).

102 *Proceedings of the St Asaph Diocesan Conference*, 1892, p. 16.

103 Parry-Jones, *A Welsh Country Parson*, p. 114.

104 Noted by Haig, *Victorian Clergy*, p. 295. He also notes the assumption that rural clergy had little to do.

105 *Report of the Royal Commission, 1911*, IV, 476-8 (47214-240). Owen noted that the number of communicants had increased in these rural areas in spite of considerable depopulation over the previous thirty years. In suggesting that the rural ministry was essential to the Church he was probably including in his thoughts the vast numbers of men from the rural parishes of his diocese who were ordained, many of whom served in the industrial areas of south Wales. Bishop Edwards presented a rather different picture to the same Commission (*ibid.*, IV, 499 [47658]). The rural parson took services on Sunday, during the week visited his school and parishioners, "but it would be quite a stretch of the imagination to describe him as a hard worked man". He accepted it needed a particular type of man to stand the monotony of a country parish and to make himself useful from day to day. Owen had grown up in a rural parish, but Edwards had little experience of the countryside.

106 *Report of the Church Congress, Brighton*, 1901, p. 252. The same speaker, P.P. Pennant, felt that the parson not only visited his parishioners but also became the confidential family lawyer and their chief advisor: *Proceedings of the St Asaph Diocesan Conference*, 1893, p. 9.

107 *Proceedings of the St Asaph Diocesan Conference*, 1903, p. 29.

108 Haig, *The Victorian Clergy*, pp. 284-7.

109 Quoted by Haig, *The Victorian Clergy*, pp. 285-6.

110 Heeney, *A Different Kind of Gentleman*, p. 20.

111 *Report of the Llandaff Church Conference*, 1890, pp. 37-8. His remedy was the use of lay people.

112 I.G. Jones, *Mid-Victorian Wales* (Cardiff, 1992), p. 4.

CHAPTER THREE: NURTURING SPIRITUAL LIFE

1 *The Lord Arch-bishop of Canterbury's Letter to the Reverend the Arch-deacons and the Rest of the Clergy of the Diocese of St David* (London, 1703), p. 13.

2 Nelson, *Life of Bishop Bull*, pp. 376-80.

3 Edward Morgan, *Home Light: or a Brief Memoir of the Rev. R. Bassett* (Carnarvon, 1860), p. 33-5.

4 David Jones, *Life and Times of Griffith Jones of Llanddowror* (London, 1902), pp. 213-4; Brown, *Evangelicals in the Church in Wales*, p. 39.

5 Burgess, *Charge (St Davids)*, 1807, p. 12.

6 Short, *Charge (St Asaph)*, 1853, pp. 19-21, 29-31.

7 SA/MB/28, fol. 95.

8 *Proceedings of the St Asaph Diocesan Conference*, 1892, pp. 13-14, 19.

9 J.A. Gauntlett, *To the Members of the Congregation of Holy Trinity Church, Swansea* (Swansea, 1884), p. 4.

10 David Howell, *Religion in the Home: Address to the St David's Diocesan Conference*, 1902; Brown, *David Howell*, pp. 284-6.

11 *Report of the Llandaff Diocesan Conference*, 1892, pp. 110-16; *Report of the Bangor Diocesan Conference*, 1910, pp. 20-4.

12 Edward Morgan, *John Elias: Life, Letters and Essays* (reprint, Edinburgh, 1973), p. 5.

13 Noted by Nigel Scotland, *Evangelical Anglicans in a Revolutionary Age* (Carlisle, 2004), pp. 348-51.

14 M.G. Morris (ed)., *Romilly's Visits to Wales* (Llandysul, 1998), p. 48.

15 John Tillotson, *Sermons on General Subjects and Occasions* (London, 1742), II, 134.

16 H.P. Jones, "An S.P.C.K. Activity in Eighteenth-Century Anglesey", *T.Anglesey A.S.*, 1963, pp. 16-42, esp. pp. 24-5; Griffiths, *Literature, Religion and Society*, pp. 67-8.

17 Clement, *Correspondence and Minutes of the S.P.C.K.*, pp. 236-8, 309, 314-5.

18 Thomas Parry (translated H.I. Bell), *A History of Welsh Literature* (Oxford, 1970), pp. 240-2.

19 D. Ll. Morgan, *The Great Awakening in Wales* (London, 1988), p. 36; and see Jenkins, *Literature, Religion and Society*, pp. 33-54 for printed books and pp. 55-84 for Bibles and Catechisms.

20 Clement, *The S.P.C.K. and Wales*, pp. 26-39; Jenkins, *Literature, Religion and Society*, pp. 113-122.

21 Jacob, *Clerical Profession*, pp. 253-5.

22 A.O. Evans, *Minutes and Proceedings of an Old Tract Society of Bangor Diocese 1804-1812* (Bangor, 1918), pp. 77-81. The society was also concerned with promoting Sunday Schools.

23 Roger L. Brown, "'One of the most Remarkable Men of his Time': Richard Davies, Archdeacon of Brecon", *Brycheiniog*, 34 (2002), 120, 123.

24 *Christian Colportage Association: Report of the Swansea Branch*, 1878-9.

25 For the history of the magazine insets see: Peter Croft, *The Parish Magazine Inset* (Blandford Forum, 1993). The local matter was generally printed on the front and end wraps by a local printer.

26 Brown, *David Howell*, pp. 82-3. It is claimed that the first parish magazine in Wales was produced by the parish of Llanelli: Gareth Hughes, *Looking around Llanelli with Harry Davies* (Llanelli, 1985), p. 207. The parish of Holy Trinity, Swansea, commenced its magazine in 1884: J.A. Gauntlett, *To the Members of the Congregation of Holy Trinity Church, Swansea* (Swansea, 1884), p. 3.

27 Melvin Humphreys, et.al., *Llanfyllin: Portrait of an Age* (Llanfyllin, 2002), p. 103.

28 Hughes, *The Very Rev. J.H. Cotton*, p. 174. The later failure of a savings bank of which he was a trustee caused him immense difficulties.

29 Brown, *Llandaff Figures and Places*, pp. 2-3.

30 Harford, *Thomas Burgess*, pp. 271-6.

31 *The Life of Reginald Herber* (by his widow: New York, 1830), I, 491-9.

32 Williams, *Thomas Price, Carnhuanawc*, II, 146-79; Brown, *Evangelicals in the Church in Wales*, p.; 107.

33 A letter of D. Richards, Llansilan: NLW, Cwrtmawr MS. 280B.

34 Jane Ross, *A Light upon the Road* (1989), p. 19.

35 Thomas Thomas (Caernarfon), *A New Year's Address, 1853*, pp. 8-9. The parish also supported the Tract Society, CPAS, SPCK, and CMS: *ibid.*, pp.20-3.

36 Hughes, *Pwllheli Church*, pp. 23-4.

37 Edward Morgan (ed.), *Letters of the Rev. Griffith Jones ... to Madam Bevan* (London, 1832), pp. 196-7; Jenkins, *Literature, Religion and Society*, p. 69.

38 David Jones, *Life and Times of Griffith Jones* (London, 1902), p. 212. He would give a dole of bread as a reward to those who could repeat a verse of Scripture, which he would then explain and apply to their circumstances. The circulating schools, noted in section 7, chapter 3, taught children and adults to read the Bible and encouraged their spiritual lives.

39 Thomas Burgess, *Sunday Evening Lectures recommended to the Clergy of the Diocese of St David's* (Carmarthen, 1806).

40 A.N. Palmer, *A History of the Parish Church of Wrexham* (reprint, Wrexham, 1984), p. 47.

41 Henry Pidgeon, *Memorials of Shrewsbury* (1837, reprint), p. 62.

42 John Ellerton (ed.), *A Manual of Parochial Work* (London, 1888), pp. 157-8 The writer suggested as the format for the service, hymn, confession, Scripture, hymn, prayer (though not from the Book of

Common Prayer), thanksgivings, address, hymn and blessing. Heeney notes Ridley's handbook which comprised a Biblical exposition followed by a summary of practical conclusions: *A Different Kind of Gentleman*, pp. 36-7.

43 *Bye-Gones*, 6 November 1912, pp. 284-5. There was also a Saturday prayer meeting and various Bible expositions. For an English background see Russell, *Clerical Profession*, pp. 68-9. Russell alleges that by the 1840s these meetings were part of parochial strategy, but by the 1860s they were being viewed with disfavour.

44 K. Hylson-Smith, *Evangelicals in the Church of England* (Edinburgh, 1988), p. 157.

45 *Memoir and Remains of the Rev. Henry Vaughan* (London, 1841), pp. 52-3, 67.

46 *Church Pastoral-Aid Society*: *11th Report,* 1846, pp. 28-9. There were also weekday services in a licensed schoolroom.

47 James Kenwood, *Ab Ithel* (Tenby, 1871), pp. 61-2, 68.

48 Davies, *Life and Opinions of Robert Roberts*, pp. 326-7.

49 Gresford Vicar's Book, fol. 265. It was held in the home of a sick person.

50 Brown, "The Curate of Berriew", pp. 143-4.

51 Jones and Williams, *The Religious Census of 1851*, I, 500.

52 Plomer, *Kilvert's Diary*, III, 349-50. John Toman notes that while Kilvert commenced a cottage meeting at Bredwardine, none is recorded at Clyro in his diary: *Kilvert: The Homeless Heart* (Logaston, 2001), pp. 255-6.

53 Hughes, *Memoir of the Rev. J.A. Jackson*, p. 27.

54 Roger L. Brown, "The Curate of Welshpool", *Sayce Papers*, 6 (2000), 41.

55 T.W. Pritchard, *Remembering Ruabon* (Wrexham, 2000), p. 82.

56 Gladstone, *Parish of Hawarden*, p. 37.

57 *Swansea Parish Magazine*, May 1905, p. 98.

58 Pryce, *One Hundred Years of Evangelical Witness*, p. 54.

59 John Walsh, "Religious Societies: Methodist and Evangelical 1738-1800", *Studies in Church History*, 23 (1986), 279-301; D.E. Jenkins (ed.), *Religious Societies (Dr Woodward's "Account")* (Liverpool, 1935), pp. 12-13.

60 Saunders, *A View of the State of Religion*, pp. 32-3.

61 J.R.. Guy, "Church and Churchmen in Llantrisant Parish", in Steward Williams, *Glamorgan Historian*, 12 (1981), 89.

62 Translated as *The Experience Meeting* by Mrs Lloyd Jones (Bridgend, 1973), whose introduction discusses these societies; Eifion Evans, *Pursued by God* (Bridgend, 1996), p. 33-6.

63 Edward Morgan, *Ministerial Record: or a Brief Account ... of the Rev. D. Jones, Llangan* (London, 1841), pp. 136-7, 144-7.

64 David Howell to the Bishop of St Asaph, 7 May 1886: Lambeth Palace Library, Benson MS. 39, fols. 200-1.

65 Bishop Carey to T.G. Roberts: NLW, MS. 22754, fol. 19.

66 "A Welsh Rector", *What says the Church?* (Bangor, 1842), pp. 5-6; "A Welsh Rector (Evan Lloyd of Llangelynys?), *A Few Words in Reply to the Remarks of a Welsh Clergyman on 'What says the Church?'* (Bangor, 1842), pp. 13-14. A reply by "A Welsh Clergyman" defended the practice: *A Few Remarks upon a Pamphlet by 'A Welsh Rector' ... "What says the Church?"* (Chester, 1842).

67 Brown, *John Griffith*, p. 23.

68 William Evan James, *Charge to the Archdeaconry of Carmarthen*, 1882, p. 11.

69 Campbell, *Charge (Bangor)*, 1860, pp. 20-3.

70 Jenkins, *Thomas Charles of Bala*, III, 302-3.

71 Perowne, *Remains of Connop Thirlwall* (1842 Charge), I, 16-19.

72 Short, *Charge (St Asaph)*, 1850, pp. 23-4, 26-30, 33-6.

73 James Kenwood, *Ab Ithel* (Tenby, 1871), p. 68.

74 *Church Pastoral-Aid Society: 11th Report,* 1846, p. 28.
75 Islwyn Jenkins, "The Church in Industrial Rhymney", *JHSCW*, 16 (1966), 83; Brown, *Evangelicals in the Church in Wales*, p. 175; Brown, *Parochial Lives*, p. 42.
76 Davies, *Life and Opinions of Robert Roberts*, pp. 292-3.
77 Brown, *Clergy and People of Welshpool*, p. 54.
78 Hughes, *Memoir of the Rev. J.A. Jackson*, p. 27.
79 *Report of the Royal Commission, 1911*, II, 105 (2659).
80 Eli Clarke, *Christ Church, Swansea: Pastoral Letter and Statement of Accounts*, 1887-8, pp. 3-4.
81 Russell, *Clerical Profession*, pp. 64-6.
82 Brown, *Evangelicals in the Church in Wales*, p. 116. He also made Llanrhystud into a centre for preaching meetings.
83 Brown, *Evangelicals in the Church in Wales*, p. 181. This was the result of a mission.
84 Daniel Richards, *Honest Memories* (Llandybie, 1985), pp. 151-2 (he also noted the services of preparation for Holy Communion).
85 Jones, *Faith and the Crisis of a Nation*, p. 100; Brown, *Parochial Lives*, p. 83.
86 *Report of the Royal Commission, 1911*, IV, 492 (47476) .The bishop also noted that such societies as MU, GFS, CLB and CETS were represented in his diocese.
87 Brown, *David Howell*, pp. 144-6. In addition he held a prayer meeting after the Sunday evening service.
88 Brown, *Clergy and People of Welshpool*, pp. 70-2. In addition, there were branches of GFS and CLB, and at a later date, MU and CEMS. By the 1910s a Pleasant Sunday Afternoon had been instituted as a sort of half-way house, with both secular and religious items.
89 *Christ Church, Swansea: Men's Bible Class*, 1901.
90 Eli Clarke, *Christ Church, Swansea: Pastoral Letter and Statement of Accounts*, 1891-2, p. 13.
91 J.R. Guy, "The Art and Architecture of the Catholic Revival in Roath", *Roath Local History Society Project Newsletter*, 6/2 (1991), 40.
92 *Yr Haul*, 1899, pp. 99-100.
93 Ward and Coe, *Father Jones of Cardiff*, pp. 48-9. For a similar position at St John the Baptist, Newport, see R.C. Wright, *The First One Hundred Years* (Newport, 2000), p. 5. There were also sisters involved in this church.
94 Brown, *Parochial Lives*, p. 61.
95 Eli Clarke, *Christ Church, Swansea: Pastoral Letter and Statement of Accounts*, 1891-2, p. 13. John Ellerton suggested these meetings could include a penny bank, a small lending library, a shoe and a clothing club and dispensary, but they should also have a spiritual aim: *A Manual of Parochial Work* (London, 1888), pp. 160-3.
96 Chrystal Davies, *Mothers' Union Alive!* (Cowbridge, 1993), esp. pp. 9, 11, 14-15; Margaret S. Walker, *From Beguildy to Rhossili* (1989), esp. pp. 6-10, 16-17; *Report of the St David's Diocesan Conference*, 1899, p. 61. Bishop Edwards' evidence about the spiritual concerns of the MU is found in the *Report of the Royal Commission, 1911*, IV, 535-6 (48488-9).
97 *Report of the Llandaff Diocesan Conference*, 1912, pp. 26-7.
98 Hughes, *Charge (Llandaff)*, 1913, p. 8.
99 *The Girls' Friendly Society: Diocese of Bangor, Annual Report for 1906.* The diocesan branch had been founded in 1880.
100 Knight, in Williams, *The Welsh Church*, p. 378.
101 Pritchard, "the Revd. S.E. Gladstone", pp. 211, 216; Gladstone, *Parish of Hawarden*, pp. 25, 27-8.
102 Ellis, *Fresh as Yesterday*, p. 92.
103 Melvin Humphreys, et.al., *Llanfyllin: Portrait of an Age* (Llanfyllin, 2002), p. 103.
104 Tilney, *Parish of Penarth with Lavernock*, p. 56.

105 Smith, *They did it their way*, pp. 76-7. For the Society of St David see: W.G.H. Thomas, *Society of St David* (Needham Market, 1972).

106 Janet Jones, *Holy Trinity Church, Aberystwyth* (1986), pp. 7-9, 12, 16.

107 Pryce, *One Hundred Years of Evangelical Witness*, pp. 52, 57.

108 Davies, *Holy Trinity Church, Ystrad Mynach*, pp. 24-5, 33-4; L.J.H. James, *To the People of Ystrad Mynach* (1914), pp. 16-17.

109 George, *St Theodore's Church*, pp. 31, 33-6. Prys Morgan notes from the Report of the Royal Commission of 1911 similar activities at St Peter's, Pentre, and Aberdare in 1905, with guilds, societies, and devotional meetings: *Glamorgan County History* (Cardiff, 1988), VI, 258.

110 I.J. Bronham, *A Record of the Life and Work of the Rev. W.J. Bronham* (1943), p. 13.

111 Roger L. Brown, "'A Man in a Hurry': Talbot Rice, vicar of Swansea", *Minerva,* 4 (1996), 39; *Parish of Swansea: Abstract of Accounts*, 1892, pp. 10-11, 14-16, 20.

112 *Report of the Royal Commission, 1911*, II, 488 (16536, 16542-3).

113 M.J. Mainwaring, *History of St Peter's Church, Senghenydd* (1946), pp. 10, 13.

114 Derrick Platt, *The Church of St Mary Magdalene, Penley* (1980), p. 15.

115 G.R. Orrin, "The Reverend Harold Stepney Williams", *Gower*, 41 (1990), 47.

116 Cowley, *St Paul's Church, Sketty*, p. 24.

117 *Report of the St David's Diocesan Conference*, 1885, p. 104.

118 *Report of the Church Congress, Manchester*, 1888, p. 69.

119 R.O. Roberts, "David Griffith, 1841-1910", *Province*, 12 (1961), 62.

120 *Report of the Royal Commission, 1911*, IV, 94 (36785-95).

121 NLW, Glansevern Ms. 13, 906.

122 Ollivant, *Charge (Llandaff)*, 1857, p. 18. Bishop Campbell also requested support for missionary societies: Campbell, *Charge (Bangor)*, 1860, p. 26.

123 Richards, "The Rural Deanery of Arllechwedd", p. 162. The diocese, working through the South American Missionary Association, helped provide a resident clergyman for the Welsh-speaking area of Chubut in Patagonia. It sent out Hugh Davies, curate of Glasfryn, in 1885, for this purpose: D. Walter Thomas to Archbishop Benson, 30 April 1885, Lambeth Palace Library, Benson Ms. 31, fol. 22. Davies was still being supported in 1896: *Report of the Bangor Diocesan Conference*, 1895, (in the *Bangor Diocesan Directory, 1896*), p. 380.

124 Jane Ross, *A Light upon the Road* (1989), p. 28,

125 Brown, "Edward Smart, Archdeacon of St Asaph", p. 122; SA/DR/54, fol. 308.

126 Williams, *Thomas Price, Carnhuanawc*, II, 73-4.

127 *Memoir and Remains of the Rev. Henry Vaughan* (London, 1841), pp. 98-114; Brown, *Evangelicals in the Church in Wales*, pp. 107-8. He founded a CMS festival at Crickhowel.

128 *Yr Haul*, 1887, pp. 148.

129 Joseph Morgan, *A Biography of The Reverend David James, Panteg* (Pontypool, 1925), p. 80. He was also a strong supporter of the BFBS.

130 Brown, *Evangelicals in the Church in Wales*, p. 211.

131 Brown, *Evangelicals in the Church in Wales*, p. 115.

132 Brown, *Clergy and People of Castle Caereinion*, p. 36.

133 Brown, *Evangelicals in the Church in Wales*, pp. 228-9.

134 J.A. Gabb ("A Clergyman"), *A Brief Memoir of James Davies* (London, 1832), pp. 17, 22; Phillips, *James Davies,* pp. 78-83.

135 Grey-Edwards, *Reminiscences of an Unknown Man*, pp. 85-93. For an account of some of the early supporters of CMS in Wales see Brown, *Evangelicals in the Church in Wales*, pp. 21-2.

136 *Returns of Collections in the Diocese of St Asaph for Home Objects, not Parochial*, 1856.

137 *Record*, 22 October 1897, p. 1081.

138 David Howell, *Foreign Missions: Their Progress during the Reign of Queen Victoria* (London, 1900), pp. 9-11. His words were echoed by Thomas Jesse Jones of Gelligaer who also noted that many parishes gave nothing to these causes because they were never requested to do so, or remained in ignorance of their needs: *Some Thoughts on how to Improve the Condition of the Welsh Church* (Merthyr Tydfil, 1893), p. 8.

139 *Proceedings of the St Asaph Diocesan Conference*, 1901, pp. 27-31.

140 *Reports of the Llandaff Diocesan Conference*, 1904, p. 29; 1911, p. 31; 1915, p. 61. The 1904 report noted that SPG had received from the parishes of the diocese £467, CMS £1,318, and UMCA £492.

141 Roger L. Brown, "The Curate of Welshpool", *Sayce Papers*, 6 (2000), 40.

142 *Report of the Llandaff Diocesan Conference*, 1907, p. 56.

143 *Parish of Swansea: Abstract of Accounts:* 1858, 1866, pp. 28-41; 1892, pp.50, 62, 65-6, 72-6. The only quasi-church organisations in 1882 were a mothers' meeting, a young men's and a young women's Christian Association, and GFS: Williams, *Move On!* pp. 30-1.

144 J.A. Gauntlett, *To the Members of the Congregation of Holy Trinity Church, Swansea* (Swansea, 1884), pp. 3-4, 13-14.

145 George, *St Theodore's Church*, p. 35.

146 *Speeches, Articles &c of Edward James Herbert, the third Earl of Powis* (London, 1892), pp. 246, 281.

147 Brown, *Clergy and People of Welshpool*, p. 74.

148 For example see: *CMG*, 29 September 1849, p. 3; 15 November 1851, p. 3; 10 November 1854, p. 3; ; 13 September 1856, p. 5; 24 April 1858, p. 6; 9 November 1861, p. 8.

149 On these occasions sermons were preached, for example: W.D. Conybeare, *A Sermon preached before the District Committee of SPCK and SPG at the Annual ... [Glamorgan] Meeting held at Cowbridge* (Cardiff, 1830); Daniel Jones, *The Day of Visitation: A Sermon preached at the parish Church of Usk at the Annual Meeting of the Monmouthshire District Committees of SPCK and SPG* (London, 1833). Connop Thirlwall's, *A Sermon preached at St Mary's Church, Haverfordwest, on behalf of the SPG* (Haverfordwest, 1842), may indicate another local auxiliary in Pembrokeshire.

150 Brown, "A Reviving Church?" p. 123.

151 Mary Clement (ed.), *Correspondence and Records of the S.P.G. relating to Wales 1701-1750* (Cardiff, 1973), pp. 2-7. For a list of missionaries from Wales 1675-1740 see Clement, *The S.P.C.K. and Wales*, pp. 178-90.

152 Mary Clement (ed.), *Correspondence and Records of the S.P.G. relating to Wales 1701-1750* (Cardiff, 1973), pp. 23, 30, 36.

153 J. Alun Thomas, "Welsh Churchmen in Colonial Pennsylvania", *JHSCW*, 4 (1954), 23-35, and 5 (1955), 52-66, es. pp. 58-61. For Evan Evans see Mary Clement (ed.), *Correspondence and Records of the S.P.G. relating to Wales, 1701-1750* (Cardiff, 1973), pp. 33-4.

154 E.D. Evans, "A Providential Rescue? Griffith Jones and the Malaber Mission", *JWRH*, 8 (2000), 35-42.

155 E.D. Evans, "The Rev. George Lewis, Rector of Dolgellau, 1715-23", *J.Mer.H.S.*, 11 (1990), 20-8, and "George Lewis and the First Protestant Mission to India", *WJRH*, 3 (2008), 29-39.

156 Daniel O'Connor (ed.), *Three Centuries of Mission* (London, 2000), p. 30.

157 W.K.D. Davies, "A Welsh Ministry at Canada's Red River Settlement", *NLW.Jnl.*, 27 (1991), 217-44.

158 D. Ambrose Jones, *A History of the Church in Wales* (Carmarthen, 1926), pp. 267-8. For Thomas Thomas, who was influenced by Thomas Byers of Lamphey, see A.H. Grey-Edwards, *Memoir of Thomas Thomas* (London, 1904), and Brown, *Evangelicals in the Church in Wales*, pp. 108-9.

159 John David Jenkins, *Passages of Church History* (Oxford, 1879), I, xi. Rice Thomas, a Welsh missionary in Cape Town is noted by the *WM*, 14 July 1874, p. 6.

160 *Memorials of John Bowen*, by his sister (London, 1862).

161 Brown, *Evangelicals in the Church in Wales*, p. 12.
162 *Bye-Gones*, 27 December 1893, p. 241.
163 E.F. Russell (ed.), *The Life of Charles Alan Smythies* (London, 1899).
164 *Bye-Gones*, 6 January 1904, p. 259. He is not noted in Crockford under this name.
165 *The Lampeter Link*, 1990, pp. 22-3.
166 H.C. Jackson, *Pastor on the Nile* (London, 1960).
167 Edward Lewis, *John Bangor: The People's Bishop* (London, 1962), pp. 50-87.
168 Brown, *Ten Clerical Lives*, pp. 41-5.
169 William Davies, *Hanes Plwyf Llanegryn* (Peniarth, 2002), p. 427.
170 Theophilus Jones, *Brecknockshire*, IV, 96.
171 Mary Curtis, *The Antiquities of Laugharne, Pendine, and their Neighbourhood* (reprint, Carmarthen, 1991), p. 256; RCAHM, *Carmarthenshire* (London, 1917), p. 244.
172 *Cardiff Rural Deanery Chapter Minutes*, October 1906.

CHAPTER FOUR: WORKING WITHIN SOCIETY

1 D.W. Howell suggests that during the eighteenth century the Church had an easy-going, non-challenging approach to personal discipline, apart from some token efforts: *The Rural Poor in the Eighteenth-Century* (Cardiff, 2000), p. 149. However, the disciplinary system of the Church relied heavily on the willingness of clergy and churchwardens to present parishioners for their misdeeds to the ecclesiastical courts, which was probably not easy to do in a small community.
2 S.J. Edwards, *Eglwys Rhos Parish Church* (1955), pp. 35-6, lists the parochial charities. For English examples see Jacob, *Clerical Profession*, pp. 215-6.
3 Brown, *Clergy and People of Welshpool*, p. 76.
4 Jacob, *Clerical Profession*, pp. 212-4, for English examples. He notes how clergy gave hospitality, drew up petitions for relief, and acted as a restraining influence on any discrimination and meanness shown by the parochial poor law authority: *ibid*, pp. 216-7.
5 Roger L. Brown, "'One of the Most Remarkable Men of his Time': Richard Davies, Archdeacon of Brecon", *Brycheiniog*, 34 (2002), 125.
6 Lewis Lloyd, *Whatever Freights may Offer* (Caernarfon, 1993), p. 329.
7 Brown, *Parochial Lives*, pp. 60-1.
8 Brown, *David Howell*, pp. 81-2.
9 Brown, *John Griffith*, pp. 135-42, 153.
10 Eli Clarke, *Christ Church, Swansea: Pastoral Letter and Statement of Accounts*, 1885-6, p. 3.
11 Brown, *Clergy and People of Welshpool*, p. 77.
12 Brown, *Clergy and People of Welshpool*, p. 76.
13 Russell, *The Clerical Profession*, p. 176.
14 *Parish of Swansea: Abstract of Accounts*, 1858, pp. 14-15. It was said that 23,743 cases had been relieved in twelve years.
15 J.G. Gauntlett, *To the Members of the Congregation of Holy Trinity Church, Swansea* (Swansea, 1884), pp. 18-20, 22 (there was also a penny bank); Eli Clarke, *Christ Church, Swansea: Pastoral Letter and Statement of Accounts*, 1878-9, p. 4.
16 G.R. Orrin, "The Reverend Harold Stepney Williams", *Gower*, 41 (1990), 47.
17 Short, *Charge (St Asaph)*, 1850, p. 28.
18 H.E. Williams, *St Paul's Church, Sketty* (1950), p. 14.
19 Brown, *David Howell*, p. 149.
20 Reynolds, *St Gabriel's Church*, p. 16.

21 G. Richards, "James Henry Cotton, Dean of Bangor", *NLW.Jnl.*, 19 (1975), 165-7; Hughes, *The Very Rev. J.H. Cotton*, pp. 26-7; J.E. Vincent (ed.), *The Memories of Sir Llewelyn Turner* (London, 1903), p. 191.

22 Pritchard, "The Revd. S.E. Gladstone", p. 208.

23 George, *St Theodore's Church*, p. 31.

24 Thomas Thomas, Caernarfon, *A New Year's Address, 1853*, p. 18.

25 *CMG*, 3 January 1852, p. 2.

26 Davies, *Holy Trinity Church, Ystrad Mynach*, pp. 18-19.

27 George, *St Theodore's Church*, p. 31.

28 *Swansea Parish Magazine*, May 1905, p. 98.

29 Brown, *Clergy and People of Welshpool*, p. 77.

30 Roger L. Brown, "The Curate of Welshpool", *Sayce Papers*, 6 (2000), 44-5.

31 Richards, "The Diocese of Bangor during the Rise of Welsh Methodism", pp. 219-20; Evans, *Religion and Politics in mid-Eighteenth Century Anglesey*, pp. 63-4; Sykes, *Church and State*, pp. 272-3.

32 Bryn Ellis, "Friendly Societies in Welshpool to 1911", *MC.*, 93 (2005), 97.

33 Lewis Lloyd, *A Real Little Seaport* (Caernarfon, 1996), II, 273.

34 Brown, "A Reviving Church?" p. 111.

35 William Crawley, *Charge to the Archdeaconry of Monmouth*, 1849, pp. 11-12.

36 *Memoir and Remains of the Rev. Henry Vaughan* (London, 1841), p. 87.

37 *CMG*, 23 August 1867, p. 5.

38 Tilney, *Parish of Penarth with Lavernock*, p. 56.

39 W.H.M. Phillips, *St Francis Church, Roath* (1958), p. 5.

40 George, *St Theodore's Church*, pp. 31, 33, 36.

41 Plomer, *Kilvert's Diary*, I, 258, 264, 301, 368. Kilvert notes a savings bank at Hay, at which he helped, and a clothing club at Clyro: Ifans, *The Diary of Francis Kilvert*, pp. 65, 68.

42 Ellis, *Fresh as Yesterday*, p. 93.

43 G.R. Orrin, "The Reverend Harold Stepney Williams", *Gower*, 41 (1990), 47.

44 *Report of the Royal Commission, 1911*, III, 126 (22285).

45 *Memoirs of John Melbourne Parry* (Chelmsford, 1920), p. 36.

46 *Record*,17 February 1905, p. 157.

47 J.R.D. Williams, *The Parish of Rhymney, Monmouthshire* (1943), p. 15.

48 F.J. Gaines, *History of St Matthias Church, Treharris* (1946), p. 57.

49 Brown, *Parochial Lives*, p. 61.

50 Theodore Johnson (ed.), *The Parish Guide: A Handbook for the use of Clergy and Lay-Helpers* (London, 1887).

51 *Report of the Royal Commission, 1911*, II, 486 (16461): the evidence of Edward Bevan.

52 R.C.B. Oliver, "Archdeacon de Winton and the building of the first Rectory in Llandrindod Wells", *T.Radn.S.*, 52 (1982), 50-3.

53 SA/DR/52, fol. 760; SA/DR/54, fols. 342, 382-3, 400-1.

54 G.R. Orrin, "The Reverend Harold Stepney Williams", *Gower*, 41 (1990), 48-51.

55 F.J. Gaines, *History of St Matthias Church, Treharris* (1946), pp. 18, 27.

56 Muriel Evans, *The Story of the Parish of St David, Ton Pentre* (1960), pp. 28-30.

57 G.R. Orrin, *A History of Bishopston* (Llandysul, 1982), p. 52.

58 M.J. Mainwaring, *History of St Peter's Church, Senghenydd* (1946), pp. 12-13.

59 G.H. James, *Manselton and its Parish Church* (1956), p. 26.

60 F.L.G. Bevan, *History of Christ Church, Cyfarthfa* (1957), pp. 35-41.

61 E. Jenkin Davies, *Speech on Thirty Years at St Thomas* (1950), p. 13.

62 *Llandaff Diocesan Magazine*, January 1911, p. 244.

63 Pryce, *One Hundred Years of Evangelical Witness*, pp. 56-7.

64 Dilys Thomas, *Memories of Old Colwyn* (Wrexham, 2000), p. 91.

65 Evans, *Religion and Politics in Mid-Eighteenth Century Anglesey*, p. 12. The 1847 educational report noted a similar position at Llandegley, where the incumbent's calves were kept in the churchyard and slept in the belfry: quoted, Phillips, *Wales*, p. 192.

66 Thomas, *St Asaph*, III, 130.

67 J.T.A., *A Collection of Welch Travels and Memoirs of Wales* (London, 1730s), p. 68; "A Countryman", *A Journey to Llandrindod Wells* (London, 1746), p. 56.

68 Quoted by J.B. Sinclair and R.W.D. Fenn, "Radnorshire Churches: An Introduction", *T.Radn.S.*, 62 (1992), 79. Activities at Diserth in 1744 are noted in J.T. Evans, *The Church Plate of Radnorshire* (Stow-on-the-Wold, 1910), pp. 26-7n.

69 "Miscellanea", *Archaeologia Cambrensis,* 1919, pp. 214-5.

70 Fisher, "Religious and Social Life in the Vale of Clwyd", pp. 152-3; David Gregory, *Yesterday in Village Church and Churchyard* (Llandysul, 1988), p. 65; B.B. Rowlands, *A Brief Account of the Ancient Church and Town of Newtown* (Newtown, 1914), p. 42 (he notes a 5s. fine was ordered by the parish vestry for those playing ball against the church in 1722, to be laid out in repairs to the church and its windows).

71 R.T.W. Denning (ed.), *The Diary of William Thomas* (SWRS, 1995), p. 78.

72 Melvin Humphreys, *The Crisis of Community* (Cardiff, 1996), p. 173.

73 Edmund Jones, *The History of Aberystruth (1779)* (Gwent, 1998), pp. 141-2. The practice at Llanfairfechan ended after a layman read extracts from the Bible to those who were playing until they were ashamed of their conduct: Ellis, *Fresh as Yesterday*, p. 36.

74 Barrie Jones, "The Reverend George Martin Maber", *Merthyr Historian*, 9 (1997), 2-3.

75 J.E. Vize, "The Parish of Forden", *MC.*, 17 (1884), 115-7.

76 *Bye-Gones*, July, 1885, p. 264; 3 February 1904, p. 279.

77 Owen, *Old Stone Crosses*, p. 38.

78 "M.N.J.", *Bygone Days in the March Wall of Wales* (London, 1926), p. 77.

79 Bishop Marsh to Bute, 5 December 1817:Glamorgan Record Office: Bute Papers, L60/38.

80 Hurdsman, *A History of the Parish of Chirk*, pp. 29-30.

81 John Fewtrell, "A Parochial History of Llanymynech", *MC.*, 12 (1879), 378; cf. G. Richards, "Snowdonia: Ecclesiastical Reflections", *T.Caerns.H.S.*, 40 (1979), 66-7.

82 Enoch, *Llanfihangel Genau'r Glyn*, p. 31.

83 G.E. Evans, *Cardiganshire* (Aberystwyth, 1903), p. 237; Mrs G.F. Dawson, *The Churches of Brecknockshire* (Swansea, 1909), p. 183. At Llantrisant in the 1820s the curate, Thomas Roderick, trying to persuade those playing fives in the churchyard to attend the church service, accepted their invitation to play for a while before he began the service. It is noted that when fives were banned from the churchyards the local hostelries erected their own courts: *The Garth Domain*, 6 (December 1999), 19.

84 J.D.K. Lloyd in *Montgomeryshire Collections*, 67 (1979), 43.

85 Gordon Beeston, *Bedwas and Machen* (Newport, 1972), p. 59. Other examples are provided by Donald Gregory, *Country Churchyards in Wales* (Llanrwst, 1991), pp. 87, 115-6, 126, 168; Brown, *Church and Clergy at Castle Caereinion*, p. 18; *Sketch of the Parish of Llanfechain* (from *Montgomeryshire Collections*: London, 1872), p. 26; J.C. Read, *A History of St John's Cardiff* (1995), p. 45, where he notes playing ball against the tower of that church in 1716.

86 D.B. Jones, *Myddfai* (Aberystwyth, 1992), pp. 167, 198.

87 Hugh Evans, *The Gorse Green* (Liverpool, 1948), p. 153.

88 D.W. Howell, *The Rural Poor in Eighteenth-Century Wales* (Cardiff, 2000), p. 142. He notes dancing went on in other churchyards.

89 Phillips, *James Davies*, p. 22.

90 J.M. Pearson, "Montgomery Folk-lore", *MC*, 37 (1915), 194-5.

91 Quoted by A. Leslie Evans, *The Story of Kenfig* (Port Talbot, 1970s), p. 54. This was also true for Berriew: Thomas, *St Asaph*, III, 130.

92 A.T. Arbor-Cooke, *Pages from the History of Llandovery* (Llandovery, 1976), p. 15. This was equally true for Cilcain: Owen, *Old Stone Crosses*, pp. 9, 38.

93 John Parker's Tour of Wales: NLW, MS. 18356C, fol. 16.

94 *CMG*, 14 April 1865, p. 8.

95 Griffith, "Visitation of the Archdeaconry of Carmarthen, 1710", II, 322.

96 Teague and Brown, "Griffith Jones' 'Pious Minister'", *T.Denb.H.S.*, pp. 33-5; J.E. Ethall, "Langernyw Church and Registers", *T.Denb.H.S.*, 18 (1969), 158-9 (there were similar occurrences at Llansannan: p. 162); SA/RD/26, fol. 42.

97 SD/MISC/972; Frederick J. Warren, *The History and Antiquities of S Mary, Haverfordwest* (Letchworth, 1914), pp. 21-2; H. Holdefast, *Haverfordwest and its Story* (Haverfordwest, 1882), pp. 167-72.

98 *Memoir and Remains of the Rev. Henry Vaughan* (London, 1841), p. 94.

99 Edward Morgan, *John Elias: Life, Letters and Essays* (reprint, Edinburgh, 1973), pp. 86-9. Elias also preached against horse races, drinking and shipwrecking: *ibid.*, pp. 143-6.

100 Griffith Thomas, *Short Notes on the History of Llangyfelach Parish Church* (1920), pp. 6-7. Donovan writing in 1809 wrote that the churchyard at Llanelli (Carms.) was used for the market, fair and sports: John Edwards (ed.), *Footprints of Faith* (Llanelli, 1980s), p. 19.

101 S.C. Passmore, "The Rev. William Wynne of Lasynys", II, *J.Mer.H.S.*, 12 (1996), 256.

102 D.W. Howell, *The Rural Poor in the Eighteenth-Century* (Cardiff, 2000), p. 150.

103 Jenkins, *Literature, Religion and Society*, pp. 90-1.

104 K.E. Kissack, "Lay Influence on Religious Life in Monmouth since the Reformation", *JHSCW*, 19 (1969), 58.

105 *Gresford Vicar's Book*, fols. 25-6.

106 *The Life of Reginald Heber* (by his widow, New York, 1830), I, 334.

107 Phillips, *James Davies*, pp. 43-4.

108 Daniel Nihill, *The Farmer's Guide to Happiness* (London, 1843), pp. 31-5.

109 E.B. Squire, *Two Sermons preached at the Parish Church being ... the day appointed by the Lord Bishop of St David's for Public Prayer and Humiliation on account of the Visitation of Cholera* (London, 1849), esp. pp. 7-10, 18-19.

110 W. Bezant Lowe, *The Heart of Northern Wales* (Llanfairfechan, 1912), I, 324.

111 Evan Jenkins, *A Sermon Preached in Dowlais Church upon the death of Sir J. John Guest, Bart.* (Llandovery, 1853), p. 23.

112 *Report of the St David's Diocesan Conference*, 1892, pp. 29-37, and esp. pp. 31, 33, 36.

113 J.P. Thompson, *Sunday Emancipation: A Paper* (Cardiff, 1887).

114 *Cardiff Rural Deanery Chapter Minutes*, January 1885. A paper on Lord's Day observance was read in October 1891.

115 Brown, *John Griffith*, pp. 162-3. In the late 1840s Griffith had alleged that Nonconformists were responsible for much drunkenness and vice in Wales: *ibid.* pp. 38-40; Lambert, *Drink and Sobriety in Victorian Wales*, p. 133.

116 *Reports of the Llandaff Diocesan Conference*, 1896, pp. 85-108, esp. pp. 87-8; 1901, pp. 71-6; 1902, pp. 34-53, esp. pp. 37, 40-1, 44-5.

117 *Proceedings of the St Asaph Diocesan Conference*, 1901, pp. 8-12.

118 Mary Curtis, *The Antiquities of Laugharne, Pendine, and their Neighbourhood* (reprint, Carmarthen, 1991), p. 39.

119 Roger L. Brown, "'A Man in a Hurry': Talbot Rice, vicar of Swansea", *Minerva*, 4 (1986), 40.

120 Hughes, *Charges (Llandaff)*, 1907, pp. 19-21; 1910, pp. 25-8.

121 *Report of the Llandaff Diocesan Conference*, 1910, pp. 52-4.
122 Jenkins, *Literature, Religion and Society*, pp. 92-7. For a general discussion see Frances Knight, "Pastoral Ministry in the Anglican Church, *c.* 1840-1950", *Review of Church History*, 83 (2003), 416-9. She suggests many Anglican clergy understood temperance to mean moderation rather than total abstinence.
123 Knight, in Williams, *The Welsh Church*, p. 379.
124 Benjamin Hall, *A Sermon preached in the Parish Church of Whitchurch ... on the Duty and Advantage of Temperance* (Cardiff, 1795).
125 Lambert, *Drink and Sobriety in Wales*, p. 92. The first society was at Holywell in 1832: *ibid.*, p. 60; *Memoir and Remains of the Rev. Henry Vaughan* (London, 1841), pp. 91-2.
126 Hughes, *Pwllheli*, p. 267. Other officials were prominent Nonconformists.
127 Pryce, *One Hundred Years of Evangelical Witness*, p. 33.
128 Lambert, *Drink and Sobriety in Wales*, pp. 132, 135. Lambert also notes Henry Griffiths of Llandrygarn and E.O. Hughes of Llanbadrig as temperance leaders.
129 Francis Jones, *Historic Carmarthenshire Homes and Families* (Carmarthen, 1987), p. 75.
130 See, for example, Thomas Phillips, *The Welsh Revival (1859)* (Edinburgh, 1989), pp. 94-8; Huw Roderick, "'A Fire made of Shavings': The 1904 Revival in Cardiganshire", *Ceredigion*¸15 (2005), 132-3.
131 Detailed in Lambert, *Drink and Sobriety in Victorian Wales*, pp. 135-7.
132 T. Meredith Williams, *Sermons of the Age* (London, 1903), p. 179.
133 Hughes, *Charge (St Asaph)*, 1874, p. 14.
134 *Proceedings of the St Asaph Diocesan Conference*, 1885, p. 7. Other debates are in subsequent reports: 1887, pp. 30-2; 1889, pp. 10-13; 1899, pp. 23-30; 1903, pp. 22-4. A grand temperance meeting was held in association with the 1901 Conference. One of the speakers was Archbishop Temple of Canterbury: *Proceedings*, 1901, pp. 13-18.
135 *Reports of the St David's Diocesan Conferences*, 1881, pp. 63, 68; 1899, p. 59.
136 *Fourth Annual Report of the Bangor Diocesan Branch of the Church of England Temperance Society*, 1903.
137 Lambert, *Drink and Sobriety in Victorian Wales*, p. 134.
138 Quoted by Knight, in Williams, *The Welsh Church*, p. 379.
139 Hughes, *Pwllheli Church*, p. 27.
140 *Church Pastoral-Aid Society: Church and People*, 3 (1891), 138.
141 J.R.D. Williams, *The Parish of Rhymney, Monmouthshire* (1943), p. 15.
142 *Report of the Llandaff Diocesan Conference*, 1909, pp. 20, 24-5; cf. 1901, pp. 79-89 (which noted the need for alternative recreations); Edwards, *Charge (St Asaph)*, 1890, pp. 33-4.
143 Brown, "A Reviving Church?" pp. 126-7.
144 Brown, *Clergy and People of Welshpool*, p. 72.
145 Lambert, *Drink and Sobriety in Wales*, p. 101.
146 Quoted by Knight, in Williams, *The Welsh Church*, p. 380.
147 Brown, *David Howell*, p. 82. He continued with this work at Wrexham: *ibid.*, pp. 149-50.
148 *Bye-Gones*, 7 January 1891, p. 3; 20 May 1891, p. 89.
149 G. Richards, "James Henry Cotton, Dean of Bangor", *NLW.Jnl.*, 19 (1975), 167; William Hughes, *Recollections of Bangor Cathedral* (Bala, 1904), pp. 63-4.
150 R.O. Roberts, "The Life of Dean H.T. Edwards", *T.Caerns.H.S.*, 40 (1979), 143; J.V. Morgan, *Welsh Religious Leaders in the Victorian Era* (London, 1905), p. 81; Knight, in Williams, *The Welsh Church*, p. 379. His temperance address, "Strike for the King", is contained in H.T. Edwards, *Wales and the Welsh Church* (London, 1889), pp. 398-413.
151 *CMG*, 10 December 1859, p. 7; 31 March 1860, p. 5.
152 Lambert, *Drink and Sobriety in Wales*, pp. 89.

153 Ward and Coe, *Father Jones of Cardiff*, pp. 109-13. He disliked the Sunday Closing Act.
154 Lambert, *Drink and Sobriety in Victorian Wales*, pp. 136-7.
155 *Yr Haul*, 1899, pp. 132.
156 Roger L. Brown, "'A Man in a Hurry': Talbot Rice, vicar of Swansea", *Minerva*, 4 (1986), 40.
157 G.A. Heald, "Pentre Foelas", *T.Denb.H.S.*, 23 (1974), 274.
158 Brown, *John Griffith*, pp. 97-9, 153-5. He also established a Temperance Hall at Aberdare, but in his speech at its opening said what its promoters probably didn't want him to say, that he believed in moderation not teetotalism and felt all the better for a glass of beer.
159 Tilney, *Parish of Penarth with Lavernock*, p. 56.
160 Reynolds, *St Gabriel's Church*, p. 28; *Swansea Parish Magazine*, May 1905, p. 106.
161 *Report of the Royal Commission, 1911*, II, 369 (12192).
162 George, *St Theodore's Church*, p. 31.
163 Pryce, *One Hundred Years of Evangelical Witness*, p. 52.
164 Brown, *Clergy and People of Welshpool*, p. 73.
165 T.G. Davies, "A Voluntary Contracted Madness", *Morgannwg*,55 (2011), 47-8.
166 David Jenkins, *The Agricultural Community in South-West Wales* (Cardiff, 1971), p. 214.
167 T.L. Evans, "David Archard Williams and his Times", *CH*, 10 (1973), 69.
168 W.R. Lambert, "The Welsh Sunday Closing Act, 1881", *WHR*, 6 (1972), 161-89, esp. pp. 174, 182. The act required that all premises selling alcohol needed to be licensed by the quarter sessions.
169 *Report of the Royal Commission appointed to Inquire into the Operation of the Sunday Closing (Wales) Act, 1881* (c. 5994: 1890), pp. 175, 194-5, 202, 249-50, 301-2.
170 Lambert, *Drink and Sobriety in Wales*, pp. 225-6.
171 Russell Davies, *Hope and Heartbreak* (Cardiff, 2005), p. 399.
172 Brown, *David Howell*, pp. 149-50.
173 Pritchard, "The Revd. S.E. Gladstone", p. 208; Ros Aitkin, *The Prime Minister's Son* (Chester, 2012), p. 97.
174 G.W.E. Russell, *Harry Drew: A Memorial Sketch* (Oxford, 1911), p. 90.
175 John Owen, *Presidential Address ... at the Opening of the Diocesan Conference, 1901: Four Aspect of the Mission of the Church*, 1901, p. 3.
176 Burgess, *Charge (St Davids)*, 1813, pp. 56-7, 62. Bishop Bull urged the magistrates to execute the laws against vice and immorality in the 1700s: Nelson, *Life of Bishop Bull*, pp. 384-5. Jenkins notes clerical reaction to swearing and cursing: *Literature, Religion and Society*, pp. 97-100.
177 *Report of the Llandaff Diocesan Conference*, 1898, pp. 65-8, being a debate on the subject.
178 George, *St Theodore's Church*, p. 31.
179 Brown, *John Griffith*, pp. 155-6.
180 Ollivant, *Charge (Llandaff)*, 1863, pp. 47-9; Brown, *John Griffith*, pp. 156-8; *First Annual Report of the House of Mercy for South Wales and Monmouthshire*, 1863. It later moved to Penarth.
181 Brown, "Henry Powell Ffoulkes", p. 136.
182 Wickham, *Charge to the Archdeaconry of St Asaph*, 1858, pp. 16-17.
183 *Report of the Llandaff Diocesan Conference*, 1901, pp. 90-104.
184 Brown, *John Griffith*, pp. 158-62.
185 S.C. Passmore, "The Rev. William Wynne of Lasynys", II, *J.Mer.H.S.*, 12 (1996), 257; Evans, *Religion and Politics in Mid-Eighteenth Century Anglesey*, pp. 63-4. Ellis also suppressed the traditional wake ceremonies.
186 Cecil Price, *The English Theatre in Wales* (Cardiff, 1948), pp. 150-1.
187 J. Allen Smith, *Is it Consistent? Or Thoughts on the Burning of Exeter Theatre* (London, 1887), esp. pp. 5, 13-16.
188 Brown, *Evangelicals in the Church in Wales*, p. 201; Roger L. Brown, "'A Man in a Hurry': Talbot Rice, vicar of Swansea", *Minerva*, 4 (1996), 40.

189 Earl of Bessborough, *Lady Charlotte Guest: Extracts from her Journal* (London, 1950), pp. 37-8.
190 *CMG*, 3 April 1863, p. 6.
191 *Montgomery and District Parish Magazine,* May 1893.
192 *Report of the Llandaff Diocesan Conference*, 1899, p. 98.
193 *Cardiff Rural Deanery Chapter Minutes*, May 1903.
194 Edward Edwards, *A Sermon Preached in Wrexham Church, ... being the Sunday after the Interment of Thomas Jones, Esq., ... who died of a Wound he received in an unfortunate Duel at Whitchurch with Mr Manning* (Wrexham, 1800), pp. 16-17.
195 Edward Davies, *Public Dues Obligatory on a Christian Conscience* (1817). He saw smuggling not only as sinful but also as an act of disloyalty and fraud against the Crown.
196 Jones, *Faith and the Crisis of a Nation*, pp. 69-73.
197 Brown, *Evangelicals in the Church in Wales*, p. 186.
198 I.J. Bronham, *A Record of the Life and Work of the Rev. W.J. Bronham* (1943), p. 13.
199 Brown, *John Griffith*, pp. 100, 161-2.
200 D.J.V. Jones, *The Last Rising* (Oxford, 1985), p. 26; K.B. Jones, "The Religious Climate of the Chartist Insurrection at Newport", *JWRH*, 5 (1997), 65-7; James Francis, *A Sermon to the Working Classes, preached in St Paul's Church, Newport* (1839), esp. pp. 25-6.
201 D.J.V. Jones, *The Last Rising* (Oxford, 1985), p. 26; David Williams, *John Frost* (Cardiff, 1939), pp. 324-5; Earl of Bessborough, *Lady Charlotte Guest: Extracts from her Journal* (London, 1950), pp. 94, 106-7.
202 Benjamin Evans, *Sin its own Punishment: A Sermon* (Carmarthen, 1857), pp. 5-10.
203 John Griffiths, *Britain's Cause: A Sermon preached at the Parish Church, Neath* (Neath, 1860), esp. pp. 18-19.
204 *Report of the Llandaff Diocesan Conference*, 1900, pp. 14-15.
205 D. Densil Morgan, "Christ and the War", *JWRH*, 5 (1997),73-91, esp. p. 77; Robert Pope in Matthew Cragoe and Chris Williams, *Wales and War* (Cardiff, 2007), pp. 170-81.
206 *Pool Deanery Magazine*, November 1914, item for Penrhos.
207 *Memoirs of John Melbourne Parry* (Chelmsford, 1920), p. 36.
208 R.L. Barnes, "In Memoriam: David Lewis Prosser", *Province*, 1/2 (1950), 42-3; D.L. Prosser, *Addresses at Church Parade Services* (London, 1915).
209 H.T. Edwards, *Politics in Wales and the Dangers of Political Pilatism* (1872), in passim, esp. pp. 7-8.
210 Edwards, *Charge (St Asaph)*, 1890, pp. 32-3.
211 David Hempton in John Wolffe (ed.), *Evangelical Faith and Public Zeal* (London, 1995), pp. 17-21.
212 Russell Davies, *Hope and Heartbreak* (Cardiff, 2005), p. 336; *Old Aberdare*, 6 (1989), 47.
213 C.B. Turner, "Ritualism, Railwaymen and the Poor: the Ministry of Canon J.D. Jenkins, Vicar of Aberdare, 1870-76", in G.H. Jenkins and J. Smith (eds.), *Politics and Society in Wales* (Cardiff, 1988), pp. 73-5.
215 Brown, *David Howell*, p. 82.
215 D.A. Pretty, *The Rural Revolt that Failed* (Cardiff, 1989), p. 81, 98, 133; cf. Lee, *Rural Society and the Anglican Clergy*, pp. 67-8, though he is writing of an earlier period.
216 F.L.G. Bevan, *History of Christ Church, Cyfarthfa* (1957), p. 38.
217 H.W.J. Edwards, *The Good Patch* (London, 1938), p. 147.
218 J. Lambert Rees (ed.), *Sermons and Hymns by Timothy Rees, Bishop of Llandaff* (London, 1946), pp.7-9, 12-14; D. Densil Morgan, *The Span of the Cross* (Cardiff, 1999), pp. 90-1; D.T.W. Price, *A History of the Church in Wales in the Twentieth-Century* (Penarth, 1990), p. 18.
219 H. Francis and D. Smith, *The Fed* (London, 1980), p. 272.
220 *Report of the Llandaff Diocesan Conference*, 1912, pp. 48-67, esp. p. 63. For Nonconformity, Labour and the social question see Robert Pope, *Building Jerusalem* (Cardiff, 1998), pp. 71-122 and

for socialism in the Church of England see K. Hylson-Smith, *High Churchmanship in the Church of England* (Edinburgh, 1993), pp. 223-7. He writes that the working class did not expect the clergy to preach political opinions.

221 *Proceedings of the St Asaph Diocesan Conference*, 1895, pp. 17-18; 1907, pp. 19-26.

222 D.A. Pretty, *The Rural Revolt that Failed* (Cardiff, 1989), p. 261.

223 Brown, *The Clergy and People of Welshpool*, pp. 36-7 (he also started a horticultural society); C.P. Gasquoine, *The Story of the Cambrian* (Wrexham, 1922), p. 38.

224 Brown, *John Griffith*, pp. 163-4.

225 Brown, *Ten Clerical Lives*, pp. 94-5.

226 Harriett Thomas (ed.), *Llewelyn Thomas: A Memoir* (London, 1897), pp. 19-20.

227 Brown, *Ten Clerical Lives*, pp. 92-3; and *Evangelicals in the Church in Wales*, p. 179. In 1850 several ships' captains agreed for services to be held on board their vessels at Cardiff Docks: Glamorgan Record Office, D/DA/34A, fol. 61.

228 For reports see *CMG*, 4 September 1852, p. 4; 20 April 1861, p. 8; 26 March 1870, p. 6.

229 *Report of the Missions to Seamen, Swansea*, 1891.

230 Lewis, *Charge (Llandaff)*, 1903, pp. 9-10; L.S. Higgins, *Newton Nottage and Porthcawl* (Llandysul, 1968), p. 86.

231 Roger Lloyd, *The Church of England 1900-1965* (London, 1966), p. 159; Russell, *The Clerical Profession*, pp. 165-6.

232 cf. Lee, *Rural Society and the Anglican Clergy*, p. 151.

A SOCIAL HISTORY OF THE WELSH CLERGY

SECTION 10: THE MISSION OF THE CHURCH

Chapters

CHAPTER ONE: A REALIZATION FOR MISSION

Although the Puritans had their doubts, and saw Wales as a mission field, the Established Church after 1660 was reasonably complacent about the Christian status of Wales. It had clergy, in theory at least, in every parish, its bishops performed their episcopal functions along with their parliamentary duties, and the bulk of the people were occasional if not regular attenders at the church services. Nevertheless, there was some cause for concern. A number of the old superstitions remained; the Welsh language might hide some lingering remnants of dissatisfaction, and was seen as a bar to progress and to national unity with England; while many clergy lacked a university education and were forced to care for a multiplicity of parishes through the poverty of their livings. As a result Thomas Gouge established his schools and the S.P.C.K. followed his work and produced numerous religious works in Welsh as well as editions of the Bible and Prayer Book.

It was Griffith Jones who showed how superficial much of the Christian heritage had become by the early eighteenth century. Spirituality had been lost as church-going, still popular, had failed to provide a personal interest rather than a corporate identity about matters of the spirit. His schools, mentioned many times already, were occasioned not by educational needs so much as by a spiritual concern, namely that church-goers were often ignorant about the basic facts of Christian doctrine, and as such were unable to apply it to their own lives.[1] His schools taught people to read the Bible and encouraged them to assimilate its truths for themselves, as well as to encourage the religion of the hearth and a more adequate appreciation of, and involvement in, the Church's liturgy. Sadly, though it had a great effect within many parishes, the movement was side-checked into Methodism, and its vital spark was lost to the Church. Thereafter, the evangelisation of the nation was left by and large to the Welsh Methodist movement together with the Baptist and other Nonconformist bodies, and although their proponents generally exaggerated the spiritual darkness of the country, they provided a spiritual warmth and fellowship the Church was unable to offer.

A FEAR OF DISSENT AND REBELLION

It was not until the early nineteenth century that the Established Church woke up to its mission. It did so partly because it saw Nonconformity as a rival that needed to be eliminated, and took the view that with a better Church order and outreach it might win back its lost adherents. Dissent fractured the unity of the parish gathered around its parish church, ended its control over the lives of people, and questioned the right of the Established Church to its ecclesiastical and political monopoly. The 1851 religious census was both a shock to, and an awakening for, the Welsh Church. While the Established Church in Wales could hold its own against any one of the Welsh Nonconformist denominations, when they were taken together it was hopelessly outclassed, save in its pastoral ministry. What no one recognised at the time was the large number of unchurched people, particularly in the industrialised areas. The first realization spurred the provision of new accommodation, the creation of new buildings, the rebuilding of others and the providing of additional seating within the churches, while the second led to the mission movement of the 1870s. All these are noted in this section.[2]

There were other reasons too which fuelled a programme of church restoration and building. For the early nineteenth century was a time of social unrest when revolution seemed to be in the air and dissent was seen as an act of disloyalty to the state. Vast areas, inhabited by a new, restless and irreligious population, lacked the ministrations of the State-Church, which had been replaced by an itinerant dissenting presence. The Church Building Society in its 1819 report held that the parochial ministry of the Established Church was the most effectual means of elevating the moral character of the people. It stated that

> [t]hey who are of opinion, that no remedy has been provided more effectual, for the evils to which human life is exposed, than the exercise of a rational piety and a sound instruction in the doctrines and duties of Christianity, will find little reason to wonder, that in the circumstances that have been here described, pauperism, vice,

and depravity should abound; that impiety and disloyalty should be widely diffused; crime increase; and the voice of human law appear often to be raised in vain.

The consequences for the State would be horrendous "if so large a portion of the community continue to be without the means of obtaining Religious Instruction".[3] It was a fear echoed as late as 1896 by William Lewis, vicar of Ystradyfodwg. His concern was to provide more church accommodation in his "thickly populated parish, to check the flood of ungodliness and immorality sweeping through it, and to train the people to a higher and better life."[4] In short, the Church was the moral policeman of the nation, keeping a people subdued, loyal and orderly. The Establishment thus realised, on a national scale, that the industrial revolution had caused towns to grow in size and new communities to be established in often out-of-the-way places. In these places the Church was totally inadequate to meet the assumed needs of the people so gathered, and to remedy this position new legislation had to be introduced and finances obtained to allow new churches to be built and new parishes to be created. All too often, especially in Wales, the Church was years behind Nonconformity in establishing its presence in these areas.

In 1839 the second marquess of Bute received a letter from Archdeacon Thomas Williams of Llandaff. He wrote that because of the lack of church accommodation at Merthyr whole families had become dissenters, and this was not from choice.[5] It was not a new situation. A parliamentary return of 1818 listed those parishes with a population of 2,000 and over where the church accommodation was less than half that population, and was probably drawn up with this fear of dissent filling the alleged gap. St Asaph had sixteen such parishes, including Berriew, Guilsfield and Holywell; Bangor seven, Dolgellau and Llanidloes amongst them, the latter having only 550 seats for a population of 2,386; St Davids had seven, of which Swansea with 500 seats for 8,963 inhabitants was the worst, though Narberth had only 550 for 2,112 inhabitants; and Llandaff surprisingly only nine, mainly as the industrial revolution had still to make its impact in its area. Here the worst localities were Aberdare and Merthyr as might be expected, but also Bedwellte, Cardiff and Blaenafon.[6] Bishop van Mildert had drawn attention to this concern in his 1821 Charge, when he noted the lack of additional church accommodation in the populous areas of his diocese. Instead, dissenting meeting houses had sprung up on every side, and many "of our own flocks are almost driven from communion with the Established Church by this lamentable deficiency."[7]

During the 1850s Bishop Ollivant continued in the same vein, declaring that many who wished to remain Church people had been forced to attend dissenting chapels because there was no church in their locality, either because of distance or as its accommodation was insufficient for its parishioners.[8] This had occurred at Llanwonno, a parish where the church was in an isolated area away from the new population. As a result people were obliged to go to dissenting chapels or remain at home.[9] Ystradyfodwg was another similar parish, embracing the whole of the upper Rhondda with a population scattered between numerous isolated hamlets. By 1869 it had two churches, two licensed schoolrooms and 33 dissenting chapels.[10] The scarcity of seats at Little Newcastle Church, Pembrokeshire, in the 1830s, offering 35 seats for 430 inhabitants, meant that most parishioners attended the Baptist chapel.[11] William North, writing in 1836 of Brecon, stated that the dissenting chapels were more comfortable and decently fitted than the churches, where people met with discomfort and even danger. Llanfaes church was in a ruinous condition and St Mary's Church lacked the accommodation thought to be required. As a result by 1844 there were seven chapels in the town, and in 1851 it was alleged that all had large congregations of whom many had been former members of the Established Church.[12] Other writers alleged that the appropriated pew by restricting the number of available seats in a church meant that the poor were "frozen out" and were driven to dissent, or even to Mormonism.[13]

The same concern related to rural parishes, especially where they were held in plurality. At Llanbadarn Trefeglwys, held in plurality with Cilcennin, there could be only one Sunday service in each church, yet within a mile of whose church there were three Calvinistic Methodist chapels, each with a Sunday school and two Sunday services. This was mentioned at the 1890 St David's diocesan conference, when it was stated that the Church simply could not compete under these circumstances.[14]

In parish after parish the inability of the Church to raise the finances required for church planting meant that Nonconformity had taken precedence over the Church in these areas, and retained an influence which the Church might have secured for itself by an earlier effort. Here, as elsewhere, the Church was failing in its national duty. It was recognised, however, that this was almost impossible to achieve due to the legal restrictions and financial requirements of church planting.[15] Until the Additional Churches Act of 1818 an act of parliament was required to alter parochial law and geography. The cost and the difficulties involved, such as compensating affected parties, meant few such acts were passed.[16] Churches had to be built in a certain style and accommodate a certain number of the population, an endowment found for a minister, and boundaries established for a new district requiring the consent of the existing incumbent and patron. A nonconformist cause could start with a cottage service, often a Sunday School, using a lay preacher. If the cause prospered a chapel could be built, sometimes as a speculative venture though more often from loans of money (unacceptable to the church authorities[17]), and a full-time minister eventually appointed. In addition lay ministry was encouraged.[18] The Llandaff Diocesan Church Extension Society in its report of 1861 stated this fact in even starker terms:

> The Non-conformists build cheap and temporary chapels; convey them to trustees, and furnish them with preachers, itinerant, or local. The Church, on the other hand, desires to meet the same wants, but she runs in the race weighed with so many rules and statutes, that she is generally distanced by her rivals. For it is the policy of the Church of England to require endowments to be secured to new churches. She will employ a priest without a church, but she will not consecrate a church without an endowment for a priest. She is opposed to the erection of thin and frail structures, unfit to stand the wear and tear of years. She expects her clergy to be men of learning, and rarely and reluctantly accepts the services of illiterate persons. She considers that though a departure from these arrangements might sometimes be advantageous, it is, upon the whole, the least of two evils to adhere to them. But there can be no doubt this policy does place the church under conditions which have often given time and superiority to Dissenters to anticipate the action of the church in new settlements.[19]

Ollivant was to remark in 1854 about the Church's rigidity in form and action. In a previous century it had driven many from her parishes, but this rigidity prevented the Church from tackling the needs of an increasing population and winning back those who had been lost.[20]

The situation might be summed up in Ted Wickham's description of Sheffield, which was equally true of Wales: "[w]here the National Church required an Act of Parliament, a grant of money, an educated gentleman and a crop of lawyers, the Methodists required only a friendly barn and a zealous preacher".[21] Consequently, the Church was in the most unfavourable position of being last in the field in many places.[22] As Archdeacon Bevan of Hay remarked in 1886, with some apparent bitterness, while the Church was making its preparations for new churches and districts, Nonconformity stepped in, unhampered by law and traditional usages, and occupied the ground. As an afterthought he claimed the Church was ready to acknowledge the services of Nonconformity to the cause of religion. Bevan accepted, however, that the work of the Ecclesiastical Commissioners in giving grants for curates and the division of parishes, together with the new diocesan initiatives, has done much to remedy this position, as did legislation and the use of auxiliary buildings.[23] In addition, when a church plant had been created, many church people who had hitherto worshipped from necessity in a Nonconformist cause, returned to the flock, as occurred at Llanfabon in the 1860s and Blaengwynfi in 1886.[24]

Another factor was that the church, by and large, failed to provide an evening service, whereas Nonconformity did. At Llansannan as the church had no lighting for an evening service many church people resorted to the chapels instead.[25] This was later addressed by ensuring that pluralities and non-residence were restricted so that most parishes had their own incumbent who was frequently reminded of his obligation to provide "double-duty" in his parish. The introduction of artificial light enabled the second service to be transferred to the evening from the afternoon.

THE GROWTH OF NEW COMMUNITIES

The nineteenth-century Church had to come to terms with the new populations arising in the industrialised areas where often the parish church was either in an unsuitable position or far too small to accommodate its expected parishioners. New churches were required.

Within fifty years of 1863 the diocese of Llandaff had increased its population threefold, almost unprecedented within the whole Church. This was made even more difficult by the need to minister in two languages, the loss of its income through impropriations and the impracticability of renting pews in mining districts.[26] In London Bishop Tait worked on the principle that there should be one church for each group of 6,000 people together with a sufficient endowment to support curates as well as an incumbent, though his predecessor, Blomfield, wished for a church for every 3,000 people.[27] At Aberdare, however, the church had accommodation for 176 people for a population of 13,000, and Bishop Ollivant sarcastically remarked in 1876 that at some time previously it had been considered a great gain to obtain nine more sittings by the removal of the pulpit.[28]

Thomas Williams, the curate of Merthyr Tydfil, remarked in 1840 that if it were not for dissent, his parish would be in little better state than that of heathen darkness. No parish in Wales was more in need of church extension.[29] By 1851 even with a new church there was still church accommodation for 2,500 in a population of 50,000, while the neighbouring Dowlais Church lacked sufficient room not only for the school children but also for its adult congregation. Ollivant, who gave these figures, also noted that many churches, such as Eglwysilan and Llanwonno, were at a great distance from the new centres of population that had arisen within their boundaries.[30] When addressing the Church Pastoral-Aid Society in 1853 Ollivant described Llanwonno as a parish with a population of four to five thousand most of whom lived five miles away from the parish church which was on the top of a bleak mountain and only accessible at times via trackless moors and deep bogs.[31] A similar case, Rhes-y-cae, in the parish of Halkyn, Flintshire, was typical of many areas where a mining population had gathered in a remote area from the parish church. Though it was only two miles away it was separated "by a bleak and dreary mountain across which no regular road had ever been formed", its surfaces broken by mines and quarries, and while it was difficult at the best of times it was positively dangerous at night or in fog and tempest.[32]

Further figures about the want of church accommodation came from a parliamentary enquiry of 1852. At Mold many householders were unable to obtain seating in the parish church, and more than half the population at Wrexham were in the same position. Llangyfelach, including the new township of Morriston, had 100 sittings for a population of 4,500, while the valley parishes had special mention as did Swansea and Cardiff.[33] It was figures such as these that were used to advertise the needs of the newly formed Llandaff Diocesan Church Extension Society, half of whose income came from the county elite who saw the Church as the antidote to social unrest and disorder.[34] On the other hand we should not discount the fact that many of the Llandaff clergy were evangelical in churchmanship, and their concern was more about religious conversion and spiritual growth than the building of new places of worship. John Griffith described these mining valleys as spiritually destitute as the cannibals of New Zealand or Sierra Leone. The "Hindooism" of Merthyr and Aberdare were in the same bracket as that of "Tinvelly and Tamjore". But little was heard of the heathenism of these "wild regions" of Wales, where one cleric per 10,000 head of population contrasted with one for every 4,000 in the West Indies.[32] Motives were clearly mixed.

THE POLICY DECRIED

It was fondly believed that if new churches were built in these rapidly developing communities, the hitherto unchurched would flock into them, and those who had moved into Nonconformity because of the lack of accommodation would return to Mother Church. Bishop Blomfield of London was of this number, and his enthusiasm was passed on to his episcopal colleagues, though he was to be bitterly disillusioned at a later date.[36] Others were much more doubtful of this policy, accepting that many had been drawn to Nonconformity not because of the lack of accommodation but because of its intrinsic merits. Bishop Copleston endeavoured to answer this criticism by asserting that the new dissenting chapel built at Abergavenny was crowded, but there had been no diminution of the numbers who attended the old places of worship of the Established Church.[35] Amongst the doubters were Golifer who wrote an open letter to Lord John Russell and John Griffith of Merthyr. Were ten new churches in the diocese of Llandaff really needed, he asked in 1850, for it was wrong to contrast church accommodation with a parish's population when the majority of them were dissenters, and many parishes only had one Sunday service. Overflowing churches, he sarcastically continued, were a "remarkable phenomenon in Wales".[37] Sumner, in his 1827 Charge to the diocese of Llandaff, accepted the same position by noting that in three parishes with adequate accommodation a total of 50 attended out of a combined population of 936 [39].

Griffith warned in the late 1840s and thereafter that the belief of church leaders that people would soon fill a newly-built church was unrealistic, and while he applauded the efforts made, the practical result was a "comparative emptiness". Where, he asked, are the fustian jackets, the men with the heavy boots and the horny hands, - "the vertebrae, the backbone of England?" They were certainly not in these new churches. Rather they were in the public houses, and yet they were not irreligious. What was the use of these buildings if they remained unoccupied by those for whom they were built? The idea that if one built churches for the working man "the working man's millennium had come to hand" was absurd. Far better to attend to their housing which forced them to "pig" it like swine and turn to crime. Men, and in his case Welsh-speaking men, needed to be trained as evangelists and preachers to bring in these absent people and so built up the Church, presumably before a new building was erected at great cost only to become a major financial liability to its parish.[40]

Griffith's comments had already been expressed in part by Benjamin Hall. Hall, speaking in 1850 argued that it was inexpedient considering the fleeting nature of the population to build new churches. Far better to fill the existing churches and require the clergy to perform double duty. The need was for pastors who could build up a congregation in schoolrooms and other buildings, and then a church could be built. This had been the policy in the diocese of Ripon.[41] However, Bishop Ollivant argued in 1863 that he believed a new church plus a pastorally orientated cleric faithful to his minister would be able to obtain a congregation.[42] Such pioneering men were not easy to find, especially as the theological colleges failed to include church planting in their curriculum.

There were others who argued that building new churches and creating new parishes was counter-productive, and it would be better in the urban parishes to spend the money required on church building to endow a second clergyman who could duplicate services in an existing church.[43] In his essay on "Church Building in Flintshire", I.G. Jones argues that the equation that an increased population needed increased church accommodation was far too simple. The need was greater not in the urban parishes but in the rural ones, parishes where pluralism and non-residency were ripe and the people were often alienated from clergy and gentry. It was people from these parishes, already unchurched or dissatisfied with the Church, who became the non-worshipping inhabitants of the new communities.[44] The 1851 religious census revealed the true extent of the alienation of the masses from religion in general rather than just the Established Church, though Bishop Cleaver of Chester had realised this in 1799 when he recorded a general decline of religious influence in the lives of many people.[45]

Such were the arguments, but if new churches were required, there was also the necessity of making the existing churches fit for use by undoing centuries of neglect. To this we now turn.

CHAPTER TWO: A CONCERN FOR BUILDINGS

For many people the typical church building is a Gothic structure, with an interior divided into specific areas: the nave for the congregation sitting in pews; the lectern and pulpit probably facing each other on either side of the chancel arch; a chancel with choir stalls and probably an organ adjoining, and a sanctuary regarded as the holy of holies wherein is found the altar or communion table. The font would be by the door, and there might be a porch, vestries, and side aisles and chapels within the building itself. However, the church interior in the eighteenth century would have been far different, as we note later, even if the building was medieval in origin. Many churches were restructured time and time again in order to accommodate the liturgical emphases of the day. In this chapter we note how the liturgical developments of the early and mid-nineteenth century changed the interior shape of most church buildings, save for a few remarkable survivals.

Although many churches were seen by the early Victorians as being in a poor condition, it needs to be realised that for the previous centuries they were probably no better or worse than the homes in which people lived. Why should those who lived in poorly constructed, damp and inconvenient houses throughout the week consider that the building in which they spent a few hours each week should be in any better condition than their homes? Improvements in comfort in many homes, led to a desire for improvements in the church building to make it more comfortable and homely. Such improvements, including in many cases leaded windows and a heating apparatus, were thought to attract people to the church services rather than allow them to stray to Nonconformity.

Many church buildings were in a disgraceful condition, often because the responsibility for repairs lay with the churchwardens, who had to set a rate for such works and the maintenance of the church's worship.[1] As they also had the task of collecting it many preferred economy to dedication. The vestry minutes which survive indicate that from time to time repairs were effected to keep a building structurally sound and in reasonable order. The roofs were repaired or replaced, the walls whitewashed, the interior fittings renewed when required, and the linen and books replaced from time to time.[2] The churchwardens' accounts of many parishes indicate that fairly substantial sums were spent on the repair of these churches, as at Marchwiel and Welshpool.[3] Thomas Prichard comments that when £5 was spent on repairs at Ystradyfodwg Church during the eighteenth century, this sum represented the wages of a labourer for one hundred days work.[4] Another reason was that in some churches the responsibility for the repair of the chancel lay with the rector or the impropriator and few took their responsibilities seriously. Erasmus Saunders noted Archbishop Laud's complaint of 1635 about his then diocese of St Davids that these impropriators either pulled down these chancels or allowed them to fall, leaving the churches cold and open so that the congregations had to endure a great deal of hardship.[5] This might have been an exaggeration, though Archdeacon Tenison of Carmarthen reported in 1710 that the chancel of Egremond Church, the responsibility of an impropriator, was propped up and as a result the interior was almost useless.[6] The wealthy Lord William Somerset as non-resident rector of Llangatwg was forced to accept his liability for these chancel repairs after a legal opinion given by Sir John Dobson, QC.[7] Others took their responsibilities seriously, as did Charles Dundas who partly paid for the restoration of the south chancel of Hawarden Church in 1817 and gave it to the parish. The remaining monies came from the sale of pews.[8]

In addition to the church rates and voluntary giving, another source of funding lay in the so-called royal briefs, allowing a church to appeal to a wider, even national community for funding for rebuilding or restoration. Gwynfryn Richards in his study of these royal briefs in their Welsh context notes that the cost of obtaining one via the local quarter sessions and of promoting it through agents was high, and could amount to around three quarters of the sum received. The agents would print the brief and distribute it to the areas mentioned within it, sometimes the whole country, otherwise limited to a number of counties, and then collect the monies received. The brief would be read in each parish church by its incumbent, and the faithful exhorted to give financial assistance, though many parishes, or their incumbents, ignored such appeals. The cost of such a brief at Llanddulas in 1732 was £432 as against £649 collected form the 9,902 briefs distributed. Richards also notes that much exaggeration took place in the details given, and in some cases a sum far in excess of what was needed was stated, £1,000 rather than the £200 required, as it was realised that the brief would only provide a limited amount of the monies needed for the rebuilding. A brief of 1767 for the parish church of Welshpool, its third such brief, claimed the church was so ruinous that there was a danger to life if it was not repaired, which was hardly the case. This brief allowed collections throughout England, Berwick on Tweed, and in the counties of Flint, Denbighshire and Radnor, and house-to-house collections in Montgomeryshire, Shropshire, Staffordshire, Worcestershire and Herefordshire.[9] Llanfyllin obtained such a brief in 1704 probably stressing the insufficiency and poor condition of the old church. It obtained from it £730 though the cost of the rebuilding was £1,325. The highest amount received was 13.5d. from St Julian's, Shrewsbury.[10] Bangor Monachorum's brief of 1723 claimed the substantial sum of £2,427 was needed for its restoration. Sums of 11d., 2s.1½d. and 2s.5½d. were recorded from such parishes as Corfe Castle, Henfield and Clocaenog.[11] A further instance was for a church at Bala as a substitute for the parish church at Llanycil in 1758. Its distance from the town prevented attendance, and the existing chapel in the town was ruinous. A sum of £1,084 was required but the parishioners were unable to raise this amount themselves from the church rate due to being burdened with numerous poor.[12]

THE STATE OF THE BUILDINGS

In spite of these resources, and generally due to the inertia of churchwardens, neglect was often the order of the day as may be seen in numerous contemporary accounts. Throughout the years reports were made about the condition of many churches. Machynlleth Church was described in 1680 as being so out of repair it was likely to become a "ruinous heape". It was still intact in 1722, by which time its steeple had fallen down and even then it was described as in a ruinous condition.[13] A visitation of 1684 revealed that many Carmarthenshire churches were in an indifferent order, as at Llanboidy; quite decayed and fallen down as was the steeple at Kidwelly; or with roofs out of repair as at Llanddarog and Llandefaelog, but others had more minor problems such as unglazed or broken windows, poor paving, with the furnishings needing repair and the pulpit cushions and communion cloths in need of replacement. Some were said to be in good repair, as was Llannon, Llanpumpsaint, Llanybyther and Pembrey.[14] In his 1710 Charge to the diocese of St Asaph, Bishop Fleetwood argued that unless there was a greater public spirit in the building and repairing of churches, within a hundred years a huge number of churches would be brought to the ground.[15] A number had been allowed to fall into decay, and it was said in the diocese of St Davids there were 147 such places. But as W.T. Morgan suggests, in most cases this had occurred as parishes had become consolidated and the more convenient church used rather than the other, though he does suggest that the policy might have been deliberate to avoid the burden of additional services and the payment of a curate.[16]

The visitation by Archdeacon Tenison of his Carmarthen archdeaconry in 1710 revealed a major concern about the floors of the churches, due to intermural burials, but at Abergwili, where the wardens charged additional fees for such burials the church was said to be in decent order. Concern was expressed that the chancel wall at Pencarreg was in danger of falling, the condition of Llandeilo Fawr was bad, and in wet weather the parishioners had to abandon Llandyfeisant church as the roof was so decayed that it was impossible to keep the officiant and worshippers dry. By and large it seems the buildings were generally regarded as passable [17]

It was a slightly different story in the deanery of Penllyn and Edeirnion. John Wynne, in his inspection of 1730, commended some churches for being in good order, such as Llanfawr and Llandderfel, but others were in a far different state. Betws Gwerful Goch church lacked light, was miserably glazed and its font was the vilest piece of church furniture he had seen (the church also lacked the book of Homilies and Foxe's Book of Martyrs while its linen cloth was indescribable). Llanuwchllyn had a chancel roof which leaked, no paving, a dangerous gallery, and a verminous pulpit cushion; the gallery and porch at Llangower was about to collapse and the building was in a deplorable condition; Gwyddelwern was another church in a poor condition, while the roof at the west end of Llansanffraid had fallen in, the gallery had collapsed, and in bad weather the parishioners were forced to quit the building.[18]

A satirical English writer of the 1730s maintained that the Welsh churches resembled Jewish tabernacles converted into pigeon houses, and compared their pews to pens for geese, calves and hogs at Smithfield.[19] At St Mary's Church, Swansea, in 1739, the roof of the nave collapsed, just before a service, and only because the incumbent was late in arriving was no-one killed.[20] John Wesley, who preached in the Breconshire church of Llanddew in 1744, wrote in his diary he had never seen such a church before. The windows were of boards with holes bored in them to give a dim light.[21]

The various reports of the St Asaph rural deans on the state of the parishes in their deaneries of 1749 and 1791 reveal many churches that were neglected and in poor repair, though some were in good order. In the 1749 reports it was alleged that Ysbyty Ifan was ready to fall into ruins and Bryneglwys was in a poor and neglected order. It would take the work of years to make Llanrhaeadr ym Mochnant seem like the house of God. The churches at Henllan and St George needed repairs to their roofs and Llanrwst had its windows, part of its roof, flags and seats in disorder, and parts of the church were almost covered with bird droppings.[22] While more churches appeared to be in good order according to the equivalent report of 1791, their arrangement of seating was condemned, and others needed rethatching or whitewashing and other similar repairs.[23]

A letter of 1770 relating to Warren Church in Pembrokeshire requested the demolition of a disused and unrequired side aisle where the water was streaming through the roof and making the whole church very damp. The parishioners refused to repair it but were prepared to take it down and fill in the arches. However, there had been an objection from a parishioner as some of his family had been buried in this aisle.[24] When he visited Bodfari Church in 1774 Dr Johnson recorded that it was below many a stable for convenience or beauty, and was surprised to find it possessed silver communion vessels.[25] John Byng called Ewenny Church in the 1780s as loathsome, dark, dirty and as rough as a fallow field.[26] He described St John's Priory Church at Brecon as like "a hogs skye", a comment reiterated by Theophilus Jones who complained in 1809 that its transepts were little better than a barn.[27] Thomas Payne, rural dean of the Third part of Brecon, visited the churches of his deanery during 1785-7. His comments were mainly about the interior fittings, as at Llanelli where the floor was ill-paved and the seats irregular and crowded, the roof out of repair. Llangynidr "wore a very indecent Appearance, and almost every corner crowded with rubbish". This was also the case at

Llanfihangel Cwmdu.[28] In 1810 S.R. Meyrick described in now familiar words Blaenpennal, a chapelry of Llanddewi Brefi, as a disgrace to the Church, more like a barn than a place of public worship.[29] The mother church, Llanddewi Brefi, also received criticism. Sir Richard Colt Hoare described it in 1802 so miserable it appeared like a ruin, rather than a building appropriated to the service of God. He also described St David's Cathedral as being in a state of absolute ruin and decay.[30]

A visitor to Wales in the 1800s, William Bingley, described the church at Llanberis as being the most ill-looking place of worship he had ever seen. He mistook it at first for a large antique cottage.[31] Writing of the mountain churches of Glamorgan, Benjamin Heath Malkin described the natives of these parts worshipping "their Maker where an Englishman would not litter the most ignoble quadruped about the house, in darkness and in damp, pelted through crevices by the elements, and immersed in dirt more profound and impenetrable than that of their most miserable hovels."[32] Ystradyfodwg Church was regarded by Malkin in 1804 as the most miserable and neglected church he had come across in his tour of south Wales.[33] It is hardly surprising that in his 1821 Charge, Bishop Van Mildert of Llandaff complained that less than one in five of the churches of his diocese were in a decent and respectable condition.[34] In 1810 Richard Fenton visited Llanallgo Church in Anglesey. The church was most slovenly kept, its windows broken and admitting pigeons and other birds who produced the most abominable litter.[35] Bishop Bethell's visitation of that county in 1837 included detailed notes about the condition of its churches. Llanfigel was so dilapidated that no services had been held there for over thirty years; Llanallgo was in serious need of overall repair, and the interior of Llanfwrog was "in a wretched state". Other churches also needed repair or refurbishment.[36] St Elvis Church, Pembrokeshire, was described in 1824 as having no seats or pews, an earthen floor, and was in such bad order that the services had to be performed in a private house as the building was too dangerous to enter.[37] There was a real fear that the church at Llanfihangel Crucorney would collapse and bury the congregation. As a result in 1833 Bishop Copleston advised the incumbent to allow his congregation to attend Llangatwg Church instead of running the risks of frequenting this dilapidated building until some restoration could be done, or services could be held more locally in a barn or a large room.[38] Thirty-one years later Stephen Glynne found that Aberporth Church was so dilapidated that it had been abandoned and a service was held in an adjoining schoolroom.[39]

The Monmouthshire church of Kilgwrrwg was used until the 1830s by a farmer as a sheepfold, and had to be cleaned out for the monthly services, when a reading desk was brought from a local farmhouse and a Bible and Prayer Book borrowed as well. Rain and snow penetrated the building.[40] A story is told of Bishop Christopher Wordsworth that when he visited a Welsh church he was informed he could not make use of the pulpit as a woman had permission to keep her goose there.[41] W.T. Morgan argues that while the answers in the various visitation returns of the diocese of St Davids of 1828 might indicate that the majority of churches were in reasonably good repair and the furniture decent and in good order, the reality was probably much worse. He quotes Dean Howell who, speaking in 1895, described the condition of many churches fifty years earlier which he had personally observed. The wretched deal communion tables would hardly have found a place in the poorest cottages, as would the dirty and moth eaten altar cloths, the roofs full of holes, grass growing in the porches, the sexton's tools and implements in open view, and common basins used for fonts.

Another observer, G.B. Hughes, also quoted by Morgan, speaking of conditions in the 1840s in the deanery of Castlemartin, observed that the churches "were miserably out of repair, ruinous in some instances; always damp, mouldy and unwholesome." The pews were often so decayed that they were incapable of occupation, and the only repairs effected were "a coat of whitewash or possibly the insertion of a hideous sash window to keep out the wind and the weather, or the application of a patch to the roof for the same purpose". These necessary repairs were often ignored for the sake of economy.[42] Writing in the 1850s, W.J. Conybeare in his essay "The Church in the Mountains" quotes from the 1847 report on education in Wales and from the *Ecclesiologist* of 1852 about churches where few services were held and where "[a]n air of slovenly carelessness, and poverty-stricken neglect, pervades the aspect of the edifice and the ministrations of the officiator". Many Brecknockshire churches were in a disgraceful condition from dirt and neglect, and the state of many churches in Pembrokeshire was "very bad, both from neglect and dilapidation."[43]

When John Keble attended a service at Llanberis Church in 1840 he wrote about the extreme dirt and negligence of the building, with its tottering three-legged communion table, the deplorable state of the minister's surplice, with the seats as dirty and uncomfortable as everything else. All showed a dislike of soap and of ecclesiastical decency, which he added, was in a place in the midst of one of the most glorious sights in nature.[44] The 1851 religious census return for Trefriw described the church as being in a most dilapidated and wretched condition, which the parishioners considered was highly injurious to their health to attend.[45]

When a group of Yorkshire Welsh clergymen visited Lanbeulan Church, Anglesey, in 1852, windows were broken, rubbish found in the transepts, the surplice mouldy, the roof imperfect, and the books torn and benches mean and backless. An old man told them the church was in a bad state, "it is painful to see it, the rain comes through." Its incumbent for the previous seventeen years was John William Trevor, and the value of the parishes he held amounted to £793, while he served as rural dean, a magistrate, one of the bishop's chaplains and treasurer of the cathedral chapter.[46] An unidentified church recorded by a speaker in 1856 was said to have walls streaming with damp, pools of stagnant water on the floor, and the churchyard path so unfrequented that the grass had grown over it knee-high.[47] Stephen Glynne in that same year of 1856 noted that St Ishmael's Church, Rhos Market, had only bare earth at the west end of its nave. Some years earlier he had visited Bleddfa Church, writing that its interior was dreary, but in a "less bad state" than many other Radnorshire churches, while Llanarmon Church in 1861 was in a miserable condition with walls and floor damp and the windows with broken glass.[48] Llangennith Church in Gower in the 1840s had a chancel roof in bad order and bare earth in the rest of the church, so that in 1865 a new rector of Llanmadoc, J.D. Davies, described this church as being meaner than the meanest hovel in the village. His other church at Cheriton was in a better condition but even then its walls were streaked with slime, the roof was bad and water penetrated into the tower.[49]

The spire of St Martin's Church, Haverfordwest, had to be taken down as it was unsafe in 1869, and it was argued that the condition of the walls was equally precarious.[50] In his recollections George Huntington of Tenby recalled stories of Pembrokeshire churches in the 1830s when parsons preached with an umbrella held over their heads, while at St Florence cocks and hens roosted in the church and a horse was kept in the porch for want of a stable.[51] By 1872 Grosmont Church was in a state of collapse due to the weight of the tower resting on four arches, while the intermural burials, some only four inches between the coffin and the surface, caused not only an unacceptable smell but also some degree of sickness.[52] Francis Kilvert, the diarist, newly appointed to the remote Radnorshire parish of St Harmon's in 1876, was horrified when he inspected his new church. It was simply hideous, its interior bare, squalid and cold, the roof admitting the rain, with its high ugly box pews, no heating apparatus and its other furnishings and contents of a similar nature to the building.[53] Some years previously he had visited Bryngwyn Church where his brother was astonished at its ruinous condition. "I told him to wait till he goes to Llanbedr Painscastle", Kilvert wrote in his diary.[54] When a new rector entered Llanllyfni Church in 1873 he found the pews and benches covered with snow.[55] As Eglwys Cymmin Church was being restored in 1877-8 it was discovered that the chancel roof had been poorly repaired with pieces of brandy cases which had "Hennessey's Cognac" clearly marked on them.[56]

Visitation queries inevitably asked about the state of a church building, and although it was easy for the wardens to provide misinformation, when it was ordered that work needed to be done and was not completed the wardens were summoned to the ecclesiastical court to explain their conduct and make good the deficiencies.[57] Bishop Barrington of Llandaff's book, compiled after his visitation of 1771, indicates a number of churches in a ruinous condition. The south aisle had collapsed at Margam; dogs and pigs entered Michaelston-super-Afan church through a hole in the wall, and the chapel at Caerphilly was in such a condition it was dangerous to hold services there. One assumes these neglectful wardens were required to make good the damage or else make answer for their neglect in the consistory court.[58] The ruinous state and neglect of some of the churches in his diocese aroused Bishop Burgess' concern in his 1807 Charge. He attributed this to the ignorance of churchwardens as to their duties, and the want of superintendence in each archdeaconry. The rural deans had been told to cite the wardens responsible for neglect in the ecclesiastical courts, but he was grateful that in general the wardens did their duty in this respect when summoned to do so. Bishop Majendie in his 1814 Charge required incumbents to admonish their wardens to do their duty regarding the church buildings and for the rural deans to follow this up.[59] It was not easy to persuade reluctant churchwardens to spend money, and one rural dean adopted the policy of providing a time-scale for the repairs needed, according to their urgency, so that the expense might not be so heavy as if all was done at once.[60]

Many churches built in the mining valleys suffered from subsidence or from the extremities of the weather. Brymbo church, built in 1837-8, collapsed in 1869 due to mine workings underneath it, and services had to be transferred to a school room while the original church was demolished and a new church built.[61] The curate of Ystradyfodwg made an impassioned plea to Lord Bute in 1842 asking for financial assistance to repair his church as the church rate, levied on poor parishioners, would not be sufficient as lightning had struck the church and it was in such a dangerous state it could not be used.[62] This church, though it had been rebuilt in 1846, was described twelve years later as damp, with a roof needing repair, a rotten door frame, a chancel laid with rough flags green with damp, though the responsibility for the chancel lay with its impropriators.[63] Even by the turn of the twentieth century some churches were in poor condition, and these included recent buildings. The iron hut used for St Paul's mission church in the parish of Penarth was described in 1905 as being worn out, the roof incapable of keeping out the rain, and the lack of head room and ventilation meant the large working class congregation remained in some discomfort throughout the services.[64] In the same period the historic Basaleg church had major problems: the roofs and glazing were in poor condition, the mullions of the windows perishing, the bell frame unsafe, and dampness pervading the whole building.[65]

To what extent these surveys and comments are typical of all the churches in Wales is uncertain. There were certainly some churches in good or reasonable condition, as already noted and as described below. However, John Guy notes that few of these churches were in the condition depicted by the Victorian restorers who made out the worst possible case to justify the need for restoration.[66] Nigel Yates observes that of the 57 churches inspected by Sir Stephen Glynne during 1841-51 only four were in a ruinous condition.[67] This is somewhat endorsed by the inspection of the chancels of those Glamorgan churches in the patronage of the dean and chapter of Gloucester (for which they were responsible) made by Josiah Tucker in that same year of 1771. While there were a number of comments about the pews which had been placed in the chancels and

Tucker which claimed were the responsibility of those who had put them there, it appears that these chancels were in a somewhat reasonable structural repair as presumably were the other parts of the buildings.[68] Bishop Majendie of Bangor, reviewing the reports made by his rural deans in the inspection of their churches in 1817, claimed that the churches in his diocese were in a much improved state of repair.[69] In his 1821 Charge Bishop van Mildert of Llandaff said that with few exceptions the churches in that diocese had undergone considerable repairs and most were in a decent and respectable condition, a matter endorsed by his successor, Bishop Sumner in 1827. Though his two immediate predecessors had complained about the dilapidated state into which some churches had been permitted to fall, this had now been remedied though this previous neglect had placed a heavy burden on the present generation.[70] Clarke, in a study of the Caernarfonshire churches at the beginning of the nineteenth century notes that while Hyde Hall in 1810 described Betws Garmon as a poor building, Capel Curig a hovel, Dolbenmaen mean and small and Llanberis even meaner, he reported favourably about most churches. Clarke suggests that many of these churches were restored not because they were in disrepair but because of the changing ecclesiological fashions of the day.[71] As Nigel Yates suggests it was the poverty and antiquity of the fittings that was the issue rather than the dilapidation of the structure or deliberate neglect.[72]

This may be verified by Archdeacon Wickham's comment in his 1855 Charge when he said that while the churches he had visited in his archdeaconry indicated a poor maintenance record, he advised churchwardens to undertake the small repairs required promptly before they became major concerns. Though damp, dirty and shabby churches did not speak of holiness to the Lord, he seemed to suggest that many of these churches were in a reasonable condition.[73] In an inspection of the Glamorgan churches in 1847, the archdeacon found that only 38 out of 111 were in good repair, 73 needed some repairs, and 33 needed extensive repairs. This probably reflected the new concern about properly maintained buildings and being on a par with domestic property, but the present state of repairs was said to be due to the parsimony of church officers and the neglect of ecclesiastical inspectors.[74] Many of the printed appeals issued on behalf of churches needing restoration probably exaggerated their dilapidated conditions and "barnlike" appearance in the hope of soliciting more funding. This may well have been the case for an appeal launched in 1879 for Betws Gwerful Goch Church, described as barnlike, dilapidated and needing a complete overhaul. It was probably typical of many such appeals causing later historians to have a false view of the condition of these churches.[75]

BURIALS WITHIN THE CHURCH

One of the reasons why churches were in poor condition was intramural burial, that is, burial within the church building itself. Those who regarded themselves as the elite of the parish generally considered it their right to be buried within the chancel, beneath their pews or in the nave aisle, allowing the more humble folk to be buried in the churchyard. When pews were moved at Vaynor Church the entrances to several family vaults were revealed.[76] Late seventeenth century wills noted by Sir Joseph Bradney in his history of Monmouthshire indicate directions that burial was to be within the church itself. Thus Isaac Tomkins who died in 1684 requested his body to be buried in Caerleon Church.[77] Clergy were often buried within the chancel, as was the father of Dean Allen of St Davids who had been rector of Burton, Pembrokeshire and who was buried, as was his wife, within the altar rails.[78] In cases involving rights to pews, it was often alleged that family burials had taken place under the disputed pew or bench. In a case involving the parish of Caeo it was said this custom also prevailed in the parishes of St Ishmael, Kidwelly and Laugharne.[79]

There were many comments and protests about this practice, which left the floors very uneven, badly paved, or even unpaved. Archdeacon Tenison's visitation of the churches in his archdeaconry of Carmarthen of 1710 reported that the floor of Abernant Church was of earth and uneven, probably for this reason.[80] At Llanarmon in 1791 the pavement of the church was bad due to the frequent burials within the church and the custom of burying within the church was noted at Llandyssil, Montgomeryshire.[81] Richard Colt Hoare, visiting St John's Church, Brecon, in 1802, wrote that the pavement had been disfigured by the burials within the church.[82] The historian of Brecknock, Theophilus Jones, left his readers in no doubt about his distaste for this practice. Writing in 1809 of Llanfihangel Cwmdu Church he added that the "pernicious" custom of burying within its walls was still continued there.[83] William Coxe, in his tour of Monmouthshire of 1801 also complained about this custom. Stones were taken up, heaps of earth strewn with flowers and evergreens which were allowed to rot, the stones seldom replaced, and the consequence was that the floor was allowed to become damp and dirty.[84] At Penley Church, and probably at many others, the burial vaults in the church during bad weather gave rise to unhealthy odours, as was reported in 1897.[85]

Measures were introduced in some churches to limit the damage these burials caused. The Llanerfyl vestry, Montgomeryshire, which agreed in 1675 to repave the church with brick, both in the aisles and under the seats, also ordered that those who wished to make a grave in the chancel or rood should pay a mark to the parson of the parish, and within a month after the burial to cause the grave to be well beaten with new earth and paved with good bricks. Those who required a grave in the nave of the church were to pay a noble in money to the parish towards the repair of the church and churchyard. Furthermore, all those who caused a grave to be cut open within the said church, should, for each week they allowed the grave to remain unpaved with bricks, after the first month of grace, to pay two shillings a week towards the same fund.[86] Owen Jenkins, vicar of St John's Church in Cardiff gave up his right to burial fees for internment within the church in 1774, and at the same time the vestry required all those who owned such burial places to keep them in good repair.[87] A new vicar of Rumney, John Latey, insisted in 1823 that a fee of one pound be paid before the ground was broken for an intramural burial, and on the restitution of the floor thereafter. Otherwise, he observed, the church would get into the same miserable condition as it was when he became vicar.[88]

There were so many intramural burials in some churches that the floor level was raised considerably above the level of the ground outside, as at Nevern Church, Pembrokeshire.[89] As churches were restored and floor levels reduced to their original level, vast numbers of human remains had to be disinterred and placed elsewhere, although there were accounts of them being discarded with the other debris from the site, as at Welshpool.[90] At Llansilin during its restoration of 1830 cart loads of human remains were taken from the church to be buried in the churchyard. Some had been buried only eighteen inches from the surface.[91]

It goes without saying that intramural burial was an unsanitary practice. Dr William Wynne, rector of Llaneilian near Mold who died in 1776 directed that his body should be buried within the churchyard and not in the church in consideration of the health of his fellow creatures. On his epitaph are these words:

> In conformity to an antient [*sic*] usage,
> from a proper regard to decency,
> and a concern for the health of his
> fellow-creatures, he was moved to give
> particular directions for being buried
> in the adjoining church-yard,
> and not in the church.[92]

The reason for this is supplied by Thomas Payne in his visitation of his deanery, the Third part of Brecon, in 1785. He commented that the curate of Llanfeugan sometimes had to leave the church even in the midst of divine service as he was overcome by the stench from putrid corpses.[93] One answer was to raise the level of the floor. This was done at Cynwyl Gaeo during the seventeenth century which, while it raised the level by four feet and sealed the floor, meant no one could stand upright.[94]

Legislation of 1818 prohibited intramural burial, but when Mrs Booth Gray of Duffryn died in 1837 a way was found around this. A hole was dug down below the east window of St Nicholas Church and her coffin was pushed into her "rightful place".[95]

Another feature of churches was barely mentioned. Crowded churches accommodating people of all classes, often infrequently cleaned, harboured insects, fleas and bugs. St John's Church, Cardiff, had to be cleansed in 1869 at a cost of £70 having been infested by insects which the local paper declaimed could not be named in polite society but "usually designated by the musical symbols of F sharp and B flat".[96]

INCONVENIENT LOCATIONS

We also need to note that many churches were built in inconvenient places, sometimes at the extremity of large parishes, which meant that many parishioners lived many miles from the church. Examples would include rural parishes such as Llanbister with its 30,000 acres, Llandingad with a circumference of 50 miles, Llanbadarn Fawr with its 80 square miles and 10,000 population, or the growing urban centres of Llanelli and Swansea whose parishes extended over a large hinterland. In addition there were those parishes where new industry had developed in the nineteenth century, such as Llangatwg, Llanwynno, Ystradyfodwg, Gelligaer and Llangynwyd, where the newly developing industrial centres were separated from the parish church by considerable distances, and in the first two instances by mountainous terrain.[97] At Llanwynno, for example, it was said that the curate having to make his way to the church could be soaked to the skin by a ten minute shower and face intense cold on his journey. He would take his food with him and eat it between services while warming and drying himself by the little fire at the grave-digger's cottage.[98] It meant that the clergy faced an uphill challenge in pastoral visiting, and the inhabitants of the more remote areas, unable to face a journey of several miles to attend the church, turned to Nonconformity which had taken the initiative in setting up causes in these places, unfettered by legal restraints or the need for an ordained ministry. The church later tried to address this issue by building additional churches and mission rooms but never really outclassed these nonconformist causes. A speaker at the St Asaph Diocesan Conference of 1892, Canon Hugh Roberts of Brymbo, thus complained that over the past thirty years people would no longer walk as far as they did to attend their parish church as they had done before the time of the railways. In addition, complained Bishop Edwards, over the previous 25 years the custom of a family worshipping together had been lost in Wales.[99]

THE INTERIOR OF THE CHURCH

It has already been noted that the interiors of many churches were whitewashed and crowded with irregularly positioned pews, and we now need to explore further. However, the descriptions we have of most church interiors, both written and illustrative, are of the eighteenth century church in its prime and beyond, rather than earlier. Few of these early interiors have survived, especially of those dating before the eighteenth century. Two that have survived, Rug Chapel and Llangar Church, are in the care of CADW.[100] In fact, there was no typical church. A town church would be far different from a rural one, as might be expected. It would be larger, and its pulpit would need to be higher, sometimes a so-called three-decker one, where the clerk who assisted with the service sat on the first level, the parson above him (and from which he probably read the lessons) and the actual pulpit, often with a sounding board, above him. A rural church could be a little more basic. Newchurch (Llannewydd), Carmarthen, had a double decker pulpit with a sounding board above it, a gallery with an outside staircase, and a communion rail so high that people had to receive the sacrament standing.[101]

The interior of the church was often whitewashed.[102] This tradition would have dated back to Reformation times when the wall paintings were obliterated by this method. In some cases the exterior was also whitewashed, though this may not have been general.[103] The decorations which were allowed were painted forms on which the Ten Commandments, the Lord's Prayer, and the Apostles' Creed were written. Some churches had a "Moses and an Aaron" but it is not known what this represented.[104] The larger churches probably had the royal coat of arms prominently displayed. Surviving examples are found at Welshpool and Castle Caereinion. Floors were badly paved, as noted, or of clay or bare earth,[105] on which rushes were often placed.[106] This occurred as late as 1839 at Gwaenysgor in the vale of Clwyd and until 1893 at Llanynys (Denbs), where they were renewed each Easter.[107] At Pentrefoelas it was known for the youngsters to start peeling them and flicking them about if the sermon went on for too long.[108] Straw mattresses were supplied by those parishioners of Llandinam who sat on the more rudimentary benches placed on an earth floor, while at Llanfair Caereinion it was said that the straw provided for the poorer members of the congregation made that part of the church strongly suggestive of a pigsty.[109]

Few churches had any form of heating system even though the main service might last for nearly two hours. This was the reason for the high-backed pews, sometimes surmounted by curtains, and for curtains to be placed at doors to keep out the draughts, as at Llantwit Major Church.[110] A few churches had a rudimentary heating system, sometimes a stove at the back of the church or in the vestry, although it was not unknown for the gentry to install a fireplace in their pews. An unknown church in south Wales had a fireplace at the back, for in the 1900s a boy remembered that he and others would step out of their pews during the service in order to warm their feet on a cold morning.[111] Some of the more substantial private pews also had their own heating arrangements, as we note later. The lack of such heating probably reduced attendances during the winter months, as Obelkevich observes in reference to South Lindsey, and people resorted to the warmer dissenting chapel.[112] In many churches the roofs had been ceiled to keep the church reasonably warm, and Sir Stephen Glynne observed these at Trallwng, Cenarth, and the chancel at Whitton, while an eighteenth century restoration had inserted ceilings at Welshpool, and at St John's Cardiff a false plaster ceiling darkened the church.[113]

A few churches still retained the Reformation practice, which Archbishop Laud had endeavoured to end in the 1630s, of having the communion table placed lengthwise in the chancel with its short end to the east. Yates notes this for Llantrisant, Anglesey, St George Denbigh, and Port Eynon,[114] and Clarke does so for the Caernarfonshire churches of Llanfaglan and Llanllyfni in 1788.[115]

The central feature of most churches was not the communion table, but the pulpit, for the eighteenth century placed a new emphasis on the art of preaching the Word of God. The pulpit was generally placed within the nave, to enable greater audibility, and it was often built to a sufficient height to be able to overlook those sitting in the high-backed pews.[116] Often the seating was arranged to this end, so that some sat with their backs to the chancel, as at Diserth where the pulpit was placed, and still remains, on the south side of the nave.[117] In 1748 it was reported of Llanfor Church that the pulpit stood in the middle of the nave on the south wall, while underneath it was the reading desk. The same was true of Llansanffraid Glyndyfrdwy in the same county of Merioneth, though here it was a poor example with no cloth on it, and only an old cushion on the desk.[118] The pulpit and reading desk of Dolgellau Church were placed between two windows on the north side of the nave.[119] Bedwas Church was described in 1854 as being unheated, possessing high backed pews as a consequence, a pulpit hiding the communion table, and so high that the preacher's head nearly touched the roof. The clerk sat on its lower deck.[120] The church at Holywell was described in 1884 as having three galleries, enclosed pews of various sizes placed all over the main body, and the pulpit and prayer desk in front of the altar.[121] At St Mary's Church, Swansea, the three decker pulpit was placed at the west end, in front of the west door, with the organ and choir above it, and the pews turned to face that direction.[122] At Llanfechain the pulpit was on the north wall, midway down the nave,[123] and at Myddfai on the south wall, and the pews were probably orientated towards it.[124] In the 1830s John Parker was distressed to find that even in the new church at Aberystwyth the pulpit and reading desk were placed in front of the chancel.[125] A description of St Mary's Church, Haverfordwest, given in 1872, noted that even after a restoration of that church thirty years earlier, it exhibited a picture as to

> how completely a church can be spoiled, and how thoroughly every idea of worship can be effaced from the mind by its internal arrangements … The altar is miserably low and small, and the great chancel … is now filled with high pews, all facing west, so that the congregation are perforce compelled to turn their backs on the Altar and on the service there performed. The pews in the nave face east, and those in the aisle south, all thus looking towards one point, and that is the triple erection … of clerk's desk, reading desk and pulpit, towering dragon-like one above the other.

It added that the church was in the hands of the "England Low Church school".[126]

A pulpit and desk of cast iron, of a Gothic pattern, graced Wrexham Church, but had been unhappily placed so as to hide the communion table, while the galleries spoilt the spaciousness of the interior, according to Glynne. He observed the same at Lamphey, where the pulpit was within the chancel arch, and at Llanaelhaearn, where the pulpit, though not in the centre of the church, had its back to the altar.[127]

Although another chapter will deal with the actual pews, we need to note how they often filled and inconvenienced the church interior. At Chepstow Church the large and high backed pews were on each side of a narrow central aisle, while there were two galleries at the west end, one used by the singers.[128] One conscientious rural dean, perhaps concerned about these matters, reported in 1791 that pews were irregularly placed at Llandrillo yn Rhos, Henllan, Llansannan, Betws Abergele and Llanelian.[129] The irregularity was often because of piecemeal development, with pews being fitted in where they could be placed as and when required and individually designed. In his descriptions of churches during the 1840s to the 1860s Sir Stephen Glynne noted many examples of this overcrowding and irregularity. At Pennant Melangell the church was very untidy and awfully crowded with pews quite up to the altar, as was the case at Trallwng, whose interior he described as truly wretched, and at Llangoed, Anglesey, where the altar was almost squeezed out of its place by pews.[130] But not only was the body of the church filled with pews, so was the chancel, as well as on either side of the communion table which was regarded as a prestigious site. Betws Gwerfyl Goch had three pews in its chancel,[131] and in the early nineteenth century the lessee of Carew Rectory, S. Allan of Cresselly, had two pews put up in the chancel for himself.[132] At Pentrefoelas, in the new church built in 1771, the parsonage pew was on one side of the communion table and the Voelas pew for the "family" on the other.[133] Llanfechain had two high pews on each side of the communion table.[134] At Burton Church, Pembrokeshire, the western arch under the tower was almost blocked by tiers of seats, rising one behind the other.[135]

Some pews were of substantial size, and their seating was often arranged along its four sides, so that some faced towards and others with their backs to the pulpit.[136] The Pentref pew at Llanymynech had seating for thirty people.[137] On the other hand, as we note later, those without pews had to make do with benches, some of them rather primitive in construction and clearly uncomfortable. At Eglwysfair Glantaf in the parish of Llanboidy, there were only eight pews but to accommodate those attending planks were placed around the church in lieu of seats.[138] Other pews, as at Llangybi, were so narrow that kneeling was impossible in them.[139]

As communion services were infrequent, sometimes once a month but generally three or four times a year, the communion table was infrequently used. As noted above, it was often surrounded by pews, as at Diserth, where the presence of a box pew on either side of it halved the available space, or at Llanganten where Theophilus Jones considered the sanctuary was so congested that a "stall fed prebendary could hardly turn around, though a lean curate could perhaps squeeze himself into it."[140] All too often it became a surface on which hats and coats could be placed.[141]

Many churches had galleries, generally one at the west end for the choir and "band", as at Llanymynech, which also had an additional gallery placed between the pillars which belonged to Carreghova Hall.[142] Chepstow has already been noted. Carno also had a singers' gallery,[143] while Llangollen had two at its west end.[144] Throughout the early nineteenth century galleries were built to accommodate school children and to further the seating of the church. This happened at Welshpool, and Glynne noted at Llanaelhaearn in 1848 that the interior had been frightfully spoilt, especially by a huge and deep gallery occupying nearly all the nave.[145]

In many churches the font was neglected, and even used as a receptacle for cleaning materials. This was sometimes because baptisms were conducted in private ceremonies in the home of the child. Archdeacon North of Cardigan castigated many of his clergy during his 1862 Visitation Charge by stating that while churches were generally in a satisfactory state, some were without fonts or those they had were neglected.[146]

A vivid description of one of these churches, whose setting was of the eighteenth century, was given by Robert Roberts in 1859. Describing the church at Cwm, Flintshire, where he was about to become curate, he wrote:

> The building was an old one, perhaps four or five hundred years old, to judge from the remains of an east window in a good perpendicular style and one or two arches apparently of the same date. But the hand of the restorer had been at work: the windows were altered to the approved church-warden pattern, round tops, iron stanchions, and plenty of whitewash. An ugly gallery was set up at one end rendering the lower part of the aisle dark and unavailable for worshippers. A still uglier erection, if possible, disfigured the north side of the aisle just where a screen had once been. A deal desk for the parish clerk formed the basement, the second story was a deal box for reading prayers and above all towered a deal pulpit, immense, tall, and hideous. The whole area of the church was filled with high square pews of the same material, and as the restorers had eschewed paint, the native hideousness of their handiwork had not even that cloak to cover its ugly nakedness. The altar was of fine carved black oak, but mildewed and as decayed as oak can decay: its covering was a bit of green baize, very brown and seedy. The altar rails were also of oak originally, but patched here and there with the deal of the restorers, so that the whole effect was somewhat piebald – old lace eked out with pack-thread.[147]

The service he attended was in line with the fabric of the church. It was against these arrangements, casual and undignified, that the reformers of the nineteenth century desired something far better that would give glory to God and holiness to the Church's worship.

THE CHANGES OF THE NINETEENTH CENTURY

The new churches built under the various parliamentary grants in the early nineteenth century were required to provide free seats as well as rented ones (the rent going for the maintenance of the incumbent and the church). To accommodate the number required, galleries were often installed on the north and south sides but not over the altar. Nigel Yates suggests that these buildings incorporated a different type of liturgical arrangement than had been the norm previously. The old three decker was replaced by a pulpit and reading desk placed on either side of the chancel entrance; the altar was given more prominence by being raised a few steps above the level of the nave, and uniform pews with doors replaced the square box pews. These were provided with kneeling boards at the front, were to be sufficiently low so to allow the occupants to see the minister, and were to face eastwards. A later preference (it seems) was for open seats, rather than closed pews, but if the latter was chosen it required a wide passageway in the aisle in which benches for the poor could be placed so they could observe the liturgical action. However, chancels were shallow, a point disliked by the later ecclesiologists.[148] Such buildings were copied by others, sometimes with variations, as at St Mary's, Cardiff, built by Lord Bute and opened in 1844. Here a central pulpit was made the main focus of the building and behind it lay a communion table almost obscured from the congregation.[149]

The Ecclesiological movement, deriving from the Cambridge Camden Society and much influenced by Pugin, wished to restore dignity, order and holiness to the Church in general, in its buildings, worship and ceremonial. Its members believed that the medieval church was its pattern book (in particular the decorative Gothic style popular between 1300-1375); the Holy Communion was the primary service; the altar, as they called it, the focal point of the church and the once central pulpit placed on the side of the chancel arch; and that the priesthood should be separated from the laity within the building because of the dignity of their calling and the holiness of their office. The nave was seen within the context of the world, whereas the chancel represented heaven itself and needed to be observed by the whole congregation. The traditional band and choir at the west end, ceiled roofs, sash windows, galleries and pews were anathema to its followers, while such items as a reredos and sedilia seats in the sanctuary, with a railed off altar, a robed and male choir in the chancel, an organ or at least a harmonium, kneeling boards in the orderly row of benches in the nave, as well as ornaments, became regarded as *de rigueur*. This new order of restoration was based on a fantasy about the medieval world.

Llangorwen Church, consecrated in 1841, was regarded as an ideal church by the Ecclesiologists. Its pulpit and desk were unobtrusive, while the chancel was placed high above the level of the nave indicating that the central focus was no longer the pulpit but the communion table, here described as an altar and built in stone. The chancel was stalled and the nave had open seats rather than pews. Its cost of £3,000 was beyond most parishes.[150] Of the 51 churches visited by Sir Stephen Glynne between 1863-73 only four fitted his description as being fully ecclesiological. However, Yates notes that he did not visit the newer churches, most of whose arrangements he would have applauded.[151] One of them was St Paul's Church, Sketty, consecrated in 1851, which fitted most of the requirements of these purists, with an elevated chancel and an even higher sanctuary, a side chapel, baptistery at the west end, and the pulpit on the north-east corner of the nave, though the seating was in low-backed pews with doors. A church which met Glynne's approval was Cilgerran which he visited in 1855. The roof was open, the seats uniform, low and open, there was no gallery, and the chancel was stalled and laid with encaustic tiles. The sanctuary was even more richly decorated.[152] George Huntington, the Tractarian rector of Tenby, described his ideal church in 1878. The holy table would be at the east end, with a cloth, candlesticks and cross on it, and there would be no pews, only chairs.[153]

It took time for these ideas to become commonplace, and they were often adopted rather piecemeal. When Llandysilio Church was restored in 1833, the pulpit and the reading desk were removed from the top of the nave into the chancel and the church was repewed.[154] Llanymynech Church, rebuilt in 1843, had its communion table raised by two steps and a communion rail provided,[155] while St David's Church, Newtown, built 1847, retained the earlier fashion of pews, galleries and a three-decker pulpit, though other arrangements were ecclesiologically shaped, with the communion table in the sanctuary and observable, and the font at the west end.[156] Not all these improvements were possible, especially in rural areas, so that when Ewen Christian came to restore Glascwm Church in 1890 he provided a new sanctuary and east window, but there was no chancel step and only one step into the sanctuary.[157] The Tractarian curate of Buckley, then in the parish of Hawarden, Henry Powell Ffoulkes, during the 1840s remodelled that church. Placing the choir stalls at the east end of the nave below the chancel, and the font at the west end, he obtained stained glass for some of its windows and a keyboard organ.[158]

Many churches were still built in an older style: a style quite contrary to the dictates of the Ecclesiological Movement. One was Rossett Church which was built in 1841. Its arrangements may have seemed orderly, but would have been condemned wholeheartedly by the ecclesiologists of that day. The communion table was under the west window, rather than the properly orientated east, a pulpit was to one side of it and the reading desk the other, and the pews ran across the middle of the church, there being no central aisle, regarded as essential by the ecclesiologists as a processional way.[159] Tastes remained conservative, so that when Llanfyllin Church was gradually restored in the 1860s a quasi-chancel was created, the pulpit and desk moved from the north wall to the south-east corner of the nave, and open seats substituted for the pews, but the chancel was not stalled nor was a central aisle provided.[160]

Nevertheless, this new style of church building pioneered by the Ecclesiological Society rapidly gained ascendancy. It was amazing how this movement spread even amongst non-Tractarian churches, though it took time to take effect. It may have been the cult of beauty and the desire for holiness in worship that enabled it to take a hold, though pride and ambition played their part, but the end result was that many churches were restored with these principles in mind, and adorned with coloured stained glass in the windows and in some cases wall paintings and decorations.[161] As Sir Kenneth Clark remarked of these ecclesiologists; for nearly fifty years every new Anglican church was built according to their instructions: "that is to say, in a manner opposed to utility, economy or good sense – a very wonderful achievement in the mid-nineteenth century."[162] One of their major concerns was to persuade churchwardens to obtain professional advice and thus prevent them from insisting that a church should be restored to its former "orthodox arrangement", and hopefully to substitute open benches for the former pews.[163]

Lord Harlech was one of many who believed that the clergy were the agents and movers of these church restorations. Speaking at the St Asaph diocesan conference of

1878 he declared:

> The old Rector dies. The church is out of repair, and the new Rector, … applies to our layman for a subscription without going into details as to the work to be done; he gives his money, and perhaps does not enquire further. On the re-opening of the church what does he find? The old square pew, where he had so often lolled, if not slumbered – has disappeared, and is replaced by long pews without doors, cushioned and comfortable enough, but without a high back against which to lean the head. The pulpit stands in the corner instead of the middle of the central aisle; the communion table is covered with a highly decorated cloth …, the choir is in surplices and has seats in the chancel – hymns of praise and thanksgiving are substituted for the miserable version of the Psalms by Tate and Brady.[164]

A caricature perhaps, but not entirely untrue, for as church restoration became fashionable and was probably seen by the hierarchy as a sign of a successful parish, the wealthy gentry and industrialists saw fit to contribute to the cost, possibly as a sign of their social conscience, but perhaps too as a means of displaying their wealth.

Bishop Thirlwall of St Davids encouraged these new arrangements. "I trust," he wrote, "I am not apt to overrate the importance of such externals, or to confound them with the essentials of religion," but "a high degree of architectural beauty is perfectly consistent with the purest simplicity of our reformed worship." He contrasted this new style to the "slight, paltry, unsightly edifices" of earlier days, occasioned by bad taste and false economy.[165] In his first visitation charge of 1877, Bishop Basil Jones enthused about the contribution of the ecclesiologists and the Oxford Movement, which had adopted their ideology, to the standard of church architecture.[166] By the 1890s, however, most churches had been rebuilt or restored in this approved style, so that Dean John Owen could suggest that the Church's zeal for decorum and dignity in the sanctuary was a valuable example to all the Christians of Wales.[167] And thus we have inherited this picture of the ecclesiological Gothic church as the very image of how a church building should be.

A NECESSARY COMFORT

It was this century which desired comfort, and thus heating systems were often installed and gas lighting introduced. The latter applied almost exclusively to town churches, where there was a gas supply, but it permitted an evening service to take place, often to compete against Nonconformity. Candles were too expensive for most churches, and oil lamps not particularly satisfactory, though these were used at Penmaen Church, Monmouthshire, in the 1890s and probably beyond.[168] A few churches possessed chandeliers, as did Welshpool (where they remain in situ), St Harmon's, Presteigne and Meifod.[169] For many rural churches the only occasion when candles were required was at the Plygain service, and many parishes asked each member of the congregation to bring their own with them.

Though it was argued in 1812 that heating was required at Chepstow Church to take off the damp and render the church more comfortable, finances prevented this amenity until 1824 when one stove was provided.[170] Older churches might be excluded from such comfort, but new churches generally had them installed as part of the building contract. Thus the new church at Llanymynech built in 1843 was provided with two large and unsightly stoves.[171] Older churches eventually obtained their own form of heating. One system was at Selattyn where in 1805 a heating pit was built in the churchyard below the east window, allowing a flue to run down through the aisle to the tower, from whence it ascended to a chimney.[172] Another was Myddfai, which possessed a number of stoves in 1815 and yet another Llandinam, though it was said to be inefficient, especially as it was placed under the west gallery.[173] The pew renters provided three coal fired stoves for Wrexham Church by 1844, but the difficulties of collecting the costs from these people meant they had not been used for two seasons.[174] Llandrinio paid £5.10s. for its stove in 1839, though it was regarded as useless by 1846, but not replaced until 1896.[175] Marchwiel did not obtain a heating system until 1891.[176] Joseph Bailey paid for a hot water system of heating at Llangatwg Church in the 1840s, allowing the parish clerk to spend his Sundays in a warm church to cook his dinner on the vestry fire.[177] Economy generally prevailed, so that the coal stove in Berriew Church was only lit at the end of November.[178] Many disliked these stoves, as often their pipe work and chimneys disfigured the church. The ecclesiologists maintained that they never gave sufficient heat save when they set a church on fire! A well attended church, it was argued, needed no heat, and if that argument did not prevail it was maintained that the former church people were self denying, and went to church to pray rather than to be comfortable.[179]

When St Mary's Church, Swansea, was lit by gas in 1822, thirty-six outlets were provided in handsome brass supporters, so that every person was able to see to read as a result.[180] Gas was installed in Oswestry Church in 1824, with forty burners including lights at the entrance doors (though it was said that its smell was offensive),[181] Pwllheli Church in 1859,[182] St John's, Cardiff, in the 1820s (though by 1848 there were complaints it was insufficient to read by),[183] Llangatwg Church in 1871 (and replaced by electricity in 1938),[184] and Llanfairfechan Church had gas installed in 1877 instead of oil lamps, but the supply was not always dependable.[185] Bangor Cathedral received its gas lights in 1849, although since 1810 there had been two evening services.[186] Gas was not liked by the earlier ecclesiologists who regarded it as dangerous, and much preferred chandeliers filled with wax candles.[187] But economy took precedence against ascetic concerns.

A newspaper report on the re-opening of St David's Church, Merthyr Tydfil, in 1869 may indicate the impression people received from these refinements. An organ chamber had been built and the chancel enlarged and fitted with stalls for the choir. The nave, side aisles and chancel were laid down with encaustic tiles. The report continued:

> Besides this, the church has been furnished with new heating stoves, on Gurney's principle, which, if an opinion is to be formed from the state of it on Sunday, have answered thoroughly. But the greatest improvement of all is in the lighting. The effect of this is most beautiful. It consists of coronae running the whole length of the church from east to west. These are of the most costly description, being of lacquered brass, in blue and vermillion and gold, jewelled. The side lights are handsome gold and bronzed brackets, each having five lights. The gallery at the west end is lighted with six large standards of the same material, each throwing out five jets. Anything more brilliant than the effect of the whole we have never seen in any church. A tolerable opinion may be formed of this, when it is considered that there are no less than 253 jets of gas in the church.[188]

We end this chapter on a more mundane note. The Breconshire parish of Tretower obtained an umbrella stand in 1885. A writer in the archdeaconry magazine declared the umbrella to be a most necessary piece of equipment for the worshippers of that county. It was left outside the church at one's peril, but it compromised one's comfort if placed in one's pew.[189]

We must now move on to consider another burning issue (sometimes all too literal) of that day, the pew question before studying the restoring and rebuilding of these churches and the building of new churches from the Victorian era onwards.

CHAPTER THREE THE QUESTION OF THE PEW

We have already noted the desire to improve church buildings in order to offer the worshippers increased comfort and even in some instances a dry interior. With the morning service lasting for two hours and more this was becoming a necessity by the early nineteenth century, especially as many parishioners were being drawn to Nonconformity with its more comfortable chapels and warmer services. Yet another obstacle remained, namely the lack of adequate seating in the churches. This was not simply because of the general increase in the population, or the growth of new communities in the industrialised areas where there was limited church accommodation for the new arrivals, but because of the appropriated pew, and to a lesser extent, the rented pew. Another issue was that there were a number of churches where parts of the building were in private ownership and thus unavailable to the parishioners in general.

The legal position of the pew was a complicated one. The duty of allocating seats in the church belonged to the diocesan bishop. It was his consistory court which issued faculties or licenses allowing individuals to build their own pews, known as faculty pews, though this was a limited and expensive option. The courts also heard the many disputes which resulted from the allocation or placing of pews. The bishop delegated the allocation of pews to the churchwardens of the parish, who were required by ecclesiastical law to provide seating for all parishioners and to seat them in the order of their social rank. However, these seats, including faculty pews, were linked not to individuals or a family, but to a house or farmstead. The chancel was reserved for the rector of the parish, whether clerical or lay, though the patron of the parish, if resident and the vicar were customarily allowed to be seated there.[1]

In all probability, most churchwardens, who served for a year, were ignorant of this duty. Few, for this reason or for the desire not to offend, saw fit to reallocate the seating of a church, a contentious issue in any case, so that the pews or seats allocated to houses became regarded as in the ownership of the householder, who saw them as their private property and believed they had the right to their exclusive use, even if they did not use them on a regular basis or occupied only a part of the pew. Some were even rented out or even sold.[2] Wardens were later reminded that if they permitted pew holders to repair their appropriated pews, they might obtain proprietary rights, equivalent to a faculty, which gave undisputed rights and was extremely difficult to challenge.[3] If John Price, rector of Llanfigan, alleged in 1890 that some pew holders had given orders that their pews were not to be entered even if they were unoccupied, they were simply following a long tradition.[4]

This position meant that the number of seats available for the more recent inhabitants was limited, especially in the fast-growing towns. In addition, as houses were split up into tenements or rented out, the question as to who was entitled to the pews allocated to these properties became acute: was it the owner, the tenant or tenants, or even the sub-tenants? Not infrequently the house owner rented out the pew to an outside party, although in law the pew belonged to the inhabitants of that property. Hence, many parishioners were unable to obtain pews for themselves in the parish church. They had three options. They could make use of the free seats, which were designed for those of such a low status that they would never be given seats of their own. These free seats, generally mean benches and sometimes marked with the words "for the poor", were placed in inconvenient areas and were often of spartan comfort. Alternatively they could find accommodation in a chapel or simply remain at home. Richard Venables of Clyro in the 1860s noted that many farmers who lacked their own pews refused to sit in the gallery, probably amongst their labourers, and were presumably lost to the Church.[5] The Cambridge Camden Society, which led the agitation against the pew system, was scathing in its criticism. It was unjust that one man could shut himself up in one pew when many could find no room at all; the system made a distinction between the rich and the poor; the pews often hid the altar, and some had been fitted up as drawing rooms.[6] In Liverpool it was considered that fifty per cent of seats were not occupied,[7] while a speaker at the Manchester Church Congress of 1863 argued that a church could be only half filled but the pew system meant that the other worshippers remained unseated.[8] It was even suggested that half the population of England and Wales were deprived of seating in their parish churches because of the appropriated pew system.[9]

A writer in a Cardiff newspaper of 1849 complained that the pews in the parish church were illegally held and illegally locked, while dozens of parishioners, including the writer and his family, all of whom had paid the church rate for that parish, were driven to dissenting places of worship. The previous Sunday some pews were crowded but others were empty because they were locked. If the wardens had done their duty and properly allocated the pews then there would be accommodation for most of those anxious to obtain seats.[10] Another writer pointed out that in that same church several large pews, with accommodation for six to ten people, were occupied by one person, while others were kept away from their parish church for want of a pew.[11] The chapels were crowded in Newtown with people who would attend the church had there been accommodation for them, wrote its curate in 1819.[12] At Hay hardly one quarter of the 500 seats were available as free seats. It was stated in 1828 that these seats were generally full and more parishioners would attend if they could be accommodated.[13]

The Victorian Church argued incessantly about the pew system. It might be argued that many church restorations were carried out in order to remove the existing high backed pews and replace them with what was termed "free and open" pews or benches, which meant that all seats would be held in common, save for the faculty pews. This was in accordance with the Ecclesiological Movement, which also wished for the chancel to be utilised for the choir. By extending the accommodation in this way and ending the hierarchy of seating it was hoped that parishioners would no longer revert to Nonconformity or remain as unchurched people, and would feel free to worship in their own parish church.

As Professor I. G. Jones comments in a study of church restorations in north Cardiganshire, "unfit for divine service" was an excuse to enable the incumbent to get rid of these pews or of a cluttered-up chancel.[14] In a printed address to his Gresford parishioners, Robert Wickham noted the new district of Gwersyllt which had been taken from his parish in 1854. While one evil had been remedied, he almost suggested another remained. Even though two new churches had been created, there was still an insufficiency of sittings for the poor in the parish church. He hinted that this was due to the appropriated pews which meant that those without seats of their own who came to the church would have difficulty in finding accommodation "where they would not be disturbed", presumably by others claiming them. This, he argued, needed to be remedied by a rearrangement of the church to make it sufficient for the whole population. It would need the expenditure of a great deal of money and would require much good temper and Christian disinterestness.[15] In his charge to the Archdeaconry of St Asaph in the following year Wickham made his appeal wider. Advocating the abolition of the pew appropriations he asked the clergy not to insist hastily on disturbing long-existing arrangements, "but by friendly representations, wherever an opportunity occurs, we should endeavour to raise up a better spirit." The mischief of the estranged poor from the services of the Church of their Fathers should be spelt out in a Christian temper, "as men who are influenced by no feelings but a desire to discharge our duty in promoting the common good", even though old-fashioned notions would delay for a time this much desired measure.[16]

Archdeacon Crawley of Monmouth in his visitation Charge of 1849, having expressed his concern at those who painted their names onto pews in various churches in order to claim private possession, often with the sanction of the churchwardens, warned these wardens against the evil of those whose selfishness in asserting their so-called rights of possession excluded "others whose claims to be accommodated are equal to their own". By this he meant their poorer neighbours, who, thrust into aisles and corners where they could neither see nor hear aright, eventually withdrew to "other places of worship, where, with the wisdom of the serpent, more attention has been paid to their suitable accommodation". He suggested that in those churches where the poor were poorly seated or even excluded because of the way pews were arranged or appropriated, the remedy lay in re-seating the church and removing the "over-grown pews", thus providing more room, or even to enlarge it.[17]

In addition Dean Bonnor frequently spoke against the evils of this "pew system". In a sermon at the reopening of Gresford Church after its restoration he expressed his delight that the pew system had been discontinued there as it was oppressive and injurious to the best interests of the Church. The same applied to Ruthin, Mold and Wrexham churches. Ten years previously no one would have predicted such a change for in these and other towns there had been a strong prejudice against free and open seats.[18]

While there were many who defended the existing system of appropriated pews, there was another and far stronger movement against them. The defenders of the system argued that the wealthy and influential pew-holders would desert the church if they lost their private pews, or if they had to sit amongst the poor they might be repelled by their smell, habits and verminous bodies. The poor were too independent to come when they were not wanted, and if the seats were free and open then families might be split up. A speaker at the Bath Church Congress of 1873 argued that the pew system protected the sittings from strangers who came from other parishes; promoted regular attendance; enabled the minister to check who was present or absent; enabled servants to be seated; kept younger persons together rather than being scattered around the building, and avoided "a distressing and incongruous" assortment of worshippers, meaning rich and poor placed together. In addition the old system encouraged a feeling of attachment, allowed the claims of age and physical infirmity, and permitted families to sit together.[19] Another speaker at the Stoke on Trent Congress alleged that farmers believed the pews had been appropriated to farms and would leave the Church if these "rights" were discontinued.[20] A further speaker, after suggesting that if the seats were all free there would be an unseemly rush to get to the better seats, argued that the problem would be resolved if the poor man's seat was as good as that of the rich man, but then alleged that the possibility of doing good to the irregular few would probably cause the dissatisfaction of the church-going many. For the well-to-do classes pews were almost a necessity to secure the regular attendance and comfort of their families. He ended by asserting that the pew system ensured that people did not become religious wanderers or spiritual vagrants but had a home in a specific church. Nevertheless, this speaker accepted that unoccupied seats should be made available to those without accommodation of their own.[21]

By 1876 another argument was being used, typified by a letter signed by "The vicar of a Free and Open Church", who was obviously disillusioned by this new system. On special occasions, such as festivals, the regular worshippers would be crowded out by those attracted by a special preacher or a famous choir. Equally, if the poor were mixed in with the general congregation, they would feel out of place with their poverty-stricken garments, especially when they had seen "garments carefully drawn aside lest they should be soiled by their contact." Being sensitive, they would not come again unless they could sit by themselves.[22]

Those who argued against the system did so generally on the grounds that the parish church was the church of all the parishioners, all of whom were entitled to seats within it, and that the Church as a national Church should place no restrictions and allow no social divisions within its buildings. The poor, with whom Christ identified, were as much entitled to seats as those who had appropriated or rented seats reserved for them. Sadly, they were excluded from many churches or placed in dark and draughty corners on uncomfortable benches.[23] This, declared Bishop Phillpotts of Exeter made "the very worship of God an occasion of injustice to man – of usurpation of the rights of the poor" who had been robbed of their rightful heritage.[24] The poor, declaimed Archdeacon Wickham, were the chief sufferers of this system. This ought not to be so, for no private rights were allowed in the church unless obtained through a faculty. However, custom had overridden law in this case, but the churchwardens' powers, delegated to them by the bishop, to reassign the pews could not be taken away.[25] Referring to an earlier judgement of Sir John Nichol, the archdeacon pointed out that "all the pews in the parish church are the common property of the parishioners, who are entitled to be seated orderly and conveniently, so as best to provide for the accommodation of all." He, again, drew attention to the waste of space occasioned by the old-fashioned pews and argued that additional sittings would be made available if the seats were rearranged and reconstructed. He also alleged that where pews had been exchanged for open seats, the proportion of "attendants from among the labouring population" had increased.[26]

A petition against the appropriation of seats in a rebuilt church addressed to the Incorporated Church Building Society stated that the system fostered pride and earthly-mindedness and gave rise to bad feelings, as by providing for the wealthy it drove away the poorer members of Christ's body, who were denied the ordinances of religion and who saw the "free" pews as an insult rather than a favour, and thus encouraged schism and promoted dissent.[27] Furthermore, it was suggested that the pew system was wasteful of space and more people could be accommodated in an open church, presumably by chairs or benches, which would also remove a barrier against many parishioners attending their parish church through want of seats. It was argued that one church that held 280 with a pew system now accommodated 400 through using open benches.[28]

Others asked how could the clergy request people to come to Church when there were no seats available for them. Far better to allocate seats as people arrived in church rather than allowing families to appropriate pews in advance for themselves.[29]

Various expedients were made to provide more accommodation or make use of the existing pews without having to resort to a whole scale revamping of the existing pews or their removal in favour of uniform benches. At Hay and St James', Swansea, all seats were declared free when the church bell had stopped; others adopted a policy of "first come, first served", and Bishop Thirlwall speaking in Convocation argued that the wardens should assign the seats from Sunday to Sunday.[30] Frederick Temple, when bishop of Exeter, advised one of his incumbents in 1871 to persuade those with appropriated pews, often left either empty or half-full, to allow the unused sittings to be utilised on a temporary basis.[31] Exhaustive enquiries took place to ensure that those who held appropriated seats were entitled to them,[32] and in other cases the pews were re-ordered and sometimes cut-down to make them more orderly and to enable more people to be seated. Galleries were built to provide additional accommodation, as at Ruthin and Welshpool, and often to offset the cost, their pews were rented.[33]

Other parishes, whose vestries found themselves unable because of vested interests to declare their churches free and open, and so maintained the appropriated pew allowing a church to be technically "full" although in reality half empty, built a chapel of ease. This happened at Oswestry and Welshpool, Cardiff and in numerous other town parishes. At Oswestry where 252 pews were capable of holding 950 people, all of which were taken, the 100 free places were on narrow benches in the centre of the aisle, nailed against the existing pews, exposed to draughts and when occupied these benches obstructed the pew-holders from getting into their pews. These free sittings provided for only one in sixty of the population, but in addition there were many families who wished to obtain their own pews, and who presumably objected to sitting with the poor. The new chapel of ease, opened in 1837, sat 700 worshippers, with 400 of the sittings being free. A re-ordering of the parish church might have eliminated this need for a chapel of ease.[34] At Welshpool the appropriation of pews required the building of Christ Church in 1845 as a chapel of ease for the labouring classes, though it seems clear from attendance figures that the number of worshippers at both churches could have been accommodated in the parish church.[35]

As a result of these concerns many church restorations dealt with these hereditary pews, and attempted to reseat parishioners in either free and open pews or alternatively in uniformed pews which could be made available for the use of others if required. Edward Smart did this at Henllan during his time there (1840-76) and ensured that the pulpit and reading desk were placed in more convenient places.[36] Some pulpits, as we noted earlier, had been placed in such a way that they obscured the chancel from the nave of the church. In his 1851 Charge, Bishop Ollivant noted that in the previous six years fifteen churches had been repaired in his diocese and "reseated".[37] This occurred at Margam under the restoration paid for by the Talbot family, when it was said that Theodore Talbot insisted on beginning the work by demolishing the squire and parson's pews saying "there must be no vested interest here".[38] At Welshpool, even before the church was restored, the difficulties of allocating pews to the new houses being built led to a resolution of 1866 that all the seats should be free and unappropriated, though this was not done until the church was heavily restored in 1870.[39]

At Montgomery in the 1860s over 105 houses in the town were without pews or any right of having sittings in the church, though twenty-four of these houses were rented from £10 onwards per year, and there were less than forty free sittings (exclusive of the gallery). A faculty issued by the diocesan chancellor for the restoration of the church permitted the annulment of all previous faculties regarding pews, and also the replacement of the existing pews with open sittings, though these were to be allocated to those who had had previous sittings and then presumably to others. It was clear that the benches provided far more sittings than the former pews.[40]

We may offer some further illustrations. Hicks Owen of Tremeirchion, who died in 1886, was eulogised in his obituary for providing heating and lighting in his church and for removing the old pews and substituting modern seats for them.[41] The 1850 restoration of Cowbridge Church ensured that the floors were levelled and the pews "equalized" from "the unsightly and irregular manner in which they stood in former years".[42] The restoration of Llanfair Duffryn Clwyd Church of 1872 saw new open seats replace the old box pews, together with a chancel screen and stalls.[43] A newspaper account of the reopening of Llangwm Church in the diocese of St Asaph after its restoration of 1874 noted that the old appropriated family pews had, with the consent of their owners, been replaced by open pitch pine seats, all of which were free and unappropriated.[44] A further report emphasised the good sense of the parishioners of Chirk for sweeping away their former old and narrow pews and replacing them with low and open seats in its restoration of 1878.[45] The restoration of Llanblethian and Llysworney Churches in the 1890s also replaced the former pews with new seats.[46] Although Yates notes that in some cases a compromise had to be allowed and seats assigned to families, the end result was often that the clutter of pews was replaced by a clutter of benches.[47]

Another debate concerned the replacement of pews with chairs, often based on a continental model which allowed it to be turned around and used as a kneeling desk.[48] But the use of chairs was virtually unknown in Wales until the turn of the twentieth century and then only in newly built churches, though they had been introduced into some of the Cardiff Tractarian churches in the 1880s, and later at Presteigne following its 1891 restoration, at St Mary's, Swansea, following its 1895 rebuilding, and in 1907 at Llanelli, Carmarthenshire, again following its rebuilding.[49]

The replacement of pews by open and free sittings, or even by a more uniform arrangement of pews, was not an easy matter and sometimes led to different problems. The consent of the pew holders had to be obtained, and in addition there was another problem, as Bishop Ollivant made clear in 1860. In his diocese it was difficult to obtain funding for the restoration of churches, with the result that some individuals offered £50 on condition that a pew was provided for their exclusive use and as they saw it as their private property they felt able to rent out to other parties even though this was illegal.[50] Another fear was that people would form a habit of using a particular seat and gradually introduce their own cushions, books and carpet, and regard it as their own.[51] That this happened is noted by Archdeacon Wickham in his 1866 Charge, who made clear that instances of this had occurred in the diocese of St Asaph. In many cases the only advantage obtained through this reseating was the additional space gained, for "[t]hose who enjoyed appropriated seats before, have stipulated for, and obtained an equal number of sittings; and the seats so allotted are taken possession of and cushioned in a manner which cannot but seem to forbid intrusion."[52] Even when a district church was established those who held pews in the parish church even though living in the new district, provided they did not attend the new church, could retain their right of seating in the mother church.[53]

THE SELLING AND RENTING OF PEWS

Another reason for the shortage of accommodation was the rented pew. It was illegal to rent pews unless permitted by a faculty to do so, generally when a gallery or extension had been built as a means of raising the money required. Churches built with parliamentary funding, as described later, were provided with pews which were rented to parishioners as a means of securing the minister's stipend. Although this was meant to be a temporary affair it soon acquired a permanent status. Other pews, when a vacancy occurred or when they were no longer required, should have been reallocated by the wardens, but all too often they were sold to the highest bidder instead, either by the wardens or by the pew holder himself.

Churchwardens, generally unaware of the illegality of their action, sometimes rented out or sold seats when a seat or pew became vacant. At Llanfyllin in 1743 the wardens offered a vacant seat for the sum of £5,[54] though when Eglwys Fach Church was rebuilt in the late 1780s, the bishop of St Asaph permitted the wardens to sell some of the seats as a means of raising the money required. Each purchaser paid five or seven guineas and was required to build his own seat, and a ballot was held to distribute the space available, though it appears there were some disputes about encroachments on other pews.[55] For some reason various pews at St Mary's, Swansea, were rented, and its vestry resolved in 1847 to equalise their rents, which were used for church expenses. Some had been let as low as 4s.6d., but others, in a less advantageous part of the church, were much higher. The new rate was an annual rent of 10s. for a pew for five or six people, depending on its position.[56] Records indicate the sale or letting of numerous pews at St Mary's Church, Welshpool and some were described in sale catalogues, such as in 1825: "a commodious seat in the middle aisle of Pool Church, within a short distance of the pulpit, capable of holding at least eight persons".[57]

Those who had pews appropriated to their houses were also inclined to let them to others if they did not require them. A correspondent to *Bye-Gones* recorded that in the 1840s his grandfather, though he had a right to a pew in Wem Church, let it for two guineas a year as he attended a Nonconformist chapel.[58] Henry Webber, a recent resident of Cardiff, had made use of a pew at St John's Church, until he was informed it was the private property of another person who required him to pay rent for it. This he refused to do, and as the wardens had not offered him alternative seating, he and his family no longer attended that church.[59] This private and "indecent" renting of pews was thoroughly condemned by Archdeacon Wickham in his 1855 Charge. It was illegal, and wardens should realise if the allocated pew was not required it reverted to the parishioners, and the wardens should place another person in it. This traffic in pews, he concluded, ought not to be permitted.[60]

Unfortunately, the Church Building Acts permitted churches built under its auspices to rent out pews as a means of obtaining an income for its minister. Though this was meant to be a temporary arrangement until other sources of income could be obtained, it became permanent due to the bureaucracy of the Ecclesiastical Commissioners, who declined to allow churches to abolish these pew rents by refusing to offer them any other augmentation, as noted later.[61] An estimate of 1863 suggested that nationally nine out of ten new churches were built with this provision for rented pews,[62] although it was only in 1857 with Lord Blandford's Act that churches built under the provisions of the Church Building Acts were required to have half the sittings free, and as convenient and well-placed position as those which were not free.[63] Such free sittings were resisted by some English bishops; Samuel Butler suggesting the poor would be more likely to attend the Church's worship if they had a seat of their own for which they paid a small rental.[64] The income was never as substantial as was anticipated: at Pontblyddyn Church, built in 1836, it amounted to £30 from its 140 rented seats (266 were free). At Gwernaffield Church, built in 1838, there were 334 free seats out of a total of 526 but of these 120 were in the gallery, while the church was built without a central aisle.[65] The free seats at St Paul's, Newport, were described by a later vicar as "skeleton benches".[66]

The Incorporated Church Building Society also gave grants for repairing and restoring churches on condition that a percentage of the seats were reserved for the poor. Cowbridge church received a grant of £150 on condition that 258 of its 645 seats were set apart and declared to be free and unappropriated for the use of the poor for ever. But those for whom these seats were intended objected to the word "poor" as it suggested inferiority and poverty whereas in the House of God all worshippers should be seen as equal. As a result the wording was omitted.[67] As "A Pauper Clergyman" wrote, it was no wonder these free seats were generally empty when to sit in one of them was an admission of pauperism.[68]

Archdeacon Thomas Williams in his 1852 Charge expressed his sadness about the existence of these rented pews, and while he understood their necessity, he believed that it hindered the "true parochial system" of the Church for all parishioners.[69] Ollivant in his 1863 Charge noted that many churches in the mining districts of his diocese were unable to impose pew rents due to the poverty of these areas and thus they lacked financial stability.[70] A writer in the *Ecclesiastic* expressed a further concern. A minister paid partly by the congregation might feel sufficiently obligated to his congregation to tone down the church teaching he wished to impart or avoid subjects that might be controversial for the sake of peace and his income.[71] And if he failed to attract a congregation or the amount from pew rents was minimal he could be "pauperised", to use Best's term.[72] The system had its defenders, as might be expected, who argued that pew rents were a perfectly legitimate source of revenue, if properly controlled, as the poor were not excluded.[73]

James Francis, incumbent of the newly built St Paul's Church, Newport, was all too aware of these difficulties. All the rentable pews in his church had been let at the same rate, which meant that while those near to the pulpit had been let, those at a distance remained unlet. The pews had been allocated under the terms of the various acts, so that those who had subscribed to the building of the church received preference in their distribution. People, it was alleged, would never pay the same for a pew in a remote part of the church as for those in the best situations. By 1840 Francis's income was so poor he was tempted to take an additional curacy, especially as it seems that the church expenses were also taken from the rental income, which should have been his. Queen Anne's Bounty was unable to assist as he had an income from the pew rents, and though he received a small augmentation from the Ecclesiastical Commissioners, further requests for assistance were declined. His successors found that the existence of these pew rents, always an uncertain figure, prevented them from claiming any further assistance; the Commissioners writing in 1864, when J. Tinson Wrenford as vicar wished to end the system of pew rents, informed him that it would be a dangerous assumption to end these rents in the expectation they might make a grant to offset such a voluntary loss of income.[74]

Many churches, where it was possible to do so, phrased out these pew rents, some regarding their existence as making the House of God into a place of merchandise. Many chose the alternative of an offertory in order to obtain money for church purposes.[75] This occurred at Hawarden in 1872, when Stephen Gladstone, its vicar, hoped it would lead to a greater reverence in the worship.[76] It was noted that at Wrexham, for example, where the pew rents had been abolished and an offertory taken instead, the small income lost had been offset by a gain of £250.[77] But the offertory system was resisted by many. It was only in the pew-rented churches that the poor in their free seats could have the Gospel preached to them for nothing. If an offertory was taken such people would "be haunted by the perpetual begging-box".[78]

At St Paul's, Sketty, the best seating in the church had been subject to pew rents, imposed to provide a substantial part of the incumbent's stipend. Paradoxically, John Coke Fowler, later a warden of this church, published in 1844 a book on church pews in which he pleaded for their abolition as exclusive pews tended to expel or keep away the poor. With the disestablishment of the Church in Wales in 1920, and the introduction of a fixed scale of stipends for clergy by the central body, the reason for these pew rents disappeared, but in was not until 1926 that all the seats in this church, with the exception of one reserved for the dowager Lady Swansea, were declared free and open.[79] Nonconformist chapels often rented out their pews, but by the 1900s most of these had been abolished. Argyle Chapel, in Swansea, was late in doing so in 1923.[80]

What again needs to be stressed is that the clergy took the leading part in initiating these changes, persuading their congregations that provision should be made for, and respect given, to the poor, and emphasising that the system of the appropriated pew was injurious to the Church's mission as well as to their own ministry. It was no easy task, and sometimes rather deviously accomplished, but the fact they succeeded speaks well of their courage, faith and consistency.

CHAPTER FOUR: RESTORATION AND REBUILDING

By the mid-nineteenth century the older churches, many with limited accommodation for their parishioners, were felt to be inadequate for a new age, an age of railways which allowed new and cheaper materials to be obtained, and an age deeply influenced by the ecclesiological movement with its desire to revert to a medieval style of building where the elevated sanctuary was reserved for the priest and the former high pews torn down for something better. The movement was noted in chapter two. It became the age when churches were restored, rebuilt, and new ones built for emerging communities. It was a costly exercise even in an age of wealth.

How could the Church have God's judgment looming over it, as some disestablishers avowed, when it was so active in repairing and renewing its places of worship? asked Bishop Short in 1851.[1] The reconstruction movement was not as fast as he anticipated, though by the late 1860s it was in full flow. Nigel Yates, however, points out that it was not until the early 1850s that the ecclesiological movement started to influence the design of churches, and ensured its principles became *de rigueur*.[3] In a study of Caernarfonshire churches during the nineteenth century, M.L. Clarke suggested that many churches were restored not because they were in poor condition, but because it had become the fashion – a sort of keeping up with the "ecclesiastical Joneses".[3] He also noted that in this county, as indeed elsewhere, most of these rebuilds and restorations were accomplished in a fourteenth century style.[4] To this may be added Bail Clarke's assertion that the ecclesiastical architects of this period endeavoured to wipe out all post-Reformation work in churches.[5] It was Dean Bonnor of St Asaph who summed up the expectations of many that these restorations (and rebuildings) would bring about a higher and more devoted tone of service, though he feared that such restorations might lead to an advanced form of ritualism.[6]

National figures indicated that between 1840-76 1,727 new churches had been built and 7,144 rebuilt, restored or enlarged at a total cost of over twenty-five million pounds. During the period 1818-70 the Incorporated Church Building Society had given, nationally, 5,617 grants totalling £770,500.[7] This society aimed to be a catalyst and stimulus to local giving, ensuring that "individuals of wealth and station" should be involved in building "at their own cost, and on no mean scale, edifices to the honour of God". Rebuilding also came into its orbit if it enabled more accommodation to be provided.[8] A strong attachment to the parish church was reviving in the hearts of people, suggested Bishop Copleston in 1848, when noting the progress in restoring, rebuilding and reseating churches.[9] But was he correct? The clergy and the squirarchy were generally behind the movement, but one suspects the enthusiasm of the people for change was not so obvious, a fact endorsed by their general lack of enthusiasm and financial contributions to these projects.[10] Yet Copleston's remark was endorsed by his successor, Ollivant, three years later, when he praised the contribution to this work made by the Diocesan Building Society, formed in 1845, which gave small grants and advice to the parishes concerned. Its main financial support came however from that same section of the community.[11] Their support meant that by 1860 Ollivant was able to claim that most of the churches in his diocese were in a condition of "decent propriety": 24 new churches had been built, 23 old ones rebuilt, and 40 restored and given additional accommodation.[12]

The work of church restoration, declared Bishop Basil Jones of St Davids in 1880, continued in full flow,[13] so that by 1884 *Forms of Prayer for certain Special Occasions authorised for use in the Diocese of St David's* included services for laying the foundation stone of a new church, opening a mission room, and reopening a church after restoration. In Radnorshire, for example, 31 churches were completely rebuilt and 16 restored between 1870 and 1900.[14] The work had gained such momentum that when Selattyn Church was restored in 1891 it was said to have been one of the few churches in the diocese of St Asaph which had remained unrestored.[15]

Many of the promoters of these restoration projects issued printed appeals requesting assistance from all and sundry. One typical example relates to Llanelian Church near Ruthin and was issued in 1889. The roof had fallen in and the discomfort in winter was intense; the pews were of the old high and boxed-up fashion, inconvenient for worship and preventing decency and heartiness in devotion, and the cost £750.[16]

ENLARGING THE BUILDING

In order to accommodate an increasing population many churches built an additional aisle or transept, or, as noted before, added galleries to the interior. New transepts were built in 1821 and 1828 at Selattyn Church to provide additional seating.[17] The old church at Llanddulas was enlarged in 1841, probably with assistance from the Incorporated Society, and as a result 110 sittings were declared to be free and unappropriated for ever.[18] A letter from John Poole of Llandysilio of 1854 to his rector, Bishop Short of St Asaph who held the parish in commendam, noted that the additional seats obtained from erecting a gallery ten years earlier was now insufficient for those wishing to attend. The local landowner was willing to assist in extending and repairing the church if the bishop permitted. Though the archdeacon drew the attention of the parishioners to the dilapidated state of the building the following year, nothing was done, save for slight repairs, until 1866, when it was decided to build an entirely new church.[19] Nerquis Church was heavily restored and enlarged by a new chancel and north aisle with a baptistery under the tower. Heating and new lighting were introduced. When it was reopened in 1888 the chancel was embellished with gifts to make it fit for ecclesiological use.[20] A new aisle was added to Llansanffraid Church in 1892,[21] and at Oystermouth the restoration of the church in 1913 added a new chancel and nave, leaving the former building as an aisle.[22]

A note of warning was sounded, however, by Archdeacon Crawley of Monmouth in his 1849 Charge. He expressed concern about additions made to a church, such as a vestry, aisle, gallery, or other alterations, "which have often been executed with little judgment or propriety to the disfigurement of the whole fabric." Such works required the consent of the bishop or a faculty, and Crawley declared that where "incongruous additions and alterations" had been made without the design having been approved and consent obtained, he would ensure proceedings were made against the wardens in the consistory court and the "offensive structure" would be removed or altered to be more in harmony with the building.[23]

Parishioners too might feel that an extension was not required, as happened at Marchwiel in 1828 when a north transept was added to the church at a cost of £411. A local farmer wrote to Squire Yorke's agent asking whether the tenants had to submit to the rector's desire to have the church made bigger or not. "There is a many of the parishioners as thinks the Church is Big enuff for the People in the Parish." His protest was not without self-interest, for one of his concerns was that some of the money required was being borrowed on land whose income was used to offset the poor rate, which would accordingly increase as a result of this loan.[24]

RESTORATION

Throughout the eighteenth century many churches were restored, or perhaps it might be better to say adapted to become preaching boxes. The appeals made via briefs for this work has been noted already. Marchwiel appears to have been restored during the 1770s, when Squire Philip Yorke of Erddig paid a substantial part of the cost. One, however, defaulted. Some years later there was concern that the steeple was unsafe, and when Squire Yorke gave a mighty sneeze an old man woke and assumed the steeple was collapsing and died of fright. It was rebuilt in 1789.[25] A further example is Llanidloes Church which went through a form of restoration in 1816 at a cost of £1,600. The aim was to make the church more comfortable, so the church was reseated with pews, but in the words of a later writer, was vandalised by incompetence.[26] Both Llanarthne and Llannon churches in Carmarthenshire were "restored" in the early nineteenth century and adapted to the "conventicle" style of building. In the first the arcade between the nave and south aisle was removed and the broad chamber that resulted was ceiled, and at Llannon the roof was also ceiled in order to make the church more comfortable.[27] As Yates suggests, many of these earlier "restorations" were in effect an attempt to make the pews more uniform and thus increase accommodation, as at Clynnog Fawr in 1827.[28]

One of the first restorations was at the priory church at Abergavenny in 1828. It was a drastic restoration, when the nave and north aisle were thrown into one and the arches which separated the two demolished. A new roof was provided, and galleries erected on four sides, with the pulpit and reading desk placed at the west end and the pews facing them. It was financed from a loan from the Public Works Loans Commissioners on the security of the rates, and from the sale of pews. By 1882 all this was old-fashioned, and the nave and north aisle were rebuilt.[29] Another early restoration was at Beddgelert in 1830, when the church was re-roofed, re-flagged, the altar raised slightly, and new seats and pews erected and paid for by a rate imposed upon the property of several landed proprietors. A later writer described this work as "vandalism", especially as the old woodwork was sold. A later restoration was carried out in an exemplary style.[30] A sum of £1,250 was required to restore Laugharne Church, rearrange its pews, and provide additional provision for the poor, described as scanty in 1854. In an appeal for assistance produced in 1856 it was noted that the church rates had produced £200, subscriptions given over a number of years amounted to £274, the Incorporated Society gave £125, Winchester Chapter as patrons offered £100 and the bishop of St Davids £50, but more was still needed.[31] A pamphlet was published in 1859 with the title "Our Village Wants a new Church", and gave a vivid description of Oystermouth Church as a place of dampness, discomfort and decay, ugly and dark, the floor of earth, the nave so narrow it was difficult to move in and out, the galleries congested, with a congregation assembling almost in risk of their lives. The funds collected were insufficient, and an appeal was made for assistance. Eventually part of the church was demolished and a new aisle added, new pews installed and the floors tiled.[32] A further restoration took place in 1913.

Restorations, as noted in the previous chapter on pews, generally saw the interior of the church gutted of its high-backed pews and replaced by benches, and wherever possible a proper ecclesiological style established. This happened in Sir Gilbert Scott's restoration of Betws Penpont, which also added an organ chamber and a baptistery under the tower.[33] St Fagan's Church, described as being in a ruinous state of decay with worshippers in some parts standing on bare earth, was restored in 1860 in the approved style, and in addition a heating apparatus was installed to render the church warm and comfortable in winter at a trifling expense; a matter clearly reported in the press.[34] In 1879 the church at Guilsfield was opened after its restoration. A spacious sanctuary with sedilia seats and a credence table had been created, the old ceiling taken down along with the two galleries, benches replaced the high backed pews, a new pulpit, screen and lectern had been installed along with choir stalls, the font moved to the west of the church and encaustic tiles placed in the aisles and chancel.[35] However, a similar restoration of 1877 at Llandrillo-yn-Edeirnion Church, near Corwen, produced a new chancel with the appropriate fittings and heating, but the seats were remodelled into open pews.[36] Kerry Church was said to be so dilapidated as to be insecure and unfit for the worship of God, and it was restored in 1882-3 at a cost of £3,005, in the approved ecclesiological style, the galleries removed as was the plaster ceiling, and with new seating, a reredos and a chancel screen.[37] Around the same time Mathern Church, Monmouthshire, was restored at a cost of £2,500. Some of its walls had to be rebuilt, the ceiling removed, a new east window installed, and the former pews replaced by benches.[38]

Llangatwg Church, Breconshire, was restored in 1885 when new seating was imposed, the west gallery demolished and the organ replaced by a new one in a different location. The cost was £2,500.[39] When Llanrhian Church, near Haverfordwest, was restored in 1891, the high-backed pews were replaced by fine oak benches, an oak chancel screen erected, and a heating apparatus installed.[40] One of the last major restorations of an old-fashioned church took place at Llanbeblig in 1910. Once again the "boxes" were replaced by comfortable seats, the plastered ceiling removed, the unsightly galleries taken away and the chancel revamped.[41] Orrin provides details of numerous churches in Glamorgan whose restoration enabled additional seating to be provided, including Coety, Cowbridge, Gilston, Llangyfelach, Newcastle, Newton Nottage, Pontarddulais, Porteynon, Pyle and Sully. In some of these projects the need to provide additional accommodation may have been the reason for the restoration as was the case at Newton Nottage and Peterston super Ely.[42]

It was probably no coincidence that the restoration of many churches took place after a new incumbent had been installed. Thus the restoration of Llanfair Duffryn Clwyd Church took place the year after Basil Morgan Jones became vicar in 1870. Once again the old pews were replaced, the west gallery removed, the oak roof exposed, and a new altar, pulpit and font together with choir stalls in the chancel, and a floor laid with encaustic tiles. What had once been a preaching box was now an ecclesiological church.[43] In similar fashion John David Davies, five years after his appointment as rector of Llanmadoc in 1860, restored that church. Parts of the building had to be taken down and rebuilt. The largest contribution came from his own pocket, but he changed the building from what he regarded as worst than the meanest hovel in his village to a church moulded to the latest liturgical fashion.[44] A new vicar of Llanfyllin was horrified when he saw his church in 1850. It had been rebuilt in a classical style of brick in 1708. Accordingly, when opportunity arose, he "normanised" the windows and arches of the church in 1863, gave the altar more prominence, and substituted open seats for the previous high backed pews, along with other improvements.[45]

The Church of St Mary, Welshpool, had undergone a major restoration in the 1770s, when the nave and two aisles were rebuilt and the interior, with its ceiled roof, was made into a preaching box with the pulpit and reading desk placed against the second pillar of the nave. A west gallery was provided and in all probability the pews were rebuilt in a more uniform manner at the expense of those to whom they had been appropriated. With an increase in population due to the flannel industry, galleries had been added and a new church built, and the dean and chapter of Christ Church, Oxford, as lay rectors, were persuaded after much haggling to rebuild the chancel described as being in "a crazy condition". With this new and improved work the rest of the building looked antiquated in its style, liturgically incorrect and it was agreed, after much opposition, that it should become a free and open church and the existing appropriations of pews swept away, thus allowing more accommodation. Again, this restoration of 1870 was led by a new vicar, John Edward Hill, and G.E. Street was appointed as architect. His proposals caused much controversy as some felt he was taking the Church in a Tractarian direction (especially the sanctuary with its "correct" furniture and the chancel with its new and elaborate choir stalls), though his proposal to demolish the two side galleries was defeated. Benches replaced the former pews, the flooring was readjusted so that the chancel and sanctuary were approached by a flight of steps, and much medieval work, including a two-storied porch, was destroyed. One third of the cost of over £4,000 was met by Lord Powis, but the response from the parishioners was not encouraging. Those who had given up their appropriated seats considered that was sufficient contribution (in some instances because they had paid £40 to £50 for them), and others were totally opposed to the scheme. Besides, John Hill as vicar had introduced Tractarian practices of which many disapproved.[46]

Local landowners often proved to be extremely generous when it was proposed to restore a church. Orrin notes that in the vale of Glamorgan the major if not the sole contributors to the restoration of many churches came from these people: he notes J. B. Bruce Pryce in respect of St Nicholas Church, Baroness Windsor for St Fagans, Mrs Traherne at St Hilary and the Turbervill family at Ewenny.[47] The Dyffryn Aled family paid half the £1,000 cost of restoring Llansannan Church in 1879,[48] and in the 1880s James Vaughan restored Llangynog Church, Breconshire, at his own expense.[49] Stephen Jackson, who became vicar of Llangynwyd in 1891, found the church in such a deplorable position – even though there had been a partial restoration in 1873 – that parts of the nave had to be rebuilt on their foundations and an unsafe gallery removed. The chancel was also refitted and the two box pews in it removed. Miss Olive Talbot of Margam paid for most of the work, £3,000, and though there was criticism that the work was out of sympathy with the older parts remaining, her generosity permitted a much more radical restoration than would have been the case otherwise.[50] The Talbot family also contributed well over half the cost of the restoration of Rhosili Church in 1891, when it was reroofed, and pitch pine benches introduced, along with an altar rail, new choir stalls, a tiled floor and heating.[51]

Bassaleg Church also benefited from the generosity of a landowner, in this case Lord Tredegar. In 1904 he paid £3,000 towards its restoration, including a new organ chamber and heating apparatus. The chancel was paid for by the Ecclesiastical Commissioners who had an interest in the parish. During the twelve months when the church was closed services were held in the National Schoolroom opposite.[52] (This was not uncommon as the work of restoration might take many months and in the case of Llanrhaeadr ym Mochnant Church four years.)[53] When Begelli Church was restored in 1886 services were authorised in the rectory barn, and at Clarbeston the schoolroom was temporarily licensed for public worship.[54])

But landowners might impose their own conditions in return for their contribution. When Thomas Briscoe, vicar of Holyhead, wished to restore St Cybi's Church in 1876 the local landowner, W.O. Stanley offered to pay £3,000 of the £5,000 estimated cost provided pews were reserved for the Penrhos servants and the Penrhos pew in the south transept retained, and that English services be held on alternative Sunday mornings. This was not to Briscoe's liking, but a vestry meeting, packed with Stanley's tenants and parishioners, including many Nonconformists, carried the poll for their landlord.[55] There were others, apart from landowners, who might be ready to assist in this work. In 1855 a frequent visitor to Llandudno, William Henry Reece, paid for the restoration of St Tudno's Church on the Great Orme, which had fallen into ruin.[56]

If an incumbent was a rector, he was generally responsible for the chancel of the church, and in any restoration or rebuilding would be expected to pay that proportion of the cost for the chancel. Thus Gilbert Harries, when the roof of Gelligaer Church collapsed in 1866 and a restoration work began, had to pay £500 from his own pocket for the necessary work on the chancel, which he found difficult to raise.[57] This was probably the reason why William Meyer, rector of St Lawrence, Pembrokeshire, and perpetual curate of St Edrin's, reacted with antagonism when Edward Peacock, a wealthy parishioner of St Lawrence and a retired cleric himself, found that church so dilapidated that he started to collect money for its restoration. The work had to wait until Meyer's death in 1875.[58]

Estimates of work required were always provisional. At Michaelston-super-Afan work was commenced in 1851, though the Incorporated Church Building Society was not amused when a transept was removed even though it was replaced by a north aisle. But the poor condition of the fabric escalated the costs by £400 to £1,100 causing William Thomas as vicar to search desperately for new donations.[59] When St Cadoc's Church, Cadoxton juxta Barry, was restored in 1885 the cost escalated from £315 to £600, though at least the new "low seats" which replaced the old box pews enabled people to view the altar.[60] The remarkable Chevalier Lloyd, as he was known, restored Llangurig Church at his own cost in 1880. But his initial estimate, partly due to the amount of stained glass he required, rose to £9,000, and so various economies had to be made and part of the work curtailed.[61] This was not unusual.

The example of Little Newcastle Church in Pembrokeshire indicated that unless strict adherence was made to the requirements of the Incorporated Church Building Society for its grant then that grant would be withdrawn. The church was in a dilapidated state with its north aisle in ruins and there was opposition in the parish for an enhanced rate to repair it. The approved plan showed five large box pews remaining with a number of the 106 free seats required for the grant in an aisle facing south in rising tiers. The vicar, Peter Davies Richardson, unfortunately gave way to the importunities of one of his farmers who wanted a box pew for himself in a place allocated for thirty other free places, and this was granted. The precedent permitted, other farmers required the same. Though it was claimed there were still sufficient free seats in the rebuilt north aisle, allowing the better folk to sit in the nave, and an excuse offered that if these pews had not been granted to these farmers they would have to sit with their servants and labourers, the grant of £25 was declined. Sadly, by 1870 the church was once again dilapidated as the lack of funds during this restoration had caused corners to be cut and inferior work allowed.[62]

Many of these restorations were held by a later generation to have been disastrous, destroying good medieval work and substituting sham-medievalism in its place. R.C.B. Oliver disputes Howse's assertion about this in respect of the churches in Radnorshire. While he accepts that some of the new work was in bad taste, he also pleads that as a result many churches were saved from ruin.[63] As early as 1845 Archdeacon Thomas Williams of Llandaff was decrying work that disfigured rather than adorned a restored church and spoke about "rude hands … slowly defacing the fingers of time".[64] There were protests about the "irreparable damage" done to Mold Church by Gilbert Scott in his 1856-7 restoration.[65] An influential churchwarden of St John's Church, Aberdare, William Thomas Lewis, a local colliery owner, objected to his vicar's plans for its restoration and resigned in the 1870s. He objected to the style proposed, presumably the replacement of pews with benches, and the amount of expenditure involved, together with a lack of consultation.[66] The restoration of Betws Cedewain Church in 1868 was said to have reduced it to a barn-like state of simplicity. The carved oak fittings were sold and the medieval font ejected to be used later as a pig's trough.[67] Bradney, in his history of Monmouthshire, notes that the churches at Llanwenarth, Llanelen, and Undy, for example, all suffered from an over-severe restoration.[68]

The restoration of Llanbadarn Fawr Church, near Aberystwyth, started in 1862, was denounced by Basil Jones, then archdeacon of York and a local landowner (later bishop of St Davids) as being more a rebuilding than a restoration, and he was particularly concerned with Seddon's proposals about the western arch and windows. He was able to prevent some of the proposed work but the mural paintings which adorned the church were destroyed by the restoration.[69] An official of the Incorporated Church Building Society, R.M. Blakiston, speaking at the 1885 St Davids diocesan conference, accepted that many churches had been badly restored in order to make them "spick and span". The difficulty, he suggested, was that with building work of many periods, it was not easy to find the right period style for the restoration.[70]

A debate at the same conference in 1891 produced further criticism. A layman, J.A. Doyle, suggested that a smaller work of restoration representing the genuine devotion of those who loved their church was far better than a more ambitious and substantial work which required "sheer importunity and undignified devices" to extort money from those with no direct personal interest in the scheme. He criticised those architects who believed that a certain architectural style was superior to all others, so that even a commonplace imitation of this style was seen as better than the genuine work of another time. The clergy too were criticised by Doyle for spending the money first and then begging for it afterwards. An Aberaeron layman, T. Davies, complained that too often a local architect was used rather than a specialist for the sake of economy. Llanddewi Aberarth Church was a case in point, where deal had been substituted for oak in the roof and furnishings, and common jerry builders' walls for the ancient stones.[71] In fact a number of clergymen acted as their own architects, such as J. Wynne Jones at Heneglwys and Trewalchmai in Anglesey, Peter Jones at Llanddona,[72] and John Parker at Llanmerewig in the 1830s and Llanyblodwel from the 1850s onwards, including the building of a tower and spire in 1855-6 at his own cost (of £1.400).[73] It is believed too that Thomas Walters, rector of Ystradgynlais, acted as his own architect and was probably clerk of works as well in the rebuilding of that church by 1861, particularly as the work was so idiosyncratic.[74]

A COMPLETE REBUILD

It is probably that many architects advised clergymen and wardens that the old church was either too dilapidated to be repaired, or the cost of repair and possibly adding a new transept or aisle to it was equal to the cost of a complete rebuild. In addition, the desire to shape the church to the latest ecclesiological fashions and provide increased accommodation, helped facilitate the decision to build a new church either on the existing site, involving the demolition of the old, or on a new site close by. The guidance given by the Incorporated Church Building Society, which gave grants towards the cost of these works, indicated and followed the liturgical fashion of the day.[75] At least one architect, Henry Kennedy, who did much work in Anglesey, rebuilt churches in a simplified 1840s style for those parishes with little money to spend.[76] In his history of Pwllheli, D.G.

Lloyd-Hughes almost hints that the reason for the rebuilding of St Peter's Church in 1886 was that the old church, opened in 1834, had such an elementary design with an interior likened to a barn, that it contrasted unfavourably with the Nonconformist chapels of the town. He also suggests that the vicar of the time had leanings towards the High Church and possibly wished for a more dignified and "correct" building.[77]

Newcastle Church, in Bridgend, is a case in point where a church required a total rebuild to accommodate more people. Its accommodation for a population of 1,239 was for 106 adults and 80 children, but all the seats were appropriated so there was no provision for the poorer part of the population who had to turn to other places of worship, that is, Nonconformity, while there were continual applications for seatings in the existing pews. In 1849 the church was demolished and a new one erected on its site, with 107 appropriated seats and 212 free seats plus the 80 seats for children, at a cost of £1,059, including gas fittings.[78]

In the 1860s a contributor to the *Church Builder* described an earlier visit to Llanfaenor, Monmouthshire, where he was horrified to see the church was akin to a dilapidated barn with the interior as pathetic as its exterior. Some years later, revisiting, he discovered in its stead "a pretty church, with porch, nave, chancel, and bell-gable, built of warn-coloured stone, with white stone dressings. I entered. There was nothing more to be desired: altar, lectern, handsome font, low open seats, all had been provided by the pious care of one [its new curate] whose taste and zeal will long be remembered in that neighbourhood; and better still, the church was crowded with a reverent congregation."[79] Here is the essence of the ecclesiological movement and its desire to restore the churches of the nation to an architectural and ecclesiastical purity, accompanied by the sober and pious devotion of its congregation.

Again, such rebuilds were not new. A detailed costing for a new church at Llangynog was presented to the Montgomeryshire Quarter Sessions in 1785, It involved the demolition of the old building, building a new one with cast iron windows, and furnishing it. The total cost was estimated at £1,016. 10s.[80] The old church of Merthyr Tydfil, far too small for the population, was demolished and a new one built on its site in 1806, with 282 free sittings, hardly sufficient for that growing town. The pew system remained, and galleries were built at a later date. The cost was £1,127, but the steeple proposed was not completed until 1825.[81] Richard Brinkley notes that a number of Pembrokeshire churches were rebuilt in the early nineteenth century, such as Capel Colman in 1800, Molygrove 1804, Maenclochog 1807 and others repaired or restored.[82]

At Slebech the parishioners decided to build a new church in 1835, regarding the old church as being far too dilapidated and poor to be worth restoration. With seats behind the pulpit it was hard to hear the clergyman. It seems a stock design of the Church Building Commissioners was used to defray costs.[83] A clergyman and local landowner, G.A. Evors, delayed the building of a replacement church at Newtown by his insistence that he should receive the same right of having his own aisle or the use of the chancel in the new church as he had in the old. He lost his case and the new church of St David – almost an elongated preaching box - was opened in 1847, and the old church of St Mary abandoned. The new church had three galleries and it appears that the pew holders of the old church retained their rights in the new.[84] This church, and many others rebuilt around this period, were seen as old fashioned within fifty years. The church at Botwnnog was rebuilt in 1835 by its incumbent, David Williams, and received a grant from the Incorporated Society allowing an additional 90 seats, of which 80 were to be free and unappropriated for ever. A later description described it an unsightly barn-like building, with a low pitched roof and wooden mullioned windows, with a west gallery but no chancel, and box seats and a centrally placed pulpit. Demolished in 1884, a new church was built on its site, in an approved ecclesiological style.[85]

It was quite clear that David Davies as rector of Castle Caereinion was instrumental in having a new church built to replace the old one, which he described as unsafe for public use, though he continued to use it for another two years. He also suggested that the Diocesan Building Society would only offer a grant if the church was rebuilt, and this was not strictly true. Before he had approached the vestry it appears he had obtained the promise of subscriptions, and had persuaded its vestry to borrow money against the rate income by offering to exonerate it from any further liability from his own resources. It is also clear that Davies wished the new building to be seen as a statement about the resurgence of church life in his parish and the surrounding area. Although it was decided all the new seating would be free and unappropriated rather than the number specified by the society, he expressed annoyance at its insistence that the churchwardens should make an annual allocation of the seats to the parishioners, claiming this would only promote annual strife and discord. The cost came to £1,762 made up of £200 granted by the diocesan building society, £90 from the Incorporated Society, the £225 promised from the parish rate, £200 odd raised by an bazaar in Welshpool, a collection of £13 obtained when the foundation stone was laid, with the remainder coming from the local squirarchy, landowners and clergy, only five of whom were resident in the parish. The parishioners seem to have given very little apart from the rate income, and one wonders how far they were in agreement with Davies' proposals.[86]

Many churches were built, as was Castle Caereinion, on the existing site, so involving the demolition of the former building. A new vicar of Ystradowen, Daniel Jones, managed to persuade those involved that the church should be rebuilt completely, on the same site as the old but slightly larger. It cost £900 and was opened in 1862, grants towards the work being obtained from the Ecclesiastical Commissioners and the Church Building Society, and other sums from the church rate and donations, many of which came from the clergy.[87] The good people of Llanfair Caereinion followed suit in 1868, rebuilding the church on the site of the old and following its plan, save that it was embellished with a proper ecclesiological taste.[88] The church at Tryddyn, near Mold, had fallen into such decay that it was thought to be structurally insecure, with the result that a new church was built in 1874 and the old one demolished.[89] Llanbadarn Fynydd Church was rebuilt on the foundations of the former church in 1893, the old chancel being in a state of near-collapse and the church regarded as hardly safe and certainly not fit for reverent worship. A printed appeal for £1,000 was circulated and widely distributed.[90]

Another rebuild was at Glyncorrwg. This was a church that had been somewhat restored and repaired in 1863 when it had been a roofless ruin for some years after an abortive attempt at repair when the finances were not equal to the work required. This church proved inadequate for the needs of a new colliery district, and was in such a bad state of repair the architect recommended a complete rebuild. A faculty allowed its demolition and rebuilding in 1905 when services were transferred to the schoolroom. Fund raising had begun with a bazaar in 1902, soon after a new vicar had been appointed. Seating was now obtained for 300 worshippers as opposed to the 89 of the old church, and it included a chancel, vestry porch, organ chamber, bell-cote and south aisle.[91]

However, many other churches were built on a new site, the former building either being demolished or used for other purposes. A desire to enlarge Cwmdauddwr Church in Radnorshire was thwarted because of the existence of graves close to the church, and thus it was decided to rebuild the church on a new site in the churchyard. Opened in 1865 with due ceremony, it had a nave, chancel, south aisle, organ chamber, west tower and spire, whereas the former church was cluttered with pews and was said to be cold and dreary.[92] Another new site, this time on glebe land, was found for the rebuilding of Llandyssil Church, Montgomeryshire, in 1865. The new church was a proper ecclesiological church as befitting its rector, Archdeacon Ffoulkes, a leading Tractarian. The churchyard of the old church still remains as the local burial ground. The new church seated one third more than the old, though Ffoulkes as rector managed to escape his responsibility for the cost of the chancel by claiming he had given already £600 to the restoration fund.[93] It was argued that the weight of a gallery at Forden Church made the church unsafe, so it was rebuilt in 1865 on a new site in the churchyard in an Early English style at a cost of £3,259, and sat 300 people.[94] St Clement's Church, Briton Ferry, was built in the churchyard of the existing church in 1866, and the old building was permitted to fall into decay until it was finally closed in 1891.[95] With an estimate for repairing the old church at Denbigh of £1,760, it was agreed it would be better to build a new church in a more convenient part of the town. St Mary's Church, opened in 1875, cost £9,500, possibly more than was realised when the work commenced.[96]

For many parishioners, the demolition of the old church and its replacement by a new one was an act of sacrilege. It was for them, using the words of the hymn, "change and decay in all around I see". The rebuilding of Monmouth parish church was no exception. Despite some alterations to its interior to make it less of a preaching box, Keith Kissack wrote that the impulse for its rebuilding came mainly from its clergy. It was maintained by them that while there was room for 600 people, the empty appropriated pews meant the average attendance was around 350, which in turn meant smaller collections whose amount was insufficient for the maintenance of the church and its worship. Though G.E. Street, as architect, described the building as "deplorably bad in every respect … dark, dismal, badly seated and badly ventilated … no style at all … extremely unattractive and uninteresting", his opinion was not necessarily shared by the congregation. Some feared that "Protestant" services would cease in a new building built in harmony with the latest ecclesiological fashions. Others argued that new churches rarely did anything to attract the ungodly, but everything to discourage the faithful. The new wealthy and High Church vicar, Wentworth Watson, refused to be daunted, ignored the protests, and carried the day. As work commenced the opposition to it became more vocal, it appears, especially when the bishop chose as his text at the opening service, "There were some who had indignation within themselves, and said, why is this waste of ointment made." He even commented on those of the company who with "cold hearts" knew "nothing of the generous emotion which prompted this manifestation of love and tenderness." Watson had to write that the congregation should be grateful to have a church to go to "without complaining because everything is not done exactly as we like". But one wonders if he included himself in that remark![97]

The rebuilding of St Mary's, Swansea, on its old site, caused equal controversy in the 1890s, but it was made clear much more accommodation was needed and this could not be obtained by extending the existing church. Nevertheless, Colonel Morgan, a local landowner and antiquarian, let it be known with the demolition of the old church the "affections and sympathies of many of the old inhabitants" had perished with it.[98]

As with church restorations a number of these rebuilds were provided by the gentry at their own expense. The Marquess of Bute had Roath Church rebuilt in 1870, together with his family mausoleum, to replace a church that was too small for a growing population.[99] A substantial part of the cost of rebuilding the ruined church at Llanfihangel Abergwesyn, £2,700 out of £3,250, was met by Mrs Thomas of Llwyn Madoc. The congregation had worshipped for some years in an iron church, but the new church, built in a Romanesque style, was badly built and by the 1950s had become unstable and had to be abandoned.[100] St Catherine's Church, Baglan, was built through the generosity of Griffith Llewelyn, the local squire who held extensive mining interests in the Rhondda. This replaced the old church some distance away, and in 1891 it became a separate parish from the mother parish of Aberafan, being endowed by the Llewelyn family.[101] The rural church of Llanbadarn Fawr in Radnorshire was entirely rebuilt in 1878-9 by the three Misses Severn in memory of their parents at a cost of £3,000.[102] A new church, costing £23,000, was built for Halkyn in 1878 by the duke of Westminster, replacing a former church that had been rebuilt in 1769-70.[103] However, Crawshay Bailey, the industrialist, dissociated himself from the rebuilding of Aberystruth Church in Monmouthshire on its original site in 1857, claiming he wanted a less expensive building.[104] His relation, Robert Thompson Crawshay, built a new church at Vaynor at his own cost, the old being dilapidated, in 1867, on condition that the amount already raised by subscriptions be placed towards a new church at Coed-y-Cymer.[105] Kilvert recorded in 1870 how the archdeacon had eulogized Mr Powell, churchwarden of Llanstephan, for rebuilding his church and subscribing £100. He was possibly a wealthy farmer and it seems he was instrumental in raising the money required rather than having paid for it himself.[106]

Yet again, an offer of assistance might be accompanied by conditions. At Penley Church, when it was decided to rebuild it in the 1880s, a Mrs Vaughan offered a site plus £500 provided her relative was appointed architect. A controversy followed which split the village, and the design produced by that relative was far too costly. Eventually another architect had to be appointed but a new church was not opened until 1901.[107]

An interesting comment was provided by the rebuilding of Nolton Church, built on a site adjacent to the old and inadequate church, thirty yards to the west of it, on land given by Lord Dunraven. There was a doubt whether a new church could be consecrated when the old one was left standing but it was eventually agreed that the old building could be used for Sunday School purposes. In 1889 Ewan Christian, the architect of the Ecclesiastical Commissioners who were required to oversee such projects, came down from London at the expense of the church's promoters, inspected it, and certified it for use as a church, thus permitting the transfer to take place.[108]

But the rebuilding of a church could be fraught with difficulties. Parishioners might not be in favour, and the difficulties of finance and the requirements of the Incorporated Society and other bodies might cause further problems. We look further at some case examples.

A vivid picture of the rebuilding of Llanrhystud Church is provided by I.G. Jones. The church was dilapidated but it was assumed it was impossible to claim a grant from the Incorporated Society on the grounds of lack of accommodation. For while the church had only 120 seats, some in appropriated pews but with a few free seats, it was sufficient for its needs, as the five local chapels had accommodation for 1,400 people out of a population of 1,800. In 1851 the vestry decided to demolish the existing church and rebuild it on its existing site. An estimate of £900 was given and it was agreed to borrow £400 against the church rate, repaying £100 per annum. The plans however became more elaborate and included a tower with a spire and a vestry with seating for 174 people with seats for 72 children under the tower. The estimated cost rose to £1,732. Discovering that other local churches had had grants from the Society an application was made and the Society offered £50 on condition that additional accommodation was provided of 126 seats with 72 of these being reserved for the poor in perpetuity. Though this additional seating was hardly required, it meant the plans had to be redrawn, the planned tower omitted, and a new south aisle added to fit in with these requirements. The church was now double the intended size in order to fit in not for local requirements but to satisfy "accepted dogma" that a church should seat a percentage of its parishioners. Worse, the cost now rose to £2,367, leaving a deficiency of £645, though an embarrassed Society offered a further grant of £160. Worse was to follow. The builder was unsatisfactory and left the roof unslated for many months so that the stonework began to drip with water, and a disagreement with the architect, Pearson, resulted in his resignation. Money had to be borrowed at five per cent but the vicar, to obtain the grant from the Society, was required to send the seating plan of the new church, and it was only with the greatest difficulty he managed to obtain it from Pearson.[109]

When Thomas Walters endeavoured to rebuild the church at Ystradgynlais in the 1850s, having become rector in 1856, he was surprised to find that the Ecclesiastical Commissioners had no powers to assist in the building or rebuilding of churches. This was the least of his worries, as a significant minority of his parishioners refused to accept there was any need for the rebuilding of the church, and instead suggested alterations in the existing building. His bishop, Thirlwall, wrote to support Walters, stating that a new church was urgently required in the place of the small, gloomy and most unsightly building (it had 200 sittings, all of which were appropriated to the local farms in an area being rapidly industrialised). The bishop continued by wondering how any friend of the Church could ever enter that building with "any other feelings than those which I have experienced on every occasion that has brought me to it, viz., mortification, shame and disgust!" A local industrialist claimed that the vestry's vote for a loan from the Public

Works Loan Commissioners of £1,000, payable from the rates over 20 years, was indecisive, argued that if Walters succeeded in obtaining this loan he would soon be asking for a further £3,500 and would ruin the parish. He was not disinterested. His works would obviously have to pay a considerable part of the enhanced rate to meet these charges. And a local minister argued that the vestry had only permitted Walters to rebuild the church on condition it was done by a voluntary rate, he having tormented the parish for a long time for permission to build this church. The vestry was packed by the industrialist's employees whose agents had canvassed their workers against the rebuilding, but Walters managed to win the vote by a narrow margin, though it is alleged the matter went through the consistory court of the diocese and to the Court of Queen's Bench before the church could be rebuilt.[110]

Many a man might be daunted by such circumstances to decline any further building work, but Walters was built of sterner stuff. In his next parish, Llansamlet, he discovered that the church was in such a deplorable condition that the chancel roof was in danger of collapse and the services had to be conducted from the nave. The gallery could not be used as the roof above was unsafe, and it was claimed that the stifling atmosphere in the church with so many people crammed into it gave people severe headaches. It was far too small for its rapidly increasing population, was inconvenient in its arrangements and "mean and ugly to the last degree". An architect testified that the condition of the building was such that rebuilding was necessary and the matter could not be delayed with safety or dignity. The earl of Jersey gave a new site for the purpose alongside the existing churchyard. One redeeming feature was that Walters could make a local claim to the Ecclesiastical Commissioners, who held the tithes and glebeland in the parish from the estate of the bishops of St Davids, for the work on the chancel. Even this had its complications as this interest had been leased, and the commissioners pointed out that while the lessee had covenanted to repair the chancel this did not cover its rebuilding. The commissioners would not assist until the lease had expired in fourteen years' time (1888). Thankfully a compromise was worked out, and a single payment of £43 released the lessee from his covenant.

With the assistance of his bishop, Walters managed to persuade the commissioners to offer a grant, but rather than the £1,116 he expected for the cost of the chancel (from a total of £6,515), only £150 was offered. More haggling followed with Walters asserting he had no resident landowners in his parish but only tenant farmers and working men. It was a time of depression and even the chairman of his building committee had been bankrupted. The offer increased to £400 but even this was insufficient. He could not ask his parishioners to find money for what was not their responsibility. Another compromise was made, and at additional expense new plans were drawn up, so that only the chancel and a portion of the nave would be built and the tower omitted beyond its foundation. It would seat 800. The old church was deteriorating rapidly, an appeal was made far and wide for the new figure of £5,000 required, and a further appeal made to the commissioners to increase its offer, made more poignant as Walter's building committee had collapsed due to the failure and liquidations of its members, and he was now solely responsible for the work. Eventually the offer was increased to £500, and so the foundation stone was laid in 1878, and it was decided to build the whole of the nave and a south aisle and vestry along with the chancel, and use the materials from the old church for rebuilding an infants' school as an annex to the existing one. Even when it was opened a deficit of £2,000 remained, and quarterly preaching services were held for many years to raise this money and continue with the work left over, so that the tower was not built until 1914.

Perhaps no one else but Walters would have had the perseverance, if not the audacity, to continue with this work at a time of depression.[111] And we may conclude, that without the stimulus given by the clergy, their risk-taking and commitment, and their cajoling of their parishioners, many churches might not have been restored or rebuilt, with the result that the church's mission might have been placed at risk. Though one is left with an uncomfortable feeling that in many cases another factor was the clerical habit of following the trend and proving one's ministry by a tangible structure.

We discuss the building of new churches for unchurched areas in the next chapter.

CHAPTER FIVE:
EXTENDING THE MISSION OF THE CHURCH

By the 1860s it was clear that restoring, extending and rebuilding an existing parish church, or even repewing it, in an attempt to win over those who had left the Church for Nonconformity or had become alienated from it, or accommodating those who were unchurched because of the lack of seating, was not very successful. Only in those places where the rift had been late and people had gone to Nonconformity by default in recent years, or when a town had expanded and new inhabitants were desirous for seating, such measures were reasonably effectual. The warnings given by John Griffith and others, as noted previously, had proved all too true. The realisation slowly dawned that the Church needed to be pro-active and provide ways and means through which people might be drawn into its life. In some cases it was necessary, because of geographical distance from a parish church, particularly in extensive and rural parishes, to build an outstation, a mission room, or to use an existing schoolroom. The same applied in poorer areas, where many people felt unable to attend a parish church for want of decent clothing, lack of familiarity with the church liturgy, or simply because they felt out of place with a "superior" congregation. When a new mission room was opened in Castle Fields, Oswestry, in 1884, it was emphatically stated it was designed for the working classes, especially those who attended no church at all, and those who disliked attending a church with a fashionable congregation.[1]

It was also realised that before building a purpose-built church, with all the trimmings and costings required, it would be better to have a "test" plant, and if this succeeded to move on to something better and more permanent. In the newly emerging colliery areas it was suggested that the first arrivals would be the rougher characters, most of whom were indifferent to religion, and only later did a better class of people arrive who might be attracted to a church plant.[2] The era of the "iron" building helped this process immensely, as it was so constructed that it could be readily dismantled and re-erected on another site. In this way the Church imitated and learnt from Nonconformity, although it had immense legal complications to face and undo before it could further this process and these we will note in passing. John Owen, bishop of St Davids, accepted in 1906 that the Church had been too slow in building new churches, especially in areas at a distance from their nearest church building.[3]

Yet it might be argued that the building of a mission room or even a chapel-of-ease was a device to avoid the difficulties of repewing a church or creating a new district with all the problems that would cause. No rights would be affected and it could still be argued that the Church was undertaking its work of mission.[282]

Until 1843, when Peel's New Parishes Act was passed, the creation of a new district required an endowment for its clergyman, a church built in a suitable style and with accommodation for a reasonable number of its parishioners, the consent of all the incumbents and their patrons from whom the district was to be carved, as well as the protection of the incumbents' financial rights from surplice fees, and consents from the diocese and other bodies involved. The act simplified these procedures (though retaining many of these obligations), allowing an area where the population was sufficient to be given a minister at £100 per annum, licensing a suitable building as a place of worship, and when a new church was consecrated enabling that area to become a district parish and the stipend to be increased to £150. Such districts were known as Peel districts and the endowments were generally provided through the Ecclesiastical Commission.[4] But even with these concessions, Ollivant, bishop of Llandaff, expressed his dismay at the rigidity of the Church in his 1854 Charge, which prevented them winning back those who had been lost by another kind of rigidity a century and less earlier.[5] His remedy was to follow a mission strategy, using mission rooms and school-chapels and allowing services to be held in private homes or even inns. He left the development of new parishes to his successors.[6] David Walter Thomas, the outspoken vicar of Llandegai, a quarrying parish in Caernarfonshire, wrote that while Nonconformists could build chapels through the use of loans, but the system required by the Church needed expensive buildings and endowments for its clergy and consequently left the Church distanced in the race between them.[7]

Although services were not permitted in unlicensed buildings if more than twenty persons were present until 1855,[8] the bishops and clergy managed a strategy of getting around this restriction by describing these services as "cottage lectures". Bishop Burgess had recommended these lectures in 1805-6 in his *The House of God the Fittest Place for Public Prayer Meetings, proposed to the Clergy of the Diocese of St David's* and *Sunday Evening Letters recommended to the Clergy of the Diocese of St David's*, as noted in an earlier chapter, and he gave an indication as to how they should proceed. These lectures, designed for non-churchgoers, took place in the parish church. To what extent these were held in his diocese is not known, but it may be assumed they formed a precedent for performing these services in places other than consecrated buildings. One of the first of these so-called cottage lectures appears to have taken place in the parish of Trevethin, when its incumbent, Thomas Davies, started a Sunday evening lecture in a house at Pontnewynydd in 1834.[9] Bishop Campbell of Bangor in his 1863 Charge accepted that these lectures would supply a felt need in the remote and scattered hamlets of many of his diocese's parishes. Six years later he described one of the objects of his diocesan Church Extension Society as providing mission rooms and finding God-fearing laymen to assist in them, aided by a moderate salary. By 1875 a number of these "humble" buildings sheltered a congregation, and when the means of supporting a clergyman were wanting, laymen, acting under the authority of the bishop, were helping to supply that deficiency.[10]

We also need to remember that the ideal was to obtain separate churches for both the Welsh and English congregations of a parish. This was not easily achieved and was costly. It was perhaps easier to achieve in the larger towns such as Merthyr and Aberdare, but as we note in a later section, in smaller bilingual parishes the Welsh congregation felt it was given inferior accommodation.[11] In many cases the church was used by the English congregation and the Welsh congregation relegated to the schoolroom, as at Aberystwyth in the 1840s, until a church was built for them,[12] while the Welsh congregation at Penmaenmawr met in a mission room before a permanent church was built for them in 1897, Eglwys Dewi Sant.[13] The Welsh congregations much resented this second-class approach to them and their exclusion from the parish church. Robin Gill, in suggesting that there was overbuilding in the diocese of St Asaph, fails to take into account the need for separate places of worship for the two linguistic congregations, nor the fact that many of these churches were built in rural areas some distance from their parish churches, especially when a Nonconformist cause had been established nearby. He notes that in 1831 there was one church in this diocese for 1,540 of the population, and by 1906 one for 885 people.[14]

There were difficulties that emerged from time to time, mainly because the Church's law had failed to reflect pastoral concerns. In some instances clergy and laity endeavoured to circumvent these laws in order to supply a need. Here are two examples.

The curate of Degannwy, in the parish of Llanrhos, William Arthur Jones, appears to have established a schoolroom, costing £800, where he commenced services as the parish church was two miles away via a rough and exposed road. He had done so with the sanction of the bishop of St Asaph. No sooner than it was erected his vicar refused him permission to officiate within it, even when his services were not required at the parish church. Eventually, the bishop made use of an act of parliament enabling him to appoint this curate as chaplain to this congregation. Though a large congregation had been drawn together, its resources were inadequate to find his stipend and pay the expenses of the church, and Jones made a printed appeal in 1885 to the Church Extension Society of the diocese for its assistance.[15]

The other example is found in a controversy about a chapel built in 1879 at Berth, in the parish of Llanfair Duffryn Clwyd, by the local squire, the eccentric Edward Owen Vaughan Lloyd. His aim was to provide a place of worship for those who lived in that part of the parish, and to win back church people who had left for Nonconformity because of the remoteness of the parish church. In this he was successful, and though he claimed he had obtained permission to conduct services himself from his relative, Archdeacon Ffoulkes, he was only able to do so as a layman as the chapel was not licensed. After Lloyd had allowed a bishop of the breakaway Reformed Episcopal Church to preach in it, the diocesan bishop, alarmed at this independence and the usurpation of the incumbent's authority, demanded that the chapel be transferred into the custody of the incumbent and the wardens of the parish, and that its services be in accordance with the Church of England and under the direction of the rector and its ritual the same as in the parish church. However, the bishop permitted a curate to be employed but by 1883 the curate had left and Lloyd resumed taking the services himself. Lloyd wanted a communion service to be held in the chapel, which meant it needed to be licensed, and this would prevent him from taking services in it. The rector had no wish to have another place of worship in his parish which in the absence of a curate he would have to serve himself. Furthermore, if Lloyd defected in the payment of a curate it would become the responsibility of the rector. A stalemate resulted, which went to Archbishop Benson for his decision. It seems he concluded that the rector could have been more accommodating, but the end result is not recorded.[16]

COTTAGE MEETINGS, MISSION ROOMS AND SCHOOL CHURCHES

In many parishes an outreach work was commenced in a private home with a cottage lecture or service, and led to the building of a mission room and eventually to a purpose built church and even possibly becoming the nucleus of a separate parish (these are noted in the next section). However, many of these mission rooms and school churches remained as part of an existing parish, available for those who either lived a distance from the parish church or who preferred a more homely rather than a more fashionable environment in which to worship. Archdeacon James of Carmarthen considered, rather reluctantly, that these services were ideal for preparing "wandering" church people to understand and join in the more elaborate system of worship in their parish churches.[17]

Cottage services were recommended by the 1885 St Davids Diocesan Conference for the remoter parts of large rural parishes. It was suggested they could be fitted in after the second service of the day, though some clergy, it was felt, considered that that service concluded their hard day's work.[18] As these particular services were barely recorded we have no idea how many were held or how successful they were, though we note later how many church congregations commenced in a private home or hostelry. Nevertheless, the diocese was a bit late in the day, as Anthony Russell suggests that in the wider church these services were well-established by the mid-1840s.[19]

Possibly as a success of these cottage initiatives, mission rooms were opened in many parishes, some being purpose built, but others consisted of an iron building or the adoption of another building. After the passing of the 1855 Act, permitting services with more than twenty persons present to be held in secular and non-consecrated buildings, it meant that these rooms could be used officially for liturgical services if authorised by the bishop and which a layman could take if permitted to do so. However, a building had to be specifically licensed to permit a service of Holy Communion in it, and this had to be conducted by an ordained person.

Significantly, Bishop Sumner of Llandaff, as early as 1827, expressed his willingness to license suitable buildings for worship on a temporary use, accepting the difficulties of dealing with a migratory population.[20] It does not appear that his offer was effected and it took time for the Church to accept this new conception of ministry. W.D. Wills estimated that Bishop Ollivant of Llandaff licensed over 60 such rooms between 1849-70.[21] One of the first in that diocese was at Devauden, which James Davies the schoolmaster fixed up in his schoolroom in 1827.[22] Those held in the parish of Eglwysilan in the 1840s brought together a large number of people who had never been seen in a church, and these led them to attending Sunday services, probably in one of the school-rooms set up in that parish.[23] Another early mission room was at Clodock, Herefordshire, then in the diocese of St Davids. In the 1840s a farmer gave an acre of his land, commenced a collection, and even walked eighty miles to interview Bishop Thirlwall, obtaining his consent to build the room and commence services. The mission room, though described as the church of St John the Baptist, Newton-in-Clodock, was opened in 1844 at a cost of £700, and much of the labour in building it was given by local men.[24] The parish of Aberdare by the 1850s was using two licensed rooms, two schoolrooms and four other places for outreach services.[25] By 1893 the parish of Dowlais had two mission rooms and also used the cemetery chapel for services and was appealing for funds to build more permanent structures,[26] while the Newport parish of Maindee in the early 1890s had not only a parish and a daughter church, but in addition a mission room, an iron church (transferred to another site when a purpose built church was erected in 1892), held cottage lectures elsewhere, and used a school, rented to the School Board, but available for use on Sundays.[27] An advertisement in the *Guardian* appealing for funds to build a stone mission room was made in 1874 by the parish of Llanasa in Flintshire, in addition to restoring the church building. The mission room was to be built at Ffynnon Groyw, three miles away, where about 700 or more miners resided. The inhabitants were poor and the landlord was a Roman Catholic.[28]

Christ Church, Swansea, established a mission hall, named after one of its principal benefactors, Charles Bath, in 1891, mainly for the unchurched. Eli Clarke, the vicar of the parish, sent out 1,000 letters to invite those who attended no place of worship and their children no Sunday School to its services. The response was not encouraging, but a congregation of 130 and a school of 100 was eventually established.[29] Two mission rooms were opened in the parish of Buckley in the 1890s on the outskirts of the parish. Both were wooden buildings and were served by lay readers. One of them, at Pentre, was replaced by an iron building in 1899 given by the wife of the rector, Mrs Mary Drew, at a cost of £327.[30] And we may note a number of so-called navvy mission rooms, such as those at Pentyrch and Ebbw Vale in the diocese of Llandaff in the 1900s, which were mentioned in the Report of the Royal Commission of 1906.[31] Not all these mission rooms were purpose built. One, in the parish of Cadoxton, near Neath, used a former grocer's shop.[32]

The opening of mission rooms became so prevalent that the diocese of St Davids devised a service for such an occasion in 1884.[33] By 1906 it was estimated that there were 78 such mission rooms in that diocese.[34] Bishop Edwards saw fit to commend their use for weekday services and prayer meetings in his 1890 Charge.[35]

A large number of these mission churches were built of iron rather than stone and were used extensively in south Wales. Their great advantage was that it was relatively easy to move them to another location, as occurred in Cardiff where the iron building erected as St James' Church was removed to form the basis of St Catherine's Church, Canton, when a purpose built edifice was built for the former in 1894;[36] or in Newport, where an iron mission church attached to St Paul's was later used for St Julian's Church, then in the parish of Maindee.[37] We note later how the use of these iron churches facilitated the Church's mission in developing areas. A catalogue of around 1870 for these buildings, issued by F. Morton and Co. Ltd., made clear an iron building cost one third of the cost of a stone one; the interior walls could be lined with wood or plaster; they were comfortable; could be moved elsewhere, and one holding 300 people would cost around £600 plus the cost of a foundation. It added a comment from a Scottish periodical that no amount of missionary work could succeed if a building was not available to establish a congregation.[38] A cheaper version, given in a presentation to the

St Asaph Diocesan Church Building Society, designed by Arthur Baker and Alfred Burder, was claimed to be far cheaper and more substantial than iron as well as warmer through the use of wooden framing over concrete slabs. A building seating 50 people would cost £166 and for 112 £296, plus the cost of foundations and carriage.[39]

A description of such an iron church, St Paul's, Grangetown, Cardiff, was given in 1872. Seventy-five feet by thirty feet, lined with wood, well-lighted by gas pendants suspended from the roof, and with Gothic windows, it had a small vestry and an organ chamber. It sat 400 people on open benches with iron frames and its cost, £600, was given by Lady Mary Clive.[40] It was almost as cheap to build an iron mission room, declared the Revd. Benjamin Lloyd, curate of the colliery parish of Mountain Ash, than hire a building, often unsuited for its purpose. An iron building could cost between £400 and £600, and with grants of £200 from societies and donations of £100 from local friends of the Church, a £200 loan on low interest rates could be guaranteed by the diocesan trust or from a friend of the Church. The interest and capital repayments for this loan would cost £25 per annum over ten years, higher but more satisfactory than paying £10 to £15 for the hire of a building.[41] Many of these iron churches are noted below but nearly every large town had their share as church plants were required for an emerging population.

A further development from the 1830s onwards was the use of schoolrooms for services, many actually being built as a combined school and church, a fact disliked by Nonconformity as many had been built with government grants. Nantgarw School-Chapel in the extensive parish of Eglwysilan, of 1845, cost £294 to build, and grants were received from the Privy Council of £75 and the National Society of £70.[42] William Roberts (Nefydd), who was the agent of the British Schools, mainly supported by Nonconformity and interdenominational, complained in 1861 that services were held in the National School at Cwmbach, Aberdare, which he believed had been erected mainly to serve as a church, although its cost had come from public funds.[43] They needed to be episcopally licensed before they could be so used and were frequently described as school-chapels. Archdeacon Wickham commended them as allowing additional services to be held, not only on Sundays but also during the week. He noted there were thirteen in the diocese of St Asaph, and more were projected. Without these buildings many in the large and scattered parishes who had been baptised and educated within the Church would be left to seek the means of grace from other sources.[44] These rooms had their limitations, however. In an appeal for a new church at Caerfallwch in the parish of Northop, dated 1873, it was stated that while services were held in a local schoolroom, it was far too small and inconvenient. The seats were designed for children, not adults, the desks were fixed, and kneeling was impossible.[45]

One of the first schools to be so used was at Buckley in 1819, though a church was built in 1822.[46] Out of the many schoolrooms noted in the 1851 religious census we may note two: at Solva, licensed in 1841 on account of the distance from the parish church of Whitchurch; and Llanfihangel Genau'r Glyn, where two schools in that extensive parish were licensed for worship, attracting a congregation of one hundred at the respective afternoon and evening services.[47] Schoolrooms were built in the large and remote parish of Berriew at Brooks and Pantyffridd during 1857-8 and served as licensed mission rooms. Both, through the assiduous pastoral care of its then curate, John James Turner, obtained large congregations, possibly from the parents of the schoolchildren.[48] In the parish of Hawarden its rector, Stephen Gladstone, probably decided as a result of the 1870 Education Act to build school-chapels, as they could not be taken over by school boards. These were built at Ewloe, Shotton and Sandycroft, where a Sunday School had already commenced in a public house.[49] At Eyton, in the parish of Bangor Monachorum, the schoolroom built in 1869 served as the nave and the chancel doubled up as a classroom.[50] Services were still being conducted by a layman in 1910 at Dolforwyn School Church in the parish of Llanmerewig. These had started in the 1850s.[51] At Fochriw, in the parish of Gelligaer, a schoolroom was used for worship and opened in 1863, with the hope that a chancel might be built at its eastern end in the future, as happened at Belan in the parish of Welshpool.[52]

MISSION LEADING TO THE BUILDING OF A PURPOSE-BUILT CHURCH

In newly established communities where a church was required it was received policy to commence a "mission" in any building that might be available and so establish a congregation. Nonconformity had practised this with great success, though the Church hoped that its own missionary endeavourers would prevent an exodus to dissent and also encourage church people who had strayed into dissent to return to "the true fold".

At Kilvey, in Swansea, the Infants School was licensed for worship in 1842, while a new church was built by the Grenfell family who were local industrialists, and opened in 1845.[53] This was unusual as the building of the church was about to start when the services commenced in that schoolroom. Generally, some time elapsed between the start of a "mission" and the building of a permanent church. Archdeacon Bevan of Hay wrote that many of the churches, especially in the coalfields, had commenced in a plain room, followed by a mission room, before a church was built.[54] Indeed, many of these missions commenced in the most unlikely of places: Pontlottyn in a stable loft holding sixty and approached by rickety stairs, Hirwaun in a public house, and Cwmaman (Glamorgan) in a rented British schoolroom.[55] Many other churches commenced in the long room of a public house, as did Broughton at the Cross Foxes Inn before St Paul's Church was built in 1889,[56] and Senghenydd, a colliery town above Caerphilly, where a room in the Leigh Hotel was used, furnished with sixty chairs, which moved to its Assembly Room when more space was required, until St Peter's Church was opened in 1897.[57] The Welsh congregation at Cadoxton-juxta-Barry, met at the Royal Hotel, until an iron building was erected for them in 1896.[58]

Other church plants made use of domestic and commercial premises, though the most popular was to use a schoolroom whenever one was available and failing that an iron building. As discussed later the Church was conspicuous in its desire to establish church or National schools, and to use them as a means of proselytising. Accordingly we look at examples drawn mainly from the diocese of Llandaff, taking a number of representative areas,

The new township of Ebbw Vale was part of the widespread parish of Llangatwg. A congregation was formed using a schoolroom in 1839, and by 1843 it had a congregation of two hundred. The church of St John's was built in 1846, and in 1861 a new parish church, dedicated to All Saints, was erected, costing £60,000, of which £15,000 went on its foundations. Most of the cost was borne by the Ebbw Vale Company, who had sold the advowsons of this and other parishes where it held property in order to pay this enormous sum.[59] An iron church was erected at Brynmawr in 1863, but the severity of the weather meant that the congregation was forced to transfer to the Corporation Hall. A new church was built in 1872, partly with help provided by Crawshay Bailey, another industrialist.[60]

In the 1870s the parish of Roath became densely populated as industry moved into the lower part of that Cardiff suburb. An iron church was used as the foundation building of three parishes, being moved from one to the other: St German's (which had started in a barn), St Saviour's Splott, and St Francis.[61] St David's Church, Ely, then in the parish of Llandaff, was consecrated in 1871, the church having previously met in a cottage.[62] The daughter of a vicar of Canton, Cardiff, Daisy Saulez, was instrumental in renting a cottage room in 1880 which she called the St Vincent Mission, after her father's Christian name. It later moved to an iron building that had started life as St Teilo's Church in Woodville Street, Cardiff, and later formed part of the parish of St Luke's, Canton. Another Cardiff church, St Sampson, commenced its life in a mission room over a bakehouse in 1897, transferring later to another building before that church was built in 1922.[63] At Tongwynlais, on the northern outskirts of Cardiff, then part of the parish of Whitchurch, services were held in the late 1850s at a farmhouse, and in 1860 a coach-house belonging to Greenmeadow House was utilised as a mission church, remaining in use until a purpose-built church was erected in 1877 at a cost of £2,000, seating 300 people.[64]

The Church at Cwmbach, in the parish of Aberdare, whose church was built in 1882, commenced in 1850s at the National School with an 11.00 am English and a 6.00 pm Welsh service.[65] Until a new church opened at Treharris, then in the parish of Merthyr Tydfil, in 1896, at a cost of £4,500, the congregation had worshipped from 1887 in a coffee tavern, and thereafter in one of the Board Schools.[66] Similarly, services commenced in a private house at Llanbradach, in the lower Rhymney Valley, and later moved to a public hall which appears to have been an iron hut. With a strong congregation a new church was built in 1897 which accommodated 350 people and Miss Clara Thomas, a local landowner, who gave the land also donated £1,000 towards its cost of £3,000.[67] At Brithdir, in the large parish of Gelligaer, now heavily industrialised, a shed was used before a church was built and a lay reader employed at £40 per annum, while in the neighbouring township of Bargoed, in the same parish, an iron church was built in 1876, to which a stone chancel was added in 1877 and a stone nave in 1893. It became a separate parish in 1904.[68]

Cottage services commenced in the Llwynypia district of the parish of Ystradyfodwg in 1871, and the National School at Tonypandy later took their place. A church was built in 1878 at a cost of £2,100, though at that price it had little ornament and the projected tower and chancel had to be excluded from the contract. From this church plants were established at Clydach Vale where a schoolroom was used, and Penygraig, where services were held in an iron building which later became the church hall when St Barnabas Church was built.[69] The church-school at Treorchi in the same area was eventually made into a church due to the difficulties of financing a new building. Even then a loan had to be taken out for its conversion.[70] By the 1880s the iron church at Ferndale was the only church for the whole of the Rhondda Fach, consisting of five or so colliery settlements, and during this period another congregation met in the reading room at Tylorstown.[71] In that decade a new community of 3,000 people developed at Maerdy at the top of this valley, where previously there had been one farmhouse. The church people of Ferndale paid their curate an additional ten pounds per annum to take a service there each Sunday, and these were held at a coffee tavern, with a Sunday school in the morning. By 1886 it was said to be full to overflowing, and it was believed that if there was a proper church there would be a threefold increase in the congregation.[72]

A schoolroom was used at Maesteg as the parish church of Llangynwyd was not only difficult of access but was also inconveniently overcrowded. While a permanent site was given in 1839 for a church in this growing town, the Maesteg Company who had given the site and promised a large donation for the building of a church went bankrupt causing substantial difficulties. Eventually, with external support, St David's Church was built with 200 sittings for £1,000 in 1853.[73] At Blaengwynfi, in the Afan Valley, split between two parishes, a service was held in a local hotel taken by a curate from Llangynwyd in 1886, though the hotel was in the parish of Glyncorrwg. A mission hall was opened in 1888, parishioners making weekly payments towards its cost, and finally, mainly through the generosity of Miss Talbot, the church of St Gabriel was opened in 1894, though it was not consecrated until 1901 until all the debts on it had been paid.[74] A licensed schoolroom formed the nucleus of a church at Skewen, leading to the building of a church in 1850 and the creation of a Peel district.[75] Although Lord Winborne gave an acre of land for a new church in 1891 at Porthcawl, an iron church was built on that land in 1892 (the congregation had previously worshipped at a school from 1873 onwards), and this remained until 1914 when All Saints Church was built at a cost of nearly £10,000 and seating 600 people.[76]

An outlying part of the parish of Swansea, Cockett, became the responsibility of a curate in the late 1840s. He was only able to find five adults who called themselves church people, and many of the inhabitants had never seen a clergyman before, but treated him with great kindness. After several months of parochial visiting he began to hold several cottage meetings and even some services underground in the coal mines, building up a congregation of fifty to sixty. By 1856 a church had been built, on a site given by J.D. Llewelyn, a local landowner, and with donations from many in the area and beyond, as Cockett was a poverty-stricken place.[77] Another iron church formed the nucleus of St Gabriel's Church, a plant recommended by a diocesan commission as a means of dividing the still extensive parish of Swansea. Three years later, in 1889, the new church was consecrated, on a totally different site, half of whose cost was given by the local landowner, Colonel Morgan, and his family. The iron building was then moved to the Mount Pleasant area of the town, and became the nucleus of St Jude's Church where a congregation had already been gathered and a Sunday School commenced in a private house.[78] Similarly the iron church that had formed the start of St Thomas's Church in the dockland area of Swansea (after an initial time in a schoolroom), was moved to Port Tennant as St Stephen's Church when a permanent church for St Thomas was built in 1887 through the generosity of the Grenfell family.[79] An iron building, erected by voluntary labour, served as a mission church at Norton in the parish of Oystermouth from 1908 for many years. The services were conducted by laymen as the clergy of the parish were fully committed elsewhere on Sundays.[80]

In the Swansea Valley the parish church of Llanguicke was some distance from the emerging industrial township of Pontardawe, so that services were held in a schoolroom in that town by 1858, but four years later were transferred to the imposing church of St Peter with its dominating spire. It was built at the expense of a local industrialist.[81] A church plant at Dafen, Llanelli, commenced in a day school in 1854, but it was not until twenty years later that a Church was consecrated for that community, whose cost was borne by the local industrialists, Phillips, Nunes and Company.[82]

In north Wales a room was licensed for worship at Greenfield, in the parish of Holywell, in 1850. Twenty years later Holy Trinity Church was built for its congregation.[83] Richard Bonnor (later dean), while vicar of Ruabon 1842-59, established a National School at Rhosllannerchrugog in his parish, and had it licensed as a place of worship. The success of this venture led to the opening of a new church there in 1853 which became a Peel district.[84] The National School at Penycae near Wrexham was licensed for worship in 1866, but eleven years elapsed before a church could be built.[85]

The history of many of the Welsh parishes created in the nineteenth century was often one of temporary buildings and mission activity before a congregation could be formed which would eventually obtain its own permanent building.

NEW CHURCHES FOR NEW COMMUNITIES

Not all churches built during the nineteenth century originated through the gradual process mentioned above. A landowner, especially mineral landowners, or an industrialist might consider he had an obligation to his tenants or workers and would build a church for them, often at his own expenses. This, of course, is noted above, but one wonders to what extent their generosity depended on the formation of an existing congregation. In large town parishes the need for an additional church to accommodate those unable to find seating in the parish church resulted in chapels-of-ease and later daughter churches being built.

Many of these churches were built through the generosity of landlords and industrialists, though not to the extent the bishops believed should be the case. While the church at Dowlais was built as a chapel-of-ease to Merthyr Tydfil in 1823 by Sir John Guest, the local industrialist, probably in the hope of winning back the many who had turned to Nonconformity for want of accommodation,[86] the Pennant family (later ennobled), as quarry owners, built St Ann's Bethesda in 1812, and later built a new church in 1865. In addition the family built Glanogwen Church, while another quarry owner, Thomas Assheton Smith, built a church at Llandinorwic.[87] When the foundation stone of a new church at Pembroke Dock was laid in 1846, it was announced that the Admiralty, which had a major naval base there, would donate £500 or its £4,000 cost as a token of its responsibility for its employees there. Thomas Lloyd regards this church as having been built in an economical style by national standards.[88] The local squire, William Williams, built a chapel of ease at Aberpergwm, near his residence, but regarded it as a private chapel, even insisting that the chancel was his own property.[89] St Margaret's Church, Bodelwyddan, was built in 1860 by Lady Willoughby de Broke at a cost of £35,000. It has since been known as "the marble church" through the richness of its construction.[90] The Gladstone family in north east Wales, the Talbots and Llewelyns in the colliery districts, and Lord Cawdor in south-west Wales, were also magnificent donors of handsome churches.[91]

The Talbot family of Margam were amongst the most generous benefactors of churches, albeit in a Tractarian direction. Miss Emily Talbot paid the £25,000 cost of St Theodore's Church, Port Talbot, in 1897, as a memorial to her brother, the heir of the estate, after whom the church was named. It became a separate parish from Margam in 1901, while Miss Talbot generously contributed to the cost of new churches at Bryn and Oakwood in that same parish.[92] St Peter's Church, Pentre, in the Rhondda Valley, whose cost of £21,000 was met by the Llewelyn family of Baglan (whose coal royalties brought in £24,000 per annum), met at first with the disapproval of Bishop Lewis, who felt that to put such a magnificent building in the midst of a colliery area was wrong. But he went on to state he was mistaken. The church had proved invaluable in educating these people about the beauty of holiness and to teach them the worship of God.[93]

The £4,600 cost of All Saints' Church, Newbridge on Wye, consecrated in 1883, was borne by George Stovin Venables of Llysdinam Hall,[94] and Sir Pryce Pryce-Jones, who founded the first mail-order company in Great Britain, in 1888 gifted a new church, All Saints, to the parish of Llanllwchaiarn, Newtown, whose parish church was at a distance from the centre of population.[95] The cost of £3,000 for the rural church of St Mark's, Brithdir, near Dolgellau, built in an Arts and Crafts style by Henry Wilson in 1897, was met by a Mrs Tooth who ensured it was a Tractarian place of worship.[96]

John Davies, in noting that the second marquess of Bute and his son's trustees spent over £35,000 on church buildings, adds that their subscription to an individual church bore the same relationship as to their total acreage in the parish. The Cawdor estate appears to have done the same,[97] and possibly other landowners adopted similar criteria. Geoffrey Orrin notes that in Glamorgan over forty churches were built by landowners and industrialists, and in nearly all cases sites for churches were given by the landowners.[98] These churches, as I.G. Jones suggests, were often built to a standard not matched by those where this benevolence was lacking, and which proved to be "utilitarian, indifferently designed, unprepossessing and badly built".[99]

CONCERNS REGARDING THE INDUSTRIALISTS

The township of Rhymney was almost a creation of the Rhymney Iron Company. To the delight of Bishop Copleston, and with his frequent praise of its beneficence, this company built a church there at a cost of £4,665 in 1842, with seating for 847 people. An endowment was also provided. However, an act of parliament had to be obtained to enable this, and though one shareholder objected that building and endowing churches was not a legitimate expense and brought an injunction to prevent it he was overruled by the judge.[100] Copleston continually used this example as a means of challenging these industrialists, and argued that those who brought vast populations to these formerly deserted places had a moral duty to provide for their inhabitants from whom they gained their wealth. Had their example, and that of the Maesteg Company, been followed at such places as Aberdare and Bedwellte, Merthyr and Mynyddislwyn, Aberystruth and Trevethin, a great change would have been wrought in the moral and religious condition of 60,000 to 70,000 people, who though materially well-off, were left vulnerable to every form of sectarian dissent and schism, mixed with heathenism and avowed infidelity. Did these industrialists believe the Gospel? Were they members of the household of faith? "and can they, year after year, draw additional crowds to the spot, and yet make no provision for their spiritual instruction, for the due administration of the Sacraments, and for the preaching of God's Word?" He prayed that his remonstrance would touch the hearts of these industrialists.[101] Perhaps it did, for J. B. Bruce Pryce bore much of the cost of Glyntaff Church, and Crawshay Bailey (for all his faults), the Ebbw Vale Company and the Tredegar Iron Company, accepted their responsibilities,[102] while much of the cost of All Saints Church in the parish of Michaelston super Afan, consecrated in 1856, with a spire that towered over the Nonconformist chapels, was born by the English Copper Company, the local employer, then owned by the Bank of England.[103]

Copleston's concern was reiterated by both William Lewis of Ystradyfodwg and H.T. Edwards when he was vicar of Aberdare. Lewis, admittedly before he received the substantial help of the Talbot and Llewelyn families, imagined that the sight of a clergyman made many landowners extremely uncomfortable, and noted that these people, though they had taken about half a million in royalties from his parish, had not contributed a penny to church building.[104] A pamphlet written by Edwards in 1867 argued that while the mission of the National Church had been committed to him at Aberdare, to the landowners and ironmasters had been committed the ministry of wealth. They thus had a responsibility for the mission of the Church in the areas where their wealth was created. A church rate had been superseded by a voluntary rate but this had not worked. If the owners were not responsible they would be creating a moral wilderness of ignorance and debasement.[105] These companies, once owned by private individuals, by the 1870s had been formed into limited liability companies. This meant that the feeling of individual responsibility had been lost, suggested Bishop Ollivant in 1875. Even if the company wished to assist the work of church planting the move might be resisted by Nonconformist members of the board or shareholders.[106]

The assistance of these landowners and industrials was not without its complications. Crawshay Bailey was persuaded to assist the building of St David's Church, Ton Pentre, in the parish of Ystradyfodwg, by Archdeacon John Griffiths, who had "dangled him on his knees as a child". He gave both the site and the substantial sum of £6,000 towards the cost of the building. This was a sum equal to half the total spent on thirteen other church buildings in the parish. The new building should have been vested with the Ecclesiastical Commission, but Bailey insisted it should be placed in the hands of trustees, including the archdeacon, causing immense complications. Being privately owned the church was unable to be consecrated. The building was jerry-built and by the 1890s the fabric was crumbling, but the good archdeacon said it was nothing to do with him as a trustee, and the Bailey estate accused the church members of neglecting the building. Eventually, the family agreed to pay for the repairs, and decided to allow the church to be vested with the commissioners. Sadly, the structure continued to deteriorate throughout the years.[107] A relation of Crawshay Bailey, Sir Joseph Bailey, built a new church at Penmyarth in the parish of Tretower. He declined to endow it, part with the site, or to give up the power of dismissing its minister, nor was it known who had given the ecclesiastical consent for its building. Eventually, instead of being consecrated, it was simply licensed for divine worship.[108]

THE CHURCH BUILDING COMMISSION

The Church Building Commission was established by the government of the day to administer the funds provided by Parliament to build new churches in areas where the population exceeded 4,000. A concerned Parliament, anxious that a troublesome population be kept in order by the Church voted one million pounds in 1818 and half a million in 1825 in order to build new churches in these places. The majority of them became chapels-of-ease, and later district churches in their own right, but the need to find a stipend for the incumbent proved difficult. Those who offered an endowment were offered the patronage of that church, and if a group subscribed towards the endowment they were eligible to become trustees and joint patrons. In addition, part of the rent of pews went towards the stipend. The Commissioners became incorporate in 1828, and after 1867 the work of the commissioners was taken over by the Ecclesiastical Commission.[109] Churches built in Wales under the auspices of the Commissioners included St Michael's Aberystwyth (a grant of £1,000 was secured),[110] Buckley and Bistre,[111] St Paul's Newport (noted below) and St Mary's Cardiff which received a grant of £1,500 from the commissioners. This church opened in 1843, ending the formal union of that parish with St John's Cardiff, the original St Mary's having been destroyed and never rebuilt. Once again, this church was built to accommodate the new population in the docks area of the town, and because there were no sittings available at St John's Church. The marquess of Bute not only gave the site, but also £1,000 towards the cost of the building, having bought the patronage of it from the dean and chapter of Gloucester after much difficulty, and having to contend with John Webb, non-resident vicar of Cardiff, who raised every objection to its building because of the loss of income to himself.[112] Like many other churches, it was a partnership between the commissioners and wealthy individuals.

FASHIONABLE CHURCHES

St James' Church was built in the fashionable suburb of the Uplands in the parish of Swansea and opened in 1867, and is a good example of a church that was designed to remain a chapel of ease in a developing part of a parish some distance from the parish church. Though designed for the more respectable parishioners, who paid pew rents, it was hoped the poorer brethren would not be forgotten. By this time the sittings in the parish church had all been taken, and it was rightly assumed that this new church would be financially viable as those living in this area would transfer to it, especially those unable to find accommodation in the parish church (in addition it had the benefit of releasing seating there). The seats were graded from 24s. to 10s. per seat and only the pew holders had the right to elect the warden.[113]

Another category of church building was for visitors to the holiday destinations in Wales, the spas and the seaside. We need to remember that many families stayed at these places for a month or longer during the season and came back year after year. The need for such churches was pointed out by Bishop Campbell of Bangor in his 1863 Charge.[114] Appeals were made for the visitors in particular to subscribe to the building of these churches, and it was anticipated that their contributions to the offertory would make these churches self-supporting. Llandudno had become one of the more fashionable watering places on the north Wales coast. The existing town church was insufficient for this purpose, even with the use of a schoolroom and a large tent "comfortably" fitted up as an overflow for the English services. A new church, Holy Trinity, was thus built mainly for this purpose. It sat 1,200 people, cost £7,000 and was built as a free church, but visitors were encouraged to give generously when the collection plate was passed around.[115] Rhyl was another popular holiday destination, and for its visitors St Thomas' Church was built in 1862, when it was hoped these visitors would contribute liberally to its building fund. George Gilbert Scott was the architect, but the estimated cost of £8,000 eventually became £26,000 by 1878 when a spire was added to the structure.[116]

Other such churches were St Seiriol's, Penmaenmawr, built in 1867, and attended by the Gladstone family who had a home in that seaside place,[117] and Holy Trinity, Llandrindod. This church opened in 1871 with a fiasco, as the Hereford Cathedral Choir, booked to attend, had to leave before the final hymn in order to catch their train. The congregation assumed it was also time to leave, and those responsible for the collection, taken at that final hymn, desperately tried to obtain it at the doors of the church, while the bishop endeavoured to give his blessing before all departed. Kilvert mentioned this fiasco in his diary. A bell tower was built about 1885 at an additional cost of £2,000, and it was hoped that the visitors to the spa would support the sales of work mounted to find this sum, as the church had been provided for them free of cost.[118] It was even suggested that Christ Church, Caernarfon, built in 1859, was not only built for the English families living in the town but for the summer visitors, though this was stated in the context of the parish church at Llanbeblig used for Welsh services being at an inconvenient distance from the town.[119]

****

When these and other churches were opened or consecrated (if they were to be a parish church) there was generally a great ceremony. A choral service, with surpliced clergy, a dinner for the dignitaries and subscribers, and a Welsh service in the evening, well-known preachers, sometimes borrowed choirs, and always an appeal for assistance in ending the debt on the church. When the church at Llanllwchaiarn, Newtown, was opened in 1888 eight days of festivities followed with special preachers on each day.[120] Nevertheless, there was much criticism in the 1840s and 1850s that the consecration service was held in English, even in Welsh-speaking parishes, and this was regarded as near Popery. Though there was generally a Welsh-speaking evening service, the dignitaries of the Church were criticised for turning their back on it.[121]

THE PROBLEMS OF FINANCE

Probably the most difficult problem in building a new church was obtaining the necessary financial resources to do so, unless one had a wealthy landowner or industrialist willing to subsidise the cost. At an earlier period money could be obtained through a church rate, and it was permitted to borrow money against the security of these rates.[122] For example, Castle Caereinion borrowed money on this security for the repair of its church in the 1810s, but found itself in great difficulties when the bank which had lent the money failed, and called the debt in.[123] When church rates were levied for building a church many parishioners felt that their contribution had already been made through this levy. Often, the problems inherent in obtaining money from the rate income became a liability. This happened at Aberystwyth. When a new church was being built in the 1830s, desperately needed because of lack of accommodation and as it was assumed the town would become a holiday resort, great difficulties were found in raising the finances required. Sadly, the Chichester family, as impropriators of the parish, declined to assist, and the grant awarded by the Church Building Commissioners had to be scaled down due to the reduced size of the building. The commissioners also required the sea wall along the church boundary to be repaired, and a rate was imposed for its building. Great trouble was caused as several refused to pay, including five Nonconformist ministers, and these were distressed for their non-payment, only for it to be discovered that the rate was illegal as the wall was not built on consecrated land. As a result great bitterness resulted, especially as many dissenters had contributed to the building fund.[124]

By the 1850s church rates were being questioned by Nonconformists and were gradually phased out, either for a voluntary rate, which was not particularly effective, or by offertories taken at each service. But the monies available from either were used for the maintenance of the church and its services and there was little left over for church building or restoration. These needed special appeals and dedicated subscriptions from the parishioners and well-wishers. While many landowners and industrialists had built churches at their own expense, this was not true for the majority of those built. Many subscribed to the funds, but help was required from the ordinary parishioner and the general public as well.[125]

A few fortunate clergy through their connections were able to obtain contributions from their friends and contacts in high places. Amongst them was the aristocratic rector of Hawarden, George Neville. In 1822 he decided to build a chapel of ease at Buckley, a remote part of his parish, where a congregation had been meeting for some years in a National Schoolroom. Not only did he manage to obtain a grant from the Church Building Commissioners of £4,000, he obtained in addition £1,967 in subscriptions from people throughout England and Wales, including the Prince Regent.[126] Other enterprising churches targeted a selected number of their parishioners. At Oswestry, where there was need for a chapel of ease to accommodate those unable to find sittings in the parish church (estimated at 77 families), it was discovered that those who paid four pounds and more for the poor rate were generally those who rented pews in the church. An appeal was made to these people for assistance in building this chapel of ease, which when opened in 1835 had 700 sittings, of which 400 were free.[127]

Though grants were available from central sources and dioceses, much of the fund raising had to be made or found locally. I.G. Jones has calculated that 80 per cent of the money for building and restoring churches had to be raised locally. The help of these diocesan and national societies, even though significant was not substantial.[128] The St Asaph Diocesan Building Society, itself funded from subscriptions and collections, gave 41 grants for new churches between 1834-61, but what were these among so many![129] Other dioceses had their own societies, such as the Llandaff Church Building Society of 1845, subsumed into the Llandaff Diocesan Church Extension Society of 1851 (which gave grants of around £100 for a new church building though by 1892 this amount had declined to between £50 and £60 from want of funds,[130] and the St David's Diocesan Church Building Board, founded in 1883.[131] The work of the Church Building Commissioners has already been noted, but its contribution was not substantial in Wales and was confined to the building of new churches rather than mission churches, though it is interesting that as early as 1821 the work of the Church Building Society was commended to the clergy of Llandaff by their bishop, Van Mildert.[132]

By 1884 the Incorporated Church Building Society, founded in 1818, had given 289 grants to the diocese of St Davids totalling £25,965, though not all these grants were for new buildings. Its constitution only allowed it to give one quarter of the cost of building and to parishes with a population under 4,000. Its secretary reminded the diocese that its contribution to the Society of £34 in the previous year was hardly sufficient and it needed more assistance from it.[133] Similarly the Society in 50 years had given £13,132 to the diocese of St Asaph for 98 building projects, though the total cost of the works amounted to £408,771.[134] Its rules were strict. If work had already commenced on a church the Society would refuse a grant, as occurred at Penclawdd in 1850.[135]

Bazaars, sales of work, and other such fund-raising efforts were used to draw in local people to assist in financing the building or restoration of churches. A great bazaar was held at Newtown for the restoration fund of Betws Cedewain Church in 1890,[136] and other examples are noted in this text. Christ Church, Machynlleth, built in 1881 as a daughter church on land donated by the marquess of Londonderry, was financed by fund raising and private subscriptions.[137] Holy Trinity Church, Aberystwyth, opened in 1886, with no rented or appropriated seats, was financed by bazaars, fetes, a guarantee fund, and even the Sunday School children raised money by building sand castles on the beach. It was assisted by money left by a Miss Mary Morice to build a church in that place, and although her bequest was contested in law by her family it was won on appeal.[138] The printed list of contributors for the new church at Rossett in the parish of Gresford, built in 1841, mentioned James Boydell who gave the site, John Townshend who gave £1,000 as an endowment, the £200 from the diocesan church building society, and other sums ranging from one shilling to £100, some from "penny boxes". The total cost was £2,577, and the balance outstanding of £329 was also given by the above John Townshend.[139]

Advertisements might also be placed in the church press requesting assistance. One, in the *Church Builder* for 1881, related to Pontycymer Iron Mission Room in the Garw Valley. The importance of erecting a church in this area with as little delay as possible was emphasised, as its population had increased in the previous year from 600 to 1,000 and was increasing rapidly. There was no church within four and a half miles. Church services and Sunday schools, conducted mainly by laymen, were held in two unsuitable buildings with an average attendance of 70 adults and 120 children. The proposed mission room would seat 200 and cost over £250, and contributions could be sent to the Rev. J. Pritchard Hughes at Newcastle Vicarage, Bridgend.[140]

All too often the response from parishioners was not particularly generous. In some cases this was more due to poverty than apathy, though at Hope the incumbent reported that six pounds was the average he could raise each year "from scanty donations grudgingly given, and painfully and laboriously collected". A similar situation was found at Ysceifiog, but here there was much poverty, and Halkyn, where in common with the other parishes mentioned, there were no resident landowners.[141] When Caerphilly new church was bring built in 1878 its vicar, T. Jenkins, was informed by the Plymouth Estate agent that while Lady Windsor had guaranteed £800 of the cost, his principal parishioners had not accepted their responsibilities to help complete the work.[142]

Bishop Ollivant, however, made it clear that he wanted all church-people to take responsibility for this work of church extension and not leave it to the wealthy. This was the theme of his sermon at the opening of Skewen Church in 1851, entitled *The Duty of those who are* not *Rich, with respect to the Extension of the Church.* All sorts and conditions of men needed to take responsibility for the mission of the Church, not just the clergy and the wealthy. If you had no minister, no worship and no church, he asked, what would you desire your fellow countrymen should do unto you?[143] However, his successor, Richard Lewis, noted in his 1891 Charge that in some parishes working men had contributed £100 and £40 for a new church, presumably collectively, and in other parishes had assisted in the digging of the foundations.[144] Assistance in kind was often given by parishioners. A list of those who carried material free of charge for the building of Gwernaffield Church in 1837 still exists, as they did for Pontblyddyn Church the previous year. Both these churches owed their origin to Charles Butler Clough as vicar of Mold.[145]

In was not unusual for the estimated cost of the work to be exceeded with the result that more fundraising had to be implemented. A new church was needed at Glyntaff in the parish of Eglwysilan, the parish church being six miles away. The area had become a centre of industry, but there was a great difficulty in persuading the landowners and industrialists to contribute towards its cost. Lord Dynevor in fact wanted to see what others were going to offer before he committed himself. When a list of subscribers was about to be published, J.B. Bruce warned Lord Bute that it would be anomalous without his name on it. The estimated cost of £1,500 rose to £2,000 because of the need to build deeper foundations due to the sandy nature of the soil.[146] St Paul's Church, Newport, consecrated in 1836, though built with substantial grants from the Commissioners for Building New Churches and the Incorporated Church Building Society, far exceeded its estimates and a trade depression had meant that a large number of promised subscriptions had been lost. At one time its building committee faced a deficit of £2,716, which its members would have to make up. Although further monies were received from the Commissioners, loans given by the committee members and modifications made to the building, it became clear that the projected endowment for the Church would have to be used and the incumbent would have to rely on pew rents for his stipend.[147]

A substantial deficit was left when Holy Trinity Church, Tylorstown, was opened in

1883. Thankfully, Thomas Edmunds, who owned the mineral rights in that area and had already contributed £400 to the building fund, wrote off this deficit from his own resources. Another deficit occurred with Christ Church, Ferndale, and it was only covered by a number of bazaars, providing collecting books (giving people three months to find 10s. or more), and by substantial loans.[148] The new church built at Newton, in the parish of Oystermouth, and opened in 1903, cost £6,000, even when its tower had been omitted, far exceeding its original estimate, as the work took eighteen months longer to complete so adding additional expense. The vicar, Harold Stepney Williams, described as a great beggar, had worked hard to obtain the money required from bazaars, sewing parties, self-denying boxes, entertainments and subscriptions, even giving specific collecting cards to members of the congregation. Over £807 was collected during the services held for its opening, possibly most of it from these collecting cards. By that time, and with this collection, another £500 had to be found to ensure the church was free from debt.[149]

It was argued in 1891 by a layman, J.A. Doyle, that too many clergy miscalculated the cost of building or overspent what they had, and then made desperate appeals to raise the finance required, even requesting further subscriptions from those who had contributed already. These appeals made him ashamed to be a churchman.[150] As a result of these problems many clergy became effectively clerical beggars, as Bishop Ollivant maintained in his 1860 Charge, often to the neglect of their proper duties, though he admitted this was sometimes because their own people declined to assist.[151] William Wickham, a Lancashire clergyman, is said to have sent 20,000 handwritten letters appealing for funds all over the country during 1880-1 and still found himself short of funds.[152] A Welsh equivalent was John Howells, curate of Cyfarthfa, who wrote 7,000 letters appealing for funds for building Christ Church between 1845-57 which was opened eventually at a cost of £2,677. A lady had already given £1,000 for the building on being told it was in the most destitute area of the diocese.[153]

Yet another clerical beggar was Hugh Roberts of Brymbo, Wrexham, who proposed to build a new church at Broughton. At present, he wrote, the congregation were meeting in a stable loft. In a holograph letter of 1888 he noted it had taken him fifteen months to collect £1,200, and had each person he had written to, given him one shilling he would have obtained his required sum of £1,600, but the time spent in writing these letters meant he had seriously neglected his parochial work. Even if the recipient could offer no large sum, he would be grateful for a few stamps to cover the cost of postage. A church was eventually built at a cost of £2,152 and opened in 1889.[154] A further example indicates another problem. In 1894 T.H. Evans, vicar of Minera, issued a plea for another £600 desperately needed for a new church at Coedpoeth to replace an iron church some distance from the parish church and with a population of 5,000. The new church had no tower and the furniture was plain, and his 45,000 letters appealing for donations had produced £1,472. Another £900 had been collected locally, but £500 had been promised by various societies, but he could not receive this money until the work had been completed, and he needed this further £600 to do so within a month. The bishop endorsed this appeal and noted its mining population was mainly of poor people.[155]

It was not unknown for an incumbent to make himself responsible for the financial liabilities of building a new church. When St Mary's Church, Aberdare, was built as the Welsh Church, its then vicar, Evan Lewis, rather stupidly made himself personally responsible for the debt of the building fund knowing that many promised donations had failed to materialise. Lewis had paid £300 to liquidate some of it from his own private means, but he still owed £606 to the builder, and was in considerable difficulties, especially as he had moved to a new parish, Dolgellau. He had even had to sell some of his furniture to avoid a court judgment. As a result the wardens of the parish endeavoured to relieve him of these liabilities by opening a subscription fund in 1876.[156] This also happened during the building of St Mary's Church, Denbigh in 1873. Several subscribers had died before giving their subscriptions while there were other "unforeseen circumstances" which probably meant that some had defaulted on their promises. There was a deficiency of £1,200 for which the rector was responsible, and as such an appeal was made to relieve him of this burden.[157] In order to open the new church of St Ethelwold at Shotton free of debt in 1902, Stephen Gladstone as rector of Hawarden made himself responsible for the remaining £700, although the tower and spire were never built.[158]

On the other hand, it was not only the clergy who found themselves in debt because of their involvement in church building. Many parishes were encumbered by debts caused by the building of a church. This was especially so in the Rhondda as William Lewis, vicar of Ystradyfodwg and its principal church builder, insisted on good quality buildings. Llwynypia Church opened with a debt of £800, forty per cent of its actual cost, and Ferndale with a deficit of £1,000, only eliminated over many years by a series of bazaars, collection books and other means.[159] Though a new church at Manselton was built in 1905, replacing an iron church of the 1880s, and R. Glynn Vivian, as patron of the mother parish of Hafod, gave £4,000 towards its £6,000 cost, a debt still remained of £830. It was finally cleared by a great bazaar in Swansea's Albert Hall in 1909, when the assistance of other churches was sought and obtained.[160]

ISSUES ABOUT ECONOMY

It is not surprising that there were often disputes about the design of buildings between the Incorporated Church Building Society, the diocesan church building societies, as grant-givers, and those who had to find the cost of a building, especially the local industrialists and landowners, generally wanted the cheapest possible option.[161] The earl of Powis, speaking in 1847, argued that if the funds were insufficient the exterior of a cathedral was hardly needed. "If we are poor, a humble church will not disgrace us."[162] Thus when a new church was proposed at Aberafan in 1857 the first object was to multiply the number of sittings before any ornamentation was allowed.[163] This concern also manifested itself in the building of St David's Church, Merthyr Tydfil. This was built to supplement the existing and insufficient parish church, which thereafter became the Welsh Church, bringing an end to prolonged disputes about times of services between the Welsh and English congregations. Built in 1847, costing £4,109, £1,150 was awarded to it by the Church Building Commissioners on condition it had 1,200 seats of which half were to be free and unappropriated. The marquess of Bute was dissatisfied, as he felt that amount of money should have produced a church capable of seating at least 1,500 people, and wanted a plainer style of architecture and all the ornamental frills abandoned. A "showy" building, he concluded, would be wasted in that area. The local ironmasters, John Guest and Anthony Hill, took the same viewpoint, and refused to subscribe unless galleries were added to increase the seating and also made the excuse they had not been given the choice of architect, though the commissioners had insisted upon T.H. Wyatt.

Such men, wrote Bishop Copleston, had no honour and accused them of delaying the building instead of promoting it.[164]

There are many instances recorded where corners were cut in the building of a church in order to economise. One writer, though in an English context, described churches built as "miserable half-finished" structures, fit for one generation only, with brick walls, green timber fostering dry rot and windows letting in the freezing wind.[165] An appendix written by the secretary of the Incorporated Church Building Society, included in the report of the 1885 St Davids diocesan conference, alleged that many churches were either built as cheaply as possible, or that the exterior was over-embellished and the interior ignored.[166] Too often the smallest tender was accepted from a local builder, and the London architect was too busy to examine it properly. A specific clerk of works should be appointed, for if a clergyman did the job himself, as many did, he would be deceived. As a result, said another speaker at the St Davids diocesan conference of 1891, a restoration would be required within twenty years.[167] This is what happened at St Elvan's church, Aberdare and at Hirwaun, where H.T. Edwards noted that within fifteen years of their construction, because both buildings had been built so cheaply, the former was seriously dilapidated and the later needed immediate restoration.[168] Two churches, built in late 1830s, Gwernaffield and Pontblyddyn, in the parish of Mold, had to be rebuilt within twenty-five years of their opening.[169] Edward Hubbard in his *Buildings of Wales: Clwyd* suggests that the architect, John Lloyd, who did much church work in that county, produced churches that were awkward in appearance, left much to be desired in their design details, and were faulty in construction, as were Bistre, Connah's Quay and Pontblyddyn, already noted above.[170] Another such church was Rhosesmor in Flintshire, which was so badly constructed that a violent storm damaged the roof of the church, unnecessarily exposed because of its steep roof, and within fifteen years after its opening in 1876 it needed a major renovation.[171]

In other cases the plans had to be modified due to lack of finance, as noted in numerous previous examples. This happened at Rhos-y-cae in the parish of Halkyn when the projected church had to be shortened.[172] In other instances a tower or aisle had to be omitted, or a building erected in stages, as at Bargoed, where a chancel was built first and many years later a nave added, replacing an iron built nave, and at Pontypridd an aisle had to be omitted from the initial building (and when it was built the roof of the main building was found to be defective).[173] At Cardiff the projected St Mary's Church, in spite of considerable grant-aid, had to have two transepts omitted through lack of funds, so the proposed cruciform plan was abandoned.[174] St Elvan's Church, Aberdare, built as a prodigious statement of Anglican ascendancy in a Nonconformist stronghold, had its plans pared down when the cheapest tender was nearly fifty per cent greater than the architect's estimate of £3,000. The thickness of the walls was reduced, much of the planned ornamentation was removed, the height of the nave reduced and the south porch and transept omitted. Even then a debt remained and a levy of £200 was placed on every member of the committee, and only the success of an eventual bazaar enabled them to be repaid. As noted earlier, substantial repairs were required on the building within fifteen years of its opening.[175] At St Andrew's, Llwynypia, the church had to be opened in 1878 without its projected chancel due to lack of funds, and forty per cent of its cost still had to be found, half of it lent by local tradespeople.[176]

A number of buildings in fact collapsed even before they were opened. The most spectacular was that of the new church at Barmouth, built at the expense of Mrs Dyson Perrins at a cost of £20,000, whose tower collapsed demolishing part of its walls as it was being built in 1891. She gave generously towards its rebuilding.[177] In 1843, while building, part of the south wall collapsed at St Mary's Church, Cardiff, causing the collapse of two piers, indicating all too clearly the hasty, cost-cutting and defective workmanship of the builders, and even before the building was consecrated its western end was saturated with damp.[178] Another example was the church at Williamstown, in the Rhondda valley. In 1891, even before the roof had been placed on the building the bell tower collapsed with the side walls injuring three members of the church. Subsidence was the official reason for the collapse.[179]

It was not unknown for an incumbent to fall out with his architect. This happened during the building of St Mary's Welsh Church, Aberystwyth, when William Butterfield quarrelled with the vicar, Evan Owen Phillips, and abandoned the job. He later refused to work on the restoration of Llanbadarn Fawr Church as Phillips was on its building committee.[180]

CREATING A NEW DISTRICT

The legal complications of creating a new district or parish were substantial. Until 1818, when the Church Building Act was passed, only a chapel of ease to an existing parish was permitted unless a new parish was created by act of parliament. This was a rare event due to the complications of respecting existing interests.[181] When Blaenafon Church was built in 1805 and created a perpetual curacy, the act permitting this specified that it did not prejudice the right of the vicar of Llanover, its original parish, to the tithes, and the fees were doubled, half going to that vicar and his successors.[182]

Peel's Act of 1843 to make better provision for the spiritual care of populous parishes, simplified this procedure, and allowed a district to be created by Order of Council on the recommendation of the Ecclesiastical Commissioners.[183] These so-called Peel districts allowed a clergyman to minister in a new district before a church was built in order to build up a congregation. The bishop's approval was required but the patron and the incumbent of the mother church only had the right to comment. The financing of these districts – in reality of their clergy - came initially from the borrowing of £600,000 of Exchequer bills from Queen Anne's Bounty by the Ecclesiastical Commissioners, and when that sum was exhausted it was not until 1856 that the commissioners had a surplus they could devote to this purpose.[184]

Until 1857 with the passing of the New Parishes Act of Lord Blandford the inhabitants of the new districts were still expected to pay church rates to the original parish church for twenty years after their creation, as well as maintain their own church by yet another church rate.[185] In addition those who lived in the new district but who held pews in the parish church were required to relinquish those pews unless they held them by faculty, had seats assigned to them, and continued to worship in the old parish church.[186] Even with the passing of this act the incumbent of the parish church was still entitled to receive the surplice fees derived from the new district, though he did not officiate on these occasions, or be compensated instead for them, because his life interest had to be preserved.[187] These rights lapsed for his successor. In many cases the incumbents of the parishes from which a new district was formed might be required to give part of their stipend to the new district, and this may be the reason why some clergy were reluctant to allow new districts to be created. We have noted already how endowments were provided for the stipends of clergy serving these parishes. In addition, the consent of patron, bishop and all those incumbents affected had to be obtained, and before the Ecclesiastical Commissioners would allow a new parish, probably formed from a district, to be created, it needed a church building with accommodation for a percentage of the population, irrespective that many might be Nonconformists, to be built in an approved style, and to be consecrated. For that to happen the building had to be free from debt and on freehold land. In addition an endowment or source of clear funding was required for the incumbent, though this might be provided by the Commissioners.[188]

Besides these complications, a debate occurred within the Church as to whether parishes should be subdivided, giving the new incumbents an insufficient income and often leaving them to deal with the debts of church building, or whether there be a large parish with a considerable number of curates, thus denying many men the chance of a parish of their own.[189] William Lewis of Ystradyfodwg, probably the most outstanding church builder in the diocese of Llandaff, preferred the former, arguing that this would better encourage the revival of church life, and acted upon this conviction.[190]

A number of parishes and consolidated chapelries (perpetual curacies) were created under the provisions of the Church Building Acts. The Church Building Commissioners were empowered from 1831 to confer parochial status on the churches built under their auspices, without any other permission save that of the diocesan bishop, and assign the patronage to those who had contributed to the building of the church or the endowment of the minister. Such a parish had to meet certain criteria: either there had to be 2,000 and more parishioners and room for no more than a third in existing churches and chapels of the parish, or there had to be at least 300 parishioners living more than two miles from one of these places of worship and less than one mile from the one being built, though this restriction was removed in 1851.[191] St Mary, Cardiff, and Dowlais became separate parishes under the terms of these acts, and amongst the consolidated chapelries were Bagillt, Llanfynydd, Llandrillo-yn-Rhos, Penrhos and Rhydycroesau in the diocese of St Asaph; St David's Carmarthen, St John's Newton-in-Clodock, Trinity chapel at Newcastle Emlyn and Cwmaman in the diocese of St Davids; Glyntaff, Caerphilly, Tredegar in the diocese of Llandaff; and Llanllwch and Llandegai in the diocese of Bangor. Most of these churches were built between 1843-51.[192]

Those districts created under Peel's 1843 Act included Brynford in the parish of Holywell; Bistre and Gwernaffield; Connah's Quay, Brymbo and Minera in the parish of Wrexham (St Asaph); St Paul's Llanelli, Brynmawr, Gorseinon, Clydach, Morriston, Trinity Church Swansea and St Paul's Sketty (St Davids); Beaufort, Nantyglo, Tredegar, Rhymney, Crynant, Skewen, Cyfarthfa, Penmaen, Abercarn, and Llantwit Fardre (Llandaff).[193] A number of their churches were built under the auspices of the Church Building Commissioners.

The Ecclesiastical Commissioners were also enabled to form and endow new districts although the main difficulty was that the population needed to be four thousand plus and in the south Wales valleys geographical difficulties made this difficult. In 1844 the district of Nantyglo was formed out of the parish of Aberystruth, one of five so formed in the colliery districts between 1844-50.[194] New districts were created from the original parish of Aberdare, St Fagan's, Mountain Ash, Hirwaun and Aberaman: though the latter two took many years as the vicars of Aberdare took umbrage because their incumbents would receive a stipend from the commissioners of £300, whereas that of Aberdare, with far greater responsibility, was set at £200 as being in private patronage.[195] Rhosymedre was formed out of the parish of Ruabon in 1844, Gorsedd from the parishes of Whitford and Ysceifiog in 1853, and Prion from the parish of Llanrhaiadr in 1860, to give some examples from the diocese of St Asaph.[196] During the episcopate of Richard Lewis as bishop of Llandaff (1883-1905) twenty-five new districts were established, most in the valley areas of his diocese.[197] By this time the rather loose distinction between a district and a parish had all but vanished, possibly due to the death of the incumbent of the mother parish whose life interest in the fee income died with him.[198]

The need for new parishes was stressed at the 1893 Llandaff diocesan conference, and by this time it was clear that a parish staffed by an incumbent and possibly one or two curates was accepted as the norm rather than a multi-church benefice.[199] Thus in his 1913 Llandaff Charge, Pritchard Hughes, noting that the population of his diocese was increasing by 30,000 annually, planned to establish 25 new parishes with an average population of 4,000 each. Already seven new parishes and seven conventional districts had been created. He accepted that these 25 new parishes might not be created immediately but he hoped that it might be possible to establish these areas as conventional districts led by a curate-in-charge. Endowments were needed for these places to become full parishes, and he thus offered any individual offering an endowment of £300 per annum the patronage of that parish.[200] One of the churches which became a conventional district was St Julian's, Newport, in 1915, which had started in an iron hut and later moved into a permanent building.[201] The First World War ended these hopes, though after it twelve new parishes had been created, five of them in the Rhondda, together with four conventional districts.[202]

When it became clear that disestablishment would happen, there was a great rush to establish these new districts and so gain those grants that would otherwise be lost. By 1914 there were plans to create two new districts out of the parish of Merthyr Tydfil, namely Merthyr Vale and Tydfil's Well, where churches had already been built. The rector, Daniel Lewis, as promoter, was required to pay the legal costs of the conveyances but prevaricated so much that time ran out and only Merthyr Vale was made into a district church.[203]

THE INCUMBENTS' DILEMMA AND TWO CASE STUDIES

Many incumbents were dissatisfied with the ease by which a district could be taken away from their parish, depriving them in some cases of the wealthier members of their congregation. Bishop Copleston wanted the new church of St Paul, Newport, to become a district church, but for two years until 1839 the incumbent of the mother church of St Woolos, Anthony Isaacson, procrastinated, fearing a loss of income even though his fees would be safeguarded by his life interest.[204] In a similar way, when Miss Clara Thomas built at her own expense a church at Cwmbach Llechryd in 1886, for her own convenience as it was near to her own home, she managed to have it established as a separate district. The rector of the "mother" parish, Llanelwedd, was not happy at having this parish carved out of his own, and probably using part of his endowment. Each year he sent to the incumbent of Cwmbach a postcard on which he placed the words, "cursed be he that removeth his neighbour's landmark".[205]

A case study may be made of the foundation of the parish of Pontypridd, formed out of the parish of Glyntaff. A growing town, in which Nonconformity had taken root, the Church congregation had commenced in some cottages before moving to a room so inconvenient that the bishop had with reluctance licensed it, and which was said to have given the impression that the church was a proscribed sect in that town. Eventually the church of St Catherine had been opened in 1869, but lack of funds meant that the proposed north aisle remained unbuilt and the interior was incomplete. By 1869 the congregation now wished for their church to become a parish church, but in so doing they met with the strong opposition of the vicar of Glyntaff, whose curate served their church. He believed that if such a large area was taken away from his parish he and his successors would be disqualified from receiving any further augmentation to their stipend from the Ecclesiastical Commissioners based on the population of their parish. Besides, he had contributed a substantial sum to the building of the church, and its congregation contained a large number of professional people compared to the more working class at Glyntaff.

The commission's secretary informed the church's committee about the conditions required before St Catherine's could become a district church. A repair fund of £150 had to be provided; and the boundaries, patronage, the private interests of the vicar of Glyntaff (that is, his fee income) had to be sorted out. Before the church could be consecrated it had to be inspected by the commission's architect to ensure it was up to standard. In addition the endowment had to be found, at least £1,000, and there the matter rested for the money could not be found until 1881, when it was agreed that the vicar of Glyntaff would retain the surplice fees as a life interest. The church still needed to be consecrated, and for this to occur it had to be on freehold land and free of debt, and this was finally accomplished by the following year. An arrangement was made whereby, because of the population of the parish, 4,500 and rising, the commissioners would offer an endowment to the parish for the stipend on terms of its population, though meanwhile the new vicar would have to subsist on a curate's stipend, partly funded by the commissioners. Another problem presented itself. To receive such an endowment the parish church needed to accommodate at least a tenth of the population, 500 people, even though this ruling was absurd in a parish where Nonconformity abounded. The church was 100 places short, with the result that money had to be found to build the long projected north aisle (when it was discovered that the roof had been so badly built it had to be reconstructed). It was not until 1884, fifteen years after the initial enquiry, that the new district was gazetted "at our Court of Balmoral".[206]

Another case study is that of the new parish of Colwyn Bay, separated from Llandrillo-yn-Rhos, after a long controversy in 1893. Already a portion of the mother parish, St Catherine's Colwyn, had become a separate district in 1844. The Colwyn Bay area developed rapidly by the 1880s, and when an iron church erected there burnt down in 1886, it was decided to build a purpose-built church fit to become the parish church of a new district. St Paul's Church, or at least its nave and north aisle as the chancel was yet to be built, was opened in 1888 with accommodation for over one thousand worshippers. A deed transferring the patronage to the diocesan bishop was signed by the vicar, Venables Williams, and others soon after, though retaining for Williams a life interest in the fees of the new parish. A new bishop, A.G. Edwards, was determined to establish this new parish and appoint a new man to it, whereas Williams believed that the previous bishop had promised he could hold it in plurality with his own, in recognition of his efforts in building the new church at a cost of between £6,000 to £7,000. It may well be that he allowed the transfer of patronage to the bishop on this understanding, for normally the first appointment would be placed in the gift of the incumbent of the mother parish, but ecclesiastical law prevented a patron presenting himself to a parish in his gift.

Edwards clearly had little time for Williams, who had procrastinated about holding Welsh services in his parish, and felt it was essential for the progress of the Church in that area for Colwyn Bay to become a separate parish and totally rejected Williams' assertion that his stipend would be affected by this division. Nevertheless, Williams maintained that he derived an income of £105 from the pew rents of the new church and these would be lost to him and he was indignant that the Bishop had proceeded with the new arrangements without even asking for his consent. Williams was clever enough to attach his case to that of the current issue of the disestablishment of the Welsh Church, claiming he was the first to be disestablished. In spite of a parliamentary report with the publication of the correspondence between Williams, the two bishops and the Ecclesiastical Commission, and an appeal to the archbishop, the support of the local and even national press who saw an old man robbed of the fruit of his labours, the division went ahead.[207]

****

The mission of the Church in establishing “church plants” (to use a modern phrase) and the building of purpose-built churches was generally accomplished by the determination of the clergy involved. Many made considerable sacrifices to do so, and encumbered themselves with much anxiety and financial burdens. A number compounded their difficulties by accepting too grandiose schemes that were unaffordable, or by failing to ensure the works were adequately supervised, and paid the penalty for their mistakes. Yet, all in all, their contribution to the life and mission of the Church was immense and enabled their Church to hold its head high during the long debates on disestablishment.

CHAPTER SIX: MISSION AND EVANGELISM

The eighteenth century Church feared enthusiasm as it seemed to be contrary to its ordered pattern and quiet way of life. The cult of enthusiasm challenged the accepted norm that all Englishmen were Christians by virtue of their birth in a Christian country, or that baptism made one a Christian. The institutional Church thus expressed horror that people needed to be evangelised or that a person might be influenced by the Holy Spirit rather than influenced by church order. The remark of Bishop Butler to John Wesley was typical of the thought of the day: "Sir, the pretending to extraordinary revelation and gifts of the Holy Ghost is a horrid thing, a very horrid thing".[1]

A century later it was clear that the country needed evangelising, especially in the large towns, hence the movement for church planting in these areas. Evangelicals and Anglo-Catholics still saw the need for evangelising not only outside the churches but within them as well, to counteract the lukewarm Christianity of many church-going people. Mission now lay not simply in erecting buildings and establishing out-stations, but involved direct appeals to people to place their whole faith in Christ. The hymns of the period reinforced this message, and stirring evangelistic hymns, appealing to the heart, became extremely prominent. Some preachers made direct and passionate appeals to people in their sermons, and even preached outdoors, while the work of mission brought about a new order of ministry, evangelists and missioners.

These methods were far different from the ordered sanitized preaching and the reciting of the metrical psalms of the previous century. The hierarchy of that day had failed to realise that many people wanted more than a static liturgy, sometimes hastily performed, and desired a heart-experience rather than a cerebral performance. Griffith Jones had realised this, and acted upon it in his open-air evangelism as a curate (for which he was severely reproved)[2] and later by his circulating schools, and the Welsh Methodists, who saw themselves as renewing the Church, had also done so. Effectively driven out of the Church, they took their converts with them. But the order had changed and in the new world of the mid-nineteenth century what had been condemned as Methodist practices became the norm in many churches: evangelistic sermons, rousing hymns, mission and preaching about the need for conversion.

DIRECT EVANGELISM

By direct evangelism is meant preaching in the open air, distributing evangelistic tracts and proclaiming the Lordship of Christ to people wherever they might be gathered outside of a church context. This obviously happened, but the actual recorded instances of this kind of evangelism are unfortunately quite rare.

Edward Smart, when at Henllan as curate and later rector1840-76, started open air services at a crossroads of a common in his parish, using his phaeton as his pulpit, and urging people to be reconciled to God. Bishop Short protested that he was aping the Methodists, but Smart held his ground and continued his activities.[3] Such open air preaching was reasonably common. The *Christian Observer* of 1856 suggested that there were few large towns where their clergy were not engaged in preaching designed "to win the souls of careless sinners for Christ", while Bishop Tait of London also did so in the following year, though he was almost unique amongst the episcopate in so doing.[4]

An account of open air preaching in an unknown South Wales valley was given in 1883, when 500 colliers were present. "I spoke to them," wrote the incumbent, "in the two languages, and it was a sight I shall not soon forget, to see the earnestness with which they listened to the message of salvation. I was assured by my parish workers that a large proportion of them have not been inside the door of a place of worship for years. Most of them had never before heard a clergyman preach, and none of them had ever before heard him preach in the open air."[5] Open air preaching by Daniel Felix, the incumbent, took place at Llanhilleth in the late 1890s, which together with the use of a board school for services and classes led to the foundation of churches at Aberberg and Six Bells.[6] Talbot Rice, vicar of Swansea, continued the tradition with open air preaching at Victoria Park during the 1900s, attended by 500 to 600 people.[7] Around the same time an office clerk, W.J. Bronham, became a part-time evangelist at Greenhill in Swansea. Gathering about him a number of lay-helpers, he organised open-air and lodging house meetings, and after ordination in 1915 built a permanent mission hall in that area, eventually becoming incumbent of St Matthew's Church where he continued to hold evangelistic services until his death in 1943.[8]

A plea for a missionary agency was made in 1851 by a North Wales incumbent in a printed letter addressed to the two north Wales bishops. With new centres of population springing up the parochial system was in danger of collapse, and he suggested that a local schoolmaster might, for some extra payment, visit the sick and poor, hold cottage lectures, baptise and read public prayer.[9]

It was John Griffith who stressed the need for evangelism in the south Wales valleys, the so called "hill district". Merthyr and Dowlais were desolate districts, and he argued in words worth repeating that "we wish to hear the *Hindooism* of Merthyr and Aberdare discussed as well as that of Tinevelly and Tanjore ... There is work here which will furnish matter for eloquent speeches, as forcible and as crying as the war hatchets and the cannibalism of New Zealand or of Sierra Leone."[10] His answer was not so much direct evangelism but clear, decisive and popular preaching. But he seems to have ignored the fact that Nonconformity was also at work, sometimes with an aggressive evangelism, in these towns. On the other hand it became clear in the larger cities, especially London, by the 1850s, that the working classes could not be integrated into the middle class churches or organised into their own churches with a middle class leadership. The answer was the use of city missioners using a direct evangelistic approach to mission.[11]

This may have formed a precedent for Bishop Ollivant of Llandaff. He had spoken about the need for a missionary agency in his diocese in his charges from the 1850s onwards, and with the need for a bilingual policy and the rapid increase in the population of his diocese, often in isolated areas, it was clear the Church was unable to cope. Though many agencies assisted the diocese, and new churches and schools had been built, more was needed to turn people away from sin and irreligion and to Christ. Missionary clergy could preach to colliers in the open air, follow them into the pits, and gather together those who lived in isolated areas. Though such an agency might appear to be at variance with the system and discipline of the Church, Ollivant argued it would be supplementary and auxiliary rather than opposed to it. Indeed, there were historical precedents for this, especially colonial practice, while he indicated that the incumbents of these areas would welcome the assistance such missioners could offer them.[12] By 1860 he had been able to appoint a missioner for the "mineral districts", but he was there to supplement the parochial system and could only enter parishes with the permission of the incumbent. By 1863 there were two "home missioners" and Ollivant claimed they were doing good work.[13] A report of what was known as the Diocesan Home Mission indicated that its three missioners had undertaken notable work at such places as Ferndale and Dinas in the Rhondda Valleys, the Ogmore Valley, and Fleur-de-Lis, where they had pioneered and developed new work.[14]

Specific missions were also established for those who were described as navvies, namely those itinerant workers who settled for a time in a makeshift camp in order to build railways or other construction works. A navvies mission was organised for the Elan Valley when the dam was being built there in the 1890s, and a missioner, the Revd. Mr Horwood, appointed by the contractors to serve the men and families brought to this isolated area by the construction.[15] The contractors of the Alwen Water Scheme for Birkenhead, in Denbighshire, provided a hall and a missioner, who was paid £65 per annum, though other denominations were allowed to use this hall.[16] In 1895 Sunday afternoon services were held for the navvies at Ewenny. This particular work showed that the Book of Common Prayer was not unacceptable and that the ministrations of parochial clergy were appreciated. Four years later another mission was held at Taffs Well for the men working on the Walnut Tree viaduct. The local mission room was used and the services were appreciated by the men and their families.[17]

PARISH MISSIONS

Parish Missions were organised events, lasting over a period of days, during which a recognised missioner was appointed, who would help a parish prepare for a mission, obtain assistant missioners to assist him, and arrange a series of meetings and services to proclaim the Lordship of Christ and the need for repentance and faith to particular groups of people, as well as to the congregation of a church. Members of that church would be encouraged not only to attend, but to publicise the mission and invite people to its meetings. In many cases an "after meeting" followed the main mission meeting, during which people were encouraged to remain and exhorted to repent and believe. The earlier missions were generally sponsored by evangelical and Tractarian parishes, and often criticised by the bishops, who feared the emotionalism they induced in people and they disliked the idea that church-going people might also need to be converted.

It is said that Bishop Wilberforce commenced parochial missions in the populous centres of his diocese, Oxford, from 1850 onwards, although it is said the first parochial mission recorded was held at St James', Wednesbury, in 1856. Others followed, mainly led by Tractarian leaders. A further initiative, once again led by Tractarian clergy under the leadership of Fr Benson of the Cowley Fathers, a monastic community, was a mission to parishes in the east end of London in 1869. Fervent services, daily eucharists, outdoor processions, extempore prayer, and earnest preaching for the conversion of souls were said to be some of its characteristic features. It met with denunciation in some quarters, but its apparent success led to another mission in 1874, this time sanctioned by the three diocesan bishops of the London area, and in which evangelical clergy took part. The Moody and Sankey missions of 1873-5 and 1881, interdenominational, well-planned and worked to a specific formula of public appeals, enquiry rooms, trained counsellors, emotional music and preaching, found favour in some quarters but derision in others. John Griffith of Merthyr, for example, declared it was no more than an "ecclesiastical jumbo" or "carnival" run by "a converted Barnum" and attended by the fashionable world as the latest novelty. Yet it was these missions and this movement that led, indirectly, to the Church Army, the Parochial Mission Society, sponsored by Robert Aitken whom Moody persuaded to become a full-time evangelist, and the establishment of a company of mission priests by Archbishop Benson based on All Hallow's Barking. By 1875 a Convocation report endorsed these missions.[18]

The Welsh bishops tended to be cautious about parochial missions. Bishop Campbell of Bangor in 1878 accepted the expediency of missions for a week or so, though they needed much preparation, but pointed out the danger of a subsequent reaction and over powerful emotions being generated. Some years later a suggestion of having mission preachers itinerating from parish to parish had been made. While Campbell accepted some men were marked out for such work, he doubted the expediency of separating the work of preaching from pastoral ministry, and feared over-emotional addresses. While a mission preacher might break up fallow ground, the man who would permanently edify his people must live among them.[19] Caution was also expressed by Bishop Ollivant of Llandaff. He almost denounced the Newport mission of 1872 for its methods, as noted later. In his 1878 Charge he noted missions in several churches in Cardiff and Roath. He had given his permission for these missions in what were clearly High Church parishes, but specifically insisted that they should not be held for upholding "party purposes", especially the use of private confession. He was grateful to hear there was a lack of controversy and excitement.[20]

Dean Burgeon of Chichester had summed up many of these fears in his pamphlet *Home Missions and Sensational Religion*. He protested that too often mission was seen as allowing an incumbent to hand over his parish to a stranger who called himself without any authority "the missioner". He might introduce such practices as confession or extreme ideas about the eucharist, and he would ensure that the preaching was of the most exciting kind, the hymns were the most emotional, the emotional feelings of people were aroused and a room of enquiry established for further emotional haranguing. Too often those who came forward under these pressures soon lapsed and returned to their old state of lethargy. Instead, the church should revive public catechising, and deal with the lost by seeking them out one by one, not with handbills and the excitement of a mission week.[21] Another critique of these missions came in 1876-7 in an anonymous article in the *Church Quarterly Review*. Though the writer accepted they could do much good, he queried the use of emotions and argued that the legality of the "after meeting" was hard to defend, as it made no pretence to be a liturgical service.[22]

A decade later this caution had been removed, possibly because experience had shown these fears were by and large unjustified. Speakers at the Carlisle Church Congress of 1884 spoke about the need for preparation, the conduct of the mission and its sequel, and speakers at the Manchester Congress of 1888 claimed that the defects of the parochial system could be remedied by continuous evangelising work (rather than by parochial missions), open air singing and preaching in addition to temperance work.[23] Dean Vaughan of Llandaff felt these missions should be occasional, every five to ten years, otherwise parish life would be too disrupted, and he believed their aim was a rousing of the careless members of the Church.[24] A debate on parochial missions took place at the Llandaff Diocesan Conference in 1887, answering the question why they were needed in a Christian country, with one speaker claiming the reason was because of the clergy's dissatisfaction with parochial work. Another speaker urged that teaching missions he held.[25] The diocese of St Davids in 1889 even gave instructions in its Calendar about holding parochial missions, advising clergy to discuss the arrangements with their parishioners, holding preparatory meetings, the advisability of using tracts, and contacting employers requesting them to give time for their employees to attend meetings.[26] By 1900 the mood had shifted, and the Llandaff Conference heard a plea that the Church should hire large halls for its missions which were to show that the Church was concerned about the social issues of the day.[27]

PAROCHIAL MISSIONS IN WALES

One of the first Welsh missions was held during 1873 at Whittington, whose rector was Walsham How. He took part in the work and appealed for people to obtain a personal religion for themselves, and in the after meetings begged people to pray for themselves. As people remained on their knees he would move up and down the church uttering words of help and encouragement, such as "Lord, I believe, help Thou my unbelief". Later he conducted missions himself but his sermons if pointed and persuasive were not sensational, and his after meetings were quiet and reverent, free from excitement.[28] In that same year a mission took place at Welshpool, whose vicar, John Hill, was a friend of Walsham How. It took place over three days with George Body as missioner assisted by How and others. Body became a noted Anglo-Catholic missioner. The day started with a service of Holy Communion, and ended with a mission service, while separate meetings were held for the clergy and an outdoor one for the men working at Lord Powis's sawmills. On the last day 140 received communion.

Another mission took place in Welshpool during 1874, again with George Body, though this was a ten-day affair. About 800 men were present for a special Sunday afternoon service for them, but many had to be turned away from the evening service as the church was packed out. There were special services for servants and children, and four addresses for clergy on the duties and difficulties of the pastoral life: the seventy clergy attending being given hospitality overnight by parishioners. Afternoon addresses on "Helps to the Spiritual Life" were described as marvellous, and Body's evening addresses left a deep impression on those attending. On the last day 182 people received communion.[29]

THE MAJOR TOWN MISSIONS OF THE 1870s

There were a number of large scale missions during the 1870s. As a result of the London mission of 1869 a group of Cardiff clergy decided to hold a mission in their town during the following year, though there had been a mission in 1866 led by David Howell, as vicar of Cardiff, Vincent Saulez, vicar of Canton, and a prominent Nonconformist minister, Alfred Tilly. While much effort was being given for mission abroad, there had been little proportionate effort "to chase away heathenism at home", wrote Howell at this time. Eleven thousand people had attended the fourteen open air meetings, nine thousand homes had been visited and eighteen thousand tracts distributed, but the results were not altogether encouraging, possibly because it was home-based and interdenominational.

In this 1871 mission Robert Aitken was the chief missioner, assisted by William Haslam and C.W. Furse, and both Tractarian and evangelical clergy from seventeen churches took part. Howell wrote in its defence that the conviction that the ordinary services and ministrations of the Church were sufficient to cope with the irreligious tendencies of the age could no longer be justified, and a supplementary agency was needed. Special services were held, entry gained to places of work, family prayer encouraged and, said Bishop Ollivant, "a solemn sense of religious things" was created. Without excitement or eccentricity the number of communicants was increased, especially in Howell's churches because of the extent of his preparation and insistence on prayer for the work, while a profound impression was made on the town. Over the whole town there were 700 converts, while at St Andrew's Church over 120 new communicants presented themselves at the altar out of a total of 322, "in a never to be forgotten service". The newly started prayer meeting held at 7.30 am on Sunday mornings at St John's Church was attended by over 200 people.[30] Another mission was held at Llanelli, where its vicar, Canon David Williams, met with considerable opposition as it was claimed the movement was English and not Welsh.[31]

The success of this 1871 Cardiff mission led J. Timson Wrenford, vicar of St Paul's

Church, Newport, to organise one that same year in his town. This mission, again led by Robert Aitken, was described as a period of extraordinary blessings, during which over 2,000 people had been converted, with after-meetings continuing until well after midnight. Preparatory meetings had been held in the YMCA open to all Christians for some time beforehand. Sadly, Bishop Ollivant did not share in Wrenford's rejoicing and said so publicly in his 1872 visitation charge, though he did not name Wrenford, only speaking of one who had failed to ask for his episcopal consent, and for whom he had a deep feeling of personal esteem and affection. He viewed these mission services with "no little anxiety and embarrassment", felt the term "conversion" was inappropriate for those who had been baptised, and depreciated the holding of after meetings when feelings were in a state of excitement, asking pointed questions to individuals, and taking those responding to the chancel rail for "fresh stimulants" to be applied to their "already excited feelings".[32]

Undaunted by these criticisms, a further mission was organised by Wrenford in 1876, during which in his parish alone there had been 1,000 conversions over four months, though he also noted the input given by other denominations.[33] The missioner, Canon Hay Aitken, wrote to his wife that at one of the meetings over 2,000 men had been packed in: "it was a glorious sight, and the power of the Lord was very present". The rails, for enquirers, were full several times over, and thirty or forty men "found what they sought then and there". At another meeting over a thousand remained for the "after-meeting" designed for enquirers and "the rails were kept in use till nearly 11 o'clock at night".[34] A report of 1898 reveals that there had been five missions in that church, conducted either by Robert Aitken, a well-known missioner, or his son, Hay M.H. Aitken.[35]

A further mission took place at Swansea in 1870, again with Robert Aitken, this time assisted by his two sons, though it appears there had been an earlier mission to the Welsh-speakers of the town. Collectively they gave forty sermons and addresses, and on some occasions over 3,000 people were crowded into St Mary's Church. Services were held in the gaol and for sailors, while drawing room meetings were arranged for the more well-to-do parishioners. After the evening meetings a prayer meeting was held in the Oxford Street Schools, allegedly attended on some occasions with over 2,000 people, helpers and penitents alike. A prayer meeting which commenced after the mission had a weekly attendance of over five hundred. Large numbers of people from all ranks of society were influenced by the mission, and as the vicar of Swansea, Edward Squire, maintained, it was a time for shaking the dry bones and establishing the believers. The missioners were surprised at the lack of any substantial opposition and the large proportion of the higher classes amongst the enquirers. Many hundreds professed faith and these became the backbone of much of the subsequent Christian life of the parish. Another result was the formation of new mission churches at Greenhill and Waun Wen, though it appears that the work at Greenhill was consolidated by a ten-day Welsh mission. A further mission with the Aitken family took place in 1874.[36] James Allan Smith, then vicar of Swansea, noted that these missions had met the special needs of a vast number of people.[37] Smith's immediate predecessor as vicar of Swansea, Samuel Christopher Morgan, was also deeply involved in the mission movement and wrote a pamphlet on conducting one. In it he emphasised the after meeting, comprising prayer and singing and presumably exhortation. Those who came from a more elevated class in society should be seen privately in the church vestry.[38]

Smith's successor as vicar of Swansea, Talbot Rice, organised another mission in 1905, using Canon Hay Aitken, Robert's son, as his missioner. Rice wrote of it: "it was an epoch in the life of the parish. A wave of spiritual blessing passed over St Mary's, and continues in the lives of many who were converted at that time". Twelve years after he could write that large numbers still attended the parish church because of the spiritual blessings they had received at that time.[39] A further mission took place in Swansea in 1917, hard on the heels of the rather abortive National Mission. It was particularly strong on children's services and open air preaching.[40]

Another town mission took place at Wrexham during 1884 when David Howell was vicar. In his initial letter he noted the contrast between the numbers attending the church services and those who were communicants, which he regarded as the real core of the Church. He asked his parishioners to put to themselves the question, "Why am I what I am? Why am I not, in the full and true sense of the word, a *Christian*?" He requested those who were Christians to make a covenant with the Lord, to consecrate themselves unreservedly to him; to trust in the Lord Jesus Christ as a personal Saviour; to be a witness for Christ; to wait upon the Lord in the ordinances of the Church to renew strength; to search daily the Holy Scriptures while resting on the promise "My Word shall not return unto me void", and finally to watch for souls and so speak of Christ's salvation to others. A return card asked people to sign if they wished to attend a confirmation class, become a communicant, a Sunday School teacher, join a Bible class or one of the organisations of the parish or wished to speak to him personally.[41]

ANGLO-CATHOLIC PAROCHIAL MISSIONS

A ten-day mission at St Mary's Cardiff was conducted by George Body during 1878. Local clergy assisted, and on its eve an address was given by the Bishop Ollivant, indicating his approval of it. The industrial workshops and the docks were visited and the workmen addressed, while a Welsh mission took place at one of the church schools.[42] Around the same time a mission took place in the parish of Mold, whose vicar was Rowland Ellis, a noted Tractarian leader. The flyer announced that the mission, led by the Revd. C.J. Ridgeway, rector of Buckhurst-hill, Essex, would be "a course of Services in which *a special effort* is made to weaken the strongholds of Satan and to extend the kingdom of Christ." It would be addressed to the utterly irreligious, who needed something to arouse their attention and make them think; to the formally religious, those habitual churchgoers but in whom the Gospel of Christ is not a living power acting on their hearts and influencing their lives and who did not know the meaning of self-denial; but also to the sincere Christian, to strengthen and build him up and give him fresh courage. The Mission would have something to say to all:

> What we want is to bring people to love the Lord Jesus Christ, with a real personal love. The power of Satan is strong in this Town and Parish – we want by the grace of God to weaken it. There are many half-hearted ones among us, many lukewarm ones, we want to make them alive to the responsibility of their position. Time is passing! Souls are dying! Satan is triumphing! We must be up and doing.

The ten-day mission included daily services of Holy Communion, morning prayer (with instruction on the spiritual life) and evensong, with a mission service, and specific services for men, women, children, and Sunday School teachers. The mission preacher was available in the Church after each service for consultation for those who desired his counsel on spiritual matters.[43]

The missions that took place in Tenby under its Tractarian rector, George Huntington, in 1878, were heavily criticised by some of his parishioners for teaching sacerdotalism and auricular confession to a priest, though it was accepted that most of those who attended were loud in their praise for the fervour and eloquence of the preachers, and felt that good was likely to result from it. The first mission was conducted by Fr Ignatius (who is noted later), and the second by F.C. Wilkinson, and both were condemned for using the term "Father" for themselves. Bishop Basil Jones, responding to these complaints, considered it unfortunate that Huntington had transferred the care of his parishes to strangers, that the names of missioners had been changed without his sanction, and that a tract on confession had been circulated which was of "a very pernicious character".[44]

Stephen Gladstone as rector of Hawarden held a number of missions in his parish during the 1880s. These were Anglo-Catholic missions, and consisted of a week or so of activities. Each day commenced with a service of Holy Communion, and mission services were once again held for particular groups of people, children, men and lads, women and servants. In that large parish with its numerous out-stations seven to eight services were held each day, so a large team of missioners was assembled, probably some from the religious orders. The idea was not only to make converts, but primarily to teach people the faith and make them more zealous for it, and to increase personal devotion to Christ and his Church. One outcome was a temperance society which encouraged people to drink in moderation.[45] Pontlottyn, a mining community in the Rhymney Valley, had a ten day mission in 1898, for which preparations had been made over three months, with weekly services and intercessions and daily communions throughout the year. Again, there were services for specific groups, children, women and men (these held on the Sunday dealt specifically with particular sins), and mission services, with the whole congregation being catechised each evening.[46]

A number of missions, most conducted by the Mirfield Fathers, an Anglican religious community, took place at St Francis' Church, Roath, between 1904-28. The mission of 1904 received some opposition as the full Catholic faith was taught, but at its end 700 people renewed their baptismal vows, and others in 1915 and 1918 were teaching missions.[47] The Mirfield Fathers, including the Welsh-speaking Timothy Rees, later bishop of Llandaff, conducted another mission at St Theodore's Church, Port Talbot, in 1905. Its aims were recorded as awakening the careless, reviving the faithful and initiating a forward movement for the parish.[48] A further mission led by Timothy Rees of Mirfield took place at Welshpool in 1920, when in a letter written beforehand Rees asked for the co-operation of the parishioners to help bring back the lapsed and unchurched. The mission was not to stir up emotionalism but rather to state the truth of the Gospel in all its simplicity, and there was a need for a new vision of sacrifice and service amongst church people. The congregation appear to have remained lukewarm and the most significant work of the mission was amongst the young people of the parish. In 1933 it was said that seventy-five per cent of the congregation in the churches was made up of young people.[49]

FURTHER PAROCHIAL MISSIONS

Probably most parishes had missions at one time or the other, but a further representative sample may be given. A mission held at Llandudno in 1887 was the origin of St Beuno's mission church;[50] and another was held at the Anglesey village of Llangadwaladr in 1893, whose missioners were David Jones, then rector of Llanfairpwllgwyngyll and James Davies, rector of St David's, Liverpool.[51] A summer mission took place at Criccieth in 1923, partly for the summer visitors as well as for local people, taken by Timothy Rees of Mirfield. It was said that his appeals could be personal and he would make people ask, "What can I do to be saved?"[52] At Ebbw Vale the Church Army assisted in a permanent mission to the people who lived in the white-washed rows of that town, presumably those who had little affiliation with organised religion.[53] During the depression years the Church Army took missions in many parishes in the depressed areas, such as Six Bells in the Monmouthshire coalfield during 1933 and 1937.[54]

DIOCESAN INITIATIVES

There was a real fear that some of these missions had lapsed from the good sober order of the Church, and had ventured upon an emotionalism that was thought to be alien to its spirit. But at the same time the diocesan "revival" was taking place, and a diocesan organisation was being established through the introduction of boards for church building, church extension, education and a diocesan conference. It was thus natural, partly to extend the activities of the diocese and to curb over-enthusiasm, for dioceses to enter into this field of evangelism and mission. Not that it was called evangelism, that surely was a word that smacked of emotionalism. Rather, mission was the approved term.

By the 1880s dioceses had started to appoint diocesan missioners to develop, co-ordinate and take parochial missions. In the Welsh dioceses this was encouraged by Joseph Cullin, the Canterbury diocesan missioner, who had organised missions in Wales, noted below, at the behest of Archbishop Benson. The work of a diocesan missioner was defined in 1881 by J.P.A. Bowers, the missioner for the diocese of Gloucester and Bristol, as conducting quiet days and retreats, taking parish missions and communicant classes, and officiating at special services for men and women. He argued that some of the results of a parochial mission could be a multiplication of communion services, a monthly communicants' preparation meeting, district visitors being found, Bible classes for men and women established, a mothers' meeting commenced, and even a course of lectures on plain cottage cooking. Bowers also noted outdoor preaching, the distribution of tracts, and parish drawing room meetings.[55] Joseph Cullen wrote an even more influential book on parochial missions in 1891. He felt there was no real distinction between an evangelistic and a teaching mission, both should be combined. After the mission monthly meetings should be held after evensong to keep up the "spirit", communicant guilds should be established, and family prayers encouraged together with daily prayers in the church.[56]

Although the following was stated in 1911 at the Llandaff Diocesan Conference, these words spoken by W. Watkin Edwards, vicar of Blaenafon, were true for the whole period under review, and underline the Anglican ethos of mission and evangelism:

> A healthy Church is always pressing on, and is never satisfied with what it has already attained. … However faithful an Incumbent may be, periods of apparent lukewarmness on the part of the communicants, and consequent stagnation of the

> spiritual life of the parish will recur. In one parish the attendance at the means of grace may possibly be far from what it should be, and Sunday School Teachers and other workers may, for the time, be increasingly difficult to obtain. In another there may be signs of that new life which is endeavouring to make itself seen, but which is retarded by the crust of old traditions. In another there may be crowded congregations and a manifold organisation, but no real spiritual life manifesting its existence in self-sacrificing efforts for the spread of Christ's Kingdom. And in another there may be a large margin of parishioners who are scarcely influenced at all by ordinary methods of parochial work. In such cases it is of the very first importance that a thorough-going spiritually minded man of God should be available for a special and sustained effort for ten or fourteen days' heart-to-heart work in the parish. His gifts and experience should enable him to meet the difficulty that presented itself to him on his advent to the district. The results that would accrue from his visit cannot be easily overestimated. They may extend to generations yet unborn.

Edwards added that the lack of such disturbing features in a rural parish should not give rise to complacency. The evil maybe less blatant but was still present, and a short visit from a missioner over two or three days "would do much towards keeping the life of our villages at its proper standard".[57] Similar words were spoken by David Howell to the 1887 St Asaph diocesan conference. A mission was needed in a parish where there was evidence of spiritual lukewarmness and deadness, displayed by "the barrenness of believers, the fewness of conversions, the want of personal devotedness and personal holiness amongst Christians, the neglect of holy communion and the worldliness of communicants, a lack of zeal for the interests of the Church and the welfare of souls, and the want of liberality in supporting Church agencies at home and abroad".[58] Howell was a keen supporter of the diocesan initiatives.

In the diocese of Llandaff Bishop Richard Lewis appointed a diocesan missioner, who would oversee the work of mission and draw together a band of colleagues, both clerical and lay, to assist in his task.[59] His work was defined in 1892 as giving Lenten instructions, organising retreats for clergy and leading missions to parishes.[60] Canon

Griffith Roberts, who became the diocesan missioner, arranged numerous parochial missions, such as a Welsh mission to Dowlais in 1889, together with a ten-day mission to five Cardiff churches plus a Welsh one for the town itself. Another mission at Abercarn in 1890, received national publicity.[61] In addition to missions of eight to ten days, there were also three day missions, starting on the evening of the first and ending with communion on the third day. The missioner also undertook Sunday work to relieve overtaxed clergy who were in sole charge of congregations, and trained some laymen and younger clergy for mission work.[62] The curate of Blackwood, J.A. Rees, in 1901, expressed his concern about the inadequacy of this mission work, arguing that in a diocese of 508 churches only eight parochial missions had been held, only one out of every eighty incumbents had requested the services of the diocesan missioner, and only 28 days had been given to such work in the previous year.[63]

By 1903 it was reported that ten day parochial missions were held the previous year, and 99 courses of Lenten instruction during which the missioner was assisted by 47 clergymen who acted as assistant missioners.[64] Canon Roberts requested clergy to remain in post for some time after a mission, or else the work of preparing converts for confirmation and others for communion might be lost.[65] But the work had slackened after Canon Roberts had moved on to the deanery of Bangor, and the want of a band of mission clergy to work in the diocese was sorely felt.[66] Later missions were held at Abercynon and Llantwit Fardre during 1913, when diocesan van missions were also noted. But by 1914, though it was agreed that at the time of war the nation had almost lost its obligation of worship, the hope of having a band of missioners exclusively for the diocese had been shelved because of lack of funds due to the war itself.[67] In one sense the work was replaced by the National Mission of Hope and Repentance called by the two archbishops as the Church's response to the First World War, but it was agreed it had not achieved its anticipated results.[68]

By 1888 the diocese of St Davids had a special mission committee; a diocesan missioner having been suggested in 1884. This committee reported on a number of missions held through its auspices, especially Welsh missions at Whitland, in the deanery of Narberth, together with quiet days for clergy. Other missions took place in the following years. In 1891 they were held in such places as Newcastle Emlyn, St Peter's

Carmarthen, Stackpole Elidor, St John's Hafod and Holy Trinity Swansea.[69] A debate at the diocesan conference of 1893 on parochial missions seems to have required the canon missioner, Robert Camber Williams, to justify their need. Are we satisfied with things as they are? he asked. He also offered some hints about preparing and organising a mission as well as the "after-work" involved. Another speaker, the suffragan bishop of Swansea, expressed the usual concern about the emotionalism and extravagances displayed at these "revival" meetings.[70] The work continued, however, though groups of parishes seem to have been involved rather than individual parishes. In 1907, for example, there were missions in South West Cardiganshire and North West Pembrokeshire, taking two days in each parish, and in the Radnorshire deanery of Melineth and Sub-Ithon.[71]

The diocese of Bangor clearly had some mission work by 1887, when its bishop noted the clear blessings from various parochial missions.[72] By 1907 missions were noted at Heneglwys and Llanberis, with a short mission at Pentraeth.[73]

In addition dioceses either sponsored or encouraged "Church Crusades", especially during the years of depression between the years. A two-week event for Monmouthshire took place in 1928,[74] following one in the previous year for the Amman Valley, which was linked to the Industrial Christian Fellowship which had a deep concern for the unemployed. There were services in all the churches of the area with guest preachers, including Timothy Rees of the Mirfield Fathers, open air preaching, processions of witness, pit-head meetings, and special services for young folk, the British Legion and friendly societies, for men, women and church workers. The most prominent speaker was Studdert Kennedy, "Woodbine Willy", a well-known cleric of his day.[75] By 1938 these arrangements appear to have become an established format, as it was repeated at the Rhondda Deanery Church Crusade of that year; the Rhondda deanery at that time included the Pontypridd area. Its mission statement suggested that the Church needed to be true to mission in times of despair by bringing a message of hope and of belief in the one Lord of all life.[76]

MISSION AGENCIES:

ARCHBISHOP BENSON'S MISSION TO THE WELSH CHURCH

In the 1880s Archbishop Benson of Canterbury was persuaded that the Welsh clergy were in a low state of morale, due to the disestablishment campaign and the tithe troubles. Though the Welsh bishops were not encouraging and almost apathetic, he sent in his missioner, who brought in others, to visit the parishes. Ostensibly, these were parochial missions, but in reality, as the reports sent back to the archbishop reveal, they were meant to encourage the clergy and enthuse them about their ministry. In addition there were flying missions to parishes, held over a few days. Both David Howell and William Evans of Rhymney were instrumental in persuading Benson to establish this mission, and he deputed Joseph Cullin, the Tait missioner for his diocese, to oversee the work. Along with a number of Welsh clergy, including Howell, Evans and Archdeacon Smart, Canon Mason (a former Truro diocesan missioner), Canon Pigou of Halifax, J.P.A. Bowers of Gloucester, noted already, and other English clergy were involved.

A flying visit was a preliminary visit to assess the potential and prepare for the main mission. The main missions lasted for ten days, and were defined as a special effort put forth by the Church, relying on the power of the Holy Spirit to reach the unchurched, to bring the impenitent to penitence and to add living stones to Christ's body. Preparation by the parish in prayer and activity was essential, taking place over four to six months, involving weekly prayer meetings, house to house visiting, the distribution of tracts and quiet days for church workers. As usual there would be services for particular groups, open air preaching, meetings at places of work if possible, and an after meeting held when such questions might be asked as "have you repented, are you baptised, confirmed, a communicant?" and resolution cards given out. The importance of following up the mission work was also stressed, such as confirmation classes, encouraging personal and family prayer, commending Bible studies and cottage lectures, establishing lay workers and district visitors; and it was emphasised that some definite result should come from the mission, such as a communicants' guild, a series of teaching sermons, a new mission chapel, or even ensuring that pew rents were abolished.

The first missions took place in September 1886 in the diocese of Llandaff, and in addition to these flying visits and parochial missions quiet days and conferences were held for church workers and the clergy. The missions were held during September and October of each year from 1886-9 and took place all over Wales wherever the missioners were invited by the incumbent, though the number held in the two north Walian dioceses was not substantial. Again and again the missioners reported on the enthusiasm and generosity of the people, their openness about spiritual matters and their spirituality, and their appreciation of doctrinal teaching and preaching. They were impressed by the number of men who attended the mission meetings and often the fluency of the extempore prayers they heard from laymen.

It was a different story regarding the clergy. Too many of the curates were ill-educated and considered themselves to be ministers of a sect and not of the Established Church, while many incumbents were discouraged and down-hearted. A spiritual upheaval was needed amongst them, reported one missioner. In many cases the clergy were stirred up and encouraged (often by having a shoulder to lean on, someone who could communicate concerns to those in authority); many parishes reported a substantial increase in confirmation candidates and people offering themselves as church workers; prayer meetings were started and family prayer commenced and, in addition, the bishops were encouraged to appoint diocesan missioners, as noted earlier. David Howell believed as a result both clergy and laity had been uplifted to a higher level of spiritual life and hope had been given to the beleagued Welsh Church.[77]

The dean of St Asaph, Dr James, reported on the effect of these missions in that diocese to its conference of 1888. Fourteen missions had been held, in both rural and urban or mining parishes, and all the clergy of these parishes reported good and encouraging results, though in varying degree. Everywhere the spiritual life of the communicants had been deepened; in many parishes this quickened spirituality showed itself in accessions to the number of church workers and attendants at Bible classes; in several the number of communicants had largely increased; some backsliders and evil-livers had been reclaimed, but what was prominent everywhere was the quickening influence upon the professed Christians (who had been aroused from their lukewarmness); and with one exception, Nonconformists had shown themselves friendly to the missions. All those attending had been well-prepared and were being diligently followed up. They had not been too emotional in character so that much of the immediate result should be permanent. The dean hoped that an organisation might be started to continue the work, but he had not been successful in obtaining diocesan clergy to offer themselves for this mission work. This was not so much because of indifference but from a consciousness of inexperience, but with some difficulty he had been able to find sufficient diocesan clergymen to assist in the mission work in a number of parishes.[78]

THE CHURCH ARMY

The Church Army, already noted, founded by Prebendary Carlile in 1882, was a lay agency devoted to the work of evangelism, although each evangelist had to be licensed by a diocesan bishop. Samuel Christopher Morgan, vicar of Swansea 1875-84, appears to have been one of the first Welsh clergy to make use of the Church Army in his parish. This is hardly surprising because it was said of him that he preached the Word of God in and out of season.[79] A Church Army van which itinerated around the parishes in the diocese of Llandaff was noted in 1898, but it was made clear it would not enter a parish without the incumbent's permission. By 1908 this van was visiting about 24 parishes each year, remaining for a week or fortnight, and in 1911 the van mission had held 289 different services within that diocese.[80] One of its evangelists, Captain Roberts, toured Wales in a van fitted up as an evangelistic centre, and came to Dowlais in 1893 where he held meetings at the Oddfellows Hall. Able to preach in both languages, he held meetings each night, and open air services on Saturdays. It seemed he eventually settled at Dowlais until his death in 1916.[81] At Wrexham the Church Army ran a mission hall in the parish, held specific Sunday evening meetings, some outdoors, and its "captains" or officers played a significant role in the life of the parish.[82]

FATHER IGNATIUS

Although the maverick Father Ignatius was hardly a mission agency, he nevertheless took missions in various parishes, often against the will of the incumbent as he was only a deacon in the Church's order and ran a monastic community at Capel-y-ffin that was ill-defined and subject to no other authority but his own whims. Born in 1837, his secular name was Joseph Leycester Lyne and he was a relation of Dr Pusey, the Tractarian leader. His great aim in life was the restoration of the Benedictine monastic order into the Church of England, but as a mission preacher he had great gifts of popular oratory and much success. In 1878 Archdeacon Bevan of Hay refused him permission to use his Church for a mission in that town, and was annoyed that he had announced his use of it before he had even sought permission. On his own authority, Bevan wrote, Ignatius had assumed the character of a monk, and he had no episcopal licence to officiate. Though he had no wish to discredit him, his admirable qualities were overruled by his lack of judgment. He would not select him for a missioner had he wanted one, but nevertheless he hoped that from this mission some good might come, though he himself would not take part in it.[83] Ignatius took part as one of the missioners at a mission in Tenby, a Tractarian parish, in 1878, as noted above.[84] However, he held an eight day mission at St Collen's Church, Llangollen in 1884, holding daily services at 3.30 pm and 8.00 pm, and proclaiming he was feeding the flock and preaching the Gospel of Salvation. Its vicar, Rhys James, wrote enthusiastically about the effect of this mission. Whole families had been converted, the parochial guild had trebled in numbers, and new life put into the church workers. "We are better, happier, and brighter Christians than before", he added.[85]

THE REVIVALS OF 1859 and 1904-5

It is often assumed that the Church stood apart from these two national revivals. That is not so, especially for the Welsh-speaking parishes which benefited greatly from them.

The 1859 revival was at first greeted with some coolness by most clergy, as they felt that the previous revival, "instituted" by Charles Finney, an American evangelist, had been artificially worked up by the use of constituted means rather than being the result of divine grace.[86] The initial hesitation was replaced by an acceptance that this revival had the finger of God within it, and many churches, especially those in Welsh speaking areas, held prayer meetings imploring God to give them a mighty outpouring of his Holy Spirit. Their prayers were answered, so that John Venn, in his account of the Welsh revival, believed that the Church gained 20,000 converts as a result, one in five of the total number. The increase, suggested Bishop Campbell, was not in the number of the congregation, but in the number of communicants, and this he thought indicated a serious concern for spiritual reality. David Herbert of Llansanffraid said 115 people had been added to his church in a calm, silent and sober work which had led to a deeper concern for the Sabbath and for family prayer. John Hughes of Llanbadarn Fawr had over 260 converts, and reported on a prevailing "deep, profound and awfully solemn impression" about spiritual things. Sixty new communicants had been added to St David's Church,

Blaenau Ffestiniog, and the lives of the older communicants had changed for the better, while Henry Grey Edwards of Llandinorwic had presented 80 adults for confirmation as the "first fruits of a Church which grew and thrived".

Archdeacon Wickham of St Asaph, who was probably not directly involved in the revival, nevertheless noted the blessings it had caused and the power of faithful prayer in drawing "a larger supply of God's grace upon his Church", while Archdeacon North of Cardigan, who was involved, could not doubt for a moment that it had left a blessing upon the Church in general.[87] However, Evan Jones was not over-impressed. Though the revival had brought many new communicants to his church at Llandysul, he felt they had little depth and believed that many had followed one another. However, when he became vicar of Llanfihangel-ar-Arth in 1860 he found that many young people had joined the Church due to the influence of the revival.[88]

The 1904-05 revival has been subjected to much debate and controversy.[575] It was argued that through it God had blessed the prayers of many within and without the Established Church who had prayed for a deepening of spiritual life in Wales from the 1880s onwards. It has also been argued that there were two simultaneous revivals: one was noisy, emotional, concentrated on the emotions with little attention paid to the Scriptures, and lacked any real teaching or spiritual depth. Too much trust was placed in shallow professions, and emotions were touched without the mind being enlightened by Scriptural knowledge and the will fortified by the Holy Spirit. The other was a deeper revival, based on the Scriptures and clear doctrinal teaching, worship based on the liturgy, and all done with dignity and sobriety, and it was this revival that affected the Church rather than the other. Talbot Rice confidently described the revival as God's blessing, and those who complained it was disorderly were reminded about "the music and dancing at the return of the prodigal" and, presumably, the attitude of the eldest son.[90] As J. Vyrnwy Morgan remarked, the Church's liturgy kept "within legitimate bounds the remorseless advances of an emotionalism that was utterly devoid of the twin-elements of reverence and spirituality".[91]

The Church's method of revival was said to be in 1905 based on Acts.2.42, "and they continued in the Apostles' fellowship, in the breaking of bread and the prayers." Informal services were encouraged as were prayer meetings, provided they adhered to the ethos of the liturgy and did not displace reason by emotionalism.[92] As the revival broke out Canon Robert Camber Williams, diocesan missioner of St David's Diocese, got together a mission team and organised twenty parochial missions, compared to the four rural deanery missions of the previous year. At Abergwili the church prayer meeting was restored as a result, while other missions were held at Eglwys Oen Duw, Builth and Hay for the more rural parishes, Aberystwyth, Cwmaman, Pontardawe, and St Peter Llanelli for the industrial parishes, Swansea St Mary's and St Gabriels, Cwmbwrla, and Oystermouth for the town parishes, and for the rural deaneries of Lampeter, Llangatwg and Fishguard. It was reported that in all 4,000 cards had been sent to those who had made resolutions during these missions.[93] It appears these cards asked such questions as have I given myself to God; seen the need for reading part of the Bible each day, for holding family prayer at home and praying for others, and what have I done to bring other people to God. Williams also made use of the revival hymns of that day.[94]

In his report to the diocese Robert Camber Williams noted the bishop's pastoral letter, "counselling an attitude of sympathy and prayer, and suggesting methods whereby the awakening might be turned to permanent spiritual advantage" (he had also urged them to remain close to the liturgy). Suggesting that the chief instrument of the revival was a Nonconformist layman, he wondered if this should lead to a readjustment about the Church's doctrine of ministry. After noting the effect of the revival on the morals of people, leading those once indifferent to religion to a more spiritual outlook, he continued:

> The clergy acted with most excellent judgment in postponing the solution of problems raised by the movement, and buying the unique opportunity it offered for deepening the convictions and moulding the lives of their people, while minds and feelings were melted and softened. To borrow a metaphor often heard and well understood in those steel-making districts, the clergy hastened to roll out the melted steel while it was malleable, without stopping to enquire the why and the how the furnace had become so readily heated.

Special services were held in all the parishes affected by the revival, and while much of the work of furthering the revival and consolidating its work was done by the parochial clergy, aided by himself and his colleagues, a number of English clergy had readily gave their help. The lessons he had learnt was the necessity of giving "conversion" a place in the Church's teaching, the need for pastoral care after conversion, and the need for people to make an open confession of Christ.

Brief reports were given of the missions undertaken. At St Gabriel's, Swansea, there was a need to restrain emotion, but each night at the close of the service clergy and laymen knelt together at the altar rails and committed the day's work to God. At Aberystwyth the missioners were impressed by the keenness and earnestness with which people listened to their message, while at the Welsh mission there the depth of fervour was extraordinary. At Swansea, the local press hardly noted the Church services by concentrating on other revival meetings, but night after night there was a reaping of a harvest of souls. Some hundreds had come forward and a Bible class for men had been started as a result.[95]

Anglican clergy took a prominent part in several localities. Timothy Rees was commissioned by the bishop of Llandaff to assist in parishes affected by the revival, and was much used in the Rhondda parishes and at Rhymney.[96] At Ystradgynlais its vicar, E.L.D. Glanley, was the leader of the revival in that town, establishing prayer meetings in the church and in the various chapels.[97] Talbot Rice of Swansea was used as a speaker, and soon adopted a less formal approach. Seventy-one people joined the church at Rhymney. At Loughor, Pontarddulais and Llanedi the church co-operated with Nonconformity in the revival meetings. Thomas Prichard of Rhosllannerchrugog saw thirty new people joining his church and he became a revival speaker. Nearly 200 people were added to St Mary's Church, Caernarfon; while the revival particularly affected the parishes of Holyhead and other churches in Anglesey and the Deanery of Arllechwedd. Here prayer life had deepened, the number of communicants had increased, and the laity had become increasingly active in the life of the Church. It was argued that as a result of the revival there had been an increase in the number of communicants for the four Welsh dioceses, from 134,234 in 1905 to 155,191 in 1912.[98]

The bishop of Bangor, Watkin Herbert Williams, stated that his clergy felt that the spiritual tone of their parishes had been deepened by the revival, and that the number of confirmation candidates had increased enormously during that year, while Pritchard Hughes, soon to become bishop of Llandaff, wrote of the great seriousness about spiritual things evident in his parish of Llantrisant.[99] As Noel Gibbard remarks, the revival movement in the Church was characterised by good order and solid teaching, unlike many Nonconformist churches, though personal testimonies were encouraged and revival hymns sung as well as those from the church books. But the Church was well aware that excitement was not conversion and acted accordingly, combining the sacramental with the evangelical graces.[100] Talbot Rice, speaking twelve years after the revival, said that in those places in Wales where there was a vigorous spiritual life it could invariably be traced back to the revival. As a result of the revival, it was argued, not only were lives transformed, but personal testimonies, new hymns and free prayer began to be included in the services of many churches.[101]

THE CHURCH REVIVAL

Nonconformity and the Church used the term "revival" differently, causing Nonconformity to scoff at the Church's use of that word. Nonconformity meant by revival a deep and lasting work of the Holy Spirit, changing lives and churches, enabling people to encounter and discover the living God. The Church, by contrast, used the term to describe its growth during the nineteenth century. If Nonconformity stressed "life" by the term revival, the Church meant buildings and services.

Episcopal charges noted over the years the number of churches built or restored. In 1885 Bishop Lewis of Llandaff said in the previous two years ten new churches had been consecrated or licensed, twelve mission rooms and school-churches opened, and six churches completely restored.[102] Archdeacon Bevan of Hay in 1895 wrote of Cardiff where once there had been two churches, now there were nine parishes with 27 places of worship and 39 clergy. Swansea with its two churches in 1831 now had nine parishes, 28 places of worship and 22 clergymen, while Llanelli which had one church and one clergyman in 1831 was now the centre of four parishes, 16 places of worship with 12 clergymen to serve them.[103] Wrexham was also used as another example of church revival. Between 1876 and 1885 the two churches and one mission room had increased to six churches and two mission rooms. The five Sunday services were now 16 in number, and the three Sunday Schools with an attendance of 300 had increased to ten with an attendance of nearly 1,700.[104] In the archdeaconry of St Davids the number of churches and mission rooms had increased from 1831 to 1906 from 113 to 137, and the number of services from 113 to 237. Between 1840-1906 £140,345 had been spent on church building and restoration. Similarly, in the archdeaconry of Carmarthen the number of churches and mission rooms during the period 1831-1906 had increased from 107 to 228.[105] Even evidence presented to the Royal Commission of 1906 was used to justify the same position, such as the claim that the seven churches in the Rhondda of 1883, with ten mission rooms accommodating 4,930 people for a population of 85,000, had grown by 1905 to 20 churches, 26 mission rooms, accommodating 17,000 people for an enhanced population of 113,735, or that in the archdeaconry of Llandaff between 1840-1906 £773,868 had been spent on church buildings, most of it derived from the pockets of its members.[106] These developments were regarded as indicating the revival of the Established Church in Wales.

All this is impressive, but to describe it as a "revival" is perhaps misleading. The real revival of the Church was in its mission not only to its own people, but to the inhabitants of its parishes. It was certainly responsive to the call of mission, but its failure to work with Nonconformity in this common task, its own shortcomings through restrictive practices and poverty, diminished its role, as did the traditional understanding of so many church people that baptism made one a Christian. It was a theological problem more than an administrative one that caused the mission of the Church if not to fail, to lose the full potential it could have had. It may be argued that much of the Church's mission work was directed more to its own congregations in an attempt to increase and make real their faith and spirituality, rather than to those outside its walls, even though mission churches were provided for their social comfort. The aggressiveness of the Calvinistic Methodist's Forward Movement was not for the Church, but nevertheless a quiet work did continue and perhaps the sound teaching and restraint of emotion shown in the 1904-5 Revival produced as much spiritual fruit in the churches it affected as within Nonconformity itself.

ENDNOTES TO SECTION TEN
THE MISSION OF THE CHURCH

CHAPTER ONE A REALISATION FOR MISSION

1 Roger L. Brown, "Spiritual Nurseries: Griffith Jones and the Circulating Schools", *NLW.Jnl.*, 30 (1996-7), 27-49.

2 As noted by I.G. Jones, *Communities*, p. 24. Popery was also included in this category. For a summary of the 1851 religious census see Jones, *Faith and the Crisis of a Nation*, pp. 31-5 and Knight in Williams, *The Welsh Church*, pp. 310-5.

3 Quoted by I.G. Jones, *Communities*, pp. 22-3.

4 Quoted Prichard, *Representative Bodies*, p. 168.

5 John Davies, *Cardiff and the Marquesses of Bute* (Cardiff, 1981), p. 98.

6 *An Account of Population and the Capacity of Churches ... in Benefices with a Population of 2,000 plus and where churches and chapels cannot contain half:* PP. 1818 xviii ( ) 93 Aberdare had 550 seats for a population of 2,912; Merthyr Tydfil 1,700 for 11,104; Cardiff 600 for 2,457; Blaenafon 800 for 2,500; Bedwellty 200 for 4,590. A report of 1857-8, *The Report of the Select Committee on Divine Worship in Populous Parishes* (PP 1857-8, ix 387), was equally disturbing. In the diocese of Llandaff it noted a lack of accommodation at such places as Llantrisant, Margam, Trevethin, Mynyddislwyn (with 147 seats for a population of 3,615): p. 583.

7 Van Mildert, *Charge (Llandaff)*, 1821, pp. 8-9 (he noted Merthyr Tydfil in particular); cf. Sumner, *Charge (Llandaff)*, 1827, pp. 17-19 (he accepted the population was a fluctuating one and did not wonder at the growth of dissent as a result of the Church's lack of presence in these areas).

8 Ollivant, *Charge (Llandaff)*, 1857, p. 6; *Llandaff Diocesan Church Extension Society: Substance of Speeches delivered at Bridgend and Newport*, 1850, p. 6; Thomas Williams, *A Letter to the Lord Bishop of Llandaff on the Peculiar Condition and Wants of the Diocese* (London, 1850), p. 10.

9 *Llandaff Diocesan Church Extension Society: Substance of Speeches*, 1863, p. 10. This argument was still being voiced in 1881 regarding the hill parishes of the diocese: *Report of the Llandaff Diocesan Conference*, 1881, pp. 48-9.

10 Prichard, *Representative Bodies*, p. 136.

11 Richard Davies, "Nineteenth Century Church Restoration, Little Newcastle Church and the Revd. Peter Davies Richardson", *J.Pembs.H.S.*, 6 (1994-5), 81.

12 Edward Parry, "The Crisis of Anglicanism in mid-Nineteenth Century Brecon", *Brycheiniog*, 37 (2008), 84, 91-2.

13 "D.C.L.", *Letters on Church Matters reprinted from the Morning Chronicle* (London, 1851), I, 301-2.

14 *Report of the St David's Diocesan Conference*, 1890, p. 18.

15 *Report of the Llandaff Diocesan Church Extension Society*, 1860, p. 6; *Reports of the St David's Diocesan Conference*, 1881, p. 54, and 1886, pp. 68-9. It was argued that had the Church taken the initiative it would have taken its place amongst the population but Nonconformity had often usurped its role. J.T.D. Llewellyn attributed this failure to the neglect of the clergy.

16 Solway, *Prelates and People*, p. 295.

17 An act of 1818 permitted parishes to raise money on the security of the church rate in order to build and enlarge churches and chapelries, but by the 1840s this probably had limited effect due to

Nonconformist opposition to the church rates: Wickham, *Charge to the Archdeaconry of St Asaph*, 1863, pp. 12-13.

18 E.T. Davies, *Religion and Society in the Nineteenth Century* (Llandybie, 1981), pp. 51-2; cf. J.C. Ryle, *Church Reform Papers* (London, 1870), p. 120n. Before the Ecclesiastical Commissioners there was no official body within the Church able to sub-divide parishes. C.R. Knight, speaking in Convocation in a debate on the Church in Wales, argued that many of the Nonconformist meeting houses had been erected as a matter of sheer speculation: *Chronicles of Convocation: Lower House, 15 February 1871*, p. 113.

19 Ollivant, *Charge (Llandaff)*, 1854, p. 43.

20 *Report of the Llandaff Diocesan Church Extension Society*, 1861, p. 7, cf. *The Position of the Established Church in Wales* of 1870 (p. 15) which speaks of the Church as akin to "heavy artillery compared to light armed skirmishers in a difficult country" and weighed down with impedimenta: quoted by Brown, *Reclaiming the Wilderness*, p. 14.

21 E.R. Wickham, *Church and People in an Industrial City* (London, 1962), p. 80.

22 *Llandaff Diocesan Church Extension Society: Substance of Speeches delivered at Bridgend and Newport*, 1850, p. 13. As late as 1892 William Lewis of Ystradyfodwg complained that in the mining areas there were often Church people there long before a Church had been started: *Report of the Llandaff Diocesan Conference*, 1892, pp. 78-81. In addition it was argued that due to financial restraints churches were built long after Nonconformist chapels had been opened: *Report of the Llandaff Diocesan Conference,* 1893, p. 71.

23 W.L. Bevan, *The Case of the Church in Wales: an Essay* (London, 1886), p. 25; and his *The Church in the South Wales Coal-field* (London, 1895), pp. 2-3.

24 *Llandaff Church Extension Society: Substance of Speeches,* 1863, p. 11; Roger L. Brown, *Through Cloud and Sunshine* (Port Talbot, 1982), pp. 126-7.

25 W. Bezant Lowe, *Llansannan* (Llanfairfechan, 1915), p. 22.

26 Ollivant, *Charge (Llandaff)*, 1863, pp. 33-4; Brown, *Reclaiming the Wilderness*, pp. 10-13, and *Evangelicals in the Church in Wales*, pp. 141-3. He notes that the parochial system had almost broken down under these circumstances.

27 Quoted by Richard Chartres in *Lambeth Palace Library: Annual Review* (2007), p. 60, and Malcolm Johnson, *Bustling Intermeddler?* (Leominster, 2001), p. 106.

28 Llandaff Diocesan Memorandum Book, II, 1868-89, for 26 June 1876.

29 *CMG*, 11 July 1840, p. 3.

30 Ollivant, *Charge (Llandaff)*, 1851, pp. 37-8; Thomas Williams, *A Letter to the Lord Bishop of Llandaff on the Peculiar Condition and Wants of the Diocese* (London, 1850), pp. 3-5, and 12, where he noted the vast extent of some parishes.

31 *Church Pastoral-Aid Society: Abstract of the Report*, 1853, p. 10. Other reports noted parish churches ten miles away and over a mountain from the main centre of population: *21st Report*, 1856, p. 37, and *50th Report*, 1885, p. 54.

32 I.G. Jones, *Communities*, p. 14. Other churches recorded as in inconvenient places included Llanbadarn Fawr (Cards), Llandingad and Llangatwg (Breconshire).

33 *Return of Particulars of Information regarding the want for 600 new Churches*: PP 1852 (51), pp. 20, 33-4, 36-7. The returns noted that Bangor required 16 new churches, Llandaff 35, St Asaph 5 and St Davids 19.

34 *Llandaff Diocesan Church Extension Society: Substance of Speeches delivered at Bridgend and Newport*, 1850, p. 4: it noted Michaelston-super-Afan had 280 seats for its population of 6,000, Newport 2,206 for 18,000, Cardiff 3,000 for 15,000 and Mynyddislwyn 296 for 6,000. See also Wills, "The Established Church in the Diocese of Llandaff", pp. 240-1, 246.

35 *CMG*, 24 October 1846, p. 3.

36 Solway, *Prelates and People*, pp. 297, 342; Alan Smith, *The Established Church and Popular Religion* (London, 1971), p. 109; D.M. Lewis, *Lighten our Darkness* (Carlisle, 2001), pp. 108-9. Bishop Blomfield believed that a new district church would become a centre for schools and other charitable institutions: Malcolm Johnson, *Bustling intermeddler?* (Leominster, 2001), pp. 106-7, 117-9.

37 Edward Copleston, *Separation either a Duty or a Sin* (London, 1840), p. iv.

38 "Golifer", *Diocese of Llandaff: Proposed New Churches. A Letter addressed to ... Lord John Russell* (London, 1850), p. 7.

39 Sumner, *Charge (Llandaff)*, 1827, p. 26. Solway notes he was one of the first to realise that many of those not attending a Church service were not worshipping elsewhere, as did Bishop Bethell then of Gloucester: *Prelates and People*, pp. 307-9.

40 *CMG*, 12 March 1870, p. 7; 24 October 1846, p 3; 20 November 1869, p. 7 (in which Griffith called for a change of policy, namely of providing preachers rather than new churches); Brown, *Reclaiming the Wilderness*, pp. 10-11; Brown, *John Griffith*, pp. 160, 204-6. Bishop Wilberforce of Oxford had come to the same conclusion: Solway, *Prelates and People*, p. 346.

41 *Llandaff Diocesan Church Extension Society: Substance of Speeches delivered at Bridgend and Newport*, 1850, p. 9; Hall, *A Letter to the Lord Bishop of Llandaff* (London, 1851),in passim.

42 Ollivant, *Charge (Llandaff)*, 1863, pp. 35-6.

43 "D.C.L.", *Letters on Church Matters reprinted from the Morning Chronicle* (London, 1851), I, 296-8; cf. Malcolm Johnson, *Bustling Intermeddler:* (Leominster, 2001), p. 119. Canon Hume of Liverpool argued that the churches were built for too large a congregation, for 2,000 rather than 800, and that the surplus money could have been used to form an endowment: Anthea Jones, *A Thousand Years of the English Parish*, p. 282.

44 I.G. Jones, *Communities*, pp. 26-7.

45 Solway, *Prelates and People*, p. 306.

CHAPTER TWO: A CONCERN FOR BUILDINGS

1 Chapels of ease and district churches were required to pay church rates to their parent body for their repair and maintenance, as well as being responsible for their own building. Nolton Church in the parish of Coety refused to pay their share of the rate for the repair of the parish church, but lost its case: R.W.D. Fenn, "Thomas Davies, Rector of Coety", *JHSCW*, 13 (1963), 45-8.

2 For a few examples see: Brown, "The Church of St Mary of the Salutation", pp. 24-5, 47-9; Brown, *Church and Clergy at Castle Caereinion*, pp. 54-60 (where excessive repairs caused financial difficulties); D.B. James, *Myddfai* (Aberystwyth, 1992), pp. 127-8, 131-2; T.E. Morris, "The Parish Book of Cefnllys, Radnorshire", *Archaeologia Cambrensis*, 19 (1919), 49-52; R. Richards and R.G. Lloyd, "The Church of St Mary, Llanfair-juxta-Harlech", offprint *Arch.Camb.*, 1936, pp. 6-9; H.R. Evans, "Llandyssul Church: Minute Book of the Vestry and Parish Meetings", *Ceredigion*, 1 (1951), 131-7; J.L. Roberts, *St Stephen's Church, Bodfari* (1978), pp. 14-15, 18-19; G. Bowen Thomas, "Llanaber Vestry Records, 1726-54", *J.Mer.H.S.*, 2 (1956), 277-8.

3 Cynthia Rees, *A History of Marchwiel* (Wrexham, 1998), pp. 9-10; Ivor Walters, *Chepstow Parish Records* (Chepstow, 1955), pp. 10-12; H.N. Oliver, *Llanllwchaiarn Church and Parish* (2000), pp. 14-17, 21-7; Brown, *Church and Clergy at Castle Caereinion,* pp. 24-6.

4 Prichard, *Representative Bodies*, pp. 90-1. Little attention was paid to the levelling of the church floor or glazing its shuttered windows, for such luxuries were excluded by the poverty of the parish.

5 Saunders, *A View of the State of Religion*, p. 16.

6 J.R. Guy and W.G. Neely, *Contrasts and Comparisons* (Welshpool, 1997), p. 58.

7 Reed, "The Llangattock Parish Scrapbook", pp. 107-8; Theophilus Jones, *Brecknockshire*, III, 164. In 1783 there was a similar dispute between Philip Yorke and the parish of Marchwiel about these chancel repairs: Cynthia Rees, *A History of the Parish of Marchwiel* (Wrexham, 1998), p. 68. At Welshpool the lessee of the tithes, Lord Powis, frequently disputed with the impropriators, Christ Church, Oxford, about the responsibility for St Mary's chancel: Church in Wales Records, SA/DR/26, fol. 165 for 1749, and NLW, Powis Castle Deeds, 14207, for a 1856 dispute. *The Ecclesiologist* criticised cathedral chapters for allowing the lessees of churches belonging to them to be responsible for these matters: vi (1846), 93.

8 T.W. Pritchard, *A History of the Old Parish of Hawarden* (Wrexham, 2002), pp. 86-7.

9 Gwynfryn Richards, "Royal Briefs for the Restoration of Churches in Wales", part I, *JHSCW*, 6 (1956), 50-69, part II, *ibid.*, 7 (1957), 25-68, noting especially I, p. 55-6, and II, p. 62-3. Berriew obtained £122 from a 1794 brief when the work cost £1,700, and Capel Garmon £200 towards its £1,005 cost (II, pp. 40-2). Richards notes that Welsh parishes were generally generous to their own countrymen. These royal briefs were later confined to certain societies but withdrawn in 1856: Bethell, *Charge (Bangor)*, 1856, pp. 15-16.

10 Richard Kretchmer, *St Myllin's and its Town* (2008), pp. 13-14.

11 David Thomas, *The Parish of Bangor Monachorum* (1962), p. 38.

12 K. Williams-Jones, *A Calendar of the Merioneth Quarter Sessions Rolls* I (Dolgellau, 1965), pp. 165-6, 174-5. Similar requests for briefs to assist in rebuildings are noted at and Llanferres and Nantglyn, and possibly briefs for more local contributions for Ruthin, Llandegla, Eglwys-fach and Llanynys, by Bryn Ellis, "Denbighshire Quarter Session Rolls in the Eighteenth Century", *T.Denb.H.S.*, 51 (2002), 81.

13 G.M. Griffiths, "Montgomeryshire in the Records of the Church in Wales", *Mont.Coll.*, 58 (1963-4), 130.

14 Evans, "Churchwardens' Presentments in Carmarthenshire", *T.Carms.A.S.*, 10 (1915), 92-100, esp. p. 94; 11 (1916), 13-34, esp. pp. 14, 16-17. The 1705 Visitation indicated that while some churches were in good order and there were many others with windows unglazed, needing whitewashing or attention to the roof and lacking a decent or any pavement, though where the chancels were out of repair, as at Pencarreg, the responsibility was that of the impropriator: *ibid*, 11 (1916), 49-84; 12 (1917-18), 7, 26-33; 14 (1919), 11-17. Presentments between 1671-9 indicated that many churches needed repair: 19 of 52 had defective windows and 17 churchyard walls needed repair: "Miscellanea", *Archaeologia Cambriensis*, 1919, pp. 209-10.

15 Fleetwood, *Charge (St Asaph)*, 1710, pp. 46-7.

16 Morgan, "The Diocese of St David's", A, p. 38. The *Report of the Association of Welsh Clergy*, 1853, pp. 21-4, suggested there were 245 discontinued churches throughout Wales. This was the case when the parish of Newton was united with Slebech in 1844. As a result the former church was allowed to decay and became ruinated: Francis Green and T.W. Barker, *Pembrokeshire Parsons*, from *West Wales Historical Records* 1915-16,II, 235-6, III, 225.

17 Griffiths, "A Visitation of the Archdeaconry of Carmarthen, 1710", in passim, but esp. I, 297; II, 318, 321-2; J.R. Guy and W.G. Neely, *Contrasts and Comparisons* (Welshpool, 1997), pp. 57-8. Paul Morgan notes that inspections of churches in the diocese of Worcester between 1674-87 reveal that many were in poor condition, especially in the deanery of Worcester itself: *Inspections of Churches and Parsonage Houses in the Diocese of Worcester* (Worcestershire Historical Society, NS 12, 1986), esp. pp. 106-10.

18 Griffiths, *Deanery of Penllyn and Edeirnion*, pp. 10, 14-15, 19, 22-3, 39, 43, 47. In the 1730s most of the Anglesey churches were in good order, though Llanbabo was akin to a tumbledown cowshed and Llanfigel so ruinated you could not tell it was a church: Evans, *Religion and Politics in mid-Eighteen Century Anglesey*, pp. 83-6.

19 "J.T.", *A Collection of Welch Travels, and Memoirs of Wales* (London, 1730s), pp. 66-7. In *A Dialogue between the Rev. Mr Jenkin Evans. ... and Mr Peter Dobson concerning Bishops, Particularly the Bishops of the Principality of Wales* (London, 1744), it was asked whether the bishops had ever surveyed the condition of the Welsh churches. Many were neglected, some partly ruinated, windows were without glass, roofs leaky, walls mouldy, floors ridged up because of burials and only covered with rushes: pp. 50-1. Theophilus Jones described some of the Breconshire churches as large barns with pews akin to sheep-pens: quoted by W.L. Bevan, *The Past and Present of a Welsh Diocese* (London, 1907), p. 26.

20 F.G. Cowley in Glanmor Williams, *Swansea: An Illustrated History* (Swansea, 1990), p. 145.

21 A.H. Williams (ed.), *John Wesley in Wales* (Cardiff, 1971), p. 20.

22 SA/RD/26 (the 1749 reports), for Marchwiel, Llanychlyn (Llanuchllyn), Llanfor, Betws Gwerfil Goch and Castle Caereinion, as a sample of those noted in good order: fols. 32-3, 41, 49, 77-9, 100, 135, 141, 149, 166; and SA/RD/28, for 1791, Meliden, "Gwernysor", Flint, Halkyn, Llangernyw, fols. 21, 29, 38, 43, 114. See also Edwards, *Memories*, pp. 50-1.

23 SA/RD/28 of 1791 notes Northop needed rethatching, fol. 40; Llangernyw, "Coed Y Druidion" (also needed rethatching), Llaneilian and Eglwys Fach needed whitewashing within, fols. 85, 113-4, 124; and concerns about poor or irregular seating at Northop, Llandrillo yn Rhos, Llansannan, Betws Abergele, Llaneilian and Eglwys Fach, fols. 40, 89, 105, 112-3, 124.

24 B.E. & K.A. Howells, *Pembrokeshire Life: 1572-1843* (Haverfordwest, 1972), p. 72.

25 Adrian Bristow (ed.), *Dr Johnson and Mrs Thrale's Tour in North Wales 1774* (Wrexham, 1995), p. 107. It was said that the old church at Beddgelert was not much better than a barn: Alan Bott and Margaret Jones, *The Priory and Parish Church of St Mary, Beddgelert* (2000), pp. 32-3.

26 John Byng, *The Torrington Diaries* (London, 1934), I, 292.

27 John Byng, *The Torrington Diaries* (London, 1934), I, 307; *A Short Account of the Church of St John the Evangelist . at Brecon* (Brecon, 1874), pp. 13-14.

28 Yates in Williams, *The Welsh Church,* pp. 249-50. However, Crickhowell, and in particular Talgarth and Llandyfaelog Tre'r Graig were commended.

29 S.R. Meyrick, *The History and Antiquities of the County of Cardigan* (London, 1810), p. 275.

30 M.W. Thompson (ed.), *The Journeys of Sir Richard Colt Hoare* (Gloucester, 1983), pp. 45, 227-8; Richard Fenton, *Tours in Wales*, wrote in 1804 that the condition of Llanddewi Brefi Church was "disgraceful to a Christian country": p. 7.

31 E.W. Parry, *Churches in Wales and their Treasures* (Pwllheli, 2011), p. 89.

32 Quoted by E.T. Davies (ed.), *The Story of the Church in Glamorgan* (London, 1962), p. 75.

33 B.H. Malkin, *The Scenery, Antiquities and Biography of South Wales* (repr. Wakefield, 1970), p. 190.

34 Varley, *The Last of the Prince Bishops*, p. 91; cf. Burgess, *Charge (St Davids),* 1807, p. 4: "The state of our Churches is obviously and deservedly one cause of complaint against the establishment."

35 Fenton, *Tours in Wales*, p. 263. Erasmus Saunders wrote that many churches had become the habitation of owls and jackdaws: *A View of the State of Religion*, pp. 23-4. As late as the 1840s it was stated that Lisvane Church had fallen into such a state of neglect that birds were nesting inside it: P. Riden and K. Edwards, *Families and Farms in Lisvane* (Cardiff. 1993), p. 34.

36 Quoted by Yates in Williams, *The Welsh Church*, pp. 262-3.

37 Francis Jones, *Treasury of Historic Pembrokeshire* (Brawdy, 1998), p. 224.

38 Brown, *Letters of Edward Copleston*, no. 148, pp. 145-6.

39 Glynne, *Notes on the Older Churches*, p. 214. He also found that the old church at Llandudno (St Tudno's) was deserted and dilapidated (1852), and Cilrhedyn Church was in complete decay and unfit for divine service (1860): pp. 275, 217. The 1852 *Report of the Association of Welsh Clergy* noted churches in the diocese of St Davids without roofs and which had been converted into places for sheep and cattle: p. 12, cf. *Report,* 1856, pp. 29-30.

40 J.A. Gabb, *A Brief Memoir of James Davies* (London, 1832), pp. 4-6; Phillips, *James Davies*, pp. 33-5.

41 *Bye-Gones*, 2 December 1891, p. 211.

42 Morgan, "Diocese of St David's, B", pp. 23-4. Morgan notes the comments of the 1847 report into Welsh education about the state of some churches. Phillips in his *Wales* also does so, noting the Carmarthenshire church of Llanafan Fechan was hardly used, and Llanddewi'r-cwm in Breconshire was so dilapidated that only its chancel could be used: *ibid.,* p. 190. Bishop Jenkinson's 1828 survey of the diocese of St Davids indicates that of 103 churches only seven clergymen reported their churches were in bad repair, eleven churches were under repair or had been recently restored, and most clergymen certified their churches were in decent, good, or tolerable repair: W.N. Yates in Evans and Wooding, *St David of Wales*, p. 347.

43 Conybeare, *Essays Ecclesiastical and Social*, pp. 23, 23-4n.

44 J.T. Coleridge, *A Memoir of the Rev. John Keble* (Oxford, 1869), II, 357-8. Augusta Pearson described this church in 1853 as a former cowhouse, whitewashed and fitted up with seats: *A Spinster's Tour through North Wales* (Llandysul, 1988), pp. 26-7.

45 Jones and Williams, *The Religious Census of 1851*, II, 214; cf. I, 359, 433-4, 484 (Eglwysfair, Llandeloy, St Elvis and Cilrhedyn were in a similar plight); Davies, *Life and Opinions of Robert Roberts*, pp. 178-9, for an Anglesey church.

46 *Report of the Association of Welsh Clergy*, 1853, pp. 10-12.

47 *Report of the Association of Welsh Clergy*, 1856, p. 30. The service was attended by the rector and his son, the clerk and his daughter, and a farmer with his three sons.

48 Glynne, *Notes on the Older Churches,* pp. 118-9, 192-3, 276. Of Ilston Church Glynne noted its general appearance contrasted agreeably with the neglected state of most of the Gower churches: p. 197.

49 G.R. Orrin, *The Gower Churches* (1979), p. 18; F.G. Cowley, *Llanmadoc and Cheriton* (1993), pp. 20, 22-4.

50 Smith, *They did it their way*, pp. 5-6.

51 Huntington, *Random Recollections*, p. 114.

52 A.W. McAdam, *St Nicholas' Church, Grosmont* (1956), pp. 6-7.

53 Plomer, *Kilvert's Diary*, III, 289.

54 Ifans, *The Diary of Francis Kilvert*, pp. 6, 10.

55 Harold Hughes, and Herbert L. North, *The Old Churches of Snowdonia* (Bangor, 1924), pp. 257-8.

56 G.G.T. Treherne, *Eglwys Cymmin* (Carmarthen, 1918), p. 11n.

57 Brown, "The Parishes of the Aberafan Area", pp. 114-15.

58 Guy, "Bishop Barrington's Book", p. 125.

59 Burgess, *Charge (St Davids)*, 1807, pp. 2-4; Majendie, *Charge (Bangor)*, 1814, pp. 24-5.

60 Yates in Williams, *The Welsh Church*, pp. 283-5.

61 Graham Rogers, *Brymbo and its Neighbourhood* (Wrexham, 1991), p. 62.

62 *Report of the Association of Welsh Clergy*, 1853, pp. 10-12.

63 Prichard, *Representative Bodies*, p. 110.

64 C. Tilney, *A History of the Parish of Penarth with Lavenock* (2nd. edn., 1988), p. 57.

65 Roger Phillips, *Bassaleg: Aspects of its History* (Bassaleg, 1991), p. 69.

66 Guy, "Bishop Barrington's Book", p. 125.

67 Nigel Yates, "Ecclesiology and Ritualism in Wales", p. 60.

68 J.R. Guy, "Church and Churchmen in Llantrisant Parish", in Stewart William, *Glamorgan Historian*, 12 (1981), 90-1.

69 Majendie, *Charge (Bangor)*, 1817, p. 23.

70 Van Mildert, *Charge (Llandaff)*, 1821, p. 7; Sumner, *Charge (Llandaff)*, 1827, pp. 14-15, 17-19.

71 M.L. Clarke, "Carnarvonshire Churches at the beginning of the Nineteenth-Century", *T.Caerns.H.S.*, 1962, pp. 57-60, 64-6. He notes that some churches were whitewashed, some were unpaved, others were thatched and some had rushes placed on the floor. Cf. Majendie, *Charge (Bangor)* 1814, pp. 24-5.

72 Yates in Williams, *The Welsh Church*, p. 280. He notes that of the churches recorded by Fenton in his survey of Pembrokeshire 48% were in good condition; as were 63.6% of those described by Hall in his work on Caernarfonshire, but only 17.6% came into that category in Theophilus Jones' account of Breconshire though 57.4% were in moderate condition. Jones, he notes, could exaggerate the defects he saw in churches: *ibid.*, pp. 215, 278-9.

73 Wickham, *Charge to the Archdeaconry of St Asaph*, 1855, pp. 5-6.

74 *CMG*, 20 February 1847, p. 2. By contrast in the Monmouth archdeaconry 50 churches were in good repair, 46 needed some repair and 48 considerable repair. David Archard Williams considered the poor condition of many churches had been due to the lack of archidiaconal visitation and inspections, but now they had a better view of church architecture: *Charge to the Archdeaconry of Carmarthen*, 1865, p. 18.

75 SA/DR/51, fol. 97. A further appeal for Nerquis in 1883 stated the church had fallen into decay and was unfit for use: *ibid.*, fol. 117.

76 Elwyn Bowen, *Vaynor* (Merthyr Tydfil, 1992), p. 323.

77 Bradney, *Monmouthshire*, IV, 308. For the practice see also Owen, *Old Stone Crosses*, pp. 78-81.

78 R.M. Grier, *John Allen, Archdeacon of Salop* (London, 1889), p. 6. William Thomas, vicar of Cadoxton, Neath, who died in 1785, was buried under its communion table: Keith Tucker, *A History of St Catwg's Church* (1990), p. 77.

79 David James, "Gleanings from Consistory Court Records", *The Carmarthenshire Antiquary*, 28 (1992), 107.

80 Griffiths, *A Visitation of the Archdeaconry of Carmarthen, 1710,* I, 295.

81 SA/RD/28, of 1791: see for Llanarmon and Llandyssil (no pagination).

82 Margaret Walker, "The Priory Church of St John the Evangelist, Brecon", *Brycheiniog,* 28 (1995-6), 116, 118.

83 Theophilus Jones, *Brecknockshire*, III, 169.

84 William Coxe, *A Historical Tour through Monmouthshire* (Davies ed., Brecon, 1904), p. 23.

85 Derrick Platt, *The Church of St Mary Magdalene, Penley* (1980), p. 26.

86 Elias Owen (ed.), *The Works of the Rev. Griffith Edwards* (London, 1895), p. 91. The Carmarthen common council decreed in 1567 that only those who had exercised senior office in the town and their families should be buried in St Peter's Church: Francis Jones, *Treasury of Historic Carmarthenshire* (Brawdy, 2002), pp. 82-3.

87 J.H. Matthews (ed.), *Cardiff Records* (Cardiff, 1898-1905), III, 474.

88 D.E. Williams, "The Parish of Rumney", *South Wales and Monmouthshire Record Society*, 4 (1957), 169. An additional charge for intermural burial was demanded in many churches, as at Llansannan in 1728: W. Bezant Lowe, *Llansannan* (Llanfairfechan, 1915), p. 21.

89 T.J. Hughes, *Wales's Best One Hundred Churches* (Bridgend, 2006), p. 34.

90 Roger L. Brown, *The Church of St Mary of the Salutation, Welshpool, Sayce Papers,* 4 (1998), 67; *Sketch of the Parish of Llanfechain*, (from *Mont.Coll.*, London, 1872), p. 32.

91 *Bye-Gones*, 17 August 1932, p. 82.

92 Thomas Pennant (ed. John Rhys), *Tours in Wales* (Carnarvon, 1883), II, 34.

93 H.T. Payne, "Visitation of the Third part of Brecon, 1785", in NLW, MS. 4278b, fol. xlii. Payne also ordered that human bones removed from graves required for new internments should be buried in a pit rather than allow dogs to gnaw at them. In 1791 the churchyard at Flint was full of human skulls: SA/RD/28, fol. 38.

94 Thomas Lloyd, et al., *The Buildings of Wales: Carmarthenshire and Ceredigion* (London, 2006), p. 172.

95 W.G. Wrenche, *Wrenche and Redcliffe. Notes on two Families of Glamorgan* (1956), p. 75. James Francis, the first vicar of St Paul's, Newport, was buried in the porch of that church in 1853: Pryce, *One Hundred Years of Evangelical Witness*, p. 32.

96 Brown, *David Howell*, p. 50.

97 Morgan, "Diocese of St David's, B", pp. 27-9, 33-4. The churchwarden of Llanrhidian, Gower, queried how their clergyman could attend to the spiritual requirements of a parish eleven miles long, while the vicar of Llanfihangel Cilycwm wrote that he could not expect his parishioners from "the extreme points" to attend his church in a parish seventeen miles long: Jones and Williams, *The Religious Census of 1851*, I, 256, 305. See also W.L. Bevan, *The Case of the Church in Wales: an Essay* (London, 1886), p. 48. Compared to English rural parishes similar parishes in Wales had the same number of population but double the amount of area.

98 *Church Builder*, 1881, pp. 16-17.

99 *Report of the St Asaph Diocesan Conference*, 1892, p. 19.

100 David Robinson (ed.), *Rug Chapel, Llangar Church, Gwydir Uchaf Chapel* (1993).

101 T.M. Morgan, *The History and Antiquities of the Parish of Newchurch, Carmarthenshire* (Carmarthen, 1910), p. 74.

102 Fisher, "Religious and Social Life in the Vale of Clwyd", pp. 150-1; Francis Jones, *Llangunnor* (1986), p. 15; Thomas, *The Parish of Holywell*, p. 38; A. Leslie Evans, *The Story of Baglan* (1970), p. 85 (in 1818; D.B. James, *Myddfai* (Aberystwyth, 1992), p. 127; W. Venables Williams, *Llandrillo yn Rhos* (repr. 1993), p. 40; Bradney, *Monmouthshire,* III, 109, 129 (he notes the custom continued at Llangibby and Llanfihangel Pont-y-moel into the 1900s) The 1791 rural deans' reports for the diocese of St Asaph mention many instances, e.g., SA/RD/28, fols. 113, 124. At Carew the walls were limed in Spanish brown and the stonework picked out in black: W.G. Spurrell, *The History of Carew* (Carmarthen, 1921), p. 49.

103 Glynne in his *Notes on the Older Churches* notes a number of churches whose exterior walls were whitewashed, such as Talbenny, Llanfihangel Nant Bran, Trallwng, Bleddfa, Cenarth, Kenfig and Flemingston (adding to this entry that this was the custom of the neighbourhood), Llantilio Pertholey and Mamhilad, pp. 120, 140, 162, 192-3, 216, 309-10, 345, 349. A number of churches were thatched, such as Northop and "Caer y Drudion" in 1791: SA/RD/28, fols. 40, 85; Llanfair Clydogau: G.E. Evans, *Cardiganshire* (Aberystwyth, 1903), p. 213; Glynne notes that at Castle Martin the windows had been transformed into sashes: p. 131, while sash windows were removed from Llangynin Church in 1842-3: Thomas Lloyd, et al, *The Buildings of Wales: Carmarthenshire and Ceredigion* (London, 2006), p. 320.

104 Griffiths, *Deanery of Penllyn and Edeirnion*, pp. 35, 44 (for Corwen and Gwyddelwern, where "Moses and Aaron were absent"). Some churches had funeral hatchments displayed, though few remain in situ today.

105 Yates notes bare earthen or clay floors at Rhosili, Llangennith and Marloes: "Ecclesiology and Ritualism", p. 62, and Glynne notes the same at St Ishmael, Rhosmarket: *Notes on the Older Churches*, pp. 118-9. As late as 1925 Llangelynin Church near Llandovery had an earthen floor: A.T. Arbor-Cooke, *Pages from the History of Llandovery* (Llandovery, 1976), II, 15.

106 Evans, *Religion and Politics in Mid-Eighteenth Century Anglesey*, p. 14 (referring to Llanfechell Church, where the rushes were replaced six times a year); Thomas, *The Parish of Holywell*, p. 38; J. Powell, *The History of Holt* (Ilfracombe, 1978), pp. 23-4, noting a festival of rushes in August until recent times). At Llanymynech straw was placed on the dilapidated floor but soon became damp: John Fewtrell, "A Parochial History of Llanymynech", *MontColl.*, 12 (1879), 128.

107 Owen, *Old Stone Crosses,* pp. 190-1 (at a cost of 3s.); L. Parry Jones, *Llanynys Church* (1988), p. 26.

108 G.O. Heald, "Pentre Foelas", *T.Denbs.H.S.*, 23 (1974), 268.

109 B.B. Rowlands, *A History of Llandinam and Parish* (Llandinam, 2011), p. 22; E.P. Hughes, "A Parochial History of Llanfair Caereinion", *Mont.Coll.*, 16 (1883), 350.

110 Marie Trevelyan, *Llantwit Major* (Newport, 1910), p. 60.

111 *Old Wales*, II (1906), 352.

112 Obelkevich, *Religion and Rural* Society, p. 110.

113 Glynne, *Notes on the Older Churches*, pp. 162, 195, 216; Roger L. Brown, *The Church of St Mary of the Salutation, Welshpool, Sayce Papers*, 4 (1998), 29 for Welshpool, and for Cardiff, Brown, *David Howell*, p. 47. Devynock is also noted by Theophilus Jones, *Brecknockshire*, IV, 116.

114 Yates, "Ecclesiology and Ritualism", p. 62.

115 M.L. Clarke, "Caernarfonshire Churches at the beginning of the Nineteenth Century", *T. Caerns.H.S.*, 1962, p. 61.

116 For the so-called long wall arrangement of the pulpit, and its central position, see Yates, in Williams, *The Welsh Church*, pp. 286-8.

117 R.W.D. Fenn and J.B. Sinclair, "Diserth Parish Church", *T.Radn.S.*, 71 (2001), 149.

118 SA/RD/26, fols. 141, 155-6.

119 Fenton, *Tours in North Wales*, p. 114.

120 Graham Beeston, *Bedwas and Machen* (Newport, 1972), p. 59; Yates, notes other examples of the pulpit being in front of the communion table at St Thomas, Haverfordwest, and Walwyn's Castle: "Ecclesiology and Ritualism", p. 62.

121 Thomas, *The Parish of Holywell*, p. 11.

122 William Jones, *A Brief Account of St Mary's Church, Swansea* (1895), p. 9.

123 "A Sketch of the Parish of Llanfechan", *Mont.Coll.*, 5 (1872), 229.

124 D.B. James, *Myddfai* (Aberystwyth, 1992), p. 128.

125 John Parker's tour of Wales: NLW, MS 18256C, fols. 314-6.

126 Quoted from the Tenby parish magazine by Nigel Yates in T. Barnes and N. Yates, *Carmarthenshire Studies* (Carmarthen, 1974), p. 239.

127 Glynne, *Notes on the Older Churches*, pp. 108-10, 125, 273.

128 W.H. James, *Chepstow Parish Church One Hundred Years Ago* (1913), pp. 8, 10.

129 SA/RD/28, fols. 89, 101, 105, 112-3.

130 Glynne, *Notes on the Older Churches*, pp. 98, 162, 248, and also Llangwyfan, Anglesey, p. 249.

131 Griffiths, *Deanery of Penllyn and Edeirnion*, p. 47.

132 W.G. Spurrell, *The History of Carew* (Carmarthen, 1926), p. 48.

133 G.O. Heald, "Pentre Foelas", *T.Denbs.H.S.*, 23 (1974), 269.

134 "A Sketch of the Parish of Llanfechain", *Mont.Coll.*, 5 (1872), 230.

135 R.M. Grier, *John Allen, Archdeacon of Salop* (London, 1889), p. 6.

136 A. Leslie Evans, *The Story of Baglan* (1970), p. 66; Betty Shaw, *A History of Selattyn and the Parish Church of St Mary the Virgin* (1991), p. 20.

137 John Fewtrell, "Parochial History of Llanymynech", *Mont.Coll.*, 12 (1879), 128.

138 Jones and Williams, *The Religious Census of 1851*, I, 359.

139 R.A. Addams-Williams, *The Church of St Cybi, Llangibby* (Bristol, 1908), p. 16.

140 R.W.D. Fenn and J.B. Sinclair, "Diserth Parish Church", *Radnorshire Society Transactions*, 71 (2001), 155.

141 E.W. Parry, *John Parker's Tour of Wales and its Churches* (Llanrwst, 1998), p. 73.

142 John Fewtrell, "Parochial History of Llanymynech", *Mont.Coll.*, 12 (1879), 127-8.

143 Mrs Andrew Davies, "History of the Parish of Carno", *Mont.Coll.*, 33 (1904), 130.

144 Edwards, *Memories*, p. 79.

145 Roger L. Brown, *The Church of St Mary of the Salutation, Welshpool, Sayce Papers*, 4 (1998), pp. 49-54; Glynne, *Notes on the Older Churches*, p. 273.

146 William North, *Charge to the Archdeaconry of Cardigan*, 1862, pp. 26-7. He also expressed concern regarding the state of communion tables.
147 Davies, *Life and Opinions of Robert Roberts*, pp. 383-4.
148 Nigel Yates, *Liturgical Space* (Aldershot, 1988), pp. 87-90.
149 Guy, *St Mary's Church, Cardiff*, p. 45. It was removed in 1879.
150 Thomas Lloyd, et al., *The Buildings of Wales: Carmarthenshire and Ceredigion* (London, 2006), pp. 522-3; Yates, "Ecclesiology and Ritualism", p. 59. Other ecclesiological churches by the 1860s were Llanbrynmair, Merthyr Cynog and Angle, *ibid.*, p. 61.
151 Yates, "Ecclesiology and Ritualism", pp. 60-1. Utilising D.R. Thomas's *History of the Diocese of St Asaph,* Yates suggests that out of 98 churches suitably described by him 34% had ecclesiological interiors, 26% combined old and new features, and 40% were "unecclesiological": p. 64.
152 Glynne, *Notes on the Older Churches*, pp. 216-7. Lampeter Velfrey, restored 1869, was also approved: p. 226.
153 George Huntington, *John Brown the Cordwainer* (London, 1878), pp. 32-3.
154 Pryce, *History of the Parish of Llandysilio*, p. 26. A plan is included.
155 Tony Villiers, *The Parish Church of Llanymynech* (1994), p. 3.
156 Yates, "Ecclesiology and Ritualism", p. 64.
157 F.W.D. Fenn and J.B. Sinclair, "Continuity and Change: A Welsh Border Parish and its Clergy 1750-1900", *T.Radn.S.*, 57 (1987), 71.
158 T.W. Pritchard, *The History of Buckley and District* (Wrexham, 2006), pp. 201-2; J.C. Jones, *Buckley Parish Church*, p. 19.
159 Roger L. Brown, "Mr Stone of Rossett", *T.Denbs.H.S.,* 1995, p. 62; cf. Nigel Yates, *Liturgical Space* (Aldershot, 2008), p. 120.
160 Yates, "Ecclesiology and Ritualism", p. 66; Thomas, *History of the Diocese of St Asaph*, II, 232.
161 Cambridge Camden Society publications: *A few Words to Churchwardens on Churches and Church Ornaments: I. Suited to Country Parishes;* and *II, Suited to Town and Manufacturing Parishes,* and *A Few Words to Church Builders* (all Cambridge, 1841: and reprinted in Christopher Webster (ed.), *'Temples ... Worthy of his Presence'* [Reading, 2003]); Christopher Webster and John Elliott (eds.), *'A Church as it Should be'* (Stamford, 2000); J.F. White, *The Cambridge Movement* (Cambridge, 1962), esp. pp. 93-7; *Ecclesiologist*, I (1843), 152-7; IV (1845), 210-3; the journal even gave practical hints as to how to remove whitewash &c: *ibid.*, VII (1847) 41-2; Yates, *Buildings, Faith and Worship*, pp. 133-4. The most successful "ecclesiological" church in Wales was thought to be Llangorwen, Cardiganshire, built in 1841: O.W. Jones, *Isaac Williams and his Circle* (London, 1971), pp. 96-7
162 Quoted Basil F.L. Clarke, *Church Builders of the Nineteenth Century* (reprint, Newton Abbot, 1969), pp. 104-5. Clarke notes how taste had changed. Archdeacon Coxe in his 1801 tour of Monmouthshire wrote of St Mary's, Monmouth, rebuilt 1736, that its interior was light and well-proportioned. But G.E. Street, its restorer, termed it unattractive and uninteresting: *ibid.*, p. 245.
163 *Ecclesiologist*, II (1842-3), 4-5.
164 *Proceedings of the St Asaph Diocesan Conference*, 1878, p. 38. He notes another successor, a strict evangelical, might introduce a very different style of worship.
165 Quoted by Cragoe, *Anglican Aristocracy*, pp. 220-1. Twenty years earlier, in 1867, a newspaper editor, referring to St Peter's Church, Carmarthen, said that any attempt to replace the high backed pews with more regular ones would have been condemned as a step towards Popish innovations.
166 Basil Jones, *Charge (St Davids),* 1877, pp. 14-16.
167 Quoted by Jones, *Faith and the Crisis of a Nation*, p. 104.
168 *Church Pastoral-Aid Society, Church and People*, 11 (1899), 206.
169 J.B. Sinclair and R.W.D. Fenn, "Radnorshire Churches. An Introduction", *T.Radns.S.*, 62 (1992), 79.
170 Ivor Walters, *Chepstow Parish Records* (Chepstow, 1955), p. 12.

171 Tony Villiers, *The Parish Church of Llanymynech* (1994), p. 3.
172 Betty Shaw, *A History of Selattyn and the Parish Church of St Mary the Virgin* (1991), p. 17.
173 D.B. James, *Myddfai* (Aberystwyth, 1992), p. 128; B.B. Rowlands, *A History of Llandinam and Parish* (Llandinam, 2011), p. 22.
174 SA/LET/972, 969. Gas was also obtained in the 1840s.
175 D.R. Thomas, "Llandrinio, 18091846", *Mont.Coll.*, 33 (1904), 189
176 Cynthia Rees, *A History of the Parish of Marchwiel* (Wrexham, 1998), p. 14.
177 Reed, "The Llangattock Parish Scrapbook", pp. 107, 109.
178 Brown, "The Curate of Berriew", p. 126.
179 C. Webster (ed.), *Temples Worthy of His Presence*, (Reading, 2003), pp. 271-2.
180 R. Jones and C.G. Reeve, *A History of Gas Production in Wales* (Cardiff, 1978), pp. 19-20. He notes Chepstow Church obtained a gas supply in 1832 and Abergele in 1869: pp. 27, 53.
181 William Cathrall, *History of Oswestry* (repr. 1987), p. 96; Watkin, *Owestry*, p. 152.
182 Hughes, *Pwllheli Church*, p. 23.
183 *CMG*, 3 January 1848, p. 3.
184 Reed "The Llangattock Parish Scrapbook", p. 112.
185 Ellis, *Fresh as Yesterday*, p. 95.
186 M.L. Clarke, *Bangor Cathedral* (Cardiff, 1969), p. 31. Oystermouth Church obtained a gas supply in 1872: G.R. Orrin and F.G. Cowley, *A History of All Saints' Church, Oystermouth* (1990), pp. 25-6; and Buckley in 1889: J.C. Jones, *Buckley Parish Church*, p. 21. At Treharris electricity replaced the flickering gas supply as early as 1921: F.J. Gaines, *History of St Matthias Church, Treharris* (1946), p. 26. St Thomas, Swansea, did so the following year: E. Jenkin Davies, *Speech on Thirty Years at St. Thomas* (1950), p. 7.
187 C. Webster (ed.), *Temples Worthy of His Presence*, (Reading, 2003), pp. 270.
188 *CMG*, 20 January 1869, p. 8. By comparison when the new church of St Mary, Denbigh, was opened in 1871 it was stated that the "handsome" brass gas standards with their 18 jets of light were amply sufficient to light the church: SA/DR/51, fol. 19.
189 Brown, "A Reviving Church?" p. 121.

CHAPTER THREE: THE QUESTION OF THE PEW

1 For a general overview see Roger L. Brown, *In Places where they Sit*. The existence of private rights in a church is noted on pp. 19-22.
2 For a system of allocation, whereby servants were placed in particular places, see Basil F.L. Clarke, *The Building of the Eighteenth-Century Church* (London, 1963), pp. 214-5.
3 Brown, *In Places where they Sit*, pp. 22-36; Wickham, *Charge to the Archdeaconry of St Asaph*, 1857, p. 13. He made clear there was no right to a private pew unless it had been obtained by a faculty.
4 *Report of the St David's Diocesan Conference*, 1890, p. 20.
5 Morgan, "The Diocese of St Davids," B, p. 26.
6 *Cambridge Camden Society: A few Words to Churchwardens on Churches and Church Ornaments: Number I* (Cambridge, 1841), pp. 11-12 (it deplored huge square pews which forced those who knelt to do so face to face as though they were worshipping each other) and *Number II*, pp. 4-6; J.F. White, *The Cambridge Movement* (Cambridge, 1962), pp. 106-9.
7 Henry Clark, *The Pew System in the National Church* (London, 1869), pp. 8-9.
8 *Report of the Church Congress, Manchester*, 1863, p. 36.
9 *Chronicles of Convocation: Upper House, 14 February 1860*, p. 142.

10 *CMG*, 1849, p. 3. He was annoyed that the parishioners of St Mary's retained seats in the old parish church of St John's.

11 *CMG*, 28 August 1847, p. 3. Also noted by *Church Builder*, 1876, p. 19, and Wickham, *Charge to the Archdeaconry of St Asaph*, 1863, pp. 17-18.

12 Melvin Humphreys, *The Crisis of Community* (Cardiff, 1996), p. 180.

13 G.L. Fairs, *A History of the Hay* (London, 1972), p. 60.

14 I.G. Jones, *Communities*, p. 38.

15 Robert Wickham, *An Address to his Parishioners* (Wrexham 1854), pp. 4-5, 7.

16 Wickham, *Charge to the Archdeaconry of St Asaph*, 1855, pp. 6-8. Bishop Howley of London was equally cautious in 1818, suggesting that if the exhortations to change were fruitless the clergy should wait for more favourable opportunities: Solway, *Prelates and People*, p. 269.

17 William Crawley, *Visitation Charge to the Archdeaconry of Monmouth*, 1849, pp. 6-9.

18 Roger L. Brown, "Dean Bonnor of St Asaph", *T.Denb.H.S.*, 51 (2002), pp. 115-7.

19 *Report of the Church Congresses, Wolverhampton*, 1867, pp. 209-11; *Bath,* 1873, pp. 295-7. Solway notes how the wealthier classes positively disliked the proximity of the poorer classes to them during the church services: *Prelates and People*, pp. 271-2. The position was lampooned by George Huntington of Tenby in his *The Autobiography of an Alms Bag* (London, 1885), pp. 19-21.

20 *Report of the Church Congress, Stoke on Trent*, 1875, p. 181. Archbishop Thomson of York in 1887 endeavoured to prevent the churchwardens of Beverley from ending the appropriated pews in their church and declaring all seats open and free to all parishioners. He invited aggravated parishioners to inform him of their social status so he could personally distribute the seats according to their "degree". His intervention met with a vigorous denunciation by the press: H. Kirk Smith, *William Thomson, Archbishop of York* (London, 1958), pp. 117-9.

21 *Report of the Church Congress, Sheffield*, 1878, pp. 90-5.

22 *Church Builder*, 1876, pp. 17-21.

23 *Report of the St David's Diocesan Conference*, 1890, pp. 15-17; *Reports of the Church Congresses, Cambridge*, 1861, p. 11; *Oxford*, 1862, pp. 170, 175-6; *Manchester*, 1863, pp. 133-4, *Bristol*, 1864, pp. 146-59 [where it was argued that the appropriation of pews caused jealousy, hereditary feuds, family estrangements and even pugilistic encounters, *ibid.*, p. 149]; and *Bath*, 1873, pp. 286-97; [a suggestion was made that seats could be free at specific or additional services in order not to disturb the wealthier classes, *ibid.*, pp. 290-1]; *Cardiff and Merthyr Guardian*: 18 January 1862, p. 7. The abortive Parish Churches Bill of 1886 would have forbidden all further faculties for pews, swept away appropriated seats, and only allow pews to be rented when permitted by law: *Report of the Church Congress, Wakefield,* 1886, pp. 431-4.

24 Quoted by Solway, *Prelates and People*, pp. 273-4.

25 Wickham, *Charge to the Archdeaconry of St Asaph*, 1855, pp. 6-8.

26 Wickham, *Charge to the Archdeaconry of St Asaph*, 1863, pp. 16-20, 35. While he did not advocate his clergy to press for immediate open seating, Wickham asked them to create a general sympathy that the existing system was incompatible with the right of all parishioners to be seated in their parish church. An appendix (pp. 31-6) pointed out the legal position regarding faculties for pews, especially those annexed to a particular house when only the occupier or tenant could make use of that pew. He indicated that some might claim a prescriptive right to a pew through long usage or its having been built or repaired at their expense. He advised that double pews should not be created, while pews occupied by non-parishioners, held by an illegal contract through purchase or rent, should be declared forfeited.

27 *Ecclesiologist*, I (1843), 157. Other protests in the same paper are at XIX (1858), 38-41, 387-9 (noting a committee formed against them), and *Report of the Church Congress, Carlisle*, 1884, pp. 110-1, where a speaker argued that if people believed they were not equal in the House of God because of the appropriated pew they would feel their presence was unwelcomed.

28 *Cambridge Camden Society: A few Words to Churchwardens on Churches and Church Ornaments: Number I* (Cambridge, 1841), p. 12.

29 Henry Clark, *The Pew System in the National Church* (London, 1869), pp. 8-11, 15-18, 25.

30 Jones and Walker, *Links with the Past*, p. 223; David Walker, *The First Hundred Years* (1967), p. 10; *Chronicles of Convocation, Upper House, 14 February 1860*, p. 146; *Report of the Church Congress, Nottingham*, 1871, pp. 52, 60-1. Another variation was that seats were free after the choir had processed in: *Report of the St David's Diocesan Conference*, 1890, p. 20. In the 1950s the parish magazine of Mold announced that all seats in the church were free, causing great umbrage to a "supposedly noble family": Mike Griffiths, *The History of the River Dee* (Llanrwst, 2000), p. 104.

31 E.G. Sandford (ed.), *Memoirs of Archbishop Temple* (London, 1906), I, 451. This would prevent the answer, "there I no room for me if I come", given in response to a clergyman pressing on a person his duty to attend the worship of the Church, and so end the existing "dog in the manger" approach of the pew holders.

32 The numerous complications caused by the existence of appropriated pews are described by Brown, "The Church of St Mary of the Salutation", pp. 43-7.

33 Yates in Williams, *The Welsh Church*, pp. 286-8; Brown, "the Church of St Mary of the Salutation", pp. 49-55.

34 Watkin, *Oswestry*, pp. 247-8.

35 Brown, *Clergy and People of Welshpool*, p. 35.

36 Roger L. Brown, "Edward Smart, Archdeacon of St Asaph", *T.Denb.H.S.*, 51 (2002), 120.

37 Ollivant, *Charge (Llandaff)*, 1851, pp. 11-13.

38 G.R. Orrin, "The Role of the Talbot Family in Church Building and Restoration in Victorian Glamorgan", *Morgannwg*, 46 (2002), 60-1.

39 SA/MISC/128.

40 J.D.K. Lloyd, "Montgomery Church", *Montgomery Collections*, 67 (1979), 20, 22.

41 SA/DR/50, fol. 204.

42 *CMG*, 25 May 1850, p. 3.

43 D. Williams, *S.S.Gwynfarch and Mary, Llanfair Duffryn Clwyd* (Denbigh, 1937), p. 6.

44 *Guardian*, 11 March 1874, p. 292.

45 SA/DR/51, fol. 82.

46 Geoffrey Orrin, *Medieval Churches of the Vale of Glamorgan* (Cowbridge, 1988), pp. 179, 262; and as at Porthceri in 1867 and Sully in 1874: *ibid.*, pp. 317, 404.

47 Yates, *Buildings, Faith and Worship*, pp. 159-60.

48 *Ecclesiologist*, XVI (1855), 5-8, 82-5, 330-2.

49 Keith Parker, *A History of Presteigne* (Logaston, 1997), p. 151; *Guardian*, 16 January 1907, p. 92.

50 *Chronicles of Convocation; Upper House, 14 February 1860*, pp. 142-3.

51 *Report of the Church Congresses, Bristol*, 1864, pp. 155-6; *Stoke on Trent*, 1875, p. 181; *Carlisle*, 1884, pp. 118-9 (it was suggested each free sitting should to be provided with a prayer book, hymn book and kneeler); *Ecclesiologist*, XVI (1855), 332.

52 Wickham, *Charge to the Archdeaconry of St Asaph*, 1866, pp. 4-6. He accepted this might be permissible in those churches where the privileged classes were few in number and the number of seats sufficient for those who required them, but this could not apply to large towns where all seats should be free and open.

53 Wickham, *Charge to the Archdeaconry of St Asaph*, 1857, pp. 6-7. Counsel's opinion in a case at Yeovil of 1850 made clear that those living in a new district had no rights of seating in the parish church: *Ecclesiologist*, NS 9 (1851), 16-19. His opinion was upheld by Lord Blandford's Act of 1857.

54 Richard Kretchmer, *St Myllin's and its Town* (2008), p. 11.

55 Elias Owen, "How Churches were built in the Eighteenth Century", *Arch.Camb*, 5th series, 5 (1888), 242-7.

56 *CMG,* 27 March 1847, p. 3. The estimated income from pew rents was between £20 and £30. The pew rents may have been imposed in lieu of a church rate.

57 Brown, "the Church of St Mary of the Salutation", pp. 42-3.

58 *Bye-Gones*, 6 August 1902, p. 416.

59 *CMG*, 28 August 1847, p. 3. The position was complicated as some of the inhabitants of St Mary's Church retained their pews at St John's Church, as at that time they were legally entitled to do so if they did not take pews in their district church. These people, he declared, did not pay a farthing of the parish rates and deprived parishioners of their pews. See also *ibid.*, 31 March 1849, p. 3 for a similar complaint.

60 Wickham, *Charge to the Archdeaconry of St Asaph*, 1855, p. 9. Though he allowed exceptions.

61 An act of 1851 permitted the Commissioners to extinguish pew rents if other sources of income were provided: M.H. Port, *Six Hundred New Churches* (London, 1961), p. 121. Port also notes an act of 1840 that allowed an income to be augmented from the surplus pew rents (*ibid.*, pp. 111-2). The *Ecclesiastical Gazette*, 8 October 1872, p. 59 notes the Church Seats Act of that year which required evidence of an endowment of an amount acceptable to the Commissioners before pew rents could be abolished.

62 *Report of the Church Congress, Manchester*, 1863, p. 35.

63 In *Sermons by the late Ven. John Hughes ... [with a] Memoir* (Aberystwyth, 1864), it is said that Hughes anticipated the Act by many years in building St Michael's Church, Aberystwyth, at a time when the majority of seats in these churches were rented and the poor placed in the most disadvantageous places, giving them the impression that the house of God was for the rich rather than the poor: pp. xii-xv.

64 Solway, *Prelates and People*, pp. 269-70.

65 M.V.J. Seaborne, "Charles Butler Clough", *NLW.Jnl.*, 29 (1996), 287-92.

66 Pryce, *One Hundred Years of Evangelical Witness*, p. 18. Half of its 1,600 seats were free and unappropriated.

67 Geoffrey Orrin, *Medieval Churches of the Vale of Glamorgan* (Cowbridge, 1988), p. 138. He adds that many seats for the poor were not marked as such.

68 "A Pauper Clergyman", *How to make better Provision of the Cure of Souls out of the Present Actual Revenues of the Church* (London, 1857), pp. 51-3. Those who attended the churches built under these acts were required to pay pew rents (unless they wished to be stigmatised as belonging to the poor), whereas those pews in the parish church were free of charge even if they were appropriated. He called for the abolition of pew rents and for all seats to be declared free.

69 Thomas Williams, *Charge to the Archdeaconry of Llandaff*, 1852, p. 8.

70 Ollivant, *Charge (Llandaff)*, 1863, pp. 33-4.

71 *Ecclesiastic*, I (1846) 361-2.

72 Best, *Temporal Pillars*, p. 409.

73 *Report of the Church Congress, Nottingham,* 1871, pp. 58-61.

74 Brown, *Reclaiming the Wilderness*, pp. 144-9. Eventually the amount obtained from these pew rents decreased and the Commissioners made an augmentation in response to a benefaction raised from the parish. The same position occurred at Nantyglo, even though the pew rents only realised between £20 and £23 per annum: *ibid.*, pp. 103-4.

75 As advocated by the *Ecclesiologist*, XIX (1858), 39-41, and *CMG*, 18 January 1862, p. 7.

76 Ros Aitkin, *The Prime Minister's Son* (Chester, 2012), pp. 101, 117.

77 Henry Clark, *The Pew System in the National Church* (London, 1869), p. 25.

78 *Report of the Church Congress, Sheffield*, 1878, p. 95. The speaker, W. Milton, a Sheffield incumbent, added that offertories were a necessary adjunct to the free and open pew system but the majority of worshippers gave little or nothing at all: *ibid.*, pp. 93-4.
79 Cowley, *St Paul's Church, Sketty*, pp. 20-2.
80 Glyn Thomas, *Argyle Presbyterian Church of Wales, Swansea* (1975), p. 6.

CHAPTER FOUR: RESTORATION AND REBUILDING

1 This is quoted from Short, *Charge (St Asaph)*, 1851, by M.L. Clarke, "Carnarvonshire Churches at the beginning of the Nineteenth Century", *T.Caerns.H.S.*, 23(1962), p. 64. However, Short did not give a charge in 1851 and I have failed to find the reference.
2 Yates, *Buildings, Faith and Worship*, pp. 151-8.
3 M.L. Clarke, "Carnarvonshire Churches at the beginning of the Nineteenth Century", *T.Caerns.H.S.*, 23(1962), p. 64-5.
4 M.L. Clarke, "Church Building and Church restoration in Carnarvonshire during the Nineteenth Century", *T.Caerns.H.S.*, 22 (1961), 27.
5 Basil F.L. Clarke, *Church Builders of the Nineteenth Century* (reprint, Newton Abbot, 1969), p. 237.
6 Roger L. Brown, "Dean Bonnor", *T.Denb.H.S.*, 51 (2002), 116.
7 I.G. Jones, "Church Reconstruction in Breconshire in the Nineteenth Century", *Brycheiniog*, 19 (1980-1), 11. The Incorporated Church Building Society was founded in 1818, funded by individual subscribers and between 1828-51 by royal letters, akin to the former system of royal briefs, in order to provide funding for the restoration and rebuilding of churches. Its work was later augmented by diocesan church building societies which worked on the same principles. The society's grants were on condition that a proportion of the new seating provided was free and open.
8 Quoted by I.G. Jones, *Communities*, p. 27.
9 Copleston, *Charge (Llandaff)*, 1848, pp. 25-6.
10 Lee notes this for an English setting (though other examples are given in my text), and states parishioners not only regarded these projects as the province of the clergyman and squire but also saw these restorations as an intrusion into their tried pattern of life. As a result they contributed little to the work: *Rural Society and the Anglican Clergy*, pp. 51-3.
11 Ollivant, *Charge (Llandaff)*, 1851, pp. 13-14.
12 Ollivant, *Charge (Llandaff)*, 1860, p. 10.
13 Basil Jones, *Charge (St Davids)*, 1880, pp. 21-2.
14 Jones and Walker, *Links with the Past*, pp. 224-6; D.T.W. Price notes 11 churches rebuilt in the 1870s alone: "The Church of England in Radnorshire in the 1870s", *T.Radn.S.,* 45 (1995), 74.
15 SA/DR/54, fols. 314. A north aisle was added.
16 SA/DR/50, fol. 222.
17 Mrs Bulkeley-Owen, *A History of Selattyn Parish* (Oswestry, n.d.), p. 266.
18 Brian Jones and Margaret Rawcliffe, *Llanddulas* (Denbigh, 1985), p. 185- .
19 SA/LET/392; Pryce, *History of the Parish of Llandysilio*, pp. 32-5, 38.
20 T.W. Pritchard (ed.), *Our Village – Nercwys* (Wrexham, 2000), pp. 116-7.
21 SA/DR/54, fol. 386.
22 G.R. Orrin, "The Reverend Harold Stepney Williams", *Gower*, 41 (1990), 50.
23 William Crawley, *Charge to the Archdeaconry of Monmouth*, 1849, p. 6.
24 Cynthia Rees, *A History of the Parish of Marchwiel* (Wrexham, 1998), p. 13.
25 Eric Griffiths, *Philip Yorke I* (Wrexham, 1995), pp. 131-3.

26 Edward Hamer, "A Parochial History of Llanidloes", *Mont.Coll.*, 6 (1873), 163-4. Wall paintings were destroyed.

27 *RCAHM, Report for Carmarthen* (London, 1917), pp. 70, 178. For other early restorations see Yates in Williams, *The Welsh Church*, pp. 280-2.

28 Yates, in Williams, *The Welsh Church*, pp. 285-8. He notes that many of the early 19th century restorations involved a long-wall arrangement by which the pulpit and reading desk were placed against the long wall of the nave and into the depth of the church, as at Dolgellau, Llanbedr Duffryn Clwyd and Ruthin. Surviving examples include Llanfihangel Helygen, Radnorshire of 1812, Llanddoged, Denbighshire 1838-9, and Llanfigel, Anglesey, about 1840. Others were rebuilt on a "T" plan with the pulpit and desk more centrally placed and the seats placed facing them in the nave and transepts.

29 Morgan Gilbert, *The Priory Church of St Mary the Virgin, Abergavenny* (1910), pp. 15-16.

30 D.E. Jenkins, *Bedd Gelert* (reprint, Beddgelert, 1997), pp. 113-5.

31 *The Restoration of St Martin's Church, Laugharne, Carmarthenshire* (1854, and 1856). In *The Proposed Restoration of the old Parish Church, Coychurch, Glamorgan*, of around the same date, an appeal was made towards the cost of restoration and reseating. The countess of Dunraven had given £300, two other landowners £250 between them, the rector £50 plus £40 for dilapidations on the chancel, a rate had produced £40, and the Llandaff diocesan society gave £25. In all £1,055 had been obtained of the £2,000 required.

32 G.R. Orrin and F.G. Cowley, *All Saints', Oystermouth* (Swansea, 1990), pp. 46-8.

33 E.H.V. Rees, *The Parish of Betws Penpont* (Brecon, 1969), pp. 10-11.

34 *CMG*, 9 September 1860, p. 5.

35 SA/DR/51, fols. 41-2.

36 SA/DR/51, fol. 75; Thomas, *St Asaph*, III, 101.

37 E. Rowley Morris, "History of the Parish of Kerry", *Mont.Coll.*, 25 (1891), 382-9; H. Noel Jarman, *Kerry, the Church and the Village* (1976), pp. 9-12. Street advised against rebuilding and commended a restoration of the church.

38 E.T. Davies, *A History of the Parish of Mathern* (Chepstow, 1950), p. 48.

39 Reed, "Llangattock Parish Scrapbook", p. 118.

40 Kathleen Lewis, *In the Steps of St Rhian* (1962), p. 13.

41 T.A. Morgan-Jones, *A Historical Sketch of the Churches of Carnarvon* (1911), p.17.

42 G.R. Orrin, *Church Building and Restoration in Victorian Glamorgan* (Cardiff, 2004), pp. 19, 35, 47-8, 58-9, 116, 135, 139, 145-7, 164, 172.

43 R.H. Griffiths, *Jottings from the Parish of Llanfair-Duffryn-Clwyd* (1984), pp. 10-11; D. Williams, *S.S. Gwnfarch and Mary, Llanfair Duffryn Clwyd* (1937), p. 6. The cost was £2,300.

44 F.G. Cowley, *Llanmadoc and Cheriton* (1993), pp. 20-2. Ten years later he restored Cheriton Church at a cost of £1,200.

45 Richard Kretchmer, *St Myllin and its Town* (2008), pp. 10-24, 29-33.

46 Brown, "Church of St Mary of the Salutation", pp. 29-31, 55-67; Brown, *Clergy and People of Welshpool*, pp. 47-50.

47 Geoffrey Orrin, *Medieval Churches of the Vale of Glamorgan* (Cowbridge, 1988), p. 42.

48 W. Bezant Lowe, *Llansannan* (Llanfairfechan, 1915), p. 21.

49 Brown, "A Reviving Church?", p. 120.

50 D.R.L. Jones, *The Restoration of Llangynwyd Church 1891-1893* (1992), pp. 4-5, 22-4, 31-2.

51 Robert Lucas, *A Gower Family* (Lewes, 1986), pp. 145-7. Miss Talbot also funded the restoration of Nicholaston Church, which J.D. Davies regarded as the most elaborately treated ecclesiastical building in Wales, if not in the west of England: *West Gower* (Swansea, 1894), IV, 410.

52 Roger Phillips, *Bassaleg: Aspects of its History* (Bassaleg, 1991), p. 70.

53 SA/DR/51, fols. 49-50.

54 Francis Green and T.W. Barker, *Pembrokeshire Parsons* (from *West Wales Historical Records*, 1911-16), I, 242, 278. The school was also temporarily licensed at Rhosili: Robert Lucas, *A Gower Family* (Lewes, 1986), p. 146.

55 Roger L. Brown, "Yr Hen Friscoe", *T,Anglesey H.S.*, 2002, pp. 66-7.

56 Roger L. Brown, "The Nineteenth Century Parish of Llandudno", *T.Caerns.H.S.*, 55 (1994), 16.

57 Brown, "The Parish of Gelligaer in the Nineteenth-Century", p. 28.

58 J.T. Evans, *The Church Plate of Pembrokeshire* (London, 1905), p. 97.

59 G. James, *The Parish of Llanfihangel Ynys Afan* (1990s), pp. 42-53.

60 B.C. Luxton, *St Cadoc's* (1980), pp. 47-9.

61 J.R. Stirk, "Chevalier J.Y.W. Lloyd", *Mont.Coll.*, 77 (1989), 137.

62 Richard Davies, "Nineteenth-Century Church Reconstruction, Little Newcastle Church", *J.Pembs.H.S.*, 6 (1994-5), 80-9.

63 R.C.B. Oliver, "Church Building and Rebuilding in Radnorshire in the later Nineteenth Century", *T.Radn.S.*, 48 (1978), 33. Howse called it a "restoration by destruction": *Radnorshire*, pp. 244-6.

64 Thomas Williams, *Charge to the Archdeaconry of Llandaff*, 1845, p. 4.

65 T.W. Pritchard, *Mold Town and County* (Wrexham, 2012), p. 189.

66 C.B. Turner, "Ritualism, Railwaymen and the poor: the Ministry of Canon J.D. Jenkins, 1870-1876", in G.H. Jenkins and J.B. Smith (eds.), *Politics and Society in Wales* (Cardiff, 1988), pp. 69-70.

67 *Bye-Gones*, 27 February 1901, p. 48.

68 Bradney, *Monmouthshire*, I, 353, 375; IV, 263.

69 O.G. Rees, "papers, Correspondence about the Restoration of Llanbadarn Fawr Parish Church, Cardiganshire, 1862-1870", *JHSCW*, 10 (1960), 54, 56-60; J.T. Evans, *The Church Plate of Cardiganshire* (Stowe on the Wold, 1904), p. 37. (Evans described the restoration as having caused "irreparable injury" and noted the "barbarous" destruction of the wall paintings).

70 *Report of the St David's Diocesan Conference*, 1885, pp. 142-3.

71 *Report of the St David's Diocesan Conference*, 1891, pp. 23-9, esp. pp. 23-4, 27-8.

72 M.L. Clarke, "Anglesey Churches in the Nineteenth Century", *T.Anglesey A.S.*, 1961, p. 54. At Glascwm, Breconshire, the vicar took over the supervision of the work as it was badly delayed: Jones and Walker, *Links with the Past*, p. 234.

73 E.W. Parry (ed.), *Rev. John Parker's Tour of Wales and its Churches* (Llanrwst, 1998), pp. 28, 33-8.

74 Brown, *Ten Clerical Lives*, p. 192.

75 I.G. Jones, "Church Reconstruction in Breconshire in the Nineteenth Century", *Brycheiniog*, 19 (1980-1), 23-4.

76 M.L. Clarke, "Anglesey Churches in the Nineteenth Century", *T.Anglesey A.S.*, 1961, p. 54.

77 Hughes, *Pwllheli*, p. 273.

78 Brown, *Reclaiming the Wilderness*, pp. 189-90. A £250 loan was secured on the rate income, £50 came from the Diocesan Board, £40 from various collections, £120 from the Incorporated Society, and £598 from subscriptions.

There were many other churches which were rebuilt or substantially restored to provide additional seating. Amongst them were: Meifod 1871-2: *Mont.Coll.*, 10 (1877), 170; Tregynon 1893; *ibid*, 30 (1898), 26; Aberhafesb in 1866, where the pews were cut down to a uniform size: Thomas, *St Asaph*, I, 507; Llanfechain and Hope 1884: SA/DR/50, fols. 132, 159; Buttington 1876 and Llanrhaeadr-ym-Mochnant 1882 where the pews were replaced by pitch pine benches: SA/DR/51, fols. 32, 50, and Tregynon: SA/DR/54, fol. 468; Llanmihangel, Porthceri, Llanblethian, Llysworney and Sully (most assisted by grants from the Incorporated Society for the provision of free places): Geoffrey Orrin, *Medieval Churches of the Vale of Glamorgan* (Cowbridge, 1988), pp. 179, 224, 262, 317, 404.

79 *Church Builder*, no 8, pp. 18-19.

80 *Mont.Coll.*, 78 (1990), 180-1. The west gallery with four pews cost £130, the pews in the church £120, and altar piece with table and banisters £90, and a reading desk and pulpit £75.

81 Barrie Jones, "The Rev. George Martin Maber", *Merthyr Historian*, 9 (1997), 6-7.
82 Brian Howells (ed.), *Pembrokeshire County History* (Haverfordwest, 1987), III, 239.
83 B. Ll. Morris (ed.), *The Slebech Story* (c. 1950), pp. 41-3.
84 Oliver Nixon, *Parish of Newtown* (1997), pp. 4-6.
85 D.T. Davies (ed.), *Hanes Eglwysi a Phlwyfi Lleyn* (Pwllheli, 1910), pp. 202-4.
86 Brown, *Church and Clergy at Castle Caereinion*, pp. 60-5.
87 H.M. Thomas, *Ystradowen* (1993), pp. 59-61.
88 E.P. Hughes, "A Parochial History of Llanfair Caereinion", *Mont.Coll.*, 16 (1883), 350-1.
89 Thomas, *St Asaph*, II, 441.
90 R.C.B. Oliver, "Church Building and Rebuilding in Radnorshire in the later Nineteenth Century", *T.Radn.S.*, 48 (1978), 34-41. He notes those who contributed to the appeal.
91 Roger L. Brown, *Through Cloud and Sunshine* (Port Talbot, 1982), pp. 93-5, 100-5. It cost £3,500, of which local landowners provided £1,350 and the parishioners £600. For other examples see G.R. Orrin, *Church Building and Restoration in Victorian Glamorgan* (Cardiff, 2004), pp. 19, 123-4, 171-3.
92 Jennifer Holland, *Cwmddauddwr Church and Parish Memories* (1990s), pp. 26, 46-9.
93 Brown, "Henry Powell Ffoulkes" p. 133. The cost was £3,000. The old church was situated on a steep bank above the village.
94 J.E. Vize, "The Parish of Forden", *Mont.Coll.*, 16 (1883), 198. Other churches rebuilt during this period in Montgomeryshire were Llandyssil, Llandysilio, Llanerfyl, Llangynog, Llanwyddelan and Llanllwchaiarn, as noted by *RCAHM Report on Montgomeryshire* (London, 1911), pp. 76-7, 80, 108, 121, 143. The commission's report on Pembrokeshire (1925) provides many further examples.
95 A.E. Parry, *St Clement's Church, Briton Ferry* (1957), pp. 4-5.
96 Cyril Williams, *Centenary of St Mary's Church, Denbigh* (1975), p. 6.
97 Kissack, *Victorian Monmouth*, pp. 95-9.
98 K. Padley, *Our Ladye Church of Swanesey* (2007), pp. 52-3; W.Ll. Morgan, *An Antiquarian Survey of East Gower* (London, 1899), p. 124. The interior of the former church was remodelled in 1849 and the congregation centred towards the chancel. The cost of the new church was £10, 748.
99 Ralph Holtham, *The Parish of Roath* (1970), p. 21.
100 Ruth Bidgood, *Parishes of the Buzzard* (Port Talbot, 2000), pp. 49-51.
101 Eben Jones, *Baglan and the Llewellyns of Baglan Hall* (1987), pp. 130-2.
102 Albert Jordan, *History of the Church and Parish of Llanbadarn Fawr* (Brecon, 1926), pp. 2, 20.
103 Bryn Ellis, *The History of Halkyn Mountain* (Halkyn, 1999), p. 160.
104 Bradney, *Monmouthshire*, I, 477.
105 Elwyn Bowen, *Vaynor* (Merthyr Tydfil, 1992), p. 238.
106 K. Hughes and D. Ifans (eds), *The Diary of Francis Kilvert, April – June 1870* (Aberystwyth, 1982), p. 71.
107 Derrick Platt, *Church of St Mary Magdalene, Penley* (1980), p. 19.
108 Brown, *Reclaiming the Wilderness*, p. 189.
109 I.G. Jones, *Communities*, pp. 47-69.
110 Brown, *Ten Clerical Lives*, pp. 191-4. I have been unable to trace the court proceedings.
111 Brown, *Ten Clerical Lives*, pp. 194-201.

CHAPTER FIVE: EXTENDING THE MISSION OF THE CHURCH

1 SA/DR/50, fol. 170.
2 Bishop of Llandaff in *Report of the Royal Commission, 1911*, IV, 520 (48095).

3 *Report of the Royal Commission, 1911*, IV, 420 (46024).

4 Thomas Williams, *Charge to the Archdeaconry of Llandaff*, 1844, pp. 22-4.

5 Ollivant, *Charge (Llandaff)*, 1854, p. 43.

6 Knight, in Williams, *The Welsh Church*, pp. 355-6.

7 David Walter Thomas, *The Church in Wales: Past and Present: Facts and Suggestions* (London, 1870), pp. 23-4.

8 Chadwick, *Victorian Church*, I, 524-5; Russell, *The Clerical Profession*, pp. 61-2. The 1855 act was entitled *An Act for the better securing of the Liberty of Religious Worship*, and was promoted, amidst bitter opposition, by Lord Shaftesbury, in order to permit open air services and services in theatres and public halls. Canon 14 of the 1603 Canons required the church services to be held in a Church building and Canon 71 forbade preaching in private houses save in case of illness; but I have failed to find in such law texts as Burn, Gibson, Watson or Cripps any account of the restriction to twenty people. Amicus rightly asked in 1833 why the clergy were not at liberty to preach in other places when their parish churches often could not accommodate half their parishioners: *Letter of Reply to Arthur James Johnes, Esq. ...[on] his Essay on the Causes of Dissent from the Established Church in Wales* (London, 1833), p. 53.

9 W.W.T. Rees, *Trevethin, Pontypool* (Pontypool, 1934), p. 23. A Sunday School was also established there.

10 Campbell, *Charges (Bangor)*, 1863, pp. 12-13; 1869, pp. 17-21; 1875, pp. 3-4.

11 Brown, *Reclaiming the Wilderness*, pp. 12-13.

12 Jane Ross, *A Light upon the Road* (1989), p. 20.

13 Joan Lent, *Anglican Churches of Arllechwedd* (1980), p. 33.

14 Robin Gill, *The Myth of the Empty Church* (London, 1993), pp. 54, 119. Gill suggests that much of this church building was due to the Church's competition with Nonconformity.

15 SA/DR/50, fol 231. It appears to have been successful.

16 Roger L. Brown, "E.O.V. Lloyd and the Squire's Chapel", *Old Denbighshire*, 1999, pp. 90-4. Thomas regards it as a mission room in the 1900s: *St Asaph*, II, 85.

17 William Evan James, *Charge to the Archdeaconry of Carmarthen*, 1882, p. 7.

18 *Report of the St David's Diocesan Conference*, 1885, pp. 104-5.

19 Russell, *The Clerical Profession*, pp. 68-70. By the 1860s these services were viewed with disfavour. Copleston had advocated weekday services for prayer and instruction in cottages or private homes: *Charge (Llandaff)*, 1836, p. 21.

20 Sumner, *Charge (Llandaff)*, 1827, pp. 18-20. His brother, John Bird Sumner, then bishop of Chester, said much the same in his Charge of 1838, arguing that these rooms would prevent the working classes from being ashamed to attend church services: Solway, *Prelates and People*, p. 271.

21 Wilton D. Wills, "The Established Church in the Diocese of Llandaff", *WHR*, 4 (1969), 250-1; *Church Pastoral-Aid Society: Abstract of Report*, 1853, p. 10. Pritchard Hughes also noted their uncomfortable and unsuitable character in 1891, stating that when a new church was built to replace one attendances increased by over fifty per cent: *Church Pastoral-Aid Society: Church and People*, 3 (1891), 137-8.

22 J.A. Gabb ("A Clergyman"), *A Brief Memoir of James Davies* (London, 1832), pp. 34-5.

23 Brown, *Evangelicals in the Church in Wales*, p. 165.

24 F.G. Llewellin, *The History of Clodock* (Manchester, 1919), pp. 194-7.

25 Brown, *John Griffith*, pp. 87-8. Three of these rooms became the seedbed of new parishes: St Margaret's, Mountain Ash, its church built at the expense of J. Bruce Pryce in 1862; St Fagan's Aberdare, its church built by the Clive family in 1854; and Hirwaun 1858.

26 T.A. and V.A. Holley, "Foundations 1893-1902", *Merthyr Historian*, 7 (1994), 82.

27 *Church Pastoral-Aid Society: Church and People*, 7 (1895), 124-6. There was also a daughter church.

28 *Guardian*, 25 March 1874, p. 374.

29 Eli Clarke, *Parish of Christ Church, Swansea: Pastoral Letter and Statement of Accounts*, 1891-92, p. 3.

30 J.C. Jones, *Buckley Parish Church*, p. 22.

31 *Report of the Royal Commission, 1911*, IV. 235 (40908).

32 B.L. Luxton, *St Cadoc's* (1980), p. 51.

33 *Forms of Prayer for certain Special Occasions issued for use in the Diocese of St David's* (Carmarthen, 1884). Bishop Basil Jones noted how his diocese used schools and mission rooms for the extension of its ministry, but wondered how to obtain the manpower required: *Report of the Church Congress, Sheffield,* 1878, p. 156.

34 *Report of the Royal Commission, 1911*, IV, 407 (45885).

35 Edwards, *Charge (St Asaph)*, 1890, p. 12. Edwards appears to have omitted Sunday services.

36 J.C. Read, *A History of St John's Cardiff* (Cardiff, 1995), p. 81.

37 Pryce, *One Hundred Years of Evangelical Witness*, p. 51.

38 F. Morton and Company, *General Remarks on the Improved Construction of Iron Churches* (1870), introduction and p. 19. An iron church erected at Ruabon was supplied by R.C. Harris of London, 45 by 20 feet, its cost was £117: T.W. Pritchard, *Remembering Ruabon* (Wrexham, 2000), p. 84. Ian Smith notes that many of these churches had a steeple or bell cote, and later galvanised iron was used as it prevented corrosion: *Tin Tabernacles* (Camrose, 2004), pp. 27-9.

39 SA/DR/51, fol. 2. The report was addressed to the St Asaph Diocesan Church Building Society in 1879.

40 *CMG*, 23 March 1872, p. 8.

41 *Report of the Llandaff Diocesan Conference*, 1890, pp. 56-7. Though it is not described as an iron building, it seems clear it was one.

42 Roger L. Brown, *The Churches in the Parish of Tongwynlais* (1988), pp. 3, 13-14. Both buildings continued as places of worship after the schools had been closed. Another school church was built in the same parish at Taffs Wells in 1868.

43 E.D. Jones, "The Journal of William Roberts", *NLW.Jnl.*, 10 (1958), 313.

44 Wickham, *Charge to the Archdeaconry of St Asaph*, 1866, p. 7.

45 SA/DR/51, fol. 4. It was also claimed that the room was at a great distance from the parish church, the congregation poor, the inhabitants mainly Dissenters, and another £200 was needed towards the cost of £1,100.

46 T.W. Pritchard, *The Making of Buckley and District* (Wrexham, 2006), pp. 197, 199. The church was later rebuilt 1897-1905 with much financial assistance from its rector, Harry Drew, and the Gladstone family: *ibid.*, pp. 207-8.

47 Jones and Williams, *The Religious Census of 1851*, I, 435, 538.

48 Brown, "The Curate of Berriew", pp. 148-9. Pantyfridd, though no longer a school is still used for services.

49 T.W. Pritchard, *A History of the Old Parish of Hawarden* (Wrexham, 2002), p. 152. There were also two mission churches: Gladstone, *Parish of Hawarden*, p. 11. Churches were built later at Sandycroft and Sholton, their cost partly funded by the Gladstone family.

50 David Thomas, *The Parish of Bangor Monachorum* (1962), p. 29.

51 *Mont.Coll.*, 35 (1910), 126.

52 *CMG*, 21 August 1863, p. 6; Women's Institute, *Belan* (1983), p. 85. The apse was provided in 1868.

53 P. Gwynn (ed.), *Saints' Alive* (1998), p. 15.

54 W.L. Bevan, *The Church in the South Wales Coal-field* (London, 1895), p. 11.

55 Wills, "The Established Church in the Diocese of Llandaff", *WHR*, 4 (1969), 251; Brown, "The Parish of Gelligaer", pp. 33-4.

56 John Bagshaw, *Broughton Then and Now* (Wrexham, 1992), p. 119.

57 M.J. Mainwaring, *History of St Peter's Church, Senghenydd* (1946), pp. 4-6.

58 B.L. Luxton, *St Cadoc's* (1980), p. 52.

59 Edward Boore and Fred Bell, *A History of the Parish Church of Ebbw Vale* (1964), pp. 4-5.

60 W.D. Jenkins, *"The Undaunted Spirit"* (1950), pp. 11-12.

61 Ralph Holtham, *The Parish of Roath* (1970), pp. 21-2; M. Warner and A.C. Hooper, *The History of Roath St German's* (Cardiff, 1934), pp. 34-6, 41 (the iron church had come from Dudley). Mission rooms in the parish of St Mary, Cardiff, built in 1876 and 1897, developed into separate parishes: Guy, *St Mary's Church, Cardiff*, p. 44.

62 Harry Old, *The Story of St David's Church, Ely* (1946), pp. 3-4. The site was given by Lady Windsor and the nave was the first part of the church to be built.

63 J.C. Read, *The Church in our City* (1953), pp. 47, 63.

64 Roger L. Brown, *The Churches in the Parish of Tongwynlais* (1988), pp. 39-40, 44-8.

65 Jeffrey Gainer, *A Short History of St Mary Magdalene's Parish Church, Cwmbach* (1982), pp. 10-11.

66 F.J. Gaines, *History of St Matthias Church, Treharris* (1946), pp. 15-17. It became a separate district in 1898.

67 Handel Thomas, *Llanbradach and its Church* (1947), pp. 5-9; Hywel Davies, *Holy Trinity Church, Ystrad Mynach*, pp. 16-17. The new parish was formed in 1904.

68 Brown, "The Parish of Gelligaer", pp. 42-4.

69 W. Haydn Rees, *A Short History of the Church and Parish of St Andrew, Llwynypia* (1948), pp. 15-16, 24-6, 33. It had 108 rented pews. A church in this parish at Ynyscynon started in a local public house in 1902.

70 Prichard, *Representative Bodies*, p. 150.

71 *Church Pastoral-Aid Society Quarterly Paper 88* (April 1886), p. 6; *Church and People*, 8 (1897), 269-70. Services had commenced in a reading room at Ferndale.

72 Prichard, *Representative Bodies*, p. 145.

73 D.R.L. Jones, *Richard and Mary Pendrill Llewelyn* (1991), pp. 16-17.

74 Roger L. Brown, *Through Cloud and Sunshine* (Port Talbot, 1982), pp. 125-34.

75 J.R. Richards, *Ecclesiastical Parish of Skewen: Historical Survey* (1950), pp. 2-4. The Church Pastoral-Aid Society had given a curate's grant for this church when it was part of the parish of Cadoxton.

76 L.S. Huggins, *Newton Nottage and Porthcawl* (Llandysul, 1968), p. 86; Alan Morgan, *Porthcawl, Newton and Nottage* (Cowbridge, 1987), pp. 62-3.

77 Williams, *Move On!*, p. 19.

78 Reynolds, *St Gabriel's*, pp. 12-14, 17-22, 25; *Parish of Swansea Report for 1889*, p. 3-4.

79 Williams, *Move On!*, p. 26; M.E. Chamberlain, "The Grenfells of Kilvey", in Stewart Williams, *Glamorgan Historian*, 9 (1970s), 135-6.

80 G.R. Orrin, "The Reverend. Harold Stepney Williams", *Gower*, 41 (1990), pp. 49-50.

81 C.D. Hughes, *St Peter's Church, Pontardawe* (1960s), pp. 11-12, 18; P.W. Jackson notes another industrialist, Arthur Gilbertson, who built All Saints' Church, Clydach, as a memorial to his father at a cost of £3,000; *The Letter Books of W. Gilbertson and Co. Ltd.* (Cardiff, 2001), p. 365.

82 *Dafen Parish Church Centenary 1874-1974.*

83 Thomas, *The Parish of Holywell*, pp. 33-4.

84 Roger L. Brown, "Dean Bonnor of St Asaph", *T.Denb.H.S.*, 51 (2002), 114.

85 Thomas, *St Asaph*, III, 270. It became a separate district in 1879.

86 Huw Williams, *A History of the Church in Dowlais* (1977), pp. 9, 13. It became a separate parish in 1839, though when difficulties had arisen beforehand about licensing the building for worship Guest threatened to make it into a dissenting place of worship.

87 Joan Lent, *The Anglican Churches of Arllechwedd* (1980), p. 2. Lord Penrhyn also built the church at Tregarth (*ibid.*, p. 36); M.L. Clarke, "Church Building and Church Restoration in Carnarvonshire during the Nineteenth Century", *T.Caerns.H.S.*, 22 (1961), 23.

88 *Guardian*, October 1846, p. 86; Thomas Lloyd, et al, *The Buildings of Wales: Pembrokeshire* (London, 2004), p. 58.

89 Elizabeth F. Belcham, *About Aberpergwm* (Glynneath, 1993), pp. 81-3, 155, 160.

90 I.G. Jones, *Communities*, pp. 27-9.

91 The names of some of these benefactors for the diocese of Llandaff is given by E.T. Davies, *Religion and Society in the Nineteenth Century* (Llandybie, 1981) p. 81, and J.M. Wooding and N. Yates (eds.), *A Guide to the Churches and Chapels of Wales* (Cardiff, 2011), pp. 29, 72, 82, 137. For Cawdor see Cragoe, *Anglican Aristocracy*, p. 223.

92 George, *St Theodore's Church*, pp. 9, 17-18; G.R. Orrin notes that her sister Emily built Kenfig Hill Church, and both sisters contributed substantially to church buildings and restorations in their area, including Llandyfodwg Church: "The Role of the Talbot Family in Church Building and Restoration in Victorian Glamorgan", *Morgannwg*, 46 (2002), pp.62-5.

93 *Report of the Church Congress, Rhyl*, 1891, p. 74; Prichard, *Representative Bodies*, pp. 160-1.

94 F.M. Slater, *Newbridge-on-Wye* (1990), p. 20.

95 SA/DR/50, fol. 255. A school-church had been built in 1856.

96 Ian Allan, "Henry Wilson's Brithdir Letters", *J.Mer.H.S.*, 8 (1980), 409-11.

97 John Davies, "The Second Marquess of Bute", in Stewart Williams, *Glamorgan Historian*, 8 (1970s), 20; Cragoe, *Anglican Aristocracy*, pp. 223-4.

98 G.R. Orrin, *Church Building and Restoration in Victorian Glamorgan* (Cardiff, 2004), p. xvii.

99 I.G. Jones, *Communities*, p. 20.

100 E.E. Edwards, *Echoes of Rhymney* (Risca, 1974), pp. 24-5.

101 Copleston, *Charge (Llandaff)*, 1845, pp. 4-7, 28-30; *Separation either a Duty or a Sin: A Sermon preached at the Consecration of Trinity Church, Abergavenny* (London, 1840), pp. i-vii, 22-4 [this church was built by Miss Rachel Herbert who also received the bishop's commendation]; Brown, *Letters of Edward Copleston*, pp. 26-9; Phillips, *Wales*, pp. 225-7. Copleston favourably commented upon the decision of the annual general meeting of the Rhymney Iron Company of 1838 to build church and schools at Rhymney: *Who are the Persons authorised to Preach the Gospel? A Sermon preached at Usk* (London, 1839), pp. 34-7. Archdeacon Thomas Williams of Llandaff made similar comments about the ironmasters' failures: *Charge to the Archdeaconry of Llandaff*, 1845, p. 3.

102 Brown, *Letters of Edward Copleston*, p. 27; E.T. Davies, *Religion in the Industrial Revolution in South Wales*, pp. 28-9.

103 G. James, *The Parish of Llanfihangel Ynys Afan* (1990s), p. 62.

104 Quoted by Davies, *Religion in the Industrial Revolution in South Wales*, pp. 107-8; *Report of the Llandaff Diocesan Conference*, 1884, p. 52; 1892, pp. 78-81; Jesse James said much the same: Brown, *Reclaiming the Wilderness*, pp. 31-2.

105 H.T. Edwards, *Church Extension in Aberdare* (1867); *Llandaff Diocesan Church Extension Society: Substance of Speeches delivered in 1863*, p. 59 (other speakers made the same points); Brown, *Reclaiming the Wilderness*, pp. 68-9.

106 Ollivant, *Charge (Llandaff)*, 1875, p. 21.

107 Muriel Evans, *The Story of the Parish of St David, Ton Pentre* (1960), pp. 12, 15-17; Prichard, *Representative Bodies*, p. 152-3.

108 Theophilus Jones, *Brecknockshire*, III, 183.

109 Solway, *Prelates and People*, pp. 290-5, 327-5; I.G. Jones, *Communities*, pp. 12-15.

110 *Sermons by the late Ven. John Hughes [with a] Memoir* (Aberystwyth, 1864), p. xii.

111 I.G. Jones, *Communities*, p. 20.

112 J.R. Guy, *St Mary's Church, Cardiff*, pp. 34-7; Brown, *Ten Clerical Lives*, pp. 84-7; John Davies estimates that the family gave £15,000 to the church in Glamorgan but the conversion of the third marquess to Roman Catholicism was a substantial loss to the Church: *Cardiff and the Marquesses of Bute* (Cardiff, 1981), p. 99.

113 David Walker, *The First Hundred Years* (1967), pp. 4, 7, 9. In 1884, 335 sittings were let at £311 per annum.

114 Campbell, *Charge (Bangor)*, 1863, p. 12.

115 Roger L. Brown, "the Nineteenth Century Parish of Llandudno", *T.Caerns.H.S.*, 55 (1984), 14-16.

116 J.G. Sunderland, *St Thomas' Church, Rhyl* (1988), pp. 6, 18.

117 Joan Lent, *Anglican Churches of Arllechwedd* (1980), p. 32.

118 R.C.B. Oliver, *The Centenary of the Church of the Holy Trinity, Llandrindod Wells* (1971), p. 10; Brown, "A Reviving Church?" p. 121.

119 *CDH*, 18 June 1859, p. 6.

120 SA/DR/54, fol. 303. The press often gave columns of type to these events, describing the church, the service and the sermon, the meal and speeches made afterwards: see, for examples: SA/DR/50, fol. 159, and SA/DR/54, fols. 354-5 (Llanrhaeadr-ym-Mochnant); Ellis, *Fresh as Yesterday*, p. 100; and J.C. Jones, *Buckley Parish Church*, pp. 10-15, for an account of the elaborate laying of the foundation stone.

121 *Report of the Association of Welsh Clergy*, 1854, pp. 38-41.

122 As at Eglwys Fach in 1786, when £200 was borrowed: Elias Owen, "How Churches were built in the Eighteenth Century", *Arch.Camb.*, 5th series, 5 (1888), 243.

123 Brown, *Church and Clergy at Castle Caereinion*, pp. 58-9.

124 I.G. Jones, *Communities,* pp. 70-87; Jane Ross, *A Light upon the Road* (1989), pp. 10-13; G.E. Evans, *Aberystwyth and its Court Leet* (Aberystwyth, 1902), pp. 40-51. Evans states that the first church opened in that town in 1789 had been previously used as a boat shed: *ibid.*, p. 40).

125 Noted by Leslie Baker-Jones, *Princelings, Privilege and Power* (Llandysul, 1999), pp. 242-4.

126 J.C. Jones, *Buckley Parish Church*, pp. 9-10, 69-73. It became a separate parish in 1874. The cost of the works also included a parsonage house.

127 Watkin, *Oswestry*, pp. 247-9. Holy Trinity became a separate district in 1842.

128 I.G. Jones, "Ecclesiastical Economy: Aspects of Church Building in Victorian Wales", in R.R. Davies, et al., *Welsh Society and Nationhood* (Cardiff, 1984), p. 225. Jones elsewhere suggests that overall 86 per cent of the cost of building was raised through voluntary giving: *Communities,* p. 15. None of the initial 1818 parliamentary grant was used in Wales and none of the 1825 grant was used in south Wales: I.G. Jones, *Mid-Victorian Wales* (Cardiff, 1992), p. 6.

129 *St Asaph Clerical Directory*, 1863. In addition 15 churches were rebuilt and 35 restored.

130 *Report of the Llandaff Diocesan Church Extension Society*, 1866, p. 8. By 1902 it had given, over the previous 51 years, £9,767 towards the building of churches and £2,855 for mission rooms: *ibid*, 1902, p. 10.

131 *St David's Diocesan Directory and Calendar*, 1889, I, 171; *Report of the St David's Diocesan Conference*, 1881, p. 50.

132 Van Mildert, *Charge (Llandaff)*, 1821, p. 8.

133 *Report of the St David's Diocesan Conference*, 1884, pp. 100-1. Cragoe notes that between 1828-37 this society gave on average four grants to the diocese: *Anglican Aristocracy*, p. 219.

134 I.G. Jones, *Communities*, p. 17.

135 G.R. Orrin, *Church Building and Restoration in Victorian Glamorgan* (Cardiff, 2004), p. 125.

136 SA/DR/54, fol. 333. Llansanffraid Church held a two day bazaar, *ibid*, fol. 362. A vivid description of a bazaar is given by George Huntington in his *Autobiography of an Alms Bag* (London, 1885), pp. 49-56.

137 David Wyn Davies, *The Goodly Heritage* (Machynlleth, 1988), p. 25.

138 Janet Jones, *Holy Trinity Church, Aberystwyth* (1986), pp. 2-3, 10-11. The court decided that a major part of the Morice bequest should be used to provide an endowment.

139 Gresford Vicar's Book, fol. 30.

140 *Church Builder*, 1881, p. 54.

141 I.G. Jones, *Communities*, pp. 19-21.

142 J.J. Tomson to T. Jenkins, 4 May 1878: South Glamorgan Record Office, D/D, Pl 836/40.

143 Alfred Ollivant, *The Duty of those who are not Rich with respect to the Extension of the Church* (London, 1851), pp. 16-17.

144 Lewis, *Charge (Llandaff)*, 1891, p. 17. He noted that one church with 900 seats in a mining area had already proved inadequate.

145 D.G. Lewis, *Holy Trinity Church, Gwernaffield* (1972), p. 6; M.V.J. Seaborne, "Charles Butler Clough", *NLW.Jnl.*, 29 (1996), 287-92. According to I.G. Jones, Gwernaffield cost £764 and Pontvlyddyn £790: *Communities*, p. 20. When Llangynog Church was restored in 1894 the farmers conveyed materials from the railway station nine miles away: SA/DR/54. fol. 455.

146 South Glamorgan Record Office, Bute Papers, L80/17, 46, 57.

147 Brown, *Reclaiming the Wilderness*, pp. 138-43.

148 Prichard, *Representative Bodies*, pp. 145-7. Tylorstown cost £1,358. Many believed that William Lewis, vicar of Ystradyfodwg, and thus of the main Rhondda valley, took too many risks in building these churches, and that his insistence in building permanent stone churches led him to be importunate with the wealthy: *ibid.*, p. 166.

149 Susan Rees, et al, *The History of St Peter's Church in the Village of Newton* (Swansea, 2010), pp. 27-30, 40-1.

150 *Report of the St David's Diocesan Conference*, 1891, p. 23.

151 Ollivant, *Charge (Llandaff)*, 1860, pp. 21-2. Bishop Ryle of Liverpool held that leaving a man with a large debt on a new church was placing a millstone around his neck and crippling his usefulness: I.D. Farley, *J.C. Ryle* (Carlisle, 2000), p. 114.

152 Kenneth Ward, *The World of William Wickham* (Havant, 1981), pp. 16-17.

153 F.L.G. Bevan, *History of Christ Church, Cyfarthfa* (1957), pp. 11-12.

154 SA/DR/50, fols. 248, 252. The vicar of Bettws Gwerful Goch in a printed manuscript letter of 1879 appealing for funds to build a church, asked for donations of one shilling in postage stamps "to promote the glory of God" and also the return of his letter. He alleged that over 25,817 letters had been sent: SA/DR/51, fol. 97-9.

155 SA/DR/54, fols. 371-2.

156 The churchwardens to the Revd. John David Jenkins, 4 March 1876: Representative Body of the Church in Wales: Ecclesiastical Commission file for Aberdare.

157 SA/DR/51, fol. 17.

158 T.W. Pritchard, *A History of the Old Parish of Hawarden* (Wrexham, 2002), pp. 248-9.

159 Brown, *Reclaiming the Wilderness*, p. 32; B.F.L. Clarke, *Church Builders of the Nineteenth-Century* (reprint, Newton Abbot, 1969), pp. 216-7. Many of the churches that were built proved to be far larger than required.

160 G.H. James, *Manselton and its Parish Church* (1956), pp. 17-18, 23.

161 Wills, "The Established Church in the Diocese of Llandaff", *WHR*, 4 (1969), 250-1. Bishop Thirlwall thought otherwise, and felt that a high degree of architectural beauty was consistent "with the purest simplicity of our reformed worship": quoted by Cragoe, *Anglican Aristocracy*, pp. 220-1.

162 *Speeches, Articles &c of Edward James Herbert, Third Earl of Powis* (London, 1892), p. 49. The church he built, for an undisclosed sum, at Pool Quay, near Welshpool, in 1862, was anything but plain and simple.

163 *CMG*, 7 February 1857, p. 5.

164 Roger L. Brown, "George Martin Maber, Rector of Merthyr", *Merthyr Historian,* 10 (1999), 66-7; Brown, *Letters of Edward Copleston*, p. 258 (letter 370); Roger L. Brown, "The Wealthiest Place and the Poorest Ministry", *Merthyr Historian*, 8 (1996), 65-7. To save cost the spire and even the doors to the pews were omitted. Later at Troedyrhiw in the same parish there were great difficulties with the mineral rights of the land when a church was proposed to be built there: *ibid.*, p. 76.

165 "D.C.L.", *Letters on Church Matters reprinted from the 'Morning Chronicle'* (London, 1851), I, 297.

166 *Report of the St David's Diocesan Conference*, 1885, p. 155.

167 *Report of the St David's Diocesan Conference*, 1891, p. 27.

168 H.T. Edwards, *Church Extension in Aberdare* (1867), p. 7.

169 I.G. Jones, *Communities*, p. 20.

170 Edward Hubbard (ed.), *The Buildings of Wales: Clwyd* (London, 1986), p. 64. He notes that the churches built with the assistance of the Church Buildings Commissioners were architecturally poor.

171 Bryn Ellis, *The History of Halkyn Mountain* (Halkyn, 1989), p. 162.

172 Bryn Ellis, *The History of Halkyn Mountain* (Halkyn, 1989), pp. 160-1.

173 Brown, "The Parish of Gelligaer", pp. 43-5; Brown, *Reclaiming the Wilderness*, pp. 122, 126.

174 Brown, *Ten Clerical Lives*, pp. 86-7.

175 Brown, *Reclaiming the Wilderness*, pp. 66-9; Brown, *John Griffith*, pp. 84-6; I.G. Jones, "Church Building in Aberdare", in his *Communities*, pp. 88-101.

176 Prichard, *Representative Bodies*, p. 144. It cost £1,960.

177 *Bye-Gones,* 23 September 1891, p. 170; Lewis Lloyd, *Whatever Freights may Offer* (Caernarfon, 1993), pp. 348, 354-5, 362-3.

178 Brown, *Ten Clerical Lives*, pp. 86-7.

179 M. Howells, *History of the Church of St Illtyd, Williamstown* (1944), p. 6.

180 Thomas Lloyd, et. al., *The Buildings of Wales: Carmarthenshire and Ceredigion* (London, 2006), p. 404.

181 Best, *Temporal Pillars*, p. 195-6. He adds that the Act was a creature of the State and the archbishop was merely sent copies of the bill to distribute to his colleagues, but the Church itself was powerless to act: *ibid.*, pp. 268-9.

182 Bradney, *Monmouthshire*, I. 403. It was built by the local ironmasters, Thomas Hill and Samuel Hopkins.

183 Basil F.L. Clarke, *Church Builders of the Nineteenth Century* (reprint, Newton Abbot, 1969), pp. 216-7. J.R. Leeming argued that smaller districts were needed: *Church Scandals and their Cure* (Rochdale, 1908), pp. 48-53.

184 Rodes, *Law and Modernization*, pp. 168-9; Solway, *Prelates and People*, pp. 345-6. Some had hoped this act would start the process of reorganising the archaic parochial structure of the Church.

185 M.H. Port, *Six Hundred New Churches* (London, 1842), pp. 25-6. A rate levied at 8d. in the pound over three years for the restoration of Cadoxton Church was lost as the notice had not been fixed to the door of its chapel of ease: Keith Tucker, *A History of St Catwg's Church* (1990), pp. 18-19.

186 Wickham, *Charge to the Archdeaconry of St Asaph*, 1857, pp. 6-7.

187 This was seen as unfair by "A Pauper Clergyman", as the old incumbent received an income for services rendered by others, and yet was relieved from paying for a curate to care for that part of the parish he had relinquished: *How to make Better Provision for the Cure of Souls out of the Present Actual Finances of the Church* (London, 1857), p. 50.

188 Prichard, *Representative Bodies*, p. 143. Many required 500 sittings. See also Rodes, *Law and Modernization*, pp. 168-9.

189 Basil F.L. Clarke, *Church Builders of the Nineteenth Century* (reprint, Newton Abbot, 1969), p. 217.

Bishop Blomfield of London believed otherwise and created many small parishes with insufficient endowments rather than establish large parishes with a number of daughter churches and a staff of curates: Malcolm Johnson, *Blustering Intermeddler?* (Leominster, 2001), p. 119.

190 *Report of the Llandaff Diocesan Conference*, 1884, pp. 51-2.

191 Rodes, *Law and Modernization*, p. 168. At first "incumbents" of these district churches were termed perpetual curates, but by 1868 those who were permitted to perform weddings and funerals in their churches were termed vicars.

192 *Detailed Statement of all the Parishes, or of the Churches therein, which have been brought within the Provisions of the Church Building Act, so far as concerns the Division of such Parishes, or the Assignment of Districts to the Churches therein: 1818-1853* (London, 1853).

193 PP, 1852 ..... (51): *Return of 30 November 1852 regarding the Subdivision of Parishes and New Churches required in Parishes where the population exceeds 3,000 souls:* pp. 20, 33-4, 36-7 (the list for Bangor does not specify areas).

194 Davies, *Religion in the Industrial Revolution in South Wales*, pp. 31-2.

195 Brown, *Reclaiming the Wilderness*, p. 77.

196 Thomas, *St Asaph*, II, 61, 183; III, 274.

197 Davies, *Religion in the Industrial Revolution in South Wales*, p. 114.

198 Rodes, *Law and Modernization*, pp. 168-9.

199 *Report of the Llandaff Diocesan Conference*, 1893, pp. 32-3.

200 Pritchard Hughes, *Charge (Llandaff)*, 1913, pp. 9-11. A conventional district resembled in some ways a former district. Its curate was licensed by the bishop, but the parishioners remained parishioners of the parish from which the district was formed. In most cases a conventional district was a preliminary to the area becoming a separate parish: Norman Doe, *The Law of the Church in Wales* (Cardiff, 2002), pp. 70-1.

201 Gordon Southeard, *St Julian's and its Parish Church* (1947), pp. 7-9.

202 E.T. Davies (ed.), *The Story of the Church in Glamorgan* (London, 1962), p. 94.

203 Roger L. Brown, "The Wealthiest Place and the Poorest Ministry", *Merthyr Historian*, 8 (1996), 77-8.

204 Brown, *Reclaiming the Wilderness*, p. 143. A similar problem occurred with Brown of Llantrisant in regard to Aberdare: *ibid.*, p. 15.

205 Jones and Walker, *Links with the Past*, p. 227.

206 Brown, *Reclaiming the Wilderness*, pp. 119-26.

207 Brown, *Ten Clerical Lives*, pp. 224-47.

CHAPTER SIX: MISSION AND EVANGELISM

1 Quoted C.J. Abbey and J.H. Overton, *The English Church in the Eighteenth Century* (London, 1878), I, 553.

2 Jones preached to several hundred people in other parishes than his own and often in the churchyard. When he was presented for such activity he declined to stop this preaching claiming that the state of the Church meant that God was dishonoured, religion despised and souls famished. His patron, Sir John Philipps, possibly interceded for him: E.D. Jones, "The Ottley Papers", *NLW.Jnl.*, 4 (1945), 66-7; *T.Carms.A.S.*, 24 (1933), 81-9.

3 Brown, "Edward Smart", 121.

4 Heeney, *A Different Sort of Gentleman*, pp. 37-8.

5 *Church Pastoral-Aid Society:40th Report for 1883*, pp. 33-4.

6 *Church Pastoral-Aid Society: Church and People*, 11 (1899), 176-8.

7 Brown, *Evangelicals in the Church in Wales*, p. 201.

8 Brown, *Evangelicals in the Church in Wales*, p. 204.

9 "A North Wales Incumbent", *A Letter to the ... Bishops of St Asaph and Bangor on Matters relating to the Well-being of the Church in their Lordships' respective Dioceses* (London, 1851), pp. 10-12, 17-18.

10 Brown, *John Griffith*, pp. 206-7.

11 D.M. Lewis, *Lighten their Darkness* (Carlisle, 2001), p. 149.

12 Alfred Ollivant, *The Mission Agency of the Church* (n.d.), esp. pp. 3-5; Ollivant, *Charge (Llandaff)*, 1851, p. 40; Brown, *Reclaiming the Wilderness*, p. 29.

13 Ollivant, *Charges (Llandaff)*, 1860, pp. 36-7; 1863, p. 50-1.

14 *Llandaff Diocesan Home Mission Report*, 1877.

15 Colin Judge, *The Elan Valley Railway* (Headington, 1997), p. 54.

16 Owen Roberts, "Politics, Engineering and Civic Pride", *T.Denb.H.S.*, 49 (2000), 118.

17 *Reports of the Llandaff Diocesan Conference*, 1895, app. p. 6; 1899, p. 112; *Report of the Royal Commission, 1911*, IV, 235 (40908).

18 Brown, *Reviving the Clergy, Renewing the Laity,* pp. 12-13; Brown, *John Griffith*, pp. 207-9. Griffith also suggested the salvation Army was a burlesque of Christianity.

19 Campbell, *Charges (Bangor)*, 1878, pp. 53-4; 1881, pp. 44-5.

20 Ollivant, *Charge (Llandaff)*, 1878, pp. 85-7.

21 J.W. Burgeon, *Home Missions and Sensational Religion* (Oxford, 1876), pp. 4-12, 15-16.

22 Article on "Parochial Missions" in the *Church Quarterly Review*, 3 (1876-7), 140-58, esp. pp. 149-50, 154-6. More affirming statements are found in *Reports of the Church Congresses, Leeds*, 1872, pp. 23-8, and *Brighton*, 1874, pp. 66-83.

23 *Report of the Church Congresses, Carlisle*, 1884, pp. 336-60 (including the speech of W.M. Hay Aitkin); *Manchester*, 1888, pp. 133-7; *Great Yarmouth*, 1907, pp. 469-73.

24 *Report of the Llandaff Diocesan Conference*, 1889, p. 47.

25 *Report of the Llandaff Diocesan Conference*, 1887, pp. 51-62, esp. pp. 58-60.

26 *St David's Diocesan Directory and Calendar* (1889), II, 56-7; *Report of the St David's Diocesan Conference*, 1897, pp. 19-21, being a paper by David Howell on parochial missions, their blessings and dangers.

27 *Report of the Llandaff Diocesan Conference*, 1900, p. 28.

28 F.D. How, *Bishop Walsham How* (London, 1899), pp. 101-3. He also took children's beach missions when he visited Barmouth on his annual holidays.

29 Roger L. Brown, "The Curate of Welshpool", *Sayce Papers*, 6 (2000), 42-4; Brown, *Clergy and People of Welshpool*, pp. 54-5, quoting the *Guardian* for 4 November 1874.

30 Brown, *Reviving the Clergy, Renewing the Laity*, pp. 13-14; Brown, *David Howell*, pp. 83-7. A further mission, organised by Tractarians, took place in 1878. Ollivant was disturbed that it had exceeded its agreed terms, especially in teaching auricular confession.

31 Brown, *Reviving the Clergy, Renewing the Laity*, p. 14.

32 Brown, *Evangelicals in the Church in Wales*, pp. 176-7; and *Reclaiming the Wilderness*, pp. 159-61. Wrenford was friendly with Frances Ridley Havergal, the hymnwriter, and probably publicised her hymn, "Take my Life and let it be, Consecrated, Lord to Thee". He also founded the All for Jesus Disciples, which spread to many parts of the world.

33 J.T. Wrenford, *God's Work at Newport* (3rd. edn., London, 1872), pp. 10-11, 14-15; Brown, *Reviving the Clergy, Renewing the Laity*, p. 14.

34 C.E. Woods, *Memoirs and Letters of Canon Hay Aitken* (London, 1928), pp. 166-7.

35 *Record*, 11 November 1898, p. 1114.

36 Brown, *Reviving the Clergy, Renewing the Laity*, p. 14; Brown, *Parochial Lives*, pp. 186-7, and *Evangelicals in the Church in Wales*, pp. 198-9.

37 *Report of the Church Congress, Birmingham*, 1893, p. 278.
38 S.C. Morgan, *Hints on Conducting a Mission* (London, 1885).
39 Brown, *Evangelicals in the Church in Wales*, p. 201; *Swansea Parish Magazine*, March and April 1905, pp. 48-9, 58, 69.
40 Roger L. Brown, "A Man in a Hurry: Talbot Rice, Vicar of Swansea", *Minerva*, 4 (1996), 39-40.
41 Brown, *David Howell*, pp. 141-4.
42 Ward and Coe, *Father Jones of Cardiff*, pp. 52-6.
43 SA/DR/51, fol. 84.
44 Brown, *Ten Clerical Lives*, pp. 151-3.
45 Pritchard, "The Revd. S.E. Gladstone", pp. 211-3; Ros Aitkin, *The Prime Minister's Son* Chester, 2012), pp. 114-7, 142-3. Gladstone stated that both church and also dissent had benefited from these missions.
46 *CT*, 29 April 1898, p. 471.
47 W.U.M. Phillips, *St Francis' Church, Roath* (1958), pp. 8, 10, 12-13.
48 George, *St Theodore's Church*, pp. 19-20.
49 Brown, *Clergy and People in Welshpool*, pp. 97-8.
50 Joan Lent, *The Anglican Churches of Arllechwedd* (1980), p. 23.
51 Morfudd Jones, *The History of St Cadwaladr's Church, Llangadwaladr* (1986), p. 19.
52 John Lambert Rees, *Timothy Rees of Mirfield and Llandaff* (London, 1945), pp. 91-5.
53 Edward Boore and Fred Bell, *A History of the Parish of Ebbw Vale* (1964), p. 9.
54 D.H. Williams, *Parish of Six Bells* (1975), p. 6; Handel Thomas notes a mission at Llanbradach in 1934, possibly by the Church Army: *Llanbradach and its Church* (1947), p. 18.
55 J.H.A. Bowers, *What is the Function and Work of a Diocesan Missioner?* (Gloucester, 1887), in passim and esp. pp. 37-9. Bowers later acted as one of Benson's missioners in Wales: *ibid.*, pp. 55-6.
56 Joseph Cullen, *Parochial Missions: their Results and AfterWork. A Manual for Clergy and People* (London, 1891), esp. pp. 34-5, 45-57, 70-9. His chapters include the benefits of mission, immediate after work and methods of instruction.
57 *Report of the Llandaff Diocesan Conference*, 1911, p. 78.
58 *Proceedings of the St Asaph Diocesan Conference*, 1887, p. 19.
59 Francis Jones, "A Victorian Bishop of Llandaff", *NLW.Jnl.*, 19 (1975), 46; Lewis, *Charge (Llandaff)*, 1888, p. 25.
60 *Report of the Llandaff Diocesan Conference*, 1892, pp. 26-9.
61 *Record*, 20 June 1890, p. 618; *Report of the Llandaff Diocesan Conference*, 1889, pp. 58-9.
62 *Reports of the Llandaff Diocesan Conference*, 1888, p. 66; 1890, pp. 20-1.
63 *Report of the Llandaff Diocesan Conference*, 1901, pp. 19-20. It was alleged that part of the problem was that missioners had cathedral and diocesan responsibilities in addition to their mission work.
64 Lewis, *Charge (Llandaff)*, 1903, p. 9.
65 *Report of the Llandaff Diocesan Conference*, 1902, p. 18.
66 *Reports of the Llandaff Diocesan Conference*, 1911, pp. 84-5; 1912, pp. 34-8 (suggesting the formation of a band of mission clergy).
67 *Reports of the Llandaff Diocesan Conference*, 1913, pp. 156-8; 1914, pp. 33-5, 59-61.
68 *Report of the Llandaff Diocesan Conference*, 1916, pp. 60-2: Albert Marrin, *The Last Crusade: The Church of England in the First World War* (Durham, North Carolina, 1974), p. 210.
69 *Reports of the St David's Diocesan Conference*, 1885, pp. 108-9; 1888, App. pp. i-ii; 1891, App. pp. ii-iii.
70 *Reports of the St David's Diocesan Conference*, 1893, pp. 28-35, 37.
71 *Guardian*, 10 July 1907, p. 1119.
72 Campbell, *Charge (Bangor)*, 1887, p. 24.
73 *Bangor Diocesan Calendar and Clergy List*, 1907, pp. 301, 304.

74 J.R.D. Williams, *The Parish of Rhymney, Monmouthshire* (1943), p. 43.

75 *Amman Valley Crusade Handbook* (1927).

76 *Rhondda Deanery Church Crusade: Official Handbook* (1938), esp. p. 11.

77 Brown, *Reviving the Clergy, Renewing the Laity*, pp. 16-52.

78 *Proceedings of the St Asaph Diocesan Conference*, 1888, p. 23.

79 Williams, *Move On!* p. 35.

80 *Reports of the Llandaff Diocesan Conference*, 1898, pp. 14-15, 22; 1899, pp. 21-2; 1908, pp. 74-5; 1911, p. 21.

81 John Williams, *A Short History of the Church in Dowlais* (1927), pp. 23-5.

82 Brown, *David Howell*, p. 144.

83 W.L. Bevan, *Father Ignatius at Hay*, 1878.

84 Brown, *Reviving the Clergy, Renewing the Laity*, p. 15.

85 SA/DR/50, fols. 174-5; J.V. Smedley (ed.), *Mission Sermons and Orations delivered by Father Ignatius* (London, 1886), pp. xii-xiv.

86 Brutus (David Owen) writing in the church periodical, *Yr Haul*, poured scorn on the revival, condemning people who screamed in their madness and acted like lunatics: Russell Davies, *Hope and Heartbreak* (Cardiff, 2005), p. 328. Evan Pughe in a sermon called on people to take care and not believe every spirit, for the work of conversion was not about sensationalism but was rational and sober as with the early apostles in the New Testament: *Sermons preached chiefly at the Cathedral Church, Bangor* (London, 1866), pp. 267-78, esp p. 276.

87 Brown, *Evangelicals in the Church in Wales*, pp. 238-40.

88 Evan Jones, *Adgofion*, pp. 31, 33. A more cautious approach came from Archdeacon Wickham, who felt there was much of the spiritual in it, but that the leaven of the world had been mixed up within it. He trusted people would not depart from the sober practices of the Church while he could not understand clergymen co-operating with Nonconformists in joint services and thus suggesting that dissent was not in schism from the Church: Wickham, *Charge to the Archdeaconry of St Asaph*, 1860, pp. 11-24; Brown, *Ten Clerical Lives*, pp. 70-71.

89 For an overview see Brown, *Evangelicals in the Church in Wales*, pp. 242-51.

90 Brown, *Evangelicals in the Church in Wales*, pp. 201, 250-1.

91 J. Vyrnwy Morgan, *The Welsh Religious Revival* (London, 1909), pp. 113-4.

92 *Proceedings of the St Asaph Diocesan Conference*, 1905, pp. 24-5.

93 *Report of the St David's Diocesan Mission, 1905*, in passim.

94 Noel Gibbard in D.W. Roberts (ed.), *Revival, Renewal and the Holy Spirit* (Milton Keynes, 2009), pp. 153-4.

95 *Report of the St David's Diocesan Mission, 1905*, pp. 5-7, 16-17.

96 Brown, *Evangelicals in the Church in Wales*, p. 244.

97 Noted by R. Tudur Jones, *Faith and the Crisis of a Nation*, p. 307.

98 Noel Gibbard in D.W. Roberts (ed.), *Revival, Renewal and the Holy Spirit* (Milton Keynes, 2009), pp. 152-8. Some parishes kept themselves apart from the revival, and these included Wrexham and Llanelli.

99 Brown, *Evangelicals in the Church in Wales*, pp. 244, 247; Knight, in Williams, *The Welsh Church*, pp. 372-4, notes that as a result of the revival the young people of some parishes in the diocese of Bangor were more ready to talk on religious subjects and take part in the prayer meetings, while services had taken on a more devotional character. In addition many hardened and indifferent sinners had been brought to seek salvation.

100 Noel Gibbard in D.W. Roberts (ed.), *Revival, Renewal and the Holy Spirit* (Milton Keynes, 2009), pp. 157-8.

101 Brown, *Evangelicals in the Church in Wales*, p. 250.

102 Lewis, *Charge (Llandaff)*, 1885, pp. 15-16; cf. *ibid.*, 1891, pp. 16-17.

103 W.L. Bevan, *The Church in the South Wales Coal-field* (London, 1895), pp. 12-13. For a further example, that of Llantrisant, see *Church Pastoral-Aid Society, Church and People*, 3 (1891), 137.

104 Brown, *David Howell*, p. 130.

105 T.W. Barker, *Diocese of St David's: Particulars relating to Endowments &c. of Living* (Carmarthen, 1907): Archdeaconries of Carmarthen, I, xv. of St Davids's, II, xiv.

106 *Report of the Royal Commission, 1911*, I, 130-1; IV, 418, 513-5 (46007, 48032-9, 48049-52).

www.ingramcontent.com/pod-product-compliance
Ingram Content Group UK Ltd.
Pitfield, Milton Keynes, MK11 3LW, UK
UKHW050615260726
13967UKWH00008B/2876